£16.99

City and Islington Sixth Form College
The Angel 283-309 Goswell Road
London EC1V 7LA
020 7520 0652

CITY AND ISLINGTON
COLLEGE

This book is due for return on or before the date last stamped below.
You may renew by telephone. Please quote the Barcode No.
May not be renewed if required by another reader.

Fine: 10p per day

7129

READING

POLITICAL

PHILOSOPHY

MACHIAVELLI

To

MILL

NIGEL WARBURTON
JON PIKE
DEREK MATRAVERS

ROUTLEDGE IN ASSOCIATION
WITH THE OPEN UNIVERSITY

Published by Routledge in association with The Open University

11 New Fetter Lane
London
EC4P 4EE

Simultaneously published in the USA and Canada
by Routledge
29 West 35th Street
New York, NY 10001

First Published 2000

Written and produced by the Open University

Walton Hall
Milton Keynes MK7 6AA

Edited, designed and typeset by The Open University.

British Library Cataloguing in Publication Data

A catalogue record for this book is available from the British Library

Library of Congress Cataloguing in Publication Data

[data confirmation forthcoming]

ISBN 0–415–21196 4 (hbk)

ISBN 0–415–21197 2 (pbk)

This book forms part of an Open University course AA311 Reading
Political Philosophy: Machiavelli to Mill. Details of this and other Open
University courses can be obtained from the Courses Reservation Centre,
PO Box 724, The Open University, Milton Keynes MK7 6ZS, United
Kingdom: tel. +44 (0)1908 653231.

For availability of this and other course components, contact Open
University Worldwide Ltd, The Berrill Building, Walton Hall, Milton
Keynes MK7 6AA, United Kingdom: tel. +44 (0)1908 858585, fax +44
(0)1908 858787, e-mail ouwenq@open.ac.uk

Alternatively, much useful information can be obtained from the Open
University's website: http://www.open.ac.uk

AA311bk1i1.1

1.1

Contents

Introduction

The history of political philosophy includes many of the greatest and most widely studied works of philosophy, from Plato's *Republic* through to John Rawls's *A Theory of Justice*. In this book we are focusing on seven works by indisputably great thinkers. These books are intrinsically interesting, in some cases qualify as significant works of literature, and, most importantly, contain ideas that have a continuing relevance beyond their original contexts of composition. Our book has been written in the firm belief that studying the history of philosophy should not be like a visit to a dusty museum of superseded thought, but rather a challenging and invigorating engagement with the ideas of the great thinkers of the past.

How to use this book

If you work through this book systematically you should emerge with an excellent grounding in political philosophy, one that should prepare you well for addressing issues within more recent political philosophy. Throughout, the emphasis is on thinking critically about the ideas expressed within these works. We have provided sufficient background material for an intelligent reading of each text studied, and have picked out what we take to be the central issues. We have indicated in our 'activity' sections when it is appropriate to read from the classic texts, and when to turn to the associated readings. Some of the 'activities' include exercises: it would be very simple to skip ahead and read our suggested answers, not bothering to answer the questions asked; however, you are unlikely to get the full value of studying this book unless you attempt to answer the questions for yourself. It has been written to be used, not absorbed passively, hence the emphasis on activities: you are strongly recommended to follow the guidance given by the authors on reading the set texts.

We have tried to pick out the most stimulating, useful and important readings on each philosopher to provide a balanced anthology of secondary reading as well as a guide to reading the primary texts. There is a brief glossary and suggestions for further reading at the end of each chapter; there is also a cumulative bibliography.

The editions of the primary texts we have chosen are particularly suitable for students at the Open University. Our grounds for selecting these editions include the usefulness of notes, glossaries, introductions and so on, and where relevant, the clarity and accuracy of the translation, and also, of course, the purchase price. The editions we have used are:

Niccolò Machiavelli, *The Prince*, George Bull (trans.), Penguin Books, 1999 (new edn).

Thomas Hobbes, *Leviathan*, Edwin Curley (ed.), Hackett, 1994.

John Locke, *Second Treatise of Government*, C.B. Macpherson (ed.), Hackett, 1980.

Jean-Jacques Rousseau, *Discourse on Political Economy and The Social Contract*, Christopher Betts (trans.), Oxford University Press, Oxford World's Classics, 1994.

Karl Marx and Frederick Engels, *The German Ideology, Part One*, C.J. Arthur (ed.), Lawrence & Wishart, 1974 (2nd edn).

John Stuart Mill, *On Liberty*, Gertrude Himmelfarb (ed.), Penguin Books, 1974.

John Stuart Mill, *The Subjection of Women*, Susan M. Okin (ed.), Hackett, 1988.

You can, of course, read this textbook using different editions. We have tried to use the simplest referencing system wherever possible, so that you can locate the relevant passages regardless of the edition you are using: Machiavelli's *The Prince* is referred to by chapter number, Hobbes's *Leviathan* by chapter and paragraph numbers, Locke's *Second Treatise* by chapter and section numbers, Rousseau's *The Social Contract* by book and chapter numbers, Marx and Engels's *The German Ideology* by heading numbers in the Arthur edition (there is an appendix on p.264 below identifying paragraphs and Arthur's headings), Mill's *On Liberty* by chapter numbers and page references to the Himmelfarb edition, and his *The Subjection of Women* by chapter numbers and page references to the Okin edition.

Acknowledgements

This book was written as the course text for the Open University course AA311 *Reading Political Philosophy: Machiavelli to Mill*. The point of the course is to guide student reading of a range of classic texts in the history of political philosophy and to provide a selection of the best secondary reading on these works, relating ideas to present-day questions wherever appropriate.

Many people commented on drafts of the book at various stages of production. We are particularly grateful to Michael Clark, the external assessor of our course, who gave swift, meticulous and extremely useful feedback to us at every stage of writing. Thanks too to Vivienne Brown, whose detailed criticisms of an earlier draft greatly improved it. We are also grateful to the anonymous publishers' readers. The contributors to the audio-cassettes which accompany the Open University course, Quentin Skinner, Jeremy Waldron, Alan Ryan, Jerry Cohen, Jonathan Wolff, Timothy O'Hagan and Janet Radcliffe Richards, helped us to refine our thinking about the philosophers they discussed, and in many cases commented on our draft material as well. We are also grateful to Carolyn Price, who read and commented on most of the chapters, to the course manager Jan Cant who helped co-ordinate our efforts, to the Open University editor Peter Wright, to Jonathan Hunt who co-ordinated co-publishing, and to Tony Bruce and Sarah Howlett of Taylor and Francis. We would also like to thank the various Open University secretaries who keyed in the chapters. Individual authors would also like to express their thanks to Matt Matravers, who commented on Chapters 4 and 5, and to Edward Garrett and Susan Robinson, who commented on Chapters 2 and 3.

Further reading

Jonathan Wolff, *An Introduction to Political Philosophy*, Oxford University Press, 1996 provides an excellent overview of all the thinkers discussed in this book except Machiavelli.

Will Kymlicka, *Contemporary Political Philosophy: An Introduction*, Oxford University Press, 1990 provides a topic-based introduction to contemporary political thought.

Iain Hampsher-Monk, *A History of Modern Political Thought: Major Political Thinkers from Hobbes to Marx*, Blackwell, 1992 gives a more historically-oriented reading of all of the thinkers included here except Machiavelli. His book also contains a very useful and detailed bibliography of secondary reading on these thinkers.

Susan Moller Okin, *Women in Western Political Thought*, Princeton University Press, 1979 explores the place of women in the history of political philosophy.

Copyright acknowledgements

Grateful acknowledgement is made to the following sources for permission to reproduce material in this book.

'Extract of a letter to Francesco Vettori' from Coyle, Martin and Richardson, Brian (eds) (1995), *Niccolò Machiavelli's The Prince*, translated by Brian Richardson, Manchester University Press. 'The Adviser to Princes' by Quentin Skinner, reprinted from Skinner, Q. (1981) *Machiavelli*, Oxford University Press, © Quentin Skinner 1981. 'Machiavelli's Political Philosophy in *The Prince*' by Maureen Ramsey, from Coyle and Richardson (1995), Manchester University Press. 'The originality of Machiavelli' by Isaiah Berlin, from *The Proper Study of Mankind*, H. Hardy and R. Hausheer (eds.), Chatto & Windus, 1997; reproduced with permission of Curtis Brown Limited, London on behalf of The Isaiah Berlin Literary Trust; copyright © Isaiah Berlin 1972. 'Dirty Hands' by C.A.J. Coady, in Goodin, R.E. and Pettit, P. (eds) (1993) *A Companion to Contemporary Political Philosophy*. Basil Blackwell Publishers Limited. 'The Theory of Human Nature in Society' by C.B. Macpherson, from his introduction to *Leviathan by Thomas Hobbes*, edited by C.B. Macpherson, Penguin Classics, 1968, pp.30–9; introduction copyright © C.B. Macpherson, 1968; reproduced by permission of Penguin Books Limited. 'Hobbes and Game Theory', 'Problems with Hobbes's Alienation Social Contract Argument' and 'Do People Actually Consent to Political Authority?' by Jean Hampton, from Hampton, J. (1996) *Political Philosophy*, printed by permission of Westview Press, a member of Perseus Books, LLC; copyright © 1996 by Westview Press. 'Hobbes and the Purely Artificial Person of the State' by Quentin Skinner; adapted from Skinner, Q. 'The inaugural Martin Hollis Memorial Lecture - Hobbes and the purely artificial person of the state', *The Journal of Political Philosophy*, 7, 1, © 1999 Blackwell Publishers Ltd. 'Hobbes and the Sexual Contract' by Carole Patemen, from Pateman, Carole (1988) *The Sexual Contract*, with the permission of the publishers, Stanford University Press; © 1991 Carol Pateman. Waldron, J. (1983) 'Two worries about mixing one's labour', *Philosophical Quarterly*, vol. 33, 130, Basil Blackwell Limited. 'Reconstructing Locke on Property' by A. John Simmons, from Simmons, A. John (1992) *The Lockean Theory of Rights*, copyright

CHAPTER I

Niccolò Machiavelli: *The Prince*

Nigel Warburton

By the end of this chapter you should:
- Have read Machiavelli's *The Prince* at least twice.
- Appreciate some relevant features of the original historical context in which *The Prince* was written.
- Have a good critical understanding of Machiavelli's position on *virtù*, cruelty, human nature, honesty and deceit, and fortune.
- Have read and understood some present-day commentators' interpretations of Machiavelli.
- Appreciate the continuing relevance to political philosophy of some of the central issues raised by Machiavelli, particularly that of 'dirty hands' in politics.

Introduction

Why bother reading Niccolò Machiavelli's *The Prince* today? It is, after all, almost five hundred years since it was written. One simple answer is that it is a key text in the history of Renaissance Italy; but that is not the way we will be approaching it here. Another answer is that it has been and continues to be an immensely influential book. This is closer to our concerns. Perhaps most relevant though is the fact that it is a forceful piece of writing that still has the power to provoke and inspire its readers. Although Machiavelli was not strictly a philosopher, but a statesman, political theorist and historian, his ideas have deep philosophical implications. *The Prince*, published posthumously in 1532, is his most famous and most controversial book. Within its pages he presents a challenge to conventional morality that is still relevant to present-day political debate. In particular he suggests that political leaders must sometimes act in apparently immoral ways, even perhaps using violence against their own supporters, in order to be effective. This raises philosophical questions about the status of individual morality, and about the alleged inevitability of 'dirty hands' in politics. Historically, many readers of *The Prince* have denounced it as a textbook for ruthless despots. Fewer readers are likely to denounce Machiavelli as the devil incarnate than in some previous ages, but his name is still used as a synonym for evil. In reading *The Prince* a central question will be the extent to which this picture of Machiavelli is an accurate one, or whether a subtler Machiavelli emerges.

Machiavelli in exile

The most significant year in Machiavelli's life, at least as far as understanding the circumstances of his writing *The Prince* is concerned, was 1513. On 12 February, aged 44, he gave himself up to the authorities of his native city state, Florence, who had accused him of plotting against the new government. Florence had just reverted from a republic to an oligarchy, once more ruled by the powerful Medici family and Machiavelli had been Second Chancellor to the Florentine republic since 1498. His fortunes changed dramatically.

While in office as a diplomat he had seen many of the most powerful statesmen and rulers at work: he had met Cesare Borgia, visited the court of the French King Louis XII and the Holy Roman Emperor Maximilian. He had a particular interest in strengthening Florentine defences, and developing a citizen militia in place of the mercenary armies on which Florence had traditionally depended, an interest which resurfaces in *The Prince,* and subsequently in the only book of his to be published in his lifetime, *The Art of War* (1521).

With the Medici's regaining control of Florence in 1512, Machiavelli first lost his post, and then his liberty. He was imprisoned and tortured. The method of torture was the *strappado,* a particularly humiliating procedure whereby the victim, whose hands were tied behind his back, was suspended on a rope tied to his wrists, sometimes for days at a time. Every so often the victim was lifted several feet and allowed to drop so that the tautening rope jerked the ligaments of his shoulders. In the circumstances it is hardly surprising that some of his alleged co-conspirators confessed and were duly executed. Machiavelli, however, survived six of these drops, and torture over several days, without admitting guilt. Despite this, he was kept prisoner for a month, and was only released as an act of charitable celebration on the occasion of Giovanni de' Medici's being elected Pope Leo X.

Machiavelli was now left outside the mainstream of political life. His name had been tarnished by association with the anti-Medici conspiracy, whether or not he had genuinely been a part of it. He was banned from the city of Florence, but not allowed to leave the region. He was an internal exile on his farm in Sant' Andrea in Percussina, about seven miles south of Florence. He desperately wanted to re-enter the political fray, and did everything in his power to bring this about. Not least of his efforts was the writing of *The Prince,* which he intended to use as a demonstration of his suitability as an adviser to a new prince taking the reigns of a city state, a barely disguised reference to the position of the incoming Medici prince. His oft-cited letter to his friend Francesco Vettori (see below), describes this intended use to which the book was probably not in the end put. There he sketches the conditions under which he wrote *The Prince.* It is clear from the letter that Machiavelli was not yet ready to retire from public life.

ACTIVITY

Read this extract from Machiavelli's letter to his friend Francesco Vettori below.

...When evening has come, I return home, and enter my study; and at the door I take off my everyday clothing, full of mud and mire, and I put on royal and courtly clothes; and, appropriately attired, I enter the ancient courts of ancient men, where, welcomed lovingly by them, I partake of that food which is mine alone, and for which I was born. Here I am not ashamed to speak with them, and to ask them about the reasons for their actions; and they, in their kindness, answer me; and for four hours I feel no affliction, I forget every trouble, I do not fear poverty, death does not make me afraid; I become completely absorbed in them. And because Dante says that there can be no knowledge without retaining what one has learned,[1] I have noted what I have gained from my acquaintance with them, and have composed a little work *De principatibus*,[2] in which I go as deeply as I can into thoughts on this subject, discussing what is a principality, of what kinds they are, how they are acquired, how they are held, why they are lost. And if ever you liked any of my whims, this one should not displease you; and to a prince, and especially to a new prince, it should be welcome; therefore I am addressing it to his Magnificence Giuliano.[3] Filippo Casavecchia has seen it; he will be able to tell you something both about the work itself and about the discussions I have had with him, although I am still filling it out and polishing it.

You would like me, magnificent ambassador, to leave this life and come to enjoy yours with you. I shall do so in any case, but what tempts me now is certain affairs of mine which will take me about six weeks to settle. What makes me hesitate is that those Soderini are there;[4] I would be obliged, if I came, to visit them and speak to them. I would be afraid that on my return I would expect to dismount at home but would in fact dismount in the Bargello,[5] because, although this regime has very strong foundations and is very secure, still it is new, and for this reason full of suspicion; nor is there a shortage of smart alecs who, to make an impression like Pagolo Bertini, would invite others to table and would leave me to foot the bill. Please allay this fear for me, and then I will in any case come to see you within the time stated.

I talked to Filippo about this little work of mine, whether it would be a good idea to present it or not to present it; and, if so, whether it would be a good idea for me to bring it or to send it. In favour of not presenting it, there was the fear that it would not even be read by Giuliano, and that this Ardinghelli[6] would take the credit for this latest effort of mine. In favour of presenting it, there was the need which is driving me, because I am wearing myself out, and I cannot go on for long like this without poverty making me despicable; there was also my desire that these Medici lords should begin to make use of me, even if they were to start by getting me to roll a stone;[7] for, if I were not then to win them over, I would regret it deeply; and through this work, if it were read, it would be evident that the fifteen years I have been studying statecraft have not been spent by me in sleeping or playing; and anyone should be glad to make use of someone who at the expense of others was full of experience. And about my good faith nobody should be in doubt, because, having always kept faith, I am not going to learn to break it now; and someone who has been faithful and good for forty-three years, as I have, cannot change his nature; and my faith and goodness are testified by my poverty.

I should therefore like you too to write to me with your opinion on this matter, and I commend myself to you. 'Be favourable.'[8]

10 December 1513

Niccolò Machiavelli in Florence

Notes

[1] Dante, *Paradiso*, V, 41–2.

[2] The work here entitled *De principatipus* ('Of Principalities') was to become *Il Principe* ('The Prince').

[3] Giuliano de' Medici (1479–1516), son of Lorenzo the Magnificent and younger brother of Pope Leo X.

[4] Piero Soderini (gonfalonier of Florence from 1502 until forced into exile on the return of the Medici in 1512) and his brother Cardinal Francesco.

[5] The *palazzo* of the Bargello (head of police), in which Machiavelli had already been imprisoned earlier in the year.

[6] Pietro Ardinghelli (1470–1526), personal secretary of Pope Leo X.

[7] A reference to the eternal labour of Sisyphus in the underworld.

[8] The Latin phrase used by Machiavelli, 'Sis felix', seems to be cited, as a counterpart to the opening quotation on divine favours, from another poetic text which both he and Vettori knew well, Virgil's *Aeneid*, I, 330: here Aeneas, driven ashore in an unknown country, has met his mother, Venus, disguised as a huntress, in a wood, and pleads for her help.

(in Coyle (1995), pp.198–9)

DISCUSSION

The letter reveals Machiavelli as unhappy with what for some would be a rural idyll. For a man of political action and intrigue, the enforced retreat must have seemed like a continuation of his torture. Nevertheless his internal exile provided him both with the time and the incentive to write his most famous works: *The Prince*, the *Discourses*, *The Art of War*, *Mandragola* and the *History of Florence*. Ensconced in his study, in the quiet of the night, he drew both on his own knowledge of political power and on the insights he gleaned from classical authors. It is interesting that he imagined conversations with the great of the past: for him the ancient past was as relevant as the recent present to understanding the ways of humanity and the complexities of political power.

The dedication of *The Prince*, as the work now survives, is to Lorenzo de' Medici, but it was probably originally intended for Giuliano de' Medici. It was a contribution to the established genre known as 'mirrors for princes': short books exhorting princes to virtue (for further details see Reading 1.1 'The Adviser to Princes' by Quentin Skinner, and Reading 1.3 'The Originality of Machiavelli' by Isaiah Berlin). However, Machiavelli's approach was very far from typical. Where contemporary readers would have expected discussions of the importance of honesty, compassion and mercy in a just ruler, he gave them justifications for acts of deceit and cruelty; where they would usually have read about paragons of moral virtue, he provided them with Cesare Borgia's acts of calculated cruelty as worthy of emulation. Indeed, so untypical of the 'mirrors for princes' genre is Machiavelli's version that some commentators have even suggested, somewhat implausibly, that the book is an ironic commentary on the genre: merely a work of satire.

Although circulated amongst his friends, the book was not published in his lifetime: it was first published posthumously in 1532. It immediately stirred up a shocked and outraged response. Machiavelli and the adjective 'machiavellian' quickly became synonyms for evil machination.

The Prince is certainly Machiavelli's most widely read and most influential work. However, his other major contribution to political thought, *The Discourses on the First Decade of Livy* (usually known simply as the *Discourses*), also published posthumously, overlaps significantly with it. The *Discourses* reveals him to have been wholeheartedly committed to republicanism, a view that it would have been imprudent to reveal in a work dedicated to members of the Medici family. Indeed, there he explicitly describes it as the best form of government. Some have accused Machiavelli of inconsistency between the two works: preferring republicanism in the *Discourses,* but siding with tyrannical rulers of principalities in *The Prince.* However, it is possible that when writing *The Prince* in 1513 he sincerely believed that strong rule by a *virtuoso* prince would be in Florence's best interests, despite his general preference for republics. Machiavelli was a practical man in that he was concerned with the actual and the possible rather than with utopian ideals. If a republic was not a realistic possibility for Florence once the Medici had returned, then it was nevertheless important for the city state to achieve the best possible form of government. He would undoubtedly have preferred strong rule by a strong prince to a weak and vulnerable republic. An alternative interpretation of *The Prince* is that it was a cynical piece of dissimulation completely consistent with the principles of behaviour laid out in that book: Machiavelli recognized that appearances are important; as he put it: 'Everyone sees what you appear to be, few experience what you really are.' (*The Prince*, XVIII, p.58). He had every reason to want to *appear* to be committed to rule by the Medici. Some indirect evidence for this interpretation exists in a passage in *The Prince* in which he makes the implausible claim that new princes

> have found men who were suspect at the start of their rule more loyal and more useful than those who, at the start, were their trusted friends.

(*The Prince*, XX, p.69)

This transparent special pleading – it after all describes his own position exactly – suggests that Machiavelli wasn't above using rhetoric to defend a position which suited him. It suggests too, perhaps, that he would have been capable of disguising his true beliefs about the relative merits of a republic if that increased his chances of being re-employed as a political aide. Rousseau's view was that Machiavelli secretly intended *The Prince* as a 'book for republicans' (*The Social Contract*, III, vi, p.106): by showing tyranny at its worse he made an indirect case for the relative merits of republican liberty. If this is so, this would have been an extremely dangerous enterprise for Machiavelli to have undertaken.

Despite his original intentions, it seems that he did not send *The Prince* to Lorenzo de' Medici, or that if he did, it did not have the desired effect. Letters he wrote at the time indicate that he was worried that if he sent Lorenzo *The Prince*, others might pass it off as their own work. Whatever his final decision on the matter, Machiavelli remained outside the cut and thrust of practical politics until shortly before his death in 1527.

Reading The Prince

Reading *The Prince* for the first time can be confusing. Machiavelli jumps from one topic to the next in a less than systematic fashion. He also uses a wide range of examples to illustrate his points, some coming from Ancient Roman history, others from the recent history of Florence and the surrounding regions. These examples reveal his belief that ancient as well as recent history can teach important lessons. For him the two sources are on a par: human nature and human foibles don't change from century to century. The behaviour of Ancient Greeks and Romans was as relevant, and could teach as much, as the actions of his contemporaries. The use of these examples also reveals his concern with what actually has happened and is likely to happen, rather than with what ought to happen in an ideal world. In stark contrast to a thinker such as Plato who, in his *Republic*, spelt out his vision of an ideal state, Machiavelli wrote about the world he inhabited and about the worlds that fellow human beings have actually inhabited.

Even in translation, Machiavelli's prose style is clear and to the point. He doesn't, on the whole, waste words. Furthermore, *The Prince* is short enough to read and re-read. Nevertheless despite the clarity of style and brevity of the book, it can sometimes be difficult to see where Machiavelli is heading. This is particularly so when you are trying to pinpoint the *philosophical* content of a book which is, for the greater part, a mixture of advice, theoretical speculation and extended illustration. It was never intended as a philosophical treatise. As a result, much of the philosophical content of *The Prince* is implied rather than stated explicitly: the onus is on the reader to interpret the significance of Machiavelli's examples and maxims. As a consequence, *The Prince* has generated a wide range of interpretations, many of them incompatible.

The sub-headings, which are Machiavelli's own, provide a useful indicator of the contents of each section. But for most readers, it will take several readings of the book before you feel at home with its structure and content.

ACTIVITY

Read *The Prince* through from beginning to end. Don't worry about the detail of what you are reading. The point of this first reading is to get an overall feel for the book and to appreciate Machiavelli's style of thought. (You should have time to re-read it in a more detailed way later on.) Try to be aware of the point of each of the sometimes lengthy historical examples.

When you have read *The Prince*, turn to Reading 1.1 'The Adviser to Princes' by Quentin Skinner. This should provide a more detailed context for understanding *The Prince*.

Virtù and cruelty

The pivotal concept in *The Prince* is *virtù,* which is usually translated as 'prowess' rather than as 'virtue', since the former translation captures the notion of effectiveness without implying adherence to conventional Christian morality. Machiavelli certainly does not believe that the Christian virtues of compassion, humility, mercy and honesty should prevail in every circumstance: acts of outright deceit and extreme violence can be considered virtuous in his sense of the term. If you are a prince it can sometimes be right to butcher those who threaten your success. It can sometimes be right to make pacts that you never intend to keep. These are hardly acts of virtue in the conventional sense. So as to avoid ambiguity, most commentators on Machiavelli use the Italian word *virtù* when discussing Machiavelli's concept.

Machiavelli nowhere provides a detailed abstract account of *virtù* – precisely what he means by it only emerges through a series of case studies and commentaries on those case studies. He does, however, make it clear that *virtù* is the quality that any new prince who wishes to maintain long-term control of the state, and thereby promote the common good, must cultivate. It is the quality most likely to protect a prince against the vicissitudes of fortune. As the translation 'prowess' suggests, *virtù* is a combination of strength and ability, courage without squeamishness. It is the quality needed above all for success as a ruler, though its possession does not guarantee it.

It is easiest to demonstrate what *virtù* is and how it differs from conventional Christian moral virtue by considering one of the most controversial parts of *The Prince*, namely, that in which Machiavelli sets up the infamous Cesare Borgia as a model of what a new prince should be and do in contrast to Agathocles, who is an example of a successful tyrant who lacked *virtù*.

ACTIVITY

Re-read chapters VII and VIII of *The Prince* (pp.20–31) and then write answers to the questions below before reading the discussion that follows. Notice how Machiavelli treats evidence from ancient history (the case of Agathocles) precisely as he treats evidence from very recent history (the case of Cesare Borgia).

1   Does Machiavelli disapprove of Cesare Borgia's cold-blooded murder of the Orsini at Sinigaglia? (p.23)

2   How did Cesare Borgia deal with Remirro de Orco and thereby avoid becoming the object of the people of Romagna's hatred? (p.24)

3   Why is Machiavelli reluctant to admit that Agathocles showed prowess (*virtù*)? (pp.27–8)

4   What is the difference between cruelty well-used and cruelty badly-used according to Machiavelli? (p.30)

5   Which kind of cruelty did Agathocles use? (p.28)

6   What is it about the actions of Agathocles which Machiavelli disapproves of as compared with those of Cesare Borgia? (p.30)

DISCUSSION

1   There isn't even a hint of disapproval in Machiavelli's description of Borgia's actions: if anything, he disapproves of the Orsini's 'simplicity'.

2   When Borgia had established authority over the people by means of his cruel henchman Remirro de Orco, he had him murdered and his body left in two pieces on the piazza at Cesena. According to Machiavelli, who seems

delighted by the skilful manipulation of the people's emotions, this had the effect of purging the people of Romagna's hatred – appeasing and stupefying them. The net effect was that they did not turn their hatred against Cesare Borgia.

3   Because, according to Machiavelli, his actions were criminal and treacherous. They were of a kind which gave him power but not glory and so were not the result of *virtù*. For a fuller discussion of this point see the following section below, 'Cesare Borgia versus Agathocles'.

4   Cruelty well used is cruelty used once and for all and which, as far as possible, is used for the good of one's subjects; cruelty badly used grows in intensity.

5   Agathocles used cruelty well. (Maureen Ramsay in Reading 1.2 seems to imply that he used it badly. For a discussion of this point, see below.)

6   This question is addressed in the following section.

Cesare Borgia versus Agathocles

It is not immediately obvious why Machiavelli wants to draw a distinction between Cesare Borgia's acts of cruelty and those of Agathocles. How can he justify treating one as a model of how new princes should behave and the other as lacking *virtù* and little more than a criminal? As we have seen, Cesare Borgia murdered his enemies, but also, when it suited him, those in his employment such as Remirro de Orco. The people of Romagna were left stupefied when they found Remirro's butchered body in the piazza; Machiavelli on the other hand can find nothing but praise for the prince's actions. Borgia's main aim in this and other cases of cruelty was to maintain his power over the newly acquired state of Romagna and to pre-empt opposition or insurrection. Agathocles, in an apparently similar fashion, used violence and cruelty both to seize power and to maintain it. His methods were brutal but effective. Furthermore Machiavelli is explicit that the reason that Agathocles was so successful in keeping control and preventing opposition was precisely that he had used violence effectively. On this last point, as I have mentioned, Maureen Ramsay, in Reading 1.2, seems to have misread Machiavelli when she writes:

> Agathocles' deeds involved uneconomic and gratuitous cruelty and led to a worse state of affairs than before.

(p.37 below)

In his discussion of Agathocles' deeds Machiavelli surely implies that they were far from uneconomic and gratuitous: they achieved their desired end precisely *because* they were at an appropriate level of intensity and violence. The desired end was maintenance of control by the new prince; the method bloody, but effective. Once he had embarked upon his violent route to power, violence was the key to maintaining his grip on Syracuse.

However, Ramsay's point about the state of affairs being worse than before is surely part of what Machiavelli was suggesting in his declaration that, in contrast with Cesare Borgia's, Agathocles' did not merit the commendation of being called acts of *virtù*. Although Machiavelli leaves the reader to fathom the distinction between the two princes, his key point seems to be that in murdering his fellow citizens Agathocles gained power but destroyed a free republic, thereby decreasing the common good, creating a situation worse than the one which existed when he took power; whereas Cesare Borgia's actions, even when cruel, were always consistent with benefiting the common good. David Wootton comments on this passage of *The Prince*:

> Both Agathocles and Oliverotto destroyed free states, murdering their friends and fellow citizens. This is the one crime Machiavelli will not forgive. Where it is concerned, success is irrelevant ...

(Wootton (ed.) (1994), p.xii)

This last point brings out the distinction between *virtù* and merely successful action, action that achieves the end it sets itself. Machiavelli is sometimes caricatured as recommending whatever action will bring success regardless of the terms in which success is measured. But the concept of *virtù,* while it differs significantly from Christian morality, is not completely neutral as to the kind of end achieved. Agathocles was successful at maintaining control of the territories in his power, yet Machiavelli is unwilling to attribute *virtù* to him; Cesare Borgia, on the other, hand not only used cruelty well, but he used it in a way that stood every chance of bringing about an appropriate end: the common good. This probably wasn't Borgia's main or only aim: there is nothing in Machiavelli's writing to suggest that Borgia was motivated in large part by anything but lust for power. However, the effects of his actions, according to Machiavelli, tended towards the common good, or would have done had fortune not undermined his preparations for strong leadership of a well-defended state. John Plamenatz, in the introduction to his edition of Machiavelli's works, brings this point out well in his assessment of the contrast between Machiavelli's treatment of Agathocles and Borgia:

> It may be that Agathocles did worse things, at least in Machiavelli's eyes, than Cesare Borgia; but I doubt whether it was any added weight of crime that moved Machiavelli to deny virtue to Agathocles while allowing it to Borgia. Agathocles achieved his ambition and Borgia did not, but it was not this lack of success that made Borgia seem the more admirable. For Machiavelli, the crucial difference between these two men is that Borgia, if he had achieved his ambition, would have created a strong state where there was not one, whereas Agathocles, in achieving his, left Syracuse worse than he found it. The point is not that Borgia wanted to do good to others while Agathocles was out only for himself; for Machiavelli, when he speaks of Borgia, never suggests that he was unselfish or concerned for the common good. It is not Borgia's having some good motives and Agathocles none that makes the difference between them; it is rather that what Borgia tried to do, whatever his motive for trying, was worth doing, not only from his own but also from a more general point of view.

(Plamenatz (ed.) (1972), p.23)

There is more, then, to *virtù,* the quality that Machiavelli so much admires, than just being ruthless: the ruthlessness must be consistent with the common good (even if not inspired by a desire for it). Machiavelli's concept of *virtù* is not *amoral* – completely outside the realm of morality – though it is sometimes misleadingly described as such. Machiavelli is not advocating pure egoism: the prince's pursuit of his own desires whatever they may be. He is arguing for the special responsibilities of princes. A prince who is squeamish and shirks swift and effective acts of violence risks bringing the state to ruin: a situation worse for everyone. Better a short, painful bout of violence, than the swift decline and collapse of the state. You may think this position *immoral*, in the sense that it goes against conventional Christian morality, or perhaps endorses cruelties which you think absolutely prohibited by any moral code meriting the name. But that is not at all the same thing as saying that Machiavelli locates politics *outside* the moral sphere. Another way of putting this is that Machiavelli does not believe that *any* ends justify *any* means of achieving them. Only the end of actually bringing about the common good justifies the cruelties that he approvingly recounts. New princes are in a position which demands strong and effective action. They are not like ordinary men, and they should not be tempted to adopt the moral standards and conventions of ordinary men, though it is usually worth them giving the impression that that is what they are doing.

Machiavelli was undoubtedly interested in the effects of actions: the appropriateness of cruelty, for example is measured entirely by its outcome. As such he fits into the category of moral theorists now known as *consequentialists*. For consequentialists (and there are numerous versions of consequentialism, the most famous being utilitarianism – the moral theory embraced by John Stuart Mill (1806–73)), the moral worth of any action is dependent solely on its effects rather than deriving from the motives from which that action was performed. In contrast, so-called *deontological* theorists stress that the rightness or wrongness of an action is a matter of absolute rules: some deontologists, such as Immanuel Kant (1724–1804), for example, think that lying is absolutely wrong, no matter what possible benefits to humanity might ensue from it. Kant famously argued that it would be morally wrong to lie to a would-be murderer asking the whereabouts of a potential victim. Consequentialists typically argue that in some special situations lying can be morally right because of the beneficial consequences that follow from it and the disastrous consequences that would be likely if a lie were not told. Machiavelli's sympathies are with the consequentialists, though the deontological/consequentialist distinction is not one with which he would have been familiar. In sixteenth-century Florence morality was Christianity based: Christianity teaches honesty and compassion above deceit and cruelty. Such a view is not the sole preserve of Christian morality: the Classical Roman author Seneca (4BC–AD65), in his essay 'Of Mercy' made the case against a ruler being cruel: for him cruelty was a vice of tyrants, and so to be avoided by a virtuous prince (see Quentin Skinner introduction to *The Prince* (Skinner (ed.) (1988), p.xvii). Machiavelli's message cuts right across this Christian and Classical tradition: when the state is under threat from possible insurrection or attack whatever will preserve it just is the correct thing to do. Mercy has its uses, but will not suit every situation. Well-used cruelty can, for Machiavelli, trump compassion:

> ... a prince must want to have a reputation for compassion rather than for cruelty: none the less, he must be careful that he does not make bad use of compassion. Cesare Borgia was accounted cruel; nevertheless, this cruelty of his reformed the Romagna, brought it unity, and restored order and obedience. On reflection, it will

be seen that there was more compassion in Cesare than in the Florentine people who, to escape being called cruel, allowed Pistoia to be devastated.

(*The Prince*, XVII, p.53)

In this quotation he seems to be saying that effective cruelty is, in many cases, actually more compassionate than refraining from cruelty. This view is closely linked to his view of human nature, which, as we have seen, he treats as stable from ancient times to his own.

ACTIVITY

Read Maureen Ramsay's 'Machiavelli's Political Philosophy in *The Prince*' (Reading 1.2). Ramsay gives a clear account of the moral and political implications of Machiavelli's position in *The Prince*.

Human nature

Most political philosophers have views about human nature which shape their account of the best forms of government. Machiavelli has a low – some would simply say realistic – view of how people behave:

> One can make this generalization about men: they are ungrateful, fickle, liars, and deceivers, they shun danger and are greedy for profit; while you treat them well, they are yours. They would shed their blood for you, risk their property, their lives, their sons, so long ... as danger is remote; but when you are in danger they turn away.

(Ibid., p.54)

Given the fickle nature of humanity, he argues that it is desirable for a prince to be loved and feared, but if he has to choose one of the two, it is better to be feared than loved. If you are surrounded by such self-interested beings, you should put your trust in the effects of fear rather than in the loyalty that may or may not be inspired by love. As he puts it:

> ... love is secured by a bond of gratitude which men, wretched creatures that they are, break when it is to their advantage to do so; but fear is strengthened by a dread of punishment which is always effective.

(Ibid.)

Machiavelli is not advocating unlimited cruelty: it is important for a prince not to be hated. But, his belief in human imperfection, based on his own observation and his study of history, leads him to mistrust love of the prince as the bond of a state and to put his faith in a more reliable mechanism. His advice here is intended to be practical and to the point.

Honesty and deceit

ACTIVITY

Re-read chapter XVIII (pp.56–8) of *The Prince*, before writing answers to the questions below.

1   Machiavelli says that there are two ways of fighting: 'by law or by force'. What do you think he means by 'by law' in this context? (p.56)

2   The two beasts that Machiavelli mentions are the fox and the lion. What attributes is he appealing to in each? (p.56)

3   Why does Machiavelli stress the wretched condition of humanity when putting forward his suggestion that a prudent prince will break some promises when it suits him? (pp.56–7)

4   What is the example of Alexander VI meant to demonstrate? (p.57)

5   What does Machiavelli mean by a 'flexible disposition' and why should a new prince have one? (p.57)

6   What does Machiavelli mean by the line 'Men in general judge by their eyes rather than by their hands' (p.58)

DISCUSSION

1   Playing by the rules – i.e. keeping one's promises, respecting treaties under all conditions, and so on.

2   Guile in the fox and strength in the lion.

3   Because an honest prince runs the risk of being duped by less than honest statesmen: if everyone were honest there would not be a problem, but since they are not, anyone who is honest runs the risk of losing out because of his honesty.

4   That a sophisticated liar can persuade others that he is telling the truth and keeping his promises while at the same time reap the benefits of his deceptions. Machiavelli seems wholeheartedly to approve of Alexander VI's strategy and appears somewhat in awe of his proficiency at dissimulation.

5   He means that a new prince should be able to perform actions which go against conventional morality (good faith, charity, kindness, religion) when appropriate. He should be able and willing to do what is called evil when it is necessary. The reason why a new prince should have this trait is that if he does not, but simply displays all and only conventionally good qualities, this will very likely be harmful for him. Machiavelli is not advocating evil for evil's sake, but rather suggesting that in certain extreme circumstances it would be wrong for a prince to abide by conventional morality (and, the implication is, this would have a detrimental effect on the common good).

6   That appearances are more important than actuality: most people don't get close enough to a prince to touch him (i.e. to discover what he is really like), but rather have to judge him at a distance and rely on how he appears.

Deceit by a prince, then, is not only excusable in certain circumstances, but seems at least on occasion to be admirable. Machiavelli suggests that it is rational for a prince to deceive others, to pretend to be more honest than he is, and to break treaties where this benefits the state. It is prudent to appear more honest than one is, but imprudent to be completely honest. This follows from his belief that since human beings are wretched, an honest promise-keeper is likely to be worse off than a skilful deceiver. Furthermore, recent history purportedly supports his argument, since, he claims:

> contemporary experience shows that princes who have achieved great things have been those who have given their word lightly, who have known how to trick men with their cunning, and who, in the end, have overcome those abiding by honest principles.

> (*The Prince*, XVIII, p.56)

Once again, Machiavelli stresses what actually happens, rather than what ought to happen. His aim is to show a new prince how to achieve success rather than simply to implement conventional morality, which would be a potential route to disaster given human nature:

> Many have dreamed up republics and principalities which have never in truth been known to exist; the gulf between how one should live and how one does live is so wide that a man who neglects what is actually done for what should be done moves towards self-destruction rather than self-preservation. The fact is that a man who wants to act virtuously in every way necessarily comes to grief among so many who are not virtuous. Therefore if a prince wants to maintain his rule he must be prepared not to be virtuous, and to make use of this or not according to need.

> (Ibid., XV, pp.49–50)

The position Machiavelli adopts here on the rationality of promise-breaking in a situation in which trust has shaky foundations anticipates Hobbes, who, as we shall see had a similarly pessimistic view of human beings and their motivations.

Machiavelli writes as if the people can easily be duped about the prince's real intentions. However, King Frederick II of Prussia who published an anonymous pamphlet *Anti-Machiavel* in the mid-eighteenth century, attacked this doctrine. First he drew attention to the special position in which princes find themselves:

> ... indeed Princes are more exposed than all other Men, to the Conjectures, Comments and Judgement of the World; they are a sort of Stars, at which a whole People of Astronomers are continually levelling their Telescopes and Cross-staves; Courtiers who are near them are daily taking their Observations; a single Gesture, a single Glance of the Eye, discovers them; and the People who observe them at a greater distance magnify them by Conjectures; in short as well may the Sun hide its spots, as great Princes their Vices and their genuine Character, from the Eyes of so many curious observers.

> (*Anti-Machiavel*, quoted in Milner (ed.) (1995), p.135)

Here King Frederick meets Machiavelli's claim based on his own observation with a contrary one, one presumably based on being a recipient of such scrutiny. Frederick goes on to conclude that a prince would not be able to deceive all those around him all of the time:

> If the mask of Dissimulation should cover, for a time, the natural deformity of a
> Prince, yet he could never keep his mask always on; he would sometimes be
> obliged, was it only for a Breathing, to throw it off; and one View of his naked
> Features would be sufficient to content the Curious ... No Man can well act any Part
> but his own; he must really have the same Character which he would bear in the
> World: Without this, the Man who thinks to impose upon the Publick, imposes
> upon none but himself

> (Ibid., pp.135–6)

Here Frederick provides what seems to be a powerful argument against Machiavelli's
position. But Machiavelli, like Frederick, had had the opportunity to observe princes
close to and to study history. He had seen that some princes had succeeded in
convincing those around them of their honesty and sincerity while clearly having very
different intentions from those they expressed. Frederick seems to be claiming that it
would be impossible to carry off such deceptions, but Machiavelli's cites examples of
people who have. For example, he writes:

> Alexander VI never did anything, or thought of anything, other than deceiving
> men; and he always found victims for his deceptions. There never was a man
> capable of such convincing asseverations, or so ready to swear to the truth of
> something, who would honour his word less. None the less his deceptions always
> had the result he intended, because he was a past master in the art.

> (*The Prince*, XVIII, p.57)

In the same chapter he alludes to the exploits of Ferdinand of Aragon:

> A certain contemporary ruler, whom it is better not to name, never preaches
> anything except peace and good faith; and he is an enemy of both one and the
> other, and if he had ever honoured either of them he would have lost either his
> standing or his state many times over.

> (Ibid., p.58)

The fact that he can see through the actions of this prince to the deceiver beneath
shows that Machiavelli did not presume that to be a successful liar a prince would
have to convince absolutely everyone: it would be enough to convince the people in
general in most situations. So to this extent Frederick's objection that *complete*
dissimulation is impossible, even if true, is irrelevant; it misses the point. Machiavelli
is not suggesting that to be successful complete deception of *everyone* has to be
achieved: a successful prince will only need to deceive the people who matter. If he
does this in the right way at the right time he is likely to thrive and the state with him.

However, even a *virtuoso* prince is subject to fortune. No matter how well-prepared
and skilful he may be, events beyond his control may annul his prowess, as was the
fate of Cesare Borgia.

Fortune

ACTIVITY

Re-read chapter XXV (pp.79–82), then answer the questions below.

1   What position is Machiavelli opposing in this chapter? (p.79)

2   How much of what we do is governed by fortune alone, according to Machiavelli? (p.79)

3   What is the point of his analogy between fortune and a flooding river? (p.80)

4   Explain the analogy between fortune and a woman. (p.82)

DISCUSSION

1   He is opposing a form of *determinism*, the view that events are entirely controlled (by fortune or by God) so as to leave no room for human influence and control over our destiny.

2   Half.

3   The analogy is meant to demonstrate that those who are well-prepared may sometimes overcome bad fortune; those who make no preparations will always fall prey to it.

4   Machiavelli – worryingly – believed that a woman needed to be beaten and coerced into submission. Similarly, being circumspect in the face of fortune is less likely to produce the desired results than being bold and impetuous. There is the implication that fortune wants to yield to those who treat her roughly.

Machiavelli's position on fortune puts him midway between determinism and the over-optimism of those who believe that everything is within our power. Some determinists are *fatalists*, that is they think the correct response to the human condition is simply to let fate (or fortune as Machiavelli would call it) take its course: they believe it a waste of effort to try to change things. In contrast, those influenced by Stoicism believe that everything of any importance is fully within our control: what we think and how we feel are up to us. Machiavelli rejects the pessimism and the manifesto for inaction of the fatalist; but equally he rejects what he would see as the naivety of the Stoics. In Machiavelli's view, part of our destiny is beyond our control; but an equal part is not. Consequently it is worth committing oneself to action: this is how we exhibit *virtù*.

Etymologically, *virtù* comes from the Latin *virtus* (virtue), which is itself derived from *vir* (meaning man). Machiavelli plays on the notion of manliness in his discussion of feminine fortune succumbing to the advances of a forceful and audacious prince.

For Machiavelli the act of writing *The Prince* was a response to fortune and an attempt by an act of will to outwit it. A set of political circumstances left him without a job and without political influence. He wrote the book ostensibly to place himself once more within the corridors of political power. It was part of a premeditated attempt to get himself reinstated as a political adviser, a demonstration of his potential worth to a new prince. The fact that he did not in the end achieve this goal he would also, presumably, have to put down to fortune. He was in the position of someone who had done everything he could to prevent the river bursting its banks, but yet still found the raging waters too strong for his defences. In this case fortune had the better of Machiavelli, despite his obvious political skills and knowledge. As we have seen, by his own account it is only half of our actions which are subject to such unavoidable swings of fortune.

Machiavelli does not provide any argument to support this claim that half of our actions are determined by fortune. He claims it simply as an observation. The view leaves open the possibility for *virtù* demonstrated by a powerful prince to be the decisive factor in determining the fate of that prince and so ultimately of the state. Where, as in the case of Cesare Borgia, fortune has the upper hand, there is little or nothing that even the most *virtuoso* prince can do to affect the outcome. But where fortune doesn't hold complete sway, she can be subdued by a prince who acts forcefully. So *virtù* isn't infallible as a means to achieving any particular end; but it is the most valuable asset a prince can have, since combined with good fortune, it can bring about great things.

Isaiah Berlin's interpretation

ACTIVITY

Read the extract from Isaiah Berlin's seminal essay 'The Originality of Machiavelli' (Reading 1.3). Make notes on its main themes before reading on.

Berlin's essay is wide-ranging, drawing on material from several of Machiavelli's works, but particularly from *The Prince* and the *Discourses*. He sets up his own interpretation of Machiavelli by contrasting it with that of Benedetto Croce (1866–1952), a famous Italian commentator on Machiavelli as well as an important philosopher in his own right. Berlin cites a passage by Cochrane summarizing Croce's views and goes on to criticize it on two counts. Berlin writes:

> Machiavelli, in Cochrane's words 'did not deny the validity of Christian morality, and he did not pretend that a crime required by political necessity was any less a crime. Rather he discovered ... that this morality simply did not hold in political affairs and that any policy based on the assumption that it did would end in disaster. His factual, objective description of contemporary political practices, then, is a sign not of cynicism or of detachment, but of anguish.'

(Reading 1.3, p.47 below)

First this interpretation of Machiavelli is misleading because Croce sets him up as distinguishing between morality, which covered one's private affairs, and politics, which was completely distinct from morality and thus not governed by any moral principles. In other words, this interpretation has it that Machiavelli recognized two autonomous realms, the one moral, the other amoral, and was only really concerned with the second of these. This view still finds its adherents today: it is not uncommon to find passing references to Machiavelli's *The Prince* as advocating not *immorality* but *amorality*.

Berlin's response to such an interpretation is that it does not recognize the subtlety of Machiavelli's implied position, the very point that makes him such an original thinker. It is not that politics, for Machiavelli, is somehow beyond good and evil; rather that political conduct is 'intrinsic to being a human being at a certain stage of civilization, and what it demands is intrinsic to living a successful human life' (ibid., p.47 below). Political activity is a form of moral activity. The morality needed, however, as Machiavelli so clearly shows, is not a Christian morality of honesty and compassion: that sort of morality puts a ruler, and thus the state, at risk from the unscrupulous who will inevitably surround him. What is needed is a combination of the lion and the fox: strength and guile. As Berlin shows, Machiavelli is not rejecting all morality in favour of amorality; rather he is rejecting one type of morality – Christian morality – in favour of another moral universe, one which ultimately derives from pagan sources, the morality of the leaders of Ancient Greece and Rome. Berlin puts his point forcefully:

> ... it is the first misinterpretation that goes deepest, that which represents Machiavelli as caring little or nothing for moral issues. This is surely not borne out by his own language. Anyone whose thought revolves round central concepts such as the good and the bad, the corrupt and the pure, has an ethical scale in mind in terms of which he gives moral praise and blame. Machiavelli's values are not Christian, but they are moral values.

(Ibid., p.49 below)

The second, connected, point made by Croce with which Berlin takes issue is that Machiavelli's fundamental reaction to the crimes committed by rulers was one of anguish (presumably brought about by his recognition of the conflict between the demands of Christian morality and the political need for a strong state – the conflicting demands of morality and expediency as Croce would have us understand it). Berlin finds no reluctance in Machiavelli, no 'trace of agony' that is consistent with this interpretation. The moral framework of *virtù* has no room for humility.

In order to assess Berlin's claims here it is important to have a clear sense of what 'moral' means. For some writers, moral action is simply action consistent with conventional rules of behaviour, such as the Ten Commandments. This is certainly not how Berlin uses the term 'moral'. For him, morality is not one particular system of values. In his essay 'The Pursuit of the Ideal' Berlin gives a convenient analysis of what he means by ethical thought (unlike some writers, Berlin uses 'ethical' and 'moral' interchangeably):

> Ethical thought consists of the systematic examination of the relations of human beings to each other, the conceptions, interests and ideals from which human ways of treating one another spring, and the systems of value on which such ends of life are based. These beliefs about how life should be lived, what men and women should be and do, are objects of moral enquiry; and when applied to groups and nations, and, indeed, mankind as a whole, are called political philosophy, which is but ethics applied to society.

(Berlin (1998), p.1)

For Berlin, Machiavelli's advice to princes evinces a moral system, because it implies a set of principles guiding one's life within which there is scope for praise and blame, and a sense of 'the good' and 'the bad'. In this sense Machiavelli's advice clearly presents a moral code. Nevertheless, it is easy to understand why some writers have thought that the set of values that Machiavelli wants his new prince to cultivate was not a *moral* system at all, so much does it subvert conventional Christian values. Some philosophers have maintained that simply because someone advocates certain principles of behaviour it does not follow that those merit the name moral principles. A comment made by the philosopher G.J. Warnock suggests this approach:

> Surely there have been individuals, and even whole societies, of whom or of which we should want to say that moral principles did not play any large part in their lives – that, perhaps, both their ideals of conduct and their actual conduct were shaped in accordance with standards that were not moral standards at all. Homer, in approving the ferocity, guile, and panache of the warrior chieftain, might be said to have been employing moral standards different from our own; but he might just as well, or better, be said not have been employing moral standards at all.

> (Warnock, G.J. (1967), p.54)

If we take Warnock's line here and apply it to the case of Machiavelli, we might decide that in describing the advice for princes as moral we may be misdescribing it: it is possible – contra Berlin – for someone to advocate standards and principles of behaviour without it following that these are moral standards and principles.

Yet, as our discussion of the comparative merits of Cesare Borgia and Agathocles show, Machiavelli distinguishes good from bad princes not simply on the basis of their success, but rather on the way in which they achieve it. There is some moral content to his advice in that it doesn't simply provide recipes for expediency, but rather attempts to distinguish between *virtù* and success achieved through treachery. Furthermore, the advice on how a prince should behave is not intended solely for the prince's benefit, but has at its heart a concern with a thriving city-state and how best it can be achieved – a concern which is clearly a moral one in that it involves consideration of others' interests and a vision of what is of value in life. Machiavelli is not advocating pagan virtue for its own sake, and for everybody, but rather on account of its worthwhile fruits when practised by new princes.

Berlin's interpretation of Machiavelli goes beyond correcting misreadings such as Croce's. From Machiavelli's writings he excavates the implied view that there are two worlds: one of personal morality, the other of political action, which is also a sphere of morality. The first world is the area within which Christian morality can operate; the second requires pagan *virtù*, not just in exceptional circumstances, but in the normal running of the state. Someone who chooses to live by the dictates of the first moral system cannot operate successfully in the realm of politics. Someone who chooses the second sphere of action will have to overcome any squeamishness, and may have to perform actions ruled impermissible by Christian morality. In other words, there are for Machiavelli two moral universes, each autonomous: the realm of Christian morality and the realm of pagan morality. Any attempt at compromise between the two will lead to ruin.

Where Berlin locates the true originality of Machiavelli's position is in its tendency to undermine a very widely held assumption of Western political thought. This is the view that there is, as Berlin terms it elsewhere, a 'final solution': some single principle which indicates how we ought to live. This principle is one which all rational beings should obey; many, for instance, have thought it to have been provided by God's word. This final solution to the great moral question 'How should we live?' might have been thought unachievable because human beings were 'too ignorant or too weak or too vicious to create it' (Reading 1.3, p.54 below). But most thinkers believed in this single answer to all moral issues. Berlin argues that Machiavelli's great originality was to have split open this rock on which so many Western beliefs and lives had been founded. Machiavelli demonstrated, albeit unwittingly, that there was something incoherent in the whole notion of a final solution. As Berlin puts it:

> There was profound disagreement about moral issues; but what none of these thinkers, not even the sceptics, had suggested was that there might exist ends – ends in themselves in terms of which alone everything else was justified – which were equally ultimate, but incompatible with one another, that there might exist no single universal overarching standard that would enable a man to choose rationally between them.

(Ibid., p.55 below)

For Berlin, Machiavelli's capacity to upset and unsettle in large part derives from this aspect of his thought. For those who are confident that any moral choice can ultimately be made by applying some kind of infallible measuring device that would indicate the right answer for any rational person, the suggestion that there could be incompatible moral systems comes as a shock. This 'awful truth' as Berlin calls it, is the source of so many readers' discomfort. It perhaps lies behind attempts to characterize Machiavelli as a cynic defending power politics, an amoralist, rather than someone whose views challenged an assumption close to the heart of the Western moral tradition.

The position which Berlin claims that Machiavelli foreshadows is usually known as *value-pluralism*. It is the view that there can be more than one set of values, and that these are incommensurable. This simply means that there is no common currency within which the two or more value systems can be compared, no straightforward way of making a comparison between them. According to Berlin, Machiavelli's position helped prepare the ground for liberal toleration. His argument is that once Machiavelli had shown that there are at least two incommensurable moralities – those of the ordinary person acting according to Christian principles and those of the Machiavellian prince – the logical next step was to move to a position of toleration. If there is no single overarching answer to the question 'How should we live?', then many of the justifications for persecuting those with whom you disagree lose their force:

> Toleration is historically the product of the realization of the irreconcilability of equally dogmatic faiths, and the practical improbability of complete victory of one over the other. Those who wished to survive realized that they had to tolerate error. They gradually came to see merits in diversity, and so became sceptical about definitive solutions in human affairs

(Ibid., p.57 below)

Whether or not Berlin has correctly identified the historical influence of Machiavelli's ideas, he has surely pinpointed the most disturbing aspect of his thought: the notion that the successful control of a state may be incompatible with the dictates of conventional morality. Honesty and mercy are precisely the qualities that are likely to bring about the downfall of a new prince, according to Machiavelli. This message is still a difficult one to stomach. This theme is taken up in C.A.J. Coady's article 'Dirty Hands' (Reading 1.4).

ACTIVITY

Read 'Dirty Hands' (Reading 1.4). This article helps to clarify precisely what the problem of 'dirty hands' in politics is. It also demonstrates the continuing relevance of Machiavelli's ideas to the contemporary debate.

When you have done this, re-read the whole of *The Prince*. You should now have a greater awareness of the philosophical implications of the book than you did on your first reading. Some passages will seem very familiar; others may still be puzzling. You should be in a better position to assess the plausibility of the various interpretations of *The Prince* you have read.

Conclusion

Reading *The Prince* as a contribution to political philosophy involves making clear his implied views on the tensions between conventional morality and the sorts of qualities he believed a successful leader needed. Although it is true that he has a dark view of human nature and sometimes advocates violent and apparently cruel solutions to political difficulties, it would not be fair to caricature him as simply an evil cynic. As Berlin's and Coady's articles make clear, his ideas can still challenge and stimulate present-day readers long after the 'mirrors for princes' his contemporaries wrote have disappeared from political discussion.

In the next chapter we will be considering a thinker who, like Machiavelli, had both a bleak view of human nature and a keen awareness of humanity's capacity to commit acts of violence – Thomas Hobbes.

Glossary

amoral

Completely outside the moral realm.

common good

Whatever is, on the whole, best for everyone. Machiavelli is far vaguer than later theorists, such as Rousseau, about what the common good is, and how we might discover it.

consequentialism

Any type of ethical theory which evaluates actions according to their likely effects rather than the motives from which they were performed.

deontological

This adjective describes any type of ethical theory that presents a code of absolute duties.

determinism

The view that we do not have genuine free will.

'dirty hands'

The issue of whether or not effective political activity must inevitably require a suspension of conventional individual moral standards is usually known as the problem of 'dirty hands' in politics.

fatalism

An attitude of abandoning oneself to the effects of chance or whatever it is one believes is determining one's apparent choices.

fortune

The usual translation of the Italian word *fortuna*. By this term Machiavelli means 'chance'. For him, half of what we do is governed by chance alone, which leaves half within our control. The part played by fortune in human affairs explains why some rulers who practised *virtù* nevertheless failed to achieve their ends. Machiavelli does, however, believe that those who act boldly are most likely to be successful in overcoming the effects of chance events, and that fortune favours youth.

immoral

Going against some established moral code.

incommensurable

Incapable of being compared directly because of a lack of common currency: two ways of life are incommensurable if there is no way of measuring them against each other.

republicanism

The view that the best form of government is one in which the people have a decisive say in running the state, or at least in who runs the state.

relativism

Relativists believe that there is no vantage point from which different moral systems can be compared, so no moral system can be said to be better (or worse) than any other.

value-pluralism

The view that there is more than one morality. Not the same as *relativism*. Berlin's value-pluralism does not imply that all moral systems are equal. It does, however, imply that there is no single correct answer to the question 'How should we live?'.

virtù

An Italian word usually translated as 'prowess'; this is the quality Machiavelli believes that a new prince should cultivate. It involves a willingness to be strong, yet cruel and deceitful where appropriate, and is the best precaution one can take against the effects of *fortune*. The adjective from *virtù* is *virtuoso*.

Further reading

Machiavelli's *The Discourses on the First Decade of Livy*, often known simply as the *Discourses* presents his defence of republicanism. There are several excellent translations of this available.

The Portable Machiavelli, edited and translated by Peter Bondanella and Mark Musa (Penguin, 1979), is a very useful collection of Machiavelli's writings including extracts from the *Discourses* and his play *Mandragola* (*The Mandrake Root*).

Sydney Anglo's *Machiavelli: A Dissection* (Paladin, 1971) is an interesting chronological account of Machiavelli's life and ideas.

The complete text of Isaiah Berlin's 'The Originality of Machiavelli' is in *The Proper Study of Mankind* (Pimlico, 1998).

Sebastian de Grazia's *Machiavelli in Hell* (Harvester, 1989) is a Pulitzer Prize-winning biography.

Thomas Nagel's 'Ruthlessness in Public Life' in *Mortal Questions* (Cambridge University Press, 1979) is an essay that takes up the Machiavellian theme of 'dirty hands'.

Quentin Skinner's *Machiavelli* (Oxford University Press, 1981) is an insightful overview of Machiavelli's life and ideas. Reading 1.1 is a substantial extract from this book. It has now been reissued as *Machiavelli: A Very Short Introduction* (Oxford University Press, 2000).

Maurizio Viroli's *Machiavelli* (Oxford University Press, 1998) interprets Machiavelli's thought in the light of the classical tradition of rhetoric.

Readings

'The Adviser to Princes'

Quentin Skinner

The Cambridge political historian Quentin Skinner explains the classical and contemporary influences on *The Prince*, providing insights into how Machiavelli's contemporaries would have understood the book.

Arms and the man: these are Machiavelli's two great themes in *The Prince*. The other lesson he accordingly wishes to bring home to the rulers of his age is that, in addition to having a sound army, a prince who aims to scale the heights of glory must cultivate the right qualities of princely leadership. The nature of these qualities had already been influentially analysed by the Roman moralists. They had argued in the first place that all great leaders need to some extent to be fortunate. For unless Fortune happens to smile, no amount of unaided human effort can hope to bring us to our highest goals. ... [H]owever, they also maintained that a special range of characteristics – those of the *vir* – tend to attract the favourable attentions of Fortune, and in this way almost guarantee us the attainment of honour, glory and fame. The assumptions underlying this belief are best summarized by Cicero in his *Tusculan Disputations*. He declares that, if we act from a thirst for *virtus* without any thought of winning glory as a result, this will give us the best chance of winning glory as well, provided that Fortune smiles; for glory is *virtus* rewarded.

This analysis was taken over without alteration by the humanists of Renaissance Italy. By the end of the fifteenth century, an extensive *genre* of humanist advice-books for princes had grown up, and had reached an unprecedentedly wide audience through the new medium of print. Such distinguished writers as Bartolomeo Sacchi, Giovanni Pontano and Francesco Patrizi all wrote treatises for the guidance of new rulers, all of which were founded on the same basic principle: that the possession of *virtus* is the key to princely success. As Pontano rather grandly proclaims in his tract on *The Prince*, any ruler who wishes to attain his noblest ends 'must rouse himself to follow the dictates of *virtus*' in all his public acts. *Virtus* is 'the most splendid thing in the world', more magnificent even than the sun, for 'the blind cannot see the sun' whereas 'even they can see *virtus* as plainly as possible'.

Machiavelli reiterates precisely the same beliefs about the relations between *virtù*, Fortune and the achievement of princely goals. He first makes these humanist allegiances clear in chapter 6 of *The Prince*, where he argues that 'in princedoms wholly new, where the prince is new, there is more or less difficulty in keeping them, according as the prince who acquires them is more or less *virtuoso*' (p.25). This is later corroborated in chapter 24, the aim of which is to explain 'Why the princes of Italy have lost their states' (p.88). Machiavelli insists that they 'should not blame Fortune' for their disgrace, because 'she only shows her power' when men of *virtù* 'do not prepare to resist her' (pp.89–90). Their losses are simply due to their failure to recognize that 'those defences alone are good' which 'depend on yourself and your own *virtù*' (p.89). Finally, the role of *virtù* is again underlined in chapter 26, the impassioned 'Exhortation' to liberate Italy that brings *The Prince* to an end. At this point Machiavelli reverts to the incomparable leaders mentioned in chapter 6 for their 'amazing *virtù*' – Moses, Cyrus and Theseus. He implies that nothing less than a union of their astonishing abilities with the greatest good Fortune will enable Italy to be saved. And he adds – in an uncharacteristic moment of preposterous flattery – that the 'glorious family' of the Medici luckily possess all the requisite qualities: they have tremendous *virtù*; they are immensely favoured by Fortune; and they are no less 'favoured by God and by the Church' (p.93).

It is often complained that Machiavelli fails to provide any definition of *virtù*, and even that ... he is 'innocent of any systematic use of the word'. But it will now be evident that he uses the term with complete consistency. Following his classical and humanist authorities, he treats it as that quality which enables a prince to withstand the blows of Fortune, to attract the goddess's favour, and to rise in consequence to the heights of princely fame, winning honour and glory for himself and security for his government.

It still remains, however, to consider what particular characteristics are to be expected in a man of *virtuoso* capacities. The Roman moralists had bequeathed a complex analysis of the concept of *virtus*, generally picturing the true *vir* as the possessor of three distinct yet affiliated sets of qualities. They took him to be endowed in the first place with the four 'cardinal' virtues of wisdom, justice, courage and temperance – the virtues that Cicero (following Plato) begins by singling out in the opening sections of *Moral Obligation*. But they also credited him with an additional range of qualities that later came to be regarded as peculiarly 'princely' in nature. The chief of these – the pivotal virtue of Cicero's *Moral Obligation* – was what Cicero called 'honesty', meaning a willingness to keep faith and deal honourably with all men at all times. This was felt to need supplementing by two further attributes, both of which were described in *Moral Obligation*, but were more extensively analysed by Seneca, who devoted special treatises to each of them. One was princely magnanimity, the theme of Seneca's *On Mercy*; the other was liberality, one of the major topics discussed in Seneca's *On Benefits*. Finally, the true *vir* was said to be characterized by his steady recognition of the fact that, if we wish to reach the goals of honour and glory, we must always be sure to behave as virtuously as possible. This contention – that it is always rational to be moral – lies at the heart of Cicero's *Moral Obligation*. He observes in Book II that many men believe 'that a thing may be morally right without being expedient, and expedient without being morally right'. But this is an illusion, for it is only by moral methods that we can hope to attain the objects of our desires. Any appearances to be contrary are wholly deceptive, for 'expediency can never conflict with moral rectitude'.

This analysis was again adopted in its entirety by the writers of advice-books for Renaissance princes. They made it their governing assumption that the general concept of *virtus* must refer to the complete list of cardinal and princely virtues, a list they proceeded to amplify and subdivide with so much attention to nuance that, in a treatise such as Patrizi's on *The Education of the King*, the overarching idea of *virtus* is eventually separated out into a series of some forty moral virtues which the ruler is expected to acquire. Next, they unhesitatingly endorsed the contention that the rational course of action for the prince to follow will always be the moral one, arguing the point with so much force that they eventually made it proverbial to say that 'honesty is the best policy'. And finally, they contributed a specifically Christian objection to any divorce between expediency and the moral realm. They insisted that, even if we succeed in advancing our interests by perpetrating injustices in this present life, we can still expect to find these apparent advantages cancelled out when we are justly visited with divine retribution in the life to come.

If we examine the moral treatises of Machiavelli's contemporaries we find these arguments tirelessly reiterated. But when we turn to *The Prince* we find this aspect of humanist morality suddenly and violently overturned. The upheaval begins in chapter 15, when Machiavelli starts to discuss the princely virtues and vices, and warns us that although 'many have written about this' already, he is going to 'depart very far from the methods of the others' (p.57). He begins by alluding to the familiar humanist commonplaces: that there is a special group of princely virtues; that these include the need to be liberal, merciful and truthful; and that all rulers have a duty to cultivate these qualities. Next he concedes – still in orthodox humanist vein – that 'it would be most praiseworthy for a prince' to be able at all times to act in such ways. But then he totally rejects the fundamental humanist assumption that these are the virtues a ruler needs to acquire if he wishes to achieve his highest ends. This belief – the nerve and heart of humanist advice-books for princes – he regards as an obvious and disastrous mistake. He agrees of course about the nature of the ends to be pursued: every prince must seek to maintain his state and obtain glory for himself. But he objects that, if these goals are to be attained, no ruler can possibly 'possess or fully practise' all the qualities that are usually 'considered good'. The position in which any prince finds himself is that of trying to protect his interests in a dark world in which most men 'are not good'. It follows that, if he 'insists on making it his business to be good' among so many who are not, he will not only fail to achieve 'great things' but 'will surely be destroyed' (p.58).

Machiavelli's criticism of classical and contemporary humanism is thus a simple but devastating one. He argues that, if a ruler wishes to reach his highest goals, he will *not* always find it rational to be moral; on the contrary, he will find that any consistent attempt to 'practise all those things for which men are considered good' will prove a ruinously irrational policy (p.66). But what of the Christian objection that this is a foolish as well as a wicked position to adopt, since it forgets the day of judgement on which all injustices will finally be punished? About this Machiavelli says nothing at all. His silence is eloquent, indeed epoch-making; it echoed around Christian Europe, at first eliciting a stunned silence in return, and then a howl of execration that has never finally died away.

If princes ought not to conduct themselves according to the dictates of conventional morality, how ought they to conduct themselves? Machiavelli's response – the core of his positive advice to new rulers – is given at the beginning of chapter 15. A wise prince will be guided above all by the dictates of necessity: 'in order to hold his position', he 'must acquire the power to be not good, and understand when to use it and when not to use it' as circumstances direct (p.58). Three chapters later, this basic doctrine is repeated. A wise prince 'holds to what is right when he can', but he 'knows how to do wrong when this is necessitated'. Moreover, he must reconcile himself to the fact that 'he will often be necessitated' to act 'contrary to truth, contrary to charity, contrary to humanity, contrary to religion' if he wishes 'to maintain his government' (p.66).

As we have seen, the crucial importance of this insight was first put to Machiavelli at an early stage in his diplomatic career. It was after conversing with the cardinal of Volterra in 1503, and with Pandolfo Petrucci some two years later, that he originally felt impelled to record what was later to become his central political belief: that the clue to successful statecraft lies in recognizing the force of circumstances, accepting what necessity dictates, and harmonizing one's behaviour with the times. A year after Pandolfo gave him this recipe for princely success, we find Machiavelli putting forward a similar set of observations as his own ideas for the first time. While stationed at Perugia in September 1506, watching the astonishing progress of Julius II's campaign, he fell to musing in a letter to his friend Giovan Soderini about the reasons for triumph and disaster in civil and military affairs. 'Nature', he declares, 'has given every man a particular talent and inspiration' which 'controls each one of us'. But 'the times are varied' and 'subject to frequent change', so that 'those who fail to alter their ways of proceeding' are bound to encounter 'good Fortune at one time and bad at another'. The moral is obvious: if a man wishes 'always to enjoy good Fortune', he must 'be wise enough to accommodate himself to the times'. Indeed, if everyone were 'to command his nature' in this way, and 'match his way of proceeding with his age', then 'it would genuinely come true that the wise man would be the ruler of the stars and of the fates' (p.73).

Writing *The Prince* seven years later, Machiavelli virtually copied out these 'Caprices', as he deprecatingly called them, in his chapter on the role of Fortune in human affairs. Everyone, he says, likes to follow his own particular bent: one person acts 'with caution, another impetuously; one by force, the other with skill'. But in the meantime, 'times and affairs change', so that a ruler who 'does not change his way of proceeding' will be bound sooner or later to encounter ill-luck. However, if 'he could change his nature with times and affairs, Fortune would not change'. So the successful prince will always be the one 'who adapts his way of proceeding to the nature of the times' (pp.90–1).

By now it will be evident that the revolution Machiavelli engineered in the *genre* of advice-books for princes was based in effect on redefining the pivotal concept of *virtù*. He endorses the conventional assumption that *virtù* is the name of that congeries of qualities which enables a prince to ally with Fortune and obtain honour, glory and fame. But he divorces the meaning of the term from any necessary connection with the cardinal and princely virtues. He argues instead that the defining characteristic of a truly *virtuoso* prince will be a willingness to do whatever is dictated by necessity – whether the action happens to be wicked or virtuous – in order to attain his highest ends. So *virtù* comes to denote precisely the requisite quality of moral flexibility in a prince: 'he must have a mind ready to turn in any direction as Fortune's winds and the variability of affairs require' (p.66).

Machiavelli takes some pains to point out that this conclusion opens up an unbridgeable gulf between himself and the whole tradition of humanist political thought, and does so in his most savagely ironic style. To the classical moralists and their innumerable followers, moral virtue had been the defining characteristic of the *vir*, the man of true manliness. Hence to abandon virtue was not merely to act irrationally; it was also to abandon one's status as a man and descend to the level of the beasts. As Cicero had put it in Book I of *Moral Obligation*, there are two ways in which wrong may be done, either by force or by fraud. Both, he declares, 'are bestial' and 'wholly unworthy of man' – force because it typifies the lion and fraud because it 'seems to belong to the cunning fox'.

To Machiavelli, by contrast, it seemed obvious that manliness is not enough. There are indeed two ways of acting, he says at the start of chapter 18, of which 'the first is suited to man, the second to the animals'. But 'because the first is often not sufficient, a prince must resort to the second' (p.64). One of the things a prince therefore needs to know is which animals to imitate. Machiavelli's celebrated advice is that he will come off best if he 'chooses among the beasts the fox and the lion', supplementing the ideals of manly decency with the indispensable arts of force and fraud (p.65). This conception is underlined in the next chapter, in which Machiavelli discusses one of his favourite historical characters, the Roman emperor Septimius Severus. First he assures us that the emperor was 'a man of very great *virtù*' (p.72). And then, explaining the judgement, he adds that Septimius' great qualities were those of 'a very savage lion and a very tricky fox', as a result of which he was 'feared and respected by everybody' (p.73).

Machiavelli rounds off his analysis by indicating the lines of conduct to be expected from a truly *virtuoso* prince. In chapter 19 he puts the point negatively, stressing that such a ruler will never do anything worthy of contempt, and will always take the greatest care 'to avoid everything that makes him hated' (p.67). In chapter 21 the positive implications are then spelled out. Such a prince will always act 'without reservation' towards his allies and enemies, boldly standing forth 'as a vigorous supporter of one side'. At the same time, he will seek to present himself to his subjects as majestically as possible, doing 'extra-ordinary things' and keeping them 'always in suspense and wonder, watching for the outcome' (pp.81–3).

In the light of this account, it is easy to understand why Machiavelli felt such admiration for Cesare Borgia, and wished to hold him up – despite his obvious limitations – as a pattern of *virtù* for other new princes. For Borgia had demonstrated, on one terrifying occasion, that he understood perfectly the paramount importance of avoiding the hatred of the people while at the same time keeping them in awe. The occasion was when he realized that his government of the Romagna, in the capable but tyrannical hands of Rimirro de Orco, was falling into the most serious danger of all, that of becoming an object of hatred to those living under it. As we have seen,

Machiavelli was an eye-witness of Borgia's cold-blooded solution to the dilemma: the summary murder of Rimirro and the exhibition of his body in the public square as a sacrifice to the people's rage.

Machiavelli's belief in the imperative need to avoid popular hatred and contempt should perhaps be dated from this moment. But even if the duke's action merely served to corroborate his own sense of political realities, there is no doubt that the episode left him deeply impressed. When he came to discuss the issues of hatred and contempt in *The Prince*, this was precisely the incident he recalled in order to illustrate his point. He makes it clear that Borgia's action had struck him on reflection as being profoundly right. It was resolute; it took courage; and it brought about exactly the desired effect, since it left the people 'gratified and awestruck' while at the same time removing their 'cause for hatred'. Summing up in his iciest tones, Machiavelli remarks that the duke's conduct seems to him, as usual, to be 'worthy of notice and of being copied by others' (p.31).

The new morality

Machiavelli is fully aware that his new analysis of princely *virtù* raises some new difficulties. He states the main dilemma in the course of chapter 15: on the one hand, a prince must 'acquire the power to be not good' and exercise it whenever this is dictated by necessity; but on the other hand, he must be careful not to acquire the reputation of being a wicked man, because this will tend to 'take his position away from him' instead of securing it (p.58). The problem is thus to avoid appearing wicked even when you cannot avoid behaving wickedly.

Moreover, the dilemma is even sharper than this implies, for the true aim of the prince is not merely to secure his position, but is of course to win honour and glory as well. As Machiavelli indicates in recounting the story of Agathocles, the tyrant of Sicily, this greatly intensifies the predicament in which any new ruler finds himself. Agathocles, we are told, 'lived a wicked life' at every stage of his career and was known as a man of 'outrageous cruelty and inhumanity'. These attributes brought him immense success, enabling him to rise from 'low and abject Fortune' to become king of Syracuse and hold on to his principality 'without any opposition from the citizens'. But as Machiavelli warns us, in a deeply revealing phrase, such unashamed cruelties may bring us 'sovereignty, but not glory'. Although Agathocles was able to maintain his state by means of these qualities, 'they cannot be called *virtù*' and they 'do not permit him to be honoured among the noblest men' (pp.35–6).

Finally, Machiavelli refuses to admit that the dilemma can be resolved by setting stringent limits to princely wickedness, and in general behaving honourably towards one's subjects and allies. This is exactly what one cannot hope to do, because all men at all times 'are ungrateful, changeable, simulators and dissimulators, runaways in danger, eager for gain', so that 'a prince who bases himself entirely on their word, if he is lacking in other preparations, falls' (p.62). The implication is that 'a prince, and above all a prince who is new' will often – not just occasionally – find himself forced by necessity to act 'contrary to humanity' if he wishes to keep his position and avoid being deceived (p.66).

These are acute difficulties, but they can certainly be overcome. The prince need only remember that, although it is not necessary to have all the qualities usually considered good, it is 'very necessary to appear to have them' (p.66). It is good to be considered liberal; it is sensible to seem merciful and not cruel; it is essential in general to be 'thought to be of great merit' (pp.59, 61, 68). The solution is thus to become 'a great simulator and dissimulator', learning 'how to addle the brains of men with trickery' and make them believe in your pretence (pp.64–5).

Machiavelli had received an early lesson in the value of addling men's brains. As we have seen, he had been present when the struggle developed between Cesare Borgia and Julius II in the closing months of 1503, and it is evident that the impressions he carried away from that occasion were still uppermost in his mind when he came to write about the question of dissimulation in *The Prince*. He immediately refers back to the episode he had witnessed, using it as his main example of the need to remain constantly on one's guard against princely duplicity. Julius, he recalls, managed to conceal his hatred of Borgia so cleverly that he caused the duke to fall into the egregious error of believing that 'men of high rank forget old injuries'. He was then able to put his powers of dissimulation to decisive use. Having won the papal election with Borgia's full support, he suddenly revealed his true feelings, turned against the duke and 'caused his final ruin'. Borgia certainly blundered at this point, and Machiavelli feels that he deserved to be blamed severely for his mistake. He ought to have known that a talent for addling men's brains is part of the armoury of any successful prince (p.34).

Machiavelli cannot have been unaware, however, that in recommending the arts of deceit as the key to success he was in danger of sounding too glib. More orthodox moralists had always been prepared to consider the suggestion that hypocrisy might be used as a short cut to glory, but had always gone on to rule out any such possibility. Cicero, for example, had explicitly canvassed the idea in Book II of *Moral Obligation*, only to dismiss it as a manifest absurdity. Anyone, he declares, who 'thinks that he can win lasting glory by pretence' is 'very much mistaken'. The reason is that 'true glory strikes deep roots and spreads its branches wide', whereas 'all pretences soon fall to the ground like fragile flowers'.

Machiavelli responds, as before, by rejecting such earnest sentiments in his most ironic style. He insists in chapter 18 that the practice of hypocrisy is not merely indispensable to princely government, but is capable of being sustained without much difficulty for as long as may be required. Two distinct reasons are offered for this deliberately provocative conclusion. One is that most men are so simple-minded, and above all so prone to self-deception, that they usually take things at face value in a wholly uncritical way (p.65). The other is that, when it comes to assessing the behaviour of princes, even the shrewdest observers are largely condemned to judge by appearances. Isolated from the populace, protected by 'the majesty of the government', the prince's position is such that 'everybody sees what you appear to be' but 'few perceive what you are' (p.67). Thus there is no reason to suppose that your sins will find you out; on the contrary, 'a prince who deceives always finds men who let themselves be deceived' (p.65).

The final issue Machiavelli discusses is what attitude we should take towards the new rules he has sought to inculcate. At first sight he appears to adopt a relatively conventional moral stance. He agrees in chapter 15 that 'it would be most praiseworthy' for new princes to exhibit those qualities which are normally considered good, and he equates the abandonment of the princely virtues with the process of learning 'to be not good' (p.58). The same scale of values recurs even in the notorious chapter on 'How princes should keep their promises'. Machiavelli begins by affirming that everybody realizes how praiseworthy it is when a ruler 'lives with sincerity and not with trickery', and goes on to insist that a prince ought not merely to seem conventionally virtuous, but ought 'actually to be so' as far as possible, 'holding to what is right when he can', and only turning away from the virtues when this is dictated by necessity (pp.64, 66).

However, two very different arguments are introduced in the course of chapter 15, each of which is subsequently developed. First of all, Machiavelli is somewhat quizzical about whether we can properly say that those qualities which are considered good, but are nevertheless ruinous, really deserve the name of virtues. Since they are prone to bring destruction, he prefers to say that they 'look like virtues'; and since their opposites are more likely to bring 'safety and well-being', he prefers to say that they 'look like vices' (p.59).

This suggestion is pursued in both the succeeding chapters. Chapter 16, entitled 'Liberality and stinginess', picks up a theme handled by all the classical moralists and turns it on its head. When Cicero discusses the virtue of liberality in *Moral Obligation*, he defines it as a desire to 'avoid any suspicion of penuriousness', together with an awareness that no vice is more offensive in a political leader than parsimony and avarice. Machiavelli replies that, if this is what we mean by liberality, it is the name not of a virtue but of a vice. He argues that a ruler who wishes to avoid a reputation for parsimony will find that he 'cannot neglect any kind of lavishness'. As a result, he will find himself having 'to burden his people excessively' to pay for his generosity, a policy which will soon make him 'hateful to his subjects'. Conversely, if he begins by abandoning any desire to act with such munificence, he may well be called miserly at the outset, but 'in course of time he will be thought more and more liberal', and will in fact be practising the true virtue of liberality (p.59).

A similar paradox appears in the following chapter, entitled 'Cruelty and mercy'. This too had been a favourite topic among the Roman moralists, Seneca's essay *On Mercy* being the most celebrated treatment of the theme. According to Seneca, a prince who is merciful will always show 'how loath he is to turn his hand' to punishment; he will resort to it only 'when great and repeated wrongdoing has overcome his patience'; and he will inflict it only 'after great reluctance' and 'much procrastination' as well as with the greatest possible clemency. Faced with this orthodoxy, Machiavelli insists once more that it represents a complete misunderstanding of the virtue involved. If you begin by trying to be merciful, so that you 'let evils continue' and only turn to punishment after 'murders or plunder' begin, your conduct will be far less clement than that of a prince who has the courage to begin by 'giving a very few examples of cruelty'. Machiavelli cites the example of the Florentines, who wanted 'to escape being called cruel' on a particular occasion, and in consequence acted in such a way that the destruction of an entire city resulted – an outcome hideously more cruel than any cruelty they could have devised. This is contrasted with the behaviour of Cesare Borgia, who 'was thought cruel', but used 'that well-known cruelty of his' so well that he 'reorganized the Romagna', united it and 'brought it to peace and loyalty', achieving all these beneficial results by means of his alleged viciousness (p.61).

This leads Machiavelli to a closely connected question which he puts forward – with a similar air of self-conscious paradox – later in the same chapter: 'is it better to be loved than feared, or the reverse?' (p.62). Again the classic answer had been furnished by Cicero in *Moral Obligation*. 'Fear is but a poor safeguard of lasting power', whereas love 'may be trusted to keep it safe for ever'. Again Machiavelli registers his total dissent. 'It is much safer', he retorts, 'for a prince to be feared than loved.' The reason is that many of the qualities that make a prince loved also tend to bring him into contempt. If your subjects have no 'dread of punishment' they will take every chance to deceive you for their own profit. But if you make yourself feared, they will hesitate to offend or injure you, as a result of which you will find it much easier to maintain your state (p.62).

The other line of argument in these chapters reflects an even more decisive rejection of conventional humanist morality. Machiavelli suggests that, even if the qualities usually considered good are indeed virtues – such that a ruler who flouts them will undoubtedly be falling into vice – he ought not to worry about such vices if he thinks them either useful or irrelevant to the conduct of his government (p.58).

Machiavelli's main concern at this point is to remind new rulers of their most basic duty of all. A wise prince 'will not worry about incurring reproaches for those vices without which he can hardly maintain his position'; he will see that such criticisms are merely an unavoidable cost he has to bear in the course of discharging his fundamental obligation, which is of course to maintain his state (p.58). The implications are first spelled out in relation to the supposed vice of parsimony. Once a wise prince perceives that stinginess is 'one of those vices that make him reign', he will judge it 'of little importance to incur the name of a stingy man' (p.60). The same applies in the case of cruelty. A willingness to act on occasion with exemplary severity is crucial to the preservation of good order in civil as in military affairs. This means that a wise prince is 'not troubled about a reproach for cruelty', and that 'it is altogether essential not to worry about being called cruel' if you are an army commander, for 'without such a reputation' you can never hope to keep your troops 'united or fit for any action' (pp.61, 63).

Lastly, Machiavelli considers whether it is important for a ruler to eschew the lesser vices and sins of the flesh if he wishes to maintain his state. The writers of advice-books for princes generally dealt with this issue in a sternly moralistic vein, echoing Cicero's insistence in Book I of *Moral Obligation* that propriety is 'essential to moral rectitude', and thus that all persons in positions of authority must avoid all lapses of conduct in their personal lives. By contrast, Machiavelli answers with a shrug. A wise prince 'protects himself from such vices if he can'; but if he finds he cannot, then 'he passes over them with little concern', not troubling himself about such ordinary susceptibilities at all (p.58).

Note

From Skinner, Quentin (1981) *Machiavelli*, Oxford University Press, Past Masters series, pp.34–47. Page references to *The Prince* are from Gilbert, Allan (trans.) (1965) *Machiavelli: The Chief Works and Others*, 3 vols, Duke University Press.

'Machiavelli's Political Philosophy in *The Prince*'

Maureen Ramsay

Maureen Ramsay examines the central philosophical issues which emerge from reading *The Prince*. She pays particular attention to Machiavelli's treatment of questions of means and ends.

The purpose [here] is to attempt to clarify Machiavelli's position on the means–end relationship and the relationship between politics and morality. In particular [this Reading] will examine the originality and uniqueness of Machiavelli's views in relation to past and present political and ethical thought, and argue that, despite their notoriety, his ideas and their attendant problems are a common feature both of political thought and practice and also of personal and political life.

Ends and means, politics and morality

Whether or not Machiavelli conceived of the means–end relationship as justificatory, as descriptive or as a technical imperative is a matter of dispute. In a sense, his glaring illustration that there is no escape from the weight of means and ends combines all three aspects of the relationship. This is because this is the way people do behave: people constantly act as though the end justifies the means, and, without judging any particular end to be good or bad, practical necessity dictates that certain means will be required to achieve them. Whether there are some means so evil that they should never be used, or whether there are some ends so good that they justify any means, is a separate question, but not one Machiavelli avoided. In fact, it is precisely his testament to these permanent questions that generates interest in Machiavelli.

For Machiavelli, the ends of political life were the acquiring and holding down of power, the stability of the state, the maintenance of order and general prosperity. To say that Machiavelli was a scientist or a technician of political life because he was not concerned with whether such ends were rational or good is to overstate the case.[1] He never explicitly justified these ends, but simply accepted them as given, because he assumed that order and security were universal ends that all human beings aspire to, and that these were necessary for human welfare. If this is so, then it is plausible to see Machiavelli as implicitly concerned with ends, the moral purpose of which is to secure the good for human beings, given what he took to be in human interests and the context of human desires. However, if the ends of order and stability are to be achieved, what means are morally permissible as well as practically expedient?

Machiavelli was not concerned to define moral rules and explain why they should be obeyed, or to define the rights, duties and obligations of princes or citizens. Rather he was concerned in *The Prince* with those qualities (capacities and dispositions) rulers must have to establish, restore or maintain order and stability. These qualities were psychological and social rather than traditional moral traits. In chapter XV he lists some of the qualities that normally bring praise or blame and admits that it would be praiseworthy for a prince to exhibit those qualities which are considered good. Machiavelli here is not denying that liberality, mercy, honesty, kindness, chastity, reliability and tolerance are virtues. He is, though, drawing attention to the fact that no ruler can possess or fully practise them because the realities of the human condition dictate behaviour which by normal standards would be condemned as immoral. The irony of the political situation is such that 'when we carefully examine the whole matter, we find some qualities that look like virtues, yet if the prince practises them – they will be his destruction, and other qualities that look like virtues, yet if the prince practises them – they will be his destruction, and other qualities that look like vices, yet – if he practises them – they will bring him safety and well-being' (chapter XV, p.101). Chapters XVI–XVIII illustrate in detail this point, that morally good human actions can lead to evil results, and immoral actions may have beneficial consequences. The classical virtue of liberality is considered to be a good, yet the consistent practice of it can be damaging. A liberal prince may use up all his resources and be forced in the end to tax his people excessively and so make him hateful to his subjects. His liberality injures the many and rewards the few as well as bringing ruin to himself. Whereas if a prince is mean initially, he will have enough income to carry out his enterprises without harming the people or becoming extortionate. Similarly with cruelty and mercy. In chapter XVII, Machiavelli writes:

> Cesare Borgia was thought cruel; nevertheless that well-known cruelty of his reorganized the Romagna, united it, brought it to peace and loyalty. If we look at this closely, we see that he was more merciful than the Florentine people, who, to escape being called cruel, allowed the ruin of Pistoia. A wise prince, then, is not troubled about a reproach for cruelty which keeps his subjects united and loyal because, giving a very few examples of cruelty, he is more merciful than those who, through too much mercy, let evils continue, from which result murder or plunder, because the latter commonly harm a whole group, but those executions that come from the prince harm individuals only.

> (*The Prince*, XVII, p.104)

Here Machiavelli is making three points. First, as in the case of liberality, he is not denying that mercy is a virtue. Just as in order to be liberal the Prince might have first to be mean, so in order to be merciful the Prince might have to be cruel. What is valued here is still the traditional virtue. Second, the selective use of cruelty can bring about the benefits of unity, peace and loyalty, whereas too much mercy can lead to ruin. This is not simply an appeal to the good consequences cruelty might promote *per se*, but a recognition that well-intentioned failure to act may have consequences far more cruel than the original inaction was designed to avoid. Where omissions have worse consequences, then cruelty is the preferable course of action. The aim is to avoid cruelty, not to promote it. This is obvious in the third point, that the lesser evil consists in harm to individuals rather than to a whole group. In political situations where choices between two evils have to be made, it is more morally responsible to act to choose the lesser evil. Machiavelli is not just simply saying that good ends outweigh immoral means; that moral squeamishness in abstaining from immoral means does not absolve responsibility for the bad consequences which result from omissions; or that in some situations the best course of action is that which avoids the worst excesses of violence and cruelty; or even that the Prince cannot conform to conventional moral standards if the interests of the state or the common good are to be preserved. He is also saying that sometimes, in employing immoral means, the Prince will be closer to displaying the virtues of conventional morality than those who, by embodying these virtues, achieve the opposite. The quality of mercy might be cruelty in disguise – we may have to be cruel in order to be kind.

Machiavelli does not disregard conventional morality as such. He exhorts his Prince to act according to the accepted virtues of truth, charity, humanity and religion when he can. That is, when the political situation is stable and secure. In these circumstances public and conventional morality are identical. However, the Prince must be adaptable and 'have a mind ready to turn in any direction as Fortune's winds and the variety of affairs require yet ... he holds to what is right when he can and knows how to do wrong when he must' (chapter XVIII, p.108). This is because politics poses questions for which conventional morality is inappropriate. In times of necessity the Prince must be unconstrained by normal ethical ideals and adopt methods which, though contrary to these ideas, will lead to beneficial consequences. Here there seems to be a split between private and public morality, so that, in certain circumstances, the latter has its own distinctive ethic.

However, there are passages where Machiavelli seems to indicate that the distinction he is making is not between private and public morality itself but rather between conventional morality and what people actually do in both the public and the private sphere. This is seen in his comments on human nature and human behaviour. These suggest it is partly because people do not act according to the dictates of conventional morality in the daily business of their lives that the Prince must behave in a similar fashion. In chapter XVIII, for instance, he argues for the breaking of promises on two grounds. The first is with reference to a consequentialist ethic, for experience shows that princes who do break their promises have done great things. The second is with reference to the corrupt nature and behaviour of human beings in general. A prudent prince cannot keep his word, first, when it works against him and, second, 'when the reasons that made him promise are annulled. If all men were good, this maxim would not be good, but because they are bad and do not keep their promises to you, you likewise do not have to keep yours to them' (chapter XVIII, p.107). Here, the Prince is not to act as he ought, according to abstract, conventional virtues, but as other people act. Similarly, when discussing cruelty and mercy, and whether it is better to be loved than feared, Machiavelli advises it is safer to be feared, given the nature of human beings:

> Because we can say this about men in general: they are ungrateful, changeable, simulators and dissimulators, runaways in danger, eager for gain; they offer you their blood, their property, their lives, their children ... when need is far off; but when it comes near you, they turn about. A prince who bases himself entirely on their words, if he is lacking other preparations, fails; because friendships gained with money, not with greatness and nobility of spirit are purchased but not possessed, and at the right times cannot be turned to account. Men have less hesitation in injuring one who makes himself loved than one who makes himself feared, for love is held by a chain of duty which, since men are bad, they break at every chance for their own profit; but fear is held by a dread of punishment that never fails you.

(*The Prince*, XVII, pp.104–5)

'Men' in general do not exhibit the qualities of conventional morality. The Prince can deceive because he 'always finds men who let themselves be deceived' (chapter XVIII, p.107). The Prince need only appear to have the conventional virtues of mercy, faith, integrity and religion 'because in general men judge more with their eyes than with their heads, since everybody can see but few can perceive' (chapter XVIII, p.109). It seems, too, that the Prince must adopt a consequentialist ethic because it is the case that 'as to the actions of all men and especially those of princes, against whom charges cannot be brought in court, everyone looks at their result' (chapter XVIII, p.109).

In order to bring about beneficial results the Prince must cultivate not conventional virtue but Machiavellian *virtù*. There is much scholarly dispute as to whether Machiavelli attached a precise or consistent meaning to *virtù*. Russell Price has shown that Machiavelli used *virtù* as a complex cluster concept which includes traditional, Christian moral virtue, military *virtù*, political *virtù*, a combination of military and political *virtù*, an instrumental *virtù*, cultural virtue as well as ancient and modern *virtù*.[2] It is clear, though, that princely *virtù* for Machiavelli was a consistent concept in so far as it embodied those qualities, capacities and dispositions necessary for the Prince to establish, restore or maintain the stability of the state, to win honour and glory for himself and to overcome the blows of fortune.[3] The quality of *virtù* is displayed in a mode of conduct which Geerken argues underlies the plurality of meanings and has three components: '(a) suitability to prevailing circumstances, (b) adequate deliberation regarding options, priorities and consequences, and, finally, (c) timely and successful action'.[4]

Virtù, then, will consist of different qualities at different times given what is necessary to attain goals in particular circumstances. Qualities which manifest *virtù* include fortitude in adversity, foresight and insight, willingness to take risks, resourcefulness and firmness of purpose. The qualities of *virtù* can be displayed in evil actions as well as good. Hence Machiavelli's admiration for Cesare Borgia who, though cruel, was an exemplar of these qualities.

However, Machiavelli did not admire all actions simply because they were bold, resolute and effective. When discussing Agothocles, the tyrant of Sicily, in chapter VIII he makes the distinction between cruelty 'well' and 'ill' used. 'Well-used' cruelties are those that are necessary and constructive, those which a conqueror must carry out and 'then does not persist in' and which he then 'transmutes into the greatest possible benefit to his subjects' (chapter VIII, p.82). 'Ill-used' cruelties are those which persist with time and which are unnecessary and destructive. Agothocles showed fortitude in adversity and was bold, resolute and resourceful, but his 'outrageous cruelty and inhumanity together with his countless wicked acts do not permit him to be honoured among the noblest men'. Acting in this manner may bring success and 'sovereignty but not glory' (chapter VIII, p.81). The difference between the deeds of Agothocles and Borgia was that if Borgia had succeeded his deeds would have resulted in a strong state and so the common good (whether or not the latter was his intention). Agothocles' deeds involved uneconomic and gratuitous cruelty and led to a worse state of affairs than before. Machiavelli is reluctant to admit that Agothocles' deeds were worthy of the name *virtù*. *Virtù* is ascribed to actions consistent with the acquisition of glory, when dictated through necessity and where they serve common interests and the needs of the public realm.

When evaluating the relationship between means and ends and between politics and morality in *The Prince*, it is necessary to see the problematic against the backdrop of Machiavelli's pessimistic assumptions about the timeless and unchanging nature of human motives and aspirations. Machiavelli's view of human beings as natural egotists with a lust for domination and power led him to see history as an arena of conflict involving deceit, treachery and violence. The roots of this conflict were psychological, but the solution was social and political. The ends of political life were to achieve the order and stability necessary to secure the fundamental human desires of self-preservation and security. Therefore political morality must be one designed to achieve these ends. Conventional morality in many circumstances is inappropriate and seems to defeat these purposes. This is because the consistent practice of traditional virtues may lead to outcomes which are not virtuous, even according to that tradition's own standard, and because observing these virtues may not lead to good consequences. Conventionally immoral actions may bring beneficial results, whereas an action done for a good motive or a well-intentioned inaction may have bad or worse consequences than the supposed immoral action. Failing to act for reasons of moral purity does not lessen the responsibility for bad consequences which result from the omission. At certain political conjunctions, it is morally necessary to employ evil means to achieve the desired result. This is not because conventional virtues are not good in themselves or desirable for both public and private practices but because people are not by nature good and do not live according to these abstract virtues in either the public or the private sphere. In order for people to live according to the virtues, certain conditions of political security and stability must pertain. When this is the case moral questions can be raised and moral virtues can be pursued within the accepted values of the established and stable community. When this is not the case, conventionally immoral actions are necessary to establish the conditions for morality and what is politically and ultimately personally valuable depends on prudential calculation. Here conventional values are questioned against the criteria of human interests and desires and the result is a consequentialist ethic. An effective political morality must be one designed for human beings as they are, in the circumstances they find themselves in, in order to create a situation where human beings will be fit for morality.

[...]

Other traditions in political and ethical thought

If Machiavelli was the first political theorist explicitly to endorse a prudential and consequentialist ethic based on beliefs about human nature and society, he certainly was not the last. Two dominant traditions in the history of both political and ethical thought take on board, albeit in more sophisticated form, certain features of Machiavelli's assumptions and conclusions.

Aspects of Machiavelli's ideas pave the way for the rise of liberal thought which opens up with the development of capitalism and which begins in a systematic, theoretical form with Hobbes. In this tradition, the abstract pre-social individual is the most fundamental and important social unit, while power and stability are the ultimate goals of social and political life. For Machiavelli, and the liberal tradition, the individual stands apart from society. Society is the backdrop against which individuals separated from their social relationships and roles act to achieve their own ends. Human beings, their motives and aspirations are defined independently of the specific social context in which these are formulated and experienced. They are essentially the same at all times and places because they are motivated by the same insatiable passions. Human beings are self-assertive, self-preserving, infinitely desirous and endlessly ambitious in a world of scarcity and limited satisfactions. The realization of the most fundamental human desires for self-preservation and security can be achieved by creating a strong and stable state. Human psychology thus becomes the cause of external conflict and the remedy for social cohesion. Self-preservation is the overriding motivational factor in creating or maintaining political arrangements which promote human desires. It follows, then, that if human beings are solely motivated by such desires, morality can be imposed by force, derived from fear of sanctions or observed only because doing so leads to their satisfaction. Moral injunctions now take the form of technical imperatives and become factual statements about the means necessary to achieve the given and required end. Reasoning in moral matters is concerned not with questioning or revising these ends but with prudential calculation, assisting human beings to attain their ends – the most basic of which is security. In brief, notwithstanding the differences in and the developments of political and moral thought, the liberal tradition continues to have at its core the key dichotomies and assumptions found in Machiavelli: the separation of the individual and society and also of the private and public sphere; the sovereignty of the individual; the pre-social, pre-political notion of an unchanging human nature; the instrumental nature of rationality and morality.

Continuities with the issues Machiavelli raises, however, are nowhere more apparent than in traditions of ethical justification and their ongoing problems. It would be absurd to attribute to Machiavelli a systematic ethical theory, but in so far as the doctrine of political expediency embodies his views on politics and morality, this has parallels with all forms of normative and political theories which rely on a utilitarian or consequentialist ethic. For Croce and his followers to argue that Machiavelli divorced morality from politics is to make a false antithesis. Isaiah Berlin suggests that what Machiavelli distinguishes is not moral from political values but two incompatible ways of life and therefore two moralities. For Berlin, these are the morality of the pagan and heroic world versus Platonic-Hebraic-Christian morality, each with its own values and claims to ultimacy. Machiavelli was not rejecting Christian values but showing the need 'to choose either a good, virtuous private life or a good, successful social existence, but not both'.[5] Dante Germino[6] has proposed that Machiavelli's position can be seen as similar to the contrast made by Weber (in *Politik als Beruf* ['Politics as a vocation']) between 'ethics of responsibility' and 'ethics of intention', in which it is irresponsible in politics to act out of pure motives of individual conscience, without weighing the consequences which actually result. But, broadly speaking, the legacy of Machiavelli is the contrast not between the political and the moral but between consequentialist ethics and all other forms. Consequentialist ethics contrast with Christian, traditional and Kantian ethics; any kind of moral purism or idealism; any ethic that has as its source and criterion of value the word of God, eternal reason or the dictates of conscience; ethics which focus on the salvation of the individual soul or the individual as an end in themselves; ethics which stress intentions, or which embody abstract conceptions of justice, fairness and rights. In short, consequentialist ethics conflict with any ethic that, in formulating rules governing how people should be treated, places restrictions on the means no amount of good consequences would sanction or permit. Machiavelli demonstrates and highlights the incompatibility of consequentialist ethics from other systems of value, and it is this collision which persists between rival ethical positions.

Though Machiavelli justified public morality on grounds of reasons of state, and though varieties of utilitarianism may differ on what ends are justified, all moral theories which justify actions according to outcomes suffer from the problems of condoning means that on other standards are bad or undesirable. The problem of means and ends is not unique to Machiavelli but is relevant to all justifications which rely on a consequentialist ethic. These range across and pervade diverse ideological frameworks and apply to all areas of public and private life. This is seen in theological and Christian formulations of just war theory; defences of *raison d'état*, imperialist and populist, Catholic and Protestant; Marxist justifications for revolution, defences of the market economy and in arguments for and against a variety of issues such as legal punishment, discrimination, abortion, infanticide and euthanasia. Consequentialist calculation is also an intimate feature of our daily lives, since in all the small lies we tell and the promises we break we constantly act as if the end justified the means. Moreover, in practical politics there has always been the problem of adopting anything other than a version of utilitarianism, when ends that are judged good (on whatever grounds) cannot be achieved without recourse to means, which judged according to the principles of alternative moral traditions would be impermissible but which, if adhered to, would make the end unrealizable. Even regimes which stress the importance of individual rights and liberties have been more than ready to sacrifice these to achieve a desired outcome. Such acts as the bombing of Hamburg and Dresden, Hiroshima and Nagasaki and American involvement in Vietnam could be justified only by appeal to their consequences, despite the fact that the perpetrators of such deeds did not subscribe to a consequentialist ethic.

The pervasiveness of means–end reasoning in moral and political, private and public life illustrates the diverse situations in which moral demands or principles conflict and the frequency with which choice has to be made between one or the other. Action directed to outcomes can involve sacrificing moral principles, but the case against moral purity does not deny that this is a sacrifice. Machiavelli acknowledges that it cannot be called good to lie, cheat, be cruel and faithless. He, like many Marxist and revolutionary thinkers following him, thought such actions were necessary to achieve a better, more humane future, but he did not deny the contradiction of achieving moral ends through immoral means. In his poem 'To Those Born Later', Brecht says that living in dark times he cannot live 'wisely', according to the morality of the 'old books', 'shun the strife of the world', 'get along without violence' or 'return good for evil'; but he laments this and makes a plea to future generations who have escaped this contradiction:

> And yet we know:
> Hatred, even of meanness
> Contorts the features.
> Anger, even against injustice
> Makes the voice hoarse. Oh, we
> Who wanted to prepare the ground for friendliness
> Could not ourselves be friendly.
>
> But you, when the time comes at last
> And man is a helper to man
> Think of us
> With forbearance. [7]

Actions which involve the sacrifice of moral values may be necessary in an imperfect world, but the efficacy of such action does not obscure their anti-moral and inhuman nature. James Connolly reiterates this point: 'No, there is no such thing as humane or civilized war! War may be forced upon a subject race or subject class to put an end to subjection of race, of class, or sex. When so waged it must be waged thoroughly and relentlessly, but with no delusions as to its elevating nature, or civilizing methods'.[8]

Trotsky confirms this view of both the necessity and the immorality of the means to liberatory ends:

> Nevertheless do lying and violence in themselves warrant condemnation? Of course as does the class society which generates them. A society without contradictions will naturally be a society without lies and violence. However, there is no bridge to that society save by revolutionary, that is violent means. The revolution is itself a product of class society and of necessity bears its traits. From the point of view of 'eternal truths' revolution is of course anti-moral. But this means that idealist morality is counter revolutionary, that is in the service of the exploiters. [9]

It is not, though, just the acknowledgement of the necessity of immoral means which forms the case against idealist morality in Machiavelli or in other consequentialist justifications. The case against moral purism argued for in contemporary literature [10] and found in embryonic form in Machiavelli depends on a rejection of the acts and omissions doctrine to show that there is no escape from the dilemma of dirty hands. The acts and omissions doctrine states that failure to perform an act with certain foreseen consequences is morally less bad than to perform an act with the same foreseen consequences. Machiavelli shows, like others who reject this doctrine, that certain omissions are as blameworthy as certain acts and sometimes more so, because those who fail to act, whatever their good intentions, are causally responsible for harm they could have prevented. If an action which employs violent, cruel or otherwise immoral means is the only way to change the world's destiny for the better, then those who fail to act will be responsible for maintaining the evil of the status quo and for allowing worse consequences to result. As Machiavelli noted, it is not the most moderate and morally pure who have provided the fewest victims in history.[11] At certain political conjunctions there can be no ethical neutrality in decision-making – 'all roads lead to the mire'. [12] In these circumstances, abstaining from immoral means is at best self-deception, at worst immoral.

It is not a particularly Machiavellian idea, nor exclusively a Marxist one that the end justifies the means or that it is impossible to apply in politics the same moral standards that are appropriate to the private sphere. Whatever ideology they are informed by, all practical politics at some time or other involves actions which would be condemned if performed by private citizens or if judged with regard to other moral considerations. Though the Anarchist tradition has argued against this and for the inseparability of means and ends, requiring that political action should be judged by personal standards, in contemporary times the emergence of radical feminism marks the sharpest break with Western political thought in this respect by questioning the legitimacy of the distinction between the private and public spheres of action. The radical feminist claim that the 'personal is political' exposes the idea that male power is not confined to the public world of politics but also extends to areas of personal life, such as the family and sexuality, which are normally seen as private and non-political. But for many radical feminists, personal politics also means that women's experience of intimate relations provides a fund of values which should inform, inspire and regulate political life.

It is easy to see, though, why an 'ethic of care'[13] arising from women's experience of connection and responsiveness, and informed by love, empathy, compassion and responsibility, would be as inappropriate to politics as Machiavelli thought traditional and princely virtues were. This is because, in the world as it is, with 'men' as they are, politics is about power, albeit in both political and private life. Change depends not on the personal reflected in the political but on the transformation of social structures which no amount of princely, personal or female virtue alone can transform or maintain.

We may agree that feminism provides insights into what is morally good. We may also agree that the mode of morality which dominates the public sphere embodies typical male views of human nature as abstract, universal and self-interested which are false to the experience of women. Though the feminist alternative virtues may be desirable in themselves, it is surely Machiavelli's point that we are involved in a world where any such morality is impossible and undesirable. Without the deceit, violence, fraud and ruthlessness that would be psychopathic in personal relations, ends cannot be achieved which make the practice of virtue possible.

We need not be committed either to a view of human nature as universal and unchanging and of conflict as endemic, nor to a view that endorses male values and conceptions to see that, in the world as it is, a consequentialist ethic and the dilemmas this brings are unavoidable if political goals are to be achieved.

And when the time comes at last and 'man is a helper to man'[14] it will still be the case that, despite the flourishing of personal virtues and their reflection in public life, there will still be occasions when these have to be sacrificed for the sake of the common good or for their very preservation itself. There will always be decisions to be made in both personal and public affairs which require prudential calculation and which will justify means which contradict those most cherished values. Traditional male conceptions of what constitute the political sphere is not the only arena in which it would be fair to say that we will still be faced with the problem of Machiavelli who has left us with 'an enigma that perhaps will never be resolved'.[15]

Notes

From Coyle, Martin (ed.) (1995) *Niccolò Machiavelli's The Prince: New Interdisciplinary Essays*, Manchester University Press, pp.174–95. Page references to *The Prince* are from Plamenatz (1972).

[1] See Ernst Cassirer, *The Myth of the State* (Yale University Press, 1946), ch. 12.

[2] Russell Price, 'The Sense of Virtù in Machiavelli', *European Studies Review*, 31 (1973), pp.315–46.

[3] Quentin Skinner, 'Machiavelli', *Great Political Thinkers* (Oxford University Press, 1992), pp.1–106 (p.44).

[4] John H. Geerken, 'Machiavelli Studies since 1969', *Journal of the History of Ideas*, 37 (1976), pp.351–68.

[5] Berlin, 'The Originality of Machiavelli', in Myron P. Gilmore (ed.) *Studies on Machiavelli* (Sansoni, 1972) pp.197–8 [Reading 1.3, pp.43–58 below].

[6] Dante Germino, 'Second Thoughts on Leo Strauss's Machiavelli', *Journal of Politics*, 28 (November 1966), pp.794–817.

[7] Bertolt Brecht, *Poems, 1913–56*, ed. John Willet and Ralph Manheim (Eyre Methuen, 1976), pp.318–20.

[8] James Connolly, 'The Worker' (30 January 1915) in *Selected Writings*, ed. P. Beresford Ellis (Penguin, 1973), p.213.

[9] Leon Trotsky, *Their Morals and Ours* (Pathfinder Press, 1973), p.46.

[10] See, for example, Jonathan Glover, *Causing Death and Saving Lives* (Penguin, 1977); John Harris, *Violence and Responsibility* (Routledge, 1980); Ted Honderich, *Violence for Equality* (Penguin, 1980).

[11] See *The Prince*, chapter XVI and XVII.

[12] Brecht, *Poems*, p.319.

[13] See, for example, Carol Gilligan, *In a Different Voice: Psychological Theory and Women's Development* (Harvard University Press, 1982).

[14] Brecht, Poems, p.320.

[15] Benedetto Croce, 'Una questione che forse non si chiuderà mai: la questione del Machiavelli', *I Quaderni della 'Critica'*, 19 (July, 1949), pp.1–9.

'The Originality of Machiavelli'

Isaiah Berlin

In this extract from his classic discussion of Machiavelli's thought, the historian and political philosopher Isaiah Berlin (1909–97) gives a critical account of some of the ways in which Machiavelli's work has been understood. His own interpretation stresses that Machiavelli's originality lies in his challenge to simple views of morality. For Berlin, Machiavelli's thought unintentionally opens the door to value pluralism and toleration.

It is commonly said, especially by those who follow Croce, that Machiavelli divided politics from morals – that he recommended, as politically necessary, courses which common opinion morally condemns: for example, treading over corpses for the benefit of the State. Leaving aside the question of what was his conception of the State, and whether he in fact possessed one, it seems to me that this is a false antithesis. For Machiavelli the ends which he advocates are those to which he thinks wise human beings, who understand reality, will dedicate their lives. Ultimate ends in this sense, whether or not they are those of the Judaeo-Christian tradition, are what is usually meant by moral values.

What Machiavelli distinguishes is not specifically moral from specifically political values,[1] what he achieves is not the emancipation of politics from ethics or religion, which Croce and many other commentators regard as his crowning achievement; what he institutes is something that cuts deeper still – a differentiation between two incompatible ideals of life, and therefore two moralities. One is the morality of the pagan world: its values are courage, vigour, fortitude in adversity, public achievement, order, discipline, happiness, strength, justice, above all assertion of one's proper claims and the knowledge and power needed to secure their satisfaction; that which for a Renaissance reader Pericles had seen embodied in his ideal Athens, Livy had found in the old Roman Republic, that of which Tacitus and Juvenal lamented the decay and death in their own time. These seem to Machiavelli the best hours of mankind and, Renaissance humanist that he is, he wishes to restore them.

Against this moral universe (moral or ethical no less in Croce's than in the traditional sense, that is, embodying ultimate human ends however these are conceived) stands in the first and foremost place Christian morality. The ideals of Christianity are charity, mercy, sacrifice, love of God, forgiveness of enemies, contempt for the goods of this world, faith in the life hereafter, belief in the salvation of the individual soul as being of incomparable value – higher than, indeed wholly incommensurable with, any social or political or other terrestrial goal, any economic or military or aesthetic consideration. Machiavelli lays it down that out of men who believe in such ideals, and practise them, no satisfactory human community, in his Roman sense, can in principle be constructed. It is not simply a question of the unattainability of an ideal because of human imperfection, original sin, or bad luck, or ignorance, or insufficiency of material means. It is not, in other words, the inability in practice on the part of ordinary human beings to rise to a sufficiently high level of Christian virtue (which may, indeed, be the inescapable lot of sinful men on earth) that makes it, for him, impracticable to establish, even to seek after, the good Christian State. It is the very opposite: Machiavelli is convinced that what are commonly thought of as the central Christian virtues, whatever their intrinsic value, are insuperable obstacles to the building of the kind of society that he wishes to see; a society which, moreover, he assumes that it is natural for all normal men to want – the kind of community that, in his view, satisfies men's permanent desires and interests.

If human beings were different from what they are, perhaps they could create an ideal Christian society. But he is clear that human beings would in that event have to differ too greatly from men as they have always been; and it is surely idle to build for, or discuss the prospects of, beings who can never be on earth; such talk is beside the point, and only breeds dreams and fatal delusions. What ought to be done must be defined in terms of what is practicable, not imaginary; statecraft is concerned with action within the limits of human possibility, however wide; men can be changed, but not to a fantastic degree. To advocate ideal measures, suitable only for angels, as previous political writers seem to him too often to have done, is visionary and irresponsible and leads to ruin.

It is important to realize that Machiavelli does not wish to deny that what Christians call good is, in fact, good, that what they call virtue and vice are in fact virtue and vice. Unlike Hobbes or Spinoza (or eighteenth-century *philosophes* or, for that matter, the first Stoics), who try to define (or redefine) moral notions in such a way as to fit in with the kind of community that, in their view, rational men must, if they are consistent, wish to build, Machiavelli does not fly in the face of common notions – the traditional, accepted moral vocabulary of mankind. He does not say or imply (as various radical philosophical reformers have done) that humility, kindness, unworldliness, faith in God, sanctity, Christian love, unwavering truthfulness, compassion are bad or unimportant attributes; or that cruelty, bad faith, power politics, sacrifice of innocent men to social needs, and so on are good ones.

But if history, and the insights of wise statesmen, especially in the ancient world, verified as they have been in practice (*verità effettuale*), are to guide us, it will be seen that it is in fact impossible to combine Christian virtues, for example meekness or the search for spiritual salvation, with a satisfactory, stable, vigorous, strong society on earth. Consequently a man must choose. To choose to lead a Christian life is to condemn oneself to political impotence: to being used and crushed by powerful, ambitious, clever, unscrupulous men; if one wishes to build a glorious community like those of Athens or Rome at their best, then one must abandon Christian education and substitute one better suited to the purpose.

Machiavelli is not a philosopher and does not deal in abstractions, but what his thesis comes to is of central concern to political theory: that it is a fact, which men will not face, that these two goals – both, evidently, capable of being believed in by human beings (and, we may add, of raising them to sublime heights) – are not compatible with one another. What usually happens, in his view, is that since men cannot bring themselves resolutely to follow either of these paths wherever they may lead ('men take certain middle ways that are very injurious; indeed, they are unable to be altogether good or altogether bad') [*Discourses*, i, 26], they try to effect compromises, vacillate, fall between two stools, and end in weakness and failure.

... Christians as he knew them in history and his own experience, that is, men who in their practice actually follow Christian precepts, are good men, but if they govern States in the light of such principles they lead them to destruction. Like Prince Myshkin in Dostoevsky's *The Idiot*, like the well-meaning *Gonfalonieri* of the Florentine Republic, like Savonarola, they are bound to be defeated by the realists (the Medici or the Pope or King Ferdinand of Spain) who understand how to create lasting institutions; build them, if need be, on the bones of innocent victims. I should like to emphasize again that he does not explicitly condemn Christian morality: he merely points out that it is, at least in rulers (but to some degree in subjects too), incompatible with those social ends which he thinks it natural and wise for men to seek. One can save one's soul, or one can found or maintain or serve a great and glorious State; but not always both at once.

This is a vast and eloquent development of Aristotle's *obiter dictum* in the *Politics* that a good man may not be identical with a good citizen (even though Aristotle was not thinking in terms of spiritual salvation). Machiavelli does not explicitly rate either way of life above the other. When he says 'hate is incurred as much by means of good deeds as of bad' [*The Prince*, chapter 19], he means by 'good deeds' what any man brought up to live by Christian values means. Again, when he says that good faith, integrity are 'praiseworthy' [ibid., chapter 18] even if they end in failure, he means by 'praiseworthy' that it is right to praise them, for of course what is good (in the ordinary sense) *is* good. When he praises the 'chastity, affability, courtesy and liberality' [ibid., chapter 14] of Scipio or Cyrus or Timoleon, or even the 'goodness' of the Medici Pope Leo X, he speaks (whether he is sincere or not) in terms of values that are common to Cicero and Dante, to Erasmus and to us. In the famous fifteenth chapter of *The Prince* he says that liberality, mercy, honour, humanity, frankness, chastity, religion, and so forth, are indeed virtues, and a life lived in the exercise of these virtues would be successful if men were all good. But they are not; and it is idle to hope that they will become so. We must take men as we find them, and seek to improve them along possible, not impossible, lines.

This may involve the benefactors of men – the founders, educators, legislators, rulers – in terrible cruelties. 'I am aware that everyone will admit that it would be most praiseworthy for a prince to exhibit such of the above-mentioned qualities as are considered good. But because no ruler can possess or fully practise them, on account of human conditions that do not permit it' [ibid., chapter 15], he must at times behave very differently in order to compass his ends. Moses and Theseus, Romulus and Cyrus all killed; what they created lasted, and was glorious; 'any man who under all conditions insists on making it his business to be good will surely be destroyed among so many who are not good. Hence a prince ... must acquire the power to be not good, and understand when to use it and when not to use it, in accord with necessity' [ibid.] 'If all men were good, this maxim [to break faith if interest dictates] would not be good, but ... they are bad' [ibid., chapter 18]. Force and guile must be met with force and guile.

The qualities of the lion and the fox are not in themselves morally admirable, but if a combination of these qualities will alone preserve the city from destruction, then these are the qualities that leaders must cultivate. They must do this not simply to serve their own interest, that is, because this is how one can become a leader, although whether men become leaders or not is a matter of indifference to the author – but because human societies in fact stand in need of leadership, and cannot become what they should be, save by the effective pursuit of power, of stability, *virtù*, greatness. These can be attained when men are led by Scipios and Timoleons or, if times are bad, men of more ruthless character. Hannibal was cruel, and cruelty is not a laudable quality, but if a sound society can be built only by conquest, and if cruelty is necessary to it, then it must not be evaded.

Machiavelli is not sadistic; he does not gloat on the need to employ ruthlessness or fraud for creating or maintaining the kind of society that he admires and recommends. His most savage examples and precepts apply only to situations in which the population is thoroughly corrupt, and needs violent measures to restore it to health, for example where a new prince takes over, or a revolution against a bad prince must be made effective. Where a society is relatively sound, or the rule is traditional and hereditary and supported by public sentiment, it would be quite wrong to practise violence for violence's sake, since its results would be destructive of social order, when the purpose of government is to create order, harmony, strength. If you are a lion and a fox you can afford virtue – chastity, affability, mercy, humanity, liberality, honour – as Agesilaus and Timoleon, Camillus, Scipio and Marcus did. But if circumstances are adverse, if you find yourself surrounded by treason, what can you do but emulate Philip and Hannibal and Severus?

Mere lust for power is destructive: Pisistratus, Dionysius, Caesar were tyrants and did harm. Agathocles, the tyrant of Syracuse, who gained power by killing his fellow citizens, betraying his friends, being 'without fidelity, without mercy, without religion', went too far, and so did not gain glory; 'his outrageous cruelty and inhumanity together with his countless wicked acts' [*The Prince*, chapter 8] led to success, but since so much vice was not needed for it, he is excluded from the pantheon; so is the savage Oliverotto da Fermo, his modern counterpart, killed by Cesare Borgia. Still, to be altogether without these qualities guarantees failure; and that makes impossible the only conditions in which Machiavelli believed that normal men could successfully develop. Saints might not need them; anchorites could perhaps practise their virtues in the desert; martyrs will obtain their reward hereafter; but Machiavelli is plainly not interested in these ways of life and does not discuss them. He is a writer about government; he is interested in public affairs; in security, independence, success, glory, strength, vigour, felicity on earth, not in heaven; in the present and future as well as the past; in the real world, not an imaginary one. And for this, given unalterable human limitations, the code preached by the Christian Church, if it is taken seriously, will not do.

Machiavelli, we are often told, was not concerned with morals. The most influential of all modern interpretations – that of Benedetto Croce, followed to some extent by Chabod, Russo and others – is that Machiavelli, in Cochrane's words:

> did not deny the validity of Christian morality, and he did not pretend that a crime required by political necessity was any less a crime. Rather he discovered ... that this morality simply did not hold in political affairs and that any policy based on the assumption that it did would end in disaster. His factual, objective description of contemporary political practices, then, is a sign not of cynicism or of detachment, but of anguish.

> (Cochrane, Eric W. (1961) 'Machiavelli: 1940–1960', *Journal of Modern History*, 33, 113–36)

This account, it seems to me, contains two basic misinterpretations. The first is that the clash is one between 'Christian morality' and 'political necessity'. The implication is that there is an incompatibility between, on the one hand, morality – the region of ultimate values sought after for their own sakes, values recognition of which alone enables us to speak of 'crimes' or morally to justify and condemn anything; and, on the other, politics – the art of adapting means to ends, the region of technical skills, of what Kant was to call 'hypothetical imperatives', which take the form 'If you want to achieve *x* do *y* (for example, betray a friend, kill an innocent man)', without necessarily asking whether *x* is itself intrinsically desirable or not. This is the heart of the divorce of politics from ethics which Croce and many others attribute to Machiavelli. But this seems to me to rest on a mistake.

If ethics is confined to, let us say, Stoic, or Christian or Kantian, or even some types of utilitarian ethics, where the source and criterion of value is the word of God, or eternal reason, or some inner sense or knowledge of good and evil, of right or wrong, voices which speak directly to individual consciousness with absolute authority, this might have been tenable. But there exists an equally time-honoured ethics, that of the Greek *polis*, of which Aristotle provided the clearest exposition. Since men are beings made by nature to live in communities, their communal purposes are the ultimate values from which the rest are derived, or with which their ends as individuals are identified. Politics – the art of living in a *polis* – is not an activity which can be dispensed with by those who prefer private life: it is not like seafaring or sculpture, which those who do not wish to do so need not undertake. Political conduct is intrinsic to being a human being at a certain stage of civilization, and what it demands is intrinsic to living a successful human life.

Ethics so conceived – the code of conduct of, or the ideal to be pursued by, the individual – cannot be known save by understanding the purpose and character of his *polis*: still less be capable of being divorced from it, even in thought. This is the kind of pre-Christian morality which Machiavelli takes for granted. 'It is well known', says Benedetto Croce [*Elementi di politica*, Bari 1925], 'that Machiavelli discovered the necessity and the autonomy of politics, politics which is beyond moral good and evil, which has its own laws against which it is futile to rebel, which cannot be exorcized and banished from the world with holy water.' Beyond good and evil in some non-Aristotelian, religious or liberal-Kantian sense; but not beyond the good and evil of those communities, ancient or modern, whose sacred values are social through and through. The arts of colonization or of mass murder (let us say) may also have their 'own laws against which it is futile to rebel' for those who wish to practise them successfully. But if or when these laws collide with those of morality, it is possible and indeed morally imperative to abandon such activities.

But if Aristotle and Machiavelli are right about what men are (and should be – and Machiavelli's ideal is, particularly in the *Discourses*, drawn in vivid colours), political activity is intrinsic to human nature, and while individuals here and there may opt out, the mass of mankind cannot do so; and its communal life determines the moral duties of its members. Hence in opposing the 'laws of politics' to 'good and evil' Machiavelli is not contrasting two 'autonomous' spheres of acting – the 'political' and the 'moral': he is contrasting his own 'political' ethics with another conception of it which governs the lives of persons who are of no interest to him. He is indeed rejecting one morality – the Christian – but not in favour of something that cannot be described as a morality at all, but only as a game of skill, an activity called political, which is not concerned with ultimate human ends, and is therefore not ethical at all.

He is indeed rejecting Christian ethics, but in favour of another system, another moral universe – the world of Pericles or of Scipio, or even of the Duke of Valentino, a society geared to ends just as ultimate as the Christian faith, a society in which men fight and are ready to die for (public) ends which they pursue for their own sakes. They are choosing not a realm of means (called politics) as opposed to a realm of ends (called morals), but opt for a rival (Roman or classical) morality, an alternative realm of ends. In other words the conflict is between two moralities, Christian and pagan (or, as some wish to call it, aesthetic), not between autonomous realms of morals and politics.

Nor is this a mere question of nomenclature, unless politics is conceived as being concerned not (as it usually is) with means, skills, methods, techniques 'know-how', Croce's *pratica* (whether or not governed by unbreakable rules of its own), but with an independent kingdom of ends of its own, sought for their own sake, a substitute for ethics.[2] When Machiavelli said (in a letter to Francesco Vettori) that he loved his native city more than his own soul, he revealed his basic moral beliefs, a position with which Croce does not credit him.[3]

The second thesis in this connection which seems to me mistaken is the idea that Machiavelli viewed the crimes of his society with anguish. (Chabod in his excellent study, unlike Croce and some Croceans, does not insist on this.) This entails that he accepts the dire necessities of the *raison d'état* with reluctance, because he sees no alternative. But there is no evidence for this: there is no trace of agony in his political works, any more than in his plays or letters.

The pagan world that Machiavelli prefers is built on recognition of the need for systematic guile and force by rulers, and he seems to think it natural and not at all exceptional or morally agonizing that they should employ these weapons wherever they are needed. Nor is the distinction he draws that between the rulers and the ruled. The subjects or citizens must be Romans too: they do not need the *virtù* of the rulers, but if they also cheat, Machiavelli's maxims will not work; they must be poor, militarized, honest and obedient; if they lead Christian lives, they will accept too uncomplainingly the rule of mere bullies and scoundrels. No sound republic can be built of such materials as these. Theseus and Romulus, Moses and Cyrus did not preach humility to their subjects, or a view of this world as but a temporary resting-place.

But it is the first misinterpretation that goes deepest, that which represents Machiavelli as caring little or nothing for moral issues. This is surely not borne out by his own language. Anyone whose thought revolves round central concepts such as the good and the bad, the corrupt and the pure, has an ethical scale in mind in terms of which he gives moral praise and blame. Machiavelli's values are not Christian, but they are moral values.

... This leaves still with us the thorny problem of the relation of *The Prince* to the *Discourses*. But whatever the disparities, the central strain which runs through both is one and the same. The vision – the dream – typical of many writers who see themselves as tough-minded realists – of the strong, united, effective, morally regenerated, splendid and victorious *patria*, whether it is saved by the *virtù* of one man or many – remains central and constant. Political judgements, attitudes to individuals or States, to *fortuna*, and *necessità,* evaluation of methods, degree of optimism, the fundamental mood – these vary between one work and another, perhaps within the same exposition. But the basic values, the ultimate end – Machiavelli's beatific vision – does not vary.

His vision is social and political. Hence the traditional view of him as simply a specialist on how to get the better of others, a vulgar cynic who says that Sunday-school precepts are all very well, but in a world full of evil men you too must lie, kill and so on if you are to get somewhere, is incorrect. The philosophy summarized by 'Eat or be eaten, beat or be beaten' – the kind of worldly wisdom to be found in, say, Mazzei[4] or Giovanni Morelli,[5] with whom he has been compared – is not what is central in him. Machiavelli is not specially concerned with the opportunism of ambitious individuals; the ideal before his eyes is a shining vision of Florence or Italy; in this respect he is a typically impassioned humanist of the Renaissance, save that his ideal is not artistic or cultural but political, unless the State – or regenerated Italy – is considered, in Burckhardt's sense, as an artistic goal. This is very different from mere advocacy of tough-mindedness as such, or of a realism irrespective of its goal.

Machiavelli's values, I should like to repeat, are not instrumental but moral and ultimate, and he calls for great sacrifices in their name. For them he rejects the rival scale – the Christian principles of *ozio* and meekness – not, indeed, as being defective in itself, but as inapplicable to the conditions of real life; and real life for him means not merely (as is sometimes alleged) life as it was lived around him in Italy – the crimes, hypocrisies, brutalities, follies of Florence, Rome, Venice, Milan. This is not the touchstone of reality. His purpose is not to leave unchanged or to reproduce this kind of life, but to lift it to a new plane, to rescue Italy from squalor and slavery, to restore her to health and sanity.

The moral ideal for which he thinks no sacrifice too great – the welfare of the *patria* – is for him the highest form of social existence attainable by man; but attainable, not unattainable; not a world outside the limits of human capacity, given human beings as we know them, that is, creatures compounded out of those emotional, intellectual and physical properties of which history and observation provide examples. He asks for men improved but not transfigured, not superhuman; not for a world of ideal beings unknown on this earth, who, even if they could be created, could not be called human.

If you object to the political methods recommended because they seem to you morally detestable, if you refuse to embark upon them because they are, to use Ritter's word, *erschreckend*, too frightening, Machiavelli has no answer, no argument. In that case you are perfectly entitled to lead a morally good life, be a private citizen (or a monk), seek some corner of your own. But, in that event, you must not make yourself responsible for the lives of others or expect good fortune; in a material sense you must expect to be ignored or destroyed.

In other words you can opt out of the public world, but in that case he has nothing to say to you, for it is to the public world and to the men in it that he addresses himself. This is expressed most clearly in his notorious advice to the victor who has to hold down a conquered province. He advises a clean sweep: new governors, new titles, new powers and new men; he should

> make the rich poor, the poor rich, as David did when he became king: 'the poor he filled with good things and the rich he sent away empty'. Besides this, he should build new cities, overthrow those already built, change the inhabitants from one place to another; and in short he should leave nothing in that province untouched, and make sure that no rank or position or office or wealth is held by anyone who does not acknowledge it as from you.

> (*Discourses*, i, 26)

He should take Philip of Macedon as his model, who 'grew in these ways until he became lord of Greece'.

Now Philip's historian informs us – Machiavelli goes on to say – that he transferred the inhabitants from one province to another 'as herdsmen transfer their herds' from one place to another. Doubtless, Machiavelli continues:

> These methods are very cruel, and enemies to all government not merely Christian but human, and any man ought to avoid them and prefer to live a private life rather than to be a king who brings such ruin on men. Notwithstanding, a ruler who does not wish to take that first good way of lawful government, if he wishes to maintain himself, must enter upon this evil one. But men take certain middle ways that are very injurious; indeed, they are unable to be altogether good or altogether bad.

> (Ibid.)

This is plain enough. There are two worlds, that of personal morality and that of public organization. There are two ethical codes, both ultimate; not two 'autonomous' regions, one of 'ethics', another of 'politics', but two (for him) exhaustive alternatives between two conflicting systems of value. If a man chooses the 'first good way', he must, presumably, give up all hope of Athens and Rome, of a noble and glorious society in which human beings can thrive and grow strong, proud, wise and productive; indeed, they must abandon all hope of a tolerable life on earth: for men cannot live outside society; they will not survive collectively if they are led by men who (like Soderini) and influenced by the first, 'private' morality; they will not be able to realize their minimal goals as men; they will end in a state of moral, not merely political, degradation. But if a man chooses, as Machiavelli himself has done, the second course, then he must suppress his private qualms, if he has any, for it is certain that those who are too squeamish during the remaking of a society, or even during the pursuit and maintenance of its power and glory, will go to the wall. Whoever has chosen to make an omelette cannot do so without breaking eggs.

... Machiavelli is possessed by a clear, intense, narrow vision of a society in which human talents can be made to contribute to a powerful and splendid whole. He prefers republican rule in which the interests of the rulers do not conflict with those of the ruled. But (as Macaulay perceived) he prefers a well-governed principate to a decadent republic; and the qualities he admires and thinks capable of being welded into – indeed, indispensable to – a durable society are not different in *The Prince* and the *Discourses*: energy, boldness, practical skill, imagination, vitality, self-discipline, shrewdness, public spirit, good fortune, *antiqua virtus, virtù* – firmness in adversity, strength of character, as celebrated by Xenophon or Livy. All his more shocking maxims – those responsible for the 'murd'rous Machiavel' of the Elizabethan stage – are descriptions of methods of realizing this single end: the classical, humanistic and patriotic vision that dominates him.

Let me cite a round dozen of his most notoriously wicked pieces of advice to princes. You must employ terrorism or kindness, as the case dictates. Severity is usually more effective, but humanity, in some situations, brings better fruit. You may excite fear but not hatred, for hatred will destroy you in the end. It is best to keep men poor and on a permanent war footing, for this will be antidote to the two great enemies of active obedience – ambition and boredom – and the ruled will then feel in constant need of great men to lead them (the twentieth century offers us only too much evidence for this sharp insight). Competition – divisions between classes – in a society is desirable, for it generates energy and ambition in the right degree.

Religion must be promoted even though it may be false, provided it is of a kind which preserves social solidarity and promotes manly virtues, as Christianity has historically failed to do. When you confer benefits (he says, following Aristotle), do so yourself; but if dirty work is to be done, let others do it, for then they, not the prince, will be blamed, and the prince can gain favour by duly cutting off their heads; for men prefer vengeance and security to liberty. Do what you must do in any case, but try to represent it as a special favour to the people. If you must commit a crime do not advertise it beforehand, since otherwise your enemies may destroy you before you destroy them. If your action must be drastic, do it in one fell swoop, not in agonizing stages. Do not be surrounded by over-powerful servants – victorious generals are best got rid of, otherwise they may get rid of you.

You may be violent and use your power to overawe, but you must not break your own laws, for that destroys confidence and disintegrates the social texture. Men should be either caressed or annihilated; appeasement and neutralism are always fatal. Excellent plans without arms are not enough or else Florence would still be a republic. Rulers must live in the constant expectation of war. Success creates more devotion than an amiable character; remember the fate of Pertinax, Savonarola, Soderini. Severus was unscrupulous and cruel, Ferdinand of Spain is treacherous and crafty: but by practising the arts of both the lion and the fox they escaped both snares and wolves. Men will be false to you unless you compel them to be true by creating circumstances in which falsehood will not pay. And so on.

These examples are typical of 'the devil's partner'. Now and then doubts assail our author: he wonders whether a man high-minded enough to labour to create a State admirable by Roman standards will be tough enough to use the violent and wicked means prescribed; and, conversely, whether a sufficiently ruthless and brutal man will be disinterested enough to compass the public good which alone justifies the evil means. Yet Moses and Theseus, Romulus and Cyrus combined these properties.[6] What has been once, can be again: the implication is optimistic.

All these maxims have one property in common: they are designed to create or resurrect or maintain an order which will satisfy what the author conceives as men's most permanent interests. Machiavelli's values may be erroneous, dangerous, odious; but he is in earnest. He is not cynical. The end is always the same: a State conceived after the analogy of Periclean Athens, or Sparta, but above all the Roman Republic. Such an end, for which men naturally crave (of this he thinks that history and observation provide conclusive evidence), 'excuses' any means; in judging means, look only to the end: if the State goes under, all is lost. Hence the famous paragraph in the forty-first chapter of the third book of the *Discourses* where he says, 'when it is absolutely a question of the safety of one's country, there must be no consideration of just or unjust, of merciful or cruel, of praiseworthy or disgraceful; instead, setting aside every scruple, one must follow to the utmost any plan that will save her life and keep her liberty'. The French have reasoned thus: and the 'majesty of their king and the power of their kingdom' have come from it. Romulus could not have founded Rome without killing Remus. Brutus would not have preserved the Republic if he had not killed his sons. Moses and Theseus, Romulus, Cyrus and the liberators of Athens had to destroy in order to build. Such conduct, so far from being condemned, is held up to admiration by the classical historians and the Bible. Machiavelli is their admirer and faithful spokesman.

What is there, then, about his words, about his tone, which has caused such tremors among his readers? Not, indeed, in his own lifetime – there was a delayed reaction of some quarter of a century, but after that it becomes one of continuous and mounting horror. Fichte, Hegel, Treitschke 'reinterpreted' his doctrines and assimilated them to their own views. But the sense of horror was not thereby greatly mitigated. It is evident that the effect of the shock which he administered was not a temporary one: it has lasted almost to our own day.

Leaving aside the historical problem of why there was no immediate contemporary criticism, let us consider the continuous discomfort caused to its readers during the four centuries that have passed since *The Prince* was placed upon the Index. The great originality and the tragic implications of Machiavelli's theses seem to me to reside in their relation to a Christian civilization. It was all very well to live by the light of pagan ideals in pagan times; but to preach paganism more than a thousand years after the triumph of Christianity was to do so after the loss of innocence – and to be forcing men to make a conscious choice. The choice is painful because it is a choice between two entire worlds. Men have lived in both, and fought and died to preserve them against each other. Machiavelli has opted for one of them, and he is prepared to commit crimes for its sake.

In killing, deceiving, betraying, Machiavelli's princes and republicans are doing evil things, not condonable in terms of common morality. It is Machiavelli's great merit that he does not deny this.[7] Marsilio, Hobbes, Spinoza, and, in their own fashion, Hegel and Marx, did try to deny it. So did many a defender of the *raison d'état*, imperialist and populist, Catholic and Protestant. These thinkers argue for a single moral system: and seek to show that the morality which justifies, and indeed demands, such deeds, is continuous with, and a more rational form of, the confused ethical beliefs of the uninstructed morality which forbids them absolutely.

From the vantage-point of the great social objectives in the name of which these (prima facie wicked) acts are to be performed, they will be seen (so the argument goes) as no longer wicked, but as rational – demanded by the very nature of things – by the common good, or man's true ends, or the dialectic of history – condemned only by those who cannot or will not see a large enough segment of the logical, or theological, or metaphysical, or historical pattern; misjudged, denounced only by the spiritually blind or short-sighted. At worst, these 'crimes' are discords demanded by the larger harmony, and therefore, to those who hear this harmony, no longer discordant.

Machiavelli is not a defender of any such abstract theory. It does not occur to him to employ such casuistry. He is transparently honest and clear. In choosing the life of a statesman, or even the life of a citizen with enough civic sense to want his State to be as successful and as splendid as possible, you commit yourself to rejection of Christian behaviour. [8] It may be that Christians are right about the well-being of the individual soul, taken outside the social or political context. But the well-being of the State is not the same as the well-being of the individual – they 'are governed in a different way'. You will have made your choice: the only crimes are weakness, cowardice, stupidity, which may cause you to draw back in mid-stream and fail.

Compromise with current morality leads to bungling, which is always despicable, and when practised by statesmen involves men in ruin. The end 'excuses' the means, however horrible these may be in terms of even pagan ethics, if it is (in terms of the ideals of Thucydides or Polybius, Cicero or Livy) lofty enough. Brutus was right to kill his children: he saved Rome. Soderini did not have the stomach to perpetrate such deeds and ruined Florence. Savonarola, who had sound ideas about austerity and moral strength and corruption, perished because he did not realize that an unarmed prophet will always go to the gallows.

If one can produce the right results by using the devotion and affection of men, let this be done by all means. There is no value in causing suffering as such. But if one cannot, then Moses, Romulus, Theseus, Cyrus are the exemplars, and fear must be employed. There is no sinister Satanism in Machiavelli, nothing of Dostoevsky's great sinner, pursuing evil for evil's sake. To Dostoevsky's famous question 'Is everything permitted?' Machiavelli (who for Dostoevsky would surely have been an atheist) answers 'Yes, if the end – that is, the pursuit of a society's basic interests in a specific situation – cannot be realized in any other way.'

... One of the deepest assumptions of Western political thought is the doctrine, scarcely questioned during its long ascendancy, that there exists some single principle which not only regulates the course of the sun and the stars, but prescribes their proper behaviour to all animate creatures. Animals and sub-rational beings of all kinds follow it by instinct; higher beings attain to consciousness of it, and are free to abandon it, but only to their doom. This doctrine, in one version or another, has dominated European thought since Plato; it has appeared in many forms, and has generated many similes and allegories; at its centre is the vision of an impersonal nature or reason or cosmic purpose, or of a divine Creator whose power has endowed all things and creatures each with a specific function; these functions are elements in a single harmonious whole, and are intelligible in terms of it alone.

... This unifying monistic pattern is at the very heart of the traditional rationalism, religious and atheistic, metaphysical and scientific, transcendental and naturalistic, that has been characteristic of Western civilization. It is the rock, upon which Western beliefs and lives had been founded, that Machiavelli seems, in effect, to have split open. So great a reversal cannot, of course, be due to the acts of a single individual. It could scarcely have taken place in a stable social and moral order; many beside him, ancient sceptics, medieval nominalists and secularists, Renaissance humanists, doubtless supplied their share of the dynamite. The purpose of this essay is to suggest that it was Machiavelli who lit the fatal fuse.

If to ask what are the ends of life is to ask a real question, it must be capable of being correctly answered. To claim rationality in matters of conduct was to claim that correct and final solutions to such questions can in principle be found. When such solutions were discussed in earlier periods, it was normally assumed that the perfect society could be conceived, at least in outline; for otherwise what standard could one use to condemn existing arrangements as imperfect? It might not be realisable here, below. Men were too ignorant or too weak or too vicious to create it. Or it was said (by some materialistic thinkers in the centuries following *The Prince*) that it was technical means that were lacking, that no one had yet discovered methods of overcoming the material obstacles to the golden age; that we were not technologically or educationally or morally sufficiently advanced. But it was never said that there was something incoherent in the very notion itself.

Plato and the Stoics, the Hebrew prophets and Christian medieval thinkers, and the writers of Utopias from More onward had a vision of what it was that men fell short of; they claimed, as it were, to be able to measure the gap between the reality and the ideal. But if Machiavelli is right, this tradition – the central current of Western thought – is fallacious. If his position is valid then it is impossible to construct even the notion of such a perfect society, for there exist at least two sets of virtues – let us call them the Christian and the pagan – which are not merely in practice, but in principle, incompatible.

If men practise Christian humility, they cannot also be inspired by the burning ambitions of the great classical founders of cultures and religions; if their gaze is centred upon the world beyond – if their ideas are infected by even lip-service to such an outlook – they will not be likely to give all that they have to an attempt to build a perfect city. If suffering and sacrifice and martyrdom are not always evil and inescapable necessities but may be of supreme value in themselves, then the glorious victories over fortune which go to the bold, the impetuous and the young might be neither won nor thought worth winning. If spiritual goods alone are worth striving for, then of how much value is the study of *necessità* – of the laws that govern nature and human lives – by the manipulation of which men might accomplish unheard-of things in the arts and the sciences and the organization of social lives?

To abandon the pursuit of secular goals may lead to disintegration and a new barbarism; but even if this is so, is it the worst that could happen? Whatever the differences between Plato and Aristotle, or of either of these thinkers from the Sophists and Epicureans or the other Greek schools of the fourth and later centuries, they and their disciples, the European rationalists and empiricists of the modern age, were agreed that the study of reality by minds undeluded by appearances could reveal the correct ends to be pursued by men – that which would make men free and happy, strong and rational.

Some thought that there was a single end for all men in all circumstances, or different ends for men of different kinds or in dissimilar historical environments. Objectivists and universalists were opposed by relativists and subjectivists, metaphysicians by empiricists, theists by atheists. There was profound disagreement about moral issues; but what none of these thinkers, not even the sceptics, had suggested was that there might exist ends – ends in themselves in terms of which alone everything else was justified – which were equally ultimate, but incompatible with one another, that there might exist no single universal overarching standard that would enable a man to choose rationally between them.

This was indeed a profoundly upsetting conclusion. It entailed that if men wished to live and act consistently, and understand what goals they were pursuing, they were obliged to examine their moral values. What if they found that they were compelled to make a choice between two incommensurable systems, to choose as they did without the aid of an infallible measuring-rod which certified one form of life as being superior to all others and could be used to demonstrate this to the satisfaction of all rational men? Is it, perhaps, this awful truth, implicit in Machiavelli's exposition, that has upset the moral consciousness of men, and has haunted their minds so permanently and obsessively ever since?

... I should like to suggest that it is Machiavelli's juxtaposition of the two outlooks – the two incompatible moral worlds, as it were – in the minds of his readers, and the collision and acute moral discomfort which follow, that, over the years, has been responsible for the desperate efforts to interpret his doctrines away, to represent him as a cynical and therefore ultimately shallow defender of power politics, or as a diabolist, or as a patriot prescribing for particularly desperate situations which seldom arise, or as a mere time-server, or as an embittered political failure, or as nothing more than a mouthpiece of truths we have always known but did not like to utter, or again as the enlightened translator of universally accepted ancient social principles into empirical terms, or as a crypto-republican satirist (a descendant of Juvenal, a forerunner of Orwell); or as a cold scientist, a mere political technologist free from moral implications; or as a typical Renaissance publicist practising a now obsolete genre; or in any of the numerous other roles that have been and are still being cast for him.

Machiavelli may have possessed some, at any rate, of these attributes, but concentration on one or other of them as constituting his essential, 'true' character seems to me to stem from reluctance to face, still more discuss, the uncomfortable truth which Machiavelli had, unintentionally, almost casually, uncovered; namely, that not all ultimate values are necessarily compatible with one another – that there might be a conceptual (what used to be called 'philosophical') and not merely a material obstacle to the notion of the single ultimate solution which, if it were only realized, would establish the perfect society.

... I do not mean that Machiavelli explicitly asserts that there is a pluralism or even a dualism of values between which conscious choices must be made. But this follows from the contrasts he draws between the conduct he admires and that which he condemns. He seems to take for granted the obvious superiority of classical civic virtue and brushes aside Christian values, as well as conventional morality, with a disparaging or patronizing sentence or two, or smooth words about the misinterpretation of Christianity.[9] This worries or infuriates those who disagree with him the more because it goes against their convictions without seeming to be aware of doing so – and recommends wicked courses as obviously the most sensible, something that only fools or visionaries will reject.

If what Machiavelli believed is true, this undermines one major assumption of Western thought: namely that somewhere in the past or the future, in this world or the next, in the church or the laboratory, in the speculations of the metaphysician or the findings of the social scientist, or in the uncorrupted heart of the simple good man, there is to be found the final solution of the question of how men should live. If this is false (and if more than one equally valid answer to the question can be returned, then it is false) the idea of the sole true, objective, universal human ideal crumbles. The very search for it becomes not merely Utopian in practice, but conceptually incoherent.

... After Machiavelli, doubt is liable to infect all monistic constructions. The sense of certainty that there is somewhere a hidden treasure – the final solution to our ills – and that some path must lead to it (for, in principle, it must be discoverable); or else, to alter the image, the conviction that the fragments constituted by our beliefs and habits are all pieces of a jigsaw puzzle, which (since there is an a priori guarantee for this) can, in principle, be solved, so that it is only because of lack of skill or stupidity or bad fortune that we have not so far succeeded in discovering the solution, whereby all interests will be brought into harmony – this fundamental belief of Western political thought has been severely shaken. Surely, in an age that looks for certainties, this is sufficient to account for the unending efforts, more numerous today than ever, to explain *The Prince* and the *Discourses*, or to explain them away?

This is the negative implication. There is also one that is positive, and might have surprised and perhaps displeased Machiavelli. So long as only one ideal is the true goal, it will always seem to men that no means can be too difficult, no price too high, to do whatever is required to realize the ultimate goal. Such certainty is one of the great justifications of fanaticism, compulsion, persecution. But if not all values are compatible with one another, and choices must be made for no better reason than that each value is what it is, and we choose it for what it is, and not because it can be shown on some single scale to be higher than another; if we choose forms of life because we believe in them, because we take them for granted, or, upon examination, find that we are morally unprepared to live in any other way (though others choose differently); if rationality and calculation can be applied only to means or subordinate ends, but never to ultimate ends; then a picture emerges different from that constructed round the ancient principle that there is only one good for men.

If there is only one solution to the puzzle, then the only problems are firstly how to find it, then how to realize it, and finally how to convert others to the solution by persuasion or by force. But if this is not so (Machiavelli contrasts two ways of life, but there could be, and, save for fanatical monists, there obviously are, more than two), then the path is open to empiricism, pluralism, toleration, compromise. Toleration is historically the product of the realization of the irreconcilability of equally dogmatic faiths, and the practical improbability of complete victory of one over the other. Those who wished to survive realized that they had to tolerate error. They gradually came to see merits in diversity, and so became sceptical about definitive solutions in human affairs.

But it is one thing to accept something in practice, another to justify it rationally. Machiavelli's 'scandalous' writings begin the latter process. This was a major turning-point, and its intellectual consequences, wholly unintended by its originator, were, by a fortunate irony of history (which some call its dialectic), the bases of the very liberalism that Machiavelli would surely have condemned as feeble and characterless, lacking in single-minded pursuit of power, in splendour, in organization, in *virtù*, in power to discipline unruly men against huge odds into one energetic whole. Yet he is, in spite of himself, one of the makers of pluralism, and of its – to him – perilous acceptance of toleration.

By breaking the original unity he helped to cause men to become aware of the necessity of having to make agonizing choices between incompatible alternatives in public and in private life (for the two could not, it became obvious, be genuinely kept distinct). His achievement is of the first order, if only because the dilemma has never given men peace since it came to light (it remains unsolved but we have learnt to live with it). Men had, no doubt, in practice, often enough experienced the conflict which Machiavelli made explicit. He converted its expression from a paradox into something approaching a commonplace.

The sword of which Meinecke spoke has not lost its edge: the wound has not healed. To know the worst is not always to be liberated from its consequences; nevertheless it is preferable to ignorance. It is this painful truth that Machiavelli forced on our attention, not by formulating it explicitly, but perhaps the more effectively by relegating much uncriticized traditional morality to the realm of Utopia. This is what, at any rate, I should like to suggest. Where more than twenty interpretations hold the field, the addition of one more cannot be deemed an impertinence. At worst it will be no more than yet another attempt to solve the problem, now more than four centuries old, of which Croce at the end of his long life spoke as 'Una questione che forse non si chiuderà mai: la questione del Machiavelli ['Machiavelli's problem: a question which will possibly never be resolved']. [10]

Notes

From Berlin, Isaiah (1998) *The Proper Study of Mankind*, Pimlico, pp.288–325.

[1] For which he is commended by de Sanctis, and ... condemned by Maurice Joly in the famous *Dialogue aux enfers entre Machiavel et Montesquieu* (Brussels, 1864), which served as the original of the forged *Protocols of the Learned Elders of Zion* (London, 1920).

[2] Meinecke, Prezzolini, Giuseppe, *Machiavelli anticristo* (Rome, 1954; tanslated into English as *Machiavelli* (New York, 1967; London, 1968) and Ernesto Landi, 'The Political Philosophy of Machiavelli', trans. Maurice Cranston, *History Today* 14 (1964), 550–5, seem to me to approach this position most closely.

[3] Benedetto Croce, 'Per un detto del Machiavelli', *La critica* 28 (1930), 310–12.

[4] Ser Lapo Mazzei, *Lettere di un notaro a un mercante del secolo XIV*, ed. Cesare Guasti (Florence, 1880).

[5] Giovanni di Pagolo Morelli, Ricordi (ed.) *Vittore Branca* (Florence,1956).

[6] Hugh Trevor-Roper has drawn my attention to the irony of the fact that the heroes of this supreme realist are all, wholly or in part, mythical.

[7] This is recognized by Jacques Maritain – see his *Moral Philosophy* (London, 1964), p.199 – who conceded that Machiavelli 'never called evil good or good evil'. *Machtpolitik* is shown to be what it is: the party with the big battalions; it does not claim that the Lord is on its side: no *Dei gesta per Francos*.

[8] At the risk of exhausting the patience of the reader, I must repeat that this is a conflict not of pagan statecraft with Christian morals, but of pagan morals (indissoluble connected with social life and inconceivable without it) with Christian ethics, which, whatever its implication for politics, can be stated independently of it; as, e.g., Aristotle's or Hegel's ethics cannot.

[9] e.g. in the passages from the *Discourses* cited above, or when he says, 'I believe the greatest good to be done and the most pleasing to God is that which one does to one's native city': *A Discourse on Remodelling the Government of Florence* (Gilbert, A. (trans.) *Machiavelli: The Chief Works and Others*, 3 vols, Duke University Press, vol. I, pp.113–14). This sentiment is by no means unique in Machiavelli's works: but, leaving aside his wish to flatter Leo X, or the liability of all authors to fall into the clichés of their own time, are we to suppose that Machiavelli means us to think that when Philip of Macedon transplanted populations in a manner that (unavoidable as it is said to have been) caused even Machiavelli a qualm, what Philip did, provided it was good for Macedon, was pleasing to God and *per contra*, that Giovanpaolo Baglioni's failure to kill the Pope and the Curia was displeasing to him? Such a notion of the Deity is, to say the least, remote from that of the New Testament. Are the needs of the *patria* automatically identical with the will of the Almighty? Are those who permit themselves to doubt this in danger of heresy? Machiavelli may at times have been represented as too Machiavellian; but to suppose that he believed that the claims of God and of Caesar were perfectly reconcilable reduces his central thesis to absurdity. Yet of course this does not prove that he lacked all Christian sentiment: the *Esortazione alla penitenza* composed in the last year of his life (if it is genuine and not a later forgery) may well be wholly sincere, as Ridolfi and Alderisio believe; Capponi may have exaggerated the extent to which he 'drove religion from his heart', even though 'it was not wholly extinct in his thought' (Gino Capponi, *Storia della repubblica di Firenze* (Florence, 1888), vol. 3, p.191). The point is that there is scarcely any trace of such *états d'ame* in his political writings, with which alone we are concerned. There is an interesting discussion of this by Giuseppe Prezzolini in his ['The Christian Roots of Machiavelli's Moral Pessimism', *Review of National Literatures*, 1 (1970), 26–37], in which this attitude is traced to Augustine, and Croce's thesis is, by implication, controverted.

[10] *Quaderni della 'Critica'*, 5, no 14 (July 1949), 1–9.

'Dirty hands'

C.A.J. Coady

The philosopher C.A.J. Coady gives a clear overview of the problem of 'dirty hands' in politics, the suggestion that successful politics requires that its practitioners set aside conventional moral practice. Machiavelli's views provide a framework for his discussion.

'All kings is mostly rapscallions.'

(Mark Twain, *The Adventures of Huckleberry Finn*)

When Huck Finn embarks upon his hilarious education of the slave Jim in the moral vagaries of the monarchies of Europe, he takes himself to be propounding the merest common sense. He may have thought large-scale villainy restricted to autocracies, but his creator was clearly not so naïve. More to the present point, Huck ends his discourse on princely rule with remarks that show he was not merely cataloguing the fact of widespread royal vice, but willing to countenance it as necessary. As he puts it, 'kings is kings, and you got to make allowances. Take them all around, they're a mighty ornery lot.'

Though Machiavelli ([*The Prince*] (1984 edn), p.52) puts the thought at its starkest, with his insistence that the Prince 'must learn how not to be good', the idea that political life essentially involves the transcendence or violation of ordinary morality has shown remarkable resilience. It was a common, though not universal, view in the nineteenth century, and has seen a revival amongst many contemporary philosophers who, echoing Sartre, characterize it as the problem of 'dirty hands'. Actually, it is not one thought but several, and they need to be disentangled. In what follows, I shall begin with some clarification of the issue, proceed to examine the claims of role morality, and then lay out the crucial situational factors that tend to produce the challenge of dirty hands. This leads on to a discussion of the complex ways that ideals and moral duties interact with the messy realities characteristic of, but not confined to, politics.

The first clarification required is the obvious one that we are not dealing merely with the claim that politics is an area in which immorality or villainy is common. This is a partly empirical claim from which nothing follows directly about a striking normative thesis like Machiavelli's. If some practice or field of endeavour is corrupt, this calls for condemnation and reform, not accommodation. Nor, to be fair, do those who rail against politicians ('they're all crooks'), usually condone all the crookedness they claim to detect. None the less, if what they say is true, there are normative problems posed by its truth. Consider the parallel with crime itself. Even though there may sometimes be 'honour among thieves' and some criminals are kind to their mothers or dogs, the claim that 'all criminals are mostly rapscallions' can be admitted without raising any qualms about the legitimate reach of ordinary morality. But politics is different: we could happily do without crime, though we do not know how to eliminate it, but politics seems an inescapable ingredient in the good life itself.

Aristotle certainly thought as much because, not only did he insist that we humans were essentially political animals, but he made the political process so central to *eudaemonia* as to maintain that the fullest achievement of virtue was available *only* to the political leader (Aristotle, *The Politics*, Book III, chapter iv). We may think Aristotle's exaltation of the political realm exaggerated: none the less, it is hard to deny that we need politics in a way that we do not need crime. If the anarchist vision is ultimately a mirage, then the political process, in something not too dissimilar to its present form, is needed to deliver so much that seems integral to the good life, e.g. health, comfort, justice, self-respect and education. The claim, therefore, that politicians are corrupt through and through rightly creates acute moral anxiety, since the idea that evil-doing is pretty much universal among the practitioners of politics implies that there is something about the very activity of politics that goes against the demands of morality as ordinarily understood. Furthermore, the anxiety remains even if we allow (as we should) for the considerable exaggeration in the line that 'they're all crooks', because enough morally shocking behaviour still seems typically political to suggest a conflict within the moral order itself: morality requires behaviour that is essentially immoral.

Morality and the political role

One line of response to this alarming conclusion is to distinguish between wrong-doing that is a natural result of the particular temptations of political life, especially those of power, but remains wrong none the less, and other apparent wrong-doing that is more integral to political activity. The latter is then seen as part of a distinctive political ethic even though it conflicts with 'ordinary morality'. The underlying premise here is that there is something so distinctive about political activity that it requires ethical thinking specific to its distinctiveness. Put like this, the idea is persuasive. Moral thinking is essentially adaptive to circumstance and context, and it is perfectly clear that different types of role, office or (as used to be said) station will affect the sorts of duty, responsibility, power and permissions that one has and ought to have. There are good reasons for allowing (some) police to carry guns and (most) ordinary citizens not to – though these good reasons do not prevail as widely as they should in the civilized world – and foresters are rightly empowered to cut down trees where ordinary citizens dare not hack. But such duties and rights hardly mark a departure from 'ordinary morality' since it is precisely in terms of 'ordinary morality' (i.e. moral reasoning readily recognizable by non-esoteric thinkers) that they are plausibly defensible. Moreover, what creates these distinctive necessities is something continuous with ordinary life, in that the special powers and duties granted to particular role-bearers, such as firemen, may be assumed by ordinary citizens in emergency situations.

What is also debatable is whether the political vocation is sufficiently distinguishable as a role for considerations of role morality or professional ethics to take us into exciting, Machiavellian territory. The political role is far more undifferentiated, even amorphous, than such roles as lawyer, doctor or fireman. This is because there are political dimensions to most, if not all, aspects of life. There are political roles in academic life, in the churches, in the law, in the crafts and trades, even (as traditional literature and modern feminism both emphasize) in the family. The point or *telos* of politics is also less clear than that of medicine or policing. We could say that its end is the concern for the common good, but this, though possibly true, raises more problems than it solves. Certainly, these facts make it difficult to read off specific moral injunctions from the phenomena of political life, as we might more easily do, say, with medical life. We may think that the good purpose of treating sickness and promoting health cannot be achieved unless those who practise medicine have certain particular duties, rights and powers, and, although there is considerable room for disagreement as to detail, the broad nature of these is clear enough. In the case of politics, especially in the context of the alleged necessity for 'dirty hands', the situation is far more obscure. This is reflected in the fact that if we determine some imperative to be part of medical ethics, e.g. that a doctor need not consult with parents before prescribing the contraceptive pill to teenage girls older than thirteen, then this determination, if correct, stands as part of ordinary morality, not in opposition to it. Any such opposition must be merely apparent. Nor are we dealing with the sort of moral impasse philosophers have discussed under the label 'moral dilemma' for these are cases where reason yields *no* right answer. For politics, the Machiavellian thought, at least in its most challenging form, is quite different; the idea is that it is sometimes legitimate for political rulers, precisely because they are rulers, to deceive, cheat, betray or even torture and murder, where these acts are clear violations of the moral code that seems to bind us all.

The qualification, 'in its most challenging form', is important. In Machiavelli himself (especially in *The Prince*), it does take this form, though at times his formulations move further in the direction of including the princely imperatives within the scope of ordinary morality. So he says of the prince that 'carefully taking everything into account, he will discover that something which appears to be a virtue, if pursued, will end in his destruction; while some other thing which seems to be a vice, if pursued, will result in his safety and well-being' (Machiavelli, [*The Prince*] (1984 edn), p.53). Here, the reference to appearances make his position a little more accommodating of morality's claim to a dominant position among reasons for acting, even if it is subversive of its normal substance. This wavering among formulations is philosophically interesting, and I have discussed it elsewhere (Coady (1993), pp.259–63). Here we need only note that because we tend to think of morality both as forming a coherent whole and as dominating all other reasons for action, there are at least two different ways of stating the 'dirty hands' thesis. We may state it as the view that political reasons sometimes legitimately override the most serious moral considerations, or as the view that morality is divided against itself, with the virtues required by political life incompatible with what we think of as normal (or 'private') virtues. There is a third option, but it is less a formulation of the dirty hands challenge than a way of sanitizing its confrontation with morality. This is the option of treating the apparent clash between political and ordinary morality as reconciled by some overarching moral principle, such as the principle of utility.

However we state it, two interesting points need settling. Are 'dirty hands' restricted to politicians, and, if they are not, is there something that makes political life a special 'showpiece' for dirty hands? It seems to me clear that the sorts of argument made by those who promote the category of 'dirty hands' are applicable beyond the arena of politics as narrowly, or even broadly, understood. When, for instance, philosophers stress the momentous consequences of political decisions, and argue that the consequences of abiding by normal moral prohibitions are sometimes so disastrous as to require the violation of moral constraints, they tend to ignore the way in which the same can be said of relatively private areas of life like the decisions facing a mother of an impoverished, crime-dominated urban ghetto, or those confronting an inmate of a concentration camp. This is not the place to examine the detail of the different arguments offered, but there are certain themes implicit, and sometimes explicit, in the argumentation, and an examination of these can show both that the dirty hands issue cannot be restricted to politics and why it is so often taken to exemplify it.

The generating of dirty hands

Machiavelli makes it clear that one of the situations generating the need for the ruler to act wickedly is the fact that others with whom one interacts cannot be relied upon to act morally, and hence conformity to morality is foolish and dangerous for survival. We might call this the problem of moral isolation. As befits someone who puts survival at the heart of morality, Thomas Hobbes gives an even clearer account of this than Machiavelli. Hobbes thought that the laws of nature gave us a valid moral code and associated virtues, but that they obliged *in foro interno* and 'not always' *in foro externo*. He meant that we ought to want the laws of nature to be obeyed, but that we would be stupid to practise morality unilaterally, Hobbes did not think the point applied solely to politics; rather, he thought it an important feature of life in a state of nature, but, as Sidgwick noted in a perceptive and neglected essay (Sidgwick (1898)), and as Hobbes would certainly have insisted, rulers often stand in relations to one another that resemble a state of nature. Hence the sphere of international relations is one that naturally lends itself to the dirty hands story. To the extent that morality depends upon the co-operation stressed by Hobbes, then where it is absent, we *may* be licensed to engage in the deception and violence of 'covert operations' against other nations. (It is worth noting, however, that the moral isolation of a state of nature may work to impose more, rather than less, stringent duties upon individuals or states. As Sidgwick ((1898), pp.77–8) saw, promises extracted by wrongful force are not binding in 'an orderly state', but are binding to some degree upon the defeated victims of an unjust war.)

The claims of 'moral isolation' have none the less to be treated with great caution. They are at their strongest in situations where the moral issues are heavily conventional. Where politeness decrees that no one need tell the truth about his feelings on meeting an unwelcome visitor, it might be folly not to lie, indeed it is not even clear that our linguistic intuitions would count as lies such falsehoods as 'I'm pleased to see you'. More interesting are the cases where broad non-compliance by others in the moral enterprise raises large issues of survival and so gives us a dispensation from strict compliance ourselves. Arguably this is so of certain dealings by the police with criminals, as in undercover investigations, and it seems particularly clear during war in activities such as spying on the enemy or providing him with misinformation. It seems reasonable to say that the drug-dealer or hit-man has, by his activities, forfeited any right to complain of such methods. Even so, issues of implicit contract, or even survival, do not exhaust the foundations of morality and there are two reasons for caution about the concessions founded on moral isolation. One concerns the matter of character and the other the possible consequences of the policy of relaxing moral prohibitions.

As to the former, it is not always folly to exercise the virtues of honesty, kindness and justice when others ignore them, since there is a personal and communal value in good character, even in such circumstances. As so many of the better spy novels teach us, the world of the spy is one of paranoia, self-deception and emotional sterility. Immersion in this world not only tends to distort the personalities of the spies, but, as recent history teaches us, it tends to damage the political culture of the wider society to which they belong. Nor are these direct consequences the only ones to be expected. If governments and their agencies are ready to relax moral standards *in extremis*, they cannot expect other groups and agencies within the community not to follow suit. This should give particular pause when we consider some of the supposed extremes in the dirty hands literature licensing serious moral exceptions in such areas as campaign funding (see Walzer (1973), p.165).

This problem is sometimes obscured by a certain romantic pomposity about the state, which sees it as the only agency of political thought and activity and as having such a special role and purpose that exemptions granted to it could hardly be extended further. A certain Gustro Rumelin, Chancellor of the University of Tübingen, put the matter splendidly in 1875: 'The state is self-sufficient. Self-regard is its appointed duty, the maintenance and development of its power and well-being – egoism, if you like to call this egoism – is the supreme principle o all politics' (quoted in Sidgwick (1898), p.64). But the example of egoism is infectious, and other corporations and groups within the state have not been slow in claiming the same prerogatives, especially where anything remotely connected with survival is at stake – survival of the party, the business, the department, the club, or the individual as indispensable leader of the group. The consequences of this, in turn, include the promotion of widespread cynicism about politicians and public life generally, and this itself makes inroads upon the achievablity of the goods that politics is supposed to promote.

Another source of this cynicism resides in the tension that seems inevitable between the supposed requirements of dirty hands and the moral underpinnings of democratic polity. The cultivation of the capacity for judicious vice in the ruler sits oddly with the values of public accountability and relative openness characteristic of genuine democracy. It is significant that Machiavelli urges his prince to keep up a public pretence of virtue while engaging in vicious acts as required, and certainly the success in ruling that Machiavelli so admired frequently requires the necessary wrong-doings to be cloaked in secrecy. But the prevalence of such secrecy, especially with regard to the breach of commonly accepted moral standards, is corrosive of the basic ideals of a democracy, and productive of cynicism about the political process. Witness the effects of the many, decidedly *unnecessary* moral enormities committed, without adequate scrutiny, under the rubric of 'national security' in so many Western democracies in recent years. For the hands to be successfully dirty, it seems they must also be democratically illegitimate. (For further discussion of this see Thompson (1987), chapter I.)

Ideals and messy realities

One thing that the discussion of moral isolation suggests is that morality often presents us with certain ideals that may have to be adapted to the messy realities of a world in which the ideals are widely disregarded or face difficulties of implementation. In much of life, we are faced with social realities that exhibit what Rawls ((1972), pp.245–8) has called 'partial compliance' to the conditions and norms of justice and other social virtues. If the champions of politics are often insensitive to the force of moral demands, the champions of morality are sometimes blind to political (and other) realities. There are two situations that need attention here, though it must regrettably be brief, and these are situations of compromise and extrication.

Problems of compromise are endemic to political life and, indeed, to all collaborative activities, for they allow joint enterprises to proceed, in spite of the conflicting goals, values and ideals of the participants. They do this because a compromise is a sort of bargain in which people who see advantages in co-operation for certain ends sacrifice other objectives, temporarily or permanently, in order to gain the ends that they believe are only achievable by co-operation. Compromise is not inherently immoral and it often has little to do with morality, but the losses may have a moral flavour about them, as when someone abandons certain ideals or sacrifices the hope of achieving certain valuable outcomes. To achieve economic stability, a politician may have to abandon much-needed reform of the health services, or a taxation scheme that would achieve more just social results. The moral losses incurred in such compromises are a necessary part of all politics, but they should not be treated lightly since persistent trading of central and cherished ideals can lead to the situation where a politician stands for nothing but personal or the party's survival in office. The problem with pragmatism is that the point of survival is swallowed up by the day-to-day necessities of compromise. Furthermore, beyond ideals, which may be modified, postponed or even legitimately abandoned, there exist basic moral standards and commitments that should be integral to an individual's character. To trade these is not just to compromise but to be compromised, and this is a description that invariably has negative force. When 'dirty hands' requires not just the limiting of moral hopes, and a certain lowering of moral outlook, but the abandonment of principle, it is an altogether more dubious and difficult demand.

Another important source for dirty hands problems are situations in which the agent needs to extricate from a moral mess of her own or others' making. In the political context, the agent may have initiated the immorality herself, or may have acquired responsibility for it, perhaps by inheriting office. Believing an existing war her country is waging to be unjust, for instance, she may, as the new leader of the government, be unable to stop the war at once without being responsible for grave harms and even wrongs, which are bound to follow on an immediate surrender or withdrawal. Gradual disengagement, however, offers good prospects for avoiding such evils, though it means that she must continue to direct an unjust war and the unjust killings it involves. More detail is required for a full discussion of this point, but it seems plausible that the example could be so constructed that the leader is morally responsible for wrong-doing whichever way she acts, but that gradual extrication is less wrong than immediate cessation. It also seems plausible that her responsibility is not the wholesale negative responsibility integral to consequentialist ethics but the responsibility inherent in ordinary moral thinking. Yet it is important to note that these are not simple cases of politics triumphing over morality since the moral verdict on the war remains dominant in showing the way to extrication. (There are fuller discussions of this issue in Coady (1989), (1990).)

There is an intriguing issue related to the dirty hands debate which is created by the role of bureaucracy in public life. This has been called the problem of 'many hands' (Thompson (1987), chapter 2) though it might just as well be called the problem of 'no hands'. It arises when, in a complex organization, so many people contribute to an outcome that the question of who is morally responsible for producing it is seriously muddled. Part of the problem is informational and part of it is attitudinal. It is particularly relevant to the role of expert advisers in political or commercial contexts. The informational point is that such advisers sometimes know little about the overall purposes for which their advice will be used; the attitudinal point is that, whether they know it or not, they frequently see themselves as having no moral responsibility for the organizational outcomes of their work. 'I am paid for my expertise', says the lawyer, soldier, accountant, or scientist. 'It is my duty to my client or employer to give them the benefits of that expertise no matter how they might use it.' It is not that the advisers are like Machiavelli's prince in considering that the end justifies the means, but rather that they disclaim any knowledge of, or concern for, the end and restrict themselves to purely technical consideration of the means. There are many complex problems raised by this phenomenon, but it is easy to see the dangers that such widespread abdication of moral responsibility poses for the relevance of morality to politics and public life generally.

Finally, it is important in considering the problem of 'dirty hands' or 'no hands' not to be trapped into considering the issue in a static way, as though the background circumstances in which hands are likely to get dirty, or empty of moral responsibility, are somehow immutable. Machiavellian thinking has a tendency to obscure the fact that the background to political life is itself a fit subject for moral scrutiny and structural change, especially when it is that background itself that contributes to the alleged need for dirty or empty hands. Talk of the necessity for hands to get dirty often assumes a complacent, even conniving, tone, and tends to stifle the moral imagination, making local necessities seem global and eternal. The Machiavellian outlook also puts morality into too defensive a posture, as though morality could only confront politics as an inhibition and a problem. But, although there are plenty of difficulties with a merely moralistic approach to politics, we must not lose sight of the power of morality as a dynamic for political change. The recent, mostly peaceful, overthrow of entrenched communist tyranny in Eastern Europe, with all its ambiguities, is a timely reminder of this (see O'Neill (1990)).

References

Aristotle (1981 edn), *The Politics*, trans. T.A. Sinclair, revised Trevor J. Saunders, Penguin Books.

Coady, C.A.J. (1989), 'Escaping from the bomb: immoral deterrence and the problem of extrication', in Shue, Henry (ed.) (1989), *Nuclear Deterrence and Moral Restraint*, Cambridge University Press.

Coady, C.A.J. (1990), 'Messy morality and the art of the possible', *Proceedings of the Aristotelian Society*, supplementary vol., 64.

Hobbes, T. (1981 edn), *Leviathan*, ed. C.B. Macpherson, Penguin Books.

Machiavelli, N. (1984 edn), *The Prince*, ed. P. Bondanella, Oxford University Press.

Machiavelli, N. (1950 edn), *The Discourses*, trans. and ed. L.J. Walker, Penguin Books.

O'Neill, O. (1990), 'Messy morality and the art of the possible', *Proceedings of the Aristotelian Society*, supplementary vol., 64.

Rawls, J. (1972), *A Theory of Justice*, Oxford University Press.

Sidgwick, H. (1898) 'Public morality', in *Practical Ethics*, Swan Sonnenschein & Co.

Thompson, D. F. (1987), *Political Ethics and Public Office*, Harvard University Press.

Walzer, M. (1973), 'Political action: the problem of dirty hands', *Philosophy and Public Affairs*, 2, 160–80.

Further reading

Acheson, D. (1965), 'Ethics in international relations today', in *The Vietnam Reader*, ed. M.G. Raskin and B. Fall, Random House.

Acheson, D. (1971), 'Homage to plain dumb luck', in *The Cuban Missile Crisis*, ed. R.A. Divine, Quadrangle Books.

Coady, C.A.J. (1993), 'Politics and the problem of dirty hands', in *A Companion to Ethics*, ed. P. Singer, Blackwell.

Day, J.P. (1989), 'Compromise', *Philosophy*, 64.

Erasmus, D. (1936), *The Education of a Christian Prince*, trans. and intro. L.K. Born, New York.

Gaita, R. (1990), 'Ethics and politics', in his *Good and Evil: An Absolute Conception*, Macmillan.

Kavka, G.S. (1987), 'Nuclear coercion', in *Moral Paradoxes of Nuclear Deterrence*, ed. G.S. Kavka, Cambridge University Press.

Hampshire, S. (ed.) (1978), *Public and Private Morality*, Cambridge University Press.

Hampshire, S. (1978a), 'Morality and pessimism', in Hampshire (1978).

Marx, K. (1967) *Writings of the Young Marx on Philosophy and Society*, ed. and trans. L.D. Easton and K.H. Guddat, Anchor Books.

Nagel, T., 'Ruthlessness in public life', in Hampshire (1978), pp.75–92.

Oberdiek, H. (1986), 'Clean and dirty hands in politics', *International Journal of Moral and Social Studies*, I, 1.

Plato, *The Republic*, any edition, especially Book I.

Rousseau, J.-J. (1986 edn), *The First and Second Discourses Together with the Replies to Critics and Essay on the Origin of Languages*, ed. V. Gourevitch, New York.

Stocker M. (1990), *Plural and Conflicting Values*, Oxford University Press.

Walzer, M. (1977/80), *Just and Unjust Wars*, Basic Books/Penguin Books.

Weber, M. (1919), 'Politics as a vocation', in *From Max Weber: Essays in Sociology*, ed. H.H. Gerth and C. Wright Mills, New York:.

Williams, B., 'Politics and moral character', in Hampshire (1978), pp.55–74.

Note

From Goodin, Robert E. and Pettit, Philip (eds) (1993) *A Companion to Contemporary Political Philosophy*, Blackwell, pp.422–30.

CHAPTER 2

Thomas Hobbes: *Leviathan*

Jon Pike

By the end of this chapter you should:
- Have read the most important chapters from Parts 1 and 2 of Hobbes's *Leviathan*.
- Have a good understanding of Hobbes's political theory and how it fits with his theory of human nature.
- Be able to offer some criticisms of Hobbes's theory.
- Be aware of some contemporary interpretations of Hobbes and of his continuing relevance to political philosophy.

Introduction

It is not difficult to justify reading *Leviathan*. If there were a poll of political philosophers to find out which book they rated as the most important and influential text of political philosophy in English, *Leviathan* would probably come out on top. In it, Thomas Hobbes provides us with the first fully worked out, systematic and modern theory of the state and of the exact nature of our obligation to obey it, in an analysis that is of enduring relevance. At the same time, *Leviathan*, published in 1651, clearly reflects its particular historical context. It is the end product of a long process of refining his science of man and politics begun by Hobbes with the *Elements of Law* (1640) and continued with a book best known by its Latin title: *De Cive* (1642). Hobbes's conclusions were certainly influenced by his recent experience of the social upheaval and conflict of the French Wars of Religion and the English Civil War (1642–9), which led to his exile. Early in 1649 the King was executed, the House of Lords was abolished, and England was proclaimed a commonwealth under the Cromwellian Council of State. *Leviathan* is, in part, a contribution to the debate over the legitimacy of that government, after the government instituted an oath of loyalty (known as the 'Engagement') on officers in the armed forces, on clergymen, and on office bearers in the state. In the Engagement controversy, Hobbes argued, perversely, that it was right to obey the new state – within limits – even though he had been on the Royalist side in the civil war.

The huge reputation of *Leviathan*, and the sheer size of the book (most editions run to at least five hundred pages) can be intimidating. But the crucial elements of the theory are relatively straightforward, and are contained in the first two parts of the work (in Parts III and IV, Hobbes discusses the religious implications of his views).

Many of Hobbes's contemporaries thought he might be an atheist. Whether he was or not is a matter of scholarly debate. Whatever the facts of the matter, his political theory as a whole can be treated as a broadly secular one without losing its essential core. In fact, this is one reason for regarding Hobbes as a specifically modern political philosopher. Like Machiavelli, Hobbes thought of politics as a secular practice, and both philosophers tried to distance political philosophizing from religious encumbrances.

I shall quickly pass over the earlier chapters of Part I, which concern Hobbes's science of man, in order to get on to the political theory proper. Having said this, *Leviathan* is a tremendous book, full of interesting puzzles, and well worth coming back to in its entirety at some time.

Hobbes's prose style is quite precise and its precision follows from his methodology. Contemporary accounts tell us that Hobbes was particularly impressed by the advances made in the field of Euclidean geometry, and he attempted to apply a broadly geometrical method to the human sciences. John Aubrey's *Brief Lives* (1651) contains an anecdote about the origin of Hobbes's love of geometry.

> Being in a gentleman's library, Euclid's *Elements* lay open, and 'twas the 47th Prop. of Book I. He read the proposition. 'By G—' said he (he would now and then swear, by way of emphasis), 'This is impossible!' So he reads the demonstration of it, which referred him back to such a proposition; which proposition he read. That referred him back to another, which he also read. And so on, until at least he was demonstratively convinced of that truth. This made him in love with geometry.
>
> (Cited in Curley (ed.) (1994), p.lxvii)

A geometrical method applied to political philosophy meant starting out with clear definitions equivalent to the axioms of the geometers, and constructing a more complex picture from these sure foundations. The analogy between geometry and political philosophy works, according to Hobbes, because both are artificial creations. In this, they both differ from natural bodies: stones or trees, for example. In his *Six Lessons to the Professors of Mathematics*, Hobbes wrote:

> Geometry, therefore is demonstrable for the lines and figures from which we reason are drawn and described by ourselves; and civil philosophy is demonstrable because we make the commonwealth ourselves. But because of natural bodies we know not the construction, but seek it from effects, there lies no demonstration of what the causes be we seek for, but only of what they may be.
>
> (*Epistle Dedicatory to Six Lessons to the Professors of Mathematics*, cited in *Body, Man, and Citizen: Thomas Hobbes* (ed. Peters) p.12)

So Hobbes spends a lot of time giving precise definitions and it is worth paying particular attention to his writing at these points, especially when a definition seems unusual, incomplete, or counterintuitive. It is also important to read Hobbes critically: he is trying to persuade you to agree with his theory, and he employs a number of tools, some of which are properly philosophical and some of which are more rhetorical, in order to gain your agreement. Reading Hobbes's account critically requires you to separate out the reason from the rhetoric, and not to be persuaded too easily.

The text of *Leviathan* contains several Latin words and phrases, and many archaic words. In some modern versions, the spelling has been modernized, the Latin is translated, and words with unusual meanings are explained either in notes or a glossary entry (see, for example, Curley, op. cit., pp.550–9). Always look them up until you remember the equivalent modern term. For example, 'diffidence' in Hobbes means something importantly different from the meaning we give it today. 'Diffidence' means for us shyness or lack of self confidence: something like self distrust, but for Hobbes the word means distrust of others and the attitude of self defence that goes with it.

Hobbes's use of the terms 'man' and 'mankind' poses problems for modern commentators. On the one hand, his mechanical account of human beings and his formal account of the origins of political authority seem to involve just individuals, regardless of the biological distinction between men and women. He thinks, for example, that the sovereign can be either a man or a woman. If this is true, he uses the term 'man' in a way that is sexist. We would have some justification in using 'human' and 'humankind' to do the same job when we comment on Hobbes. This would avoid the sexist mistake of using 'man' to refer to humans of either sex.

But Hobbes also uses 'man' in a sexually specific way to mean males. For example, he says in Chapter XX, 4[1] that 'as to the generation, God hath ordained to man a helper ...' So there is a tension in his use of the terms. Sometimes Hobbes's 'man' is clearly male, at others, he, or she, is not. The actual use of the terms and the assumptions behind them should be carefully identified in each case.

Hobbes's writing is stylish, and often funny. It is well worth persevering with his seventeenth-century prose in order to reap the benefits of a first-hand acquaintance with *Leviathan*.

Hobbes aims to build up his theory step by step. Here is a very brief summary.

First (Introduction, Chapters I–VI) he provides a mechanical account of the nature of human beings. Life is nothing more than 'an motion of limbs' and careful examination will determine what sort of motion. Human action is determined, and we are driven by appetites and aversions. The biggest aversion is fear of death. This would not matter if we were able to live together harmoniously – but unfortunately we are not. Instead, we seek increasing power over one another (Chapter X) because we can never feel safe with the power we have. When we live together in the absence of a common power, each of us continually fights against everyone else (Chapter XIII). This shows us that, to keep the peace, we require an overall power stronger than any one of us. So it is reasonable to agree together to hand over our power to a powerful sovereign (Chapter XIV). Under these circumstances, but not before, it is appropriate for us to behave morally towards one another. We come together in the form of a state or commonwealth which is represented by a sovereign (Chapter XVI). The sovereign has very wide authority (Chapter XVIII), and the best sort of sovereign is a monarch (Chapter XIX). But we are still entitled to resist orders that put at risk our own lives. (Chapter XXI). Overall it is Hobbes's desire for peace, and his account of human nature that underpins his political theory.

You do not first need to read *Leviathan* quickly because it is almost impossible to read Hobbes quickly! Instead, I will take *Leviathan* a chapter or two at a time, and the chapters themselves are relatively short.

Hobbes's materialism

Hobbes builds his political philosophy, and in particular his account of the need for a state, on the foundation of his view of human nature. This view is solidly materialist: humankind is no more than moving matter.

ACTIVITY

Read: Hobbes's Introduction to *Leviathan* and then answer the following two questions.

1 What does the state consist of?
2 What does Hobbes consider to be the fundamental nature of mankind?

DISCUSSION

1 Hobbes says that Part I describes the *matter* of the state, i.e. what it consists of. It is clear that Hobbes sees the content of the state filled out entirely by individual human beings, with no other independent entities entering into the scheme of things. There are no 'estates' or 'classes' or 'castes' at the foundations of Hobbes's account. He thinks that the appropriate way to think about the state is to think first about the 'atoms' that compose it. The view that social entities should be analysed only in terms of the individuals that constitute them is called *methodological individualism* but within political philosophy it is a contested analysis. Marx, for example, would insist that classes and capital were part of the social world. Locke sometimes seems to see 'the people' or 'the community' as a collectivity beyond and distinct from individuals, so that the whole is more than the sum of its parts: a view not shared by Hobbes. As we shall see, Hobbes adheres to methodological individualism more consistently than any other political philosopher in this book. This approach is illustrated graphically in the original frontispiece to *Leviathan* (Fig. I). It shows a huge monarchical figure wielding a sword high over the land. It is clear that this figure is leviathan or the state, but if you look closely you will see that the single figure is made up of thousands of tiny individual human figures.

2 Hobbes asserts that the fundamental nature of mankind is one of human beings being simply physical objects and that their actions can be explained by analogy with the movements of machines. I say that Hobbes asserts this because he does not provide an *argument* here. This is evident from the grammatical structure of his claim – it is a rhetorical question: 'what is the heart but a spring, and the nerves so many strings and the joints so many wheels, giving motion to the whole body ... ?' Hobbes assumes that the answer is 'nothing else', and he is clearly denying that there is anything else to mankind beyond matter – no 'incorporeal substance' or non-material 'mind', for example. Hobbes's view of the fundamental nature of human beings is, then, a materialist and mechanical one.

Figure 1 Title page to Hobbes's Leviathan.

There are a number of difficulties for any materialist account of mind, but two are particularly pertinent to reading Hobbes:

1   The materialist description of human beings as machines in motion seems to be a matter of physiology, but that they have thoughts and of what kind, is a matter of psychology. An important feature of thoughts is that they are *about something*, whereas mechanical motions cannot be thought of as being about anything; they happen because of what caused them. Hobbes, as a materialist, holds that there is only a mechanical description of our thoughts, but how can this mechanical motion be *about* anything?

2   If all human actions can be explained in the same way as the movements of machines, as only causes and effects in which the effects follow on necessarily from their physical causes, then there seems no room for free will – for the possibility that we could change our minds. Yet we have the impression that we can choose what we do or do not do. How can this be?

ACTIVITY

Read Chapter VI of *Leviathan* and answer these two questions (for the second question, it will help if you also read the first four paragraphs of Chapter XXI):

1   What particular features of Hobbes's account suggests that mechanical motion *could* be about something?

2   How does Hobbes deal with the problem of free will?

DISCUSSION

1   Chapter VI presents Hobbes's account of the 'passions'. These passions are an important category for early modern philosophers, and are recognizable to us as something we might call 'motivations'. He presents us with a classification scheme, first distinguishing *vital* from *voluntary* motions. Vital motions are involuntary bodily functions such as breathing and blood circulation; voluntary motions, unlike vital ones, are bodily motions preceded by a thought, such as to speak, to kiss or to spurn. At first sight this looks like a common-sense account of action: something is an action when we decide what to do and then we act. But Hobbes's account is different: for him, the preceding thought is a movement, which he calls an *endeavour*. Hobbes separates passions into appetites or desires and aversions, which are, according to this argument, just different directions of the endeavours – 'these small beginnings of motion within the body of man'.

How does the theory of endeavours help us with the first problem faced by a materialist account of mind? Certainly, Hobbes thinks that he has moved on from physiology to psychology by means of endeavours: that a passion is about something is indicated by the direction of the endeavour towards or away from that thing. But it might be objected that the meaning of 'about' does not seem to be fully conveyed by directional terms – by thoughts being towards or away from some object. Perhaps if one thinks about the washing up, this thought can be reduced to a tiny interior movement away from the sink, so that an aversion can be accounted for in this directional manner.

But this will not do. Any direction is both toward *and* away (and alongside, and half away from, and so on) from many points. Suppose 'the washing up' is singled out as the object from which direction is mapped. Then, it is the 'singling out' of the washing up that makes the thought 'about' the washing up. The 'aboutness' is smuggled into the argument when the objects of the passions are identified in the first place. It does not come from some neutral account of direction.

2   It is important for his political philosophy that Hobbes deal with the problem of free will. What must be satisfied to be able to say that people are free? Is it, for example, a matter of people deciding how they should live together, by being in a democracy? Or is it simply a matter of whether they are chained up or not? The materialist and mechanical account of physiology entails a deterministic account of action; our actions are caused, and the causes of our actions are caused too, as part of a necessary chain of causes and effects going back in time. So, for Hobbes our actions are determined: they occur of necessity. Despite this, he claims that they are (usually) free. How can this be so? To understand this, we need to look carefully at how Hobbes defines the will. In Chapter VI, 53, Hobbes defines the will as 'the last appetite or aversion immediately adhering to the action, or to the omission thereof, is that we call the WILL, the act (not the faculty) of *willing*'. He goes on to say that 'a voluntary act is that which proceedeth from the will, and no other'.

The account amounts, then, to this. Suppose I am pondering whether or not I take a specific action X. In fact, what is happening is that various appetites and aversions – which are tiny movements – are battling it out. One of these appetites or aversions wins, and attaches itself to the action, or omission. I do, or do not do, X. This victorious appetite or aversion is called the will. But this is not a capacity or ability to *will* – to choose, independently of my appetites and aversions whether or not to do X. I do not have such a capacity according to Hobbes. How then are my actions free? They are free if I am able to act according to my last appetite or aversion: that is, they are free if I can act according to my will. They would not be free if I was tied up, and unable to do what I wanted to do. Free action is a matter of being able to do what I want to do. But it would be a mistake to go one step back from this and say that I could decide what I wanted to do.

So, for Hobbes free action and determinism are compatible, that is, he holds a *compatibilist* position. The example that he gives later, in Chapter XXI, is meant to show how this can be so. A river is free to run down a hillside, in the sense that it is not constrained – it is not dammed, for example – but its flow is none the less determined by physical laws.

ACTIVITY

Does Hobbes make a convincing case for the compatibility of freedom and determinism?

Hint: consider the prisoner tied up in his cell – does he have free will to the same extent as a free person?

DISCUSSION

It is true that the prisoner's actions are constrained when he is tied and locked up. But this does not show that he lacks the sort of freedom that counts in the debate over free will and determinism, that is the freedom to do otherwise, or to put it another way, the freedom to make up his mind. Hobbes seems to conflate freedom with political freedom, and denies the possibility of free will. This is because of what he wants 'freedom' to do in political philosophy: Freedom is just a matter of not being in chains: it is not a matter of deciding who should rule. Hobbes systematically downplays free choice: his mechanistic materialism leads him to deny this sort of freedom, and thus we would have to doubt the coherence of the idea that we *could* act in a way that was different from the way that we were *caused* to act.

Hobbes on power

We have seen how human beings work, according to Hobbes, being drawn towards or away from external objects. But how do we relate to each other? It is common today to talk of 'power relationships' and Hobbes would recognize this phrase. He thinks that power is an essential part of our relationships with one another. His account of power is the next foundational element in his political philosophy.

ACTIVITY

Read through Chapters X and XI, paying less attention to the classical allusions than the bones of Hobbes's argument. As you read make a note of the following:

1   Hobbes's definitions of 'power' in man.
2   Hobbes's account of the worth or value of a man.
3   What Hobbes thinks the general inclination of all mankind is.

DISCUSSION

1   Hobbes distinguishes between natural and instrumental power: We have, it seems, some power because of our natural attributes, and we get other power by using these attributes. This second kind of power itself is a resource for accruing power, which increases at an accelerating rate.

    But there is another distinction that Hobbes employs in this passage, between two different definitions, of power in man. At paragraph 1 power is the 'present means to obtain some future apparent good'. But in the next paragraph he outlines natural power as 'the eminence of the faculties of body or mind' and the use of this eminence to acquire more power. The important point is that if I have eminence in a particular faculty, then I am better, in relation to someone else, at exercising this faculty. Eminence is a relative notion.

2   Value is determined in the market. Hobbes says 'The value or worth of a man is, as of all other things, his price, that is to say, so much as would be given for the use of his power; and therefore is not absolute, but a thing dependent on the need and judgement of another'.

> 3 By the time we get to Chapter XI Hobbes thinks he has established as a 'general inclination of all mankind a perpetual and restless desire for of power after power that ceaseth only in death'.

The difference is between the two concepts of power is significant. According to the first definition, if a man improves his prospects of securing a comfortable future, then he has increased his power, and his increased power does not seem to affect anyone else. Think perhaps of someone getting a pay rise, and putting some of it into a pension. This does the person some good, and is an increase of power in the sense of present means to acquire some future good, but it does not have any negative effect upon anyone else. But according to the second definition, power as *eminence*, an increase in someone's power certainly does affect others. If power is eminence, it is the amount by which a person's faculties exceed others' that matters. Power as eminence is a relative notion, relative to the faculties of others. The distribution of power as eminence is a 'zero-sum game' (i.e. the gain of one participant is the loss of another), so if one person's power increases, others' falls and vice versa: the sum is always zero. So if I gain some power-as-eminence in some way in relation to you, you lose some power-as-eminence in relation to me. Suppose you take a French class, and improve your faculty to speak French. Then, regardless of my faculty to speak French, you have either closed the gap behind me, or opened one ahead of me. You gain and I lose. According to this conception of power, any gain in power for you has a corresponding negative effect on me.

ACTIVITY

Read C.B. Macpherson's 'The Theory of Human Nature in Society' (Reading 2.1). and answer the following question.

Macpherson argues that Hobbes makes some illicit assumptions about man in the natural state. What are these assumptions?

DISCUSSION

Macpherson argues that the man that Hobbes describes is not man in the state of nature at all, but contemporary man. This man is abstracted from a society and its political relations but he continues to carry with him assumptions about men in that society. For Hobbes these assumptions are uncontroversial. They are assumptions about the natural properties of humankind. For Macpherson these properties are not natural, but social. Hobbes's assumptions are smuggled in under the guise of the definition of power as eminence. The assumptions are:

1 That every man's power resists and hinders the effects of other men's power.

2 That all acquired power consists in command over some of the powers of other men.

3 That some men's desires are without limit.

Macpherson identifies the society in which these claims are true as a 'possessive market society'. This sort of society, which corresponds roughly to capitalist society, is one in which labour is a commodity and therefore can be bought and sold. If labour can be bought and sold, then there is far more scope for one man to command the powers of another (Macpherson (1962), Chapter 2).

Macpherson's argument here is influenced by Marx. A Marxist would argue (contra Hobbes) that the profit motive and the relentless drive to competition is not a natural feature of mankind or human nature, but something that is fostered and encouraged by capitalist market relations.

Macpherson argues that the conception of power as eminence is not self evident, but rather a deduction from possessive market society. In the terms of game theory, his case is that power games are not necessarily zero-sum games; they only appear that way in a possessive market society. In fact, gaining power could be a positive-sum game in which an increase in one person's stock of power can be accompanied by an increase – or at least no change in – another's stock of power.

So, is power primarily distributed in a zero-sum way or a positive-sum way? It depends on the sorts of resources in question. Both material resources such as food, and non-material resources such as reputation and glory are types of power, since they are 'present means to acquire some future good'. If we are considering food, the positive-sum account seems plausible: a person can increase his stock of food without affecting others' stock. But if the resource concerned is glory, then a zero-sum account seems correct.

At my school speech day, some years ago, there was a long list of prizes. These prizes were given out to sixth-form pupils, including prizes for general achievement and team work. So, virtually everyone ended up with a prize for something or other. As a result – and to my chagrin – my own particularly glorious achievements went relatively unrecognized. Of course, I got a prize, but then so did everyone else. In order for my achievements to win the glory they deserved, I needed a large number of people not to get prizes. So, glory looks to be the sort of power that is distributed according to a zero-sum game.

However, my desire for glory sounds rather ignoble, and could itself be a product of the fact that I grew up in a possessive market society. That is probably what Macpherson would say. He needs to show that the distribution of power can be a positive-sum game, otherwise we are going to be locked into a competitive Hobbesian struggle for 'power after power'. I have suggested that it is not an *exclusively* positive-sum game: there are some irreducibly zero-sum distributions of power.

Hobbes spends some time analysing power because he thinks that the network of power relationships between people has consequences for how they will behave. In order to see how they will behave he posits a society without government – the famous (or infamous) 'state of nature'.

Hobbes's conception of the state of nature

Let's review the point that we have reached in *Leviathan*. Hobbes has presented a mechanistic account of human beings driven by appetites and aversions, constantly seeking happiness ('felicity'). After thinking about the isolated individual man, Hobbes goes on to consider 'man in multitudes'. One way of thinking about this is to consider Hobbes as a child who examines his clockwork toy soldiers one by one, investigating what makes them move, and then sets them down and reports what happens when they are all wound up and let go together. Now we reach the most famous and memorable chapter of *Leviathan*. In Chapter XIII – 'Of the natural condition of mankind, as concerning their felicity, and misery' – Hobbes describes the state of nature: what our lives would be like without a state that constrains our behaviour. His famous conclusion is that the state of nature is a state of war in which constant competition, pre-emptive strikes, insecurity and distrust leave us with lives that are 'solitary, poor, nasty, brutish, and short' (paragraph 9). The idea of a state of nature is central to three of the philosophers discussed in this book: Hobbes, Locke and Rousseau. All use the device to help them structure their different approaches to the state.

ACTIVITY

Before you read Chapter XIII, do the thought experiment yourself. How do you think we would behave in a state of nature? Would we be able to muddle along together cooperating when we needed to, and helping each other out in projects that needed more than one person involved? Or would we end up fighting one another and stealing if there were no central power keeping us under control?

Now read Chapter XIII, in which Hobbes gives his view of life in the state of nature. As you do so, answer the following questions.

1   How does Hobbes define 'the state of nature'? Note that in Chapter XIII he does not actually use the term 'state of nature' at all: this is just a convenient shorthand used later to refer back to the situation he describes in Chapter XIII.

2   What are the three principal sources of disagreement in the nature of man?

3   Does Hobbes assume that we all naturally pursue more goods and land than we need?

4   Is Hobbes relating how we once lived, or how we live now? That is, is he giving a *factual* account, either historical or anthropological? Or is he offering us an abstract model, or thought experiment: a *hypothetical* account?

5   Finally, do you agree with Hobbes? Give as many reasons as possible for your view. Suppose you thought that human kind is naturally sociable and cooperative and that, in fact, it is the state that corrupts us and makes us competitive and antagonistic towards one another; how would you reply to Hobbes's arguments? That is, what are the possible objections from an *anarchist* perspective.

DISCUSSION

1   Hobbes talks about the state of nature in two different ways. In the chapter title, he refers to 'the natural condition of mankind' and in paragraph 8 he speaks of 'the time men live without a common power to keep them all in awe'. So the state of nature is defined both as a separate and distinctive state: the 'natural condition', and also as a lack of a common power.

2   '[C]ompetition, diffidence and glory' (paragraph 6) are the principal sources of disagreement.

3   No. In paragraph 4 he accepts that there are some who 'would be glad to be at ease within modest bounds' were it not for the existence of those who take pleasure in contemplating their own power.

4   I think Hobbes is ambiguous on this issue: Chapter XIII mostly consists of a thought experiment, but there are also some factual points brought in later on, e.g. 'the savage people in many places of America' (paragraph 11).

Arguing for the state of nature

As I see it, Hobbes has three arguments for the state of nature being a state of war of all against all:

1   that is how people behave when government actually crumbles (call this 'the argument from observation');

2   that is the evidence provided by reflection upon our own actions (call this 'the argument from introspection');

3   we can infer the state of nature from first principles about mankind (call this 'the argument from the passions').

The argument from observation

Hobbes suggests that we can know about the state of nature by looking at what happens in the absence of government. He does not go into great detail, and some might say that his account was not historically accurate. Hobbes confronts this objection head on. He imagines an opponent who says 'there never was such a time nor condition of war as this' and concedes that this was generally true. But he also thinks that in parts of America people do live in this brutish state. What is more, we can also get empirical evidence about the state of nature by looking at what happens when people who have lived peacefully together enter into civil war. Clearly he would have had in mind here the French Wars of Religion and the English Civil War which ended with the execution of King Charles in 1649, only two years before the publication of *Leviathan*. So Hobbes is providing some empirical evidence to support his view of the brutish state of nature.

This evidence is meant to persuade us of the *precariousness* of political, and more generally, social life. Political life, Hobbes thinks, is a delicate and fragile state of affairs. It does not come naturally to human beings: rather the opposite. We are not, as Aristotle thought, political animals who fulfil ourselves in political organizations, but rather our natural state is as isolated and self seeking atoms in a state of constant conflict. At first glance it might look as if political institutions have a life of their own, and are relatively stable. Not so, according to Hobbes. Political institutions are created by an immense act of will, which he compares in the Introduction to the act of will carried out by God when He created the earth. The existence of these institutions is precarious, always liable to collapse into the war of all against all, because the natural condition of mankind acts like a force which tends to pull apart artificial institutions such as the state. Because of the strength of this force, the institutions have to be correspondingly robust in order to withstand it. This is the fundamental reason for Hobbes's advocacy of an authoritarian state. In the second part of *Leviathan* he frequently criticizes specific proposals for political institutions on the basis that they allow the possibility of dissent and faction fighting, from which can proceed only an accelerating conflict and a degeneration back to the state of nature, which is a state that must be avoided at all costs. *Anything* is better than that! Thus we must hand (almost) all our rights to the sovereign, because of the risk of political institutions unravelling if we hang on to any serious rights. This idea of the political institutions as a careful and fragile construction, always liable to collapse back into the state of nature is one of the key explanatory devices in *Leviathan*. And Hobbes's observation of the European civil wars gave the most immediate evidence for the belief that this collapse is likely to take place.

The argument from self reflection and the careful anarchist

Recall what Hobbes said about introspection in the Introduction to *Leviathan*. He suggested there that *nosce teipsum* ('read thy self') was a useful watchword: 'whosoever looketh into himself ... he shall thereby read and know, what are the thoughts and passions of all other men on the like occasions' (paragraph 3). In Chapter XIII he applies this introspective method, asking readers to look into themselves. Hobbes acknowledges that we may find the picture of the state of war unpalatable so he tries a persuasive strategy that relies on introspection.

ACTIVITY

Reread Chapter XIII, paragraph 10. By what argument does Hobbes attempt to persuade us that we in fact see others as a threat?

Hobbes tries to persuade us by pointing to a hidden assumption that is required to make sense of our everyday actions. Why do we lock our doors when we go on a journey? The only answer possible is that we lock our doors in order to prevent strangers from taking our property. This only makes sense if we expect other people to steal our belongings when our backs are turned. So our everyday actions are explained by putting them as the conclusion of an argument like this:

> People are essentially untrustworthy and will take my property if they can.
> I do not want my property to be taken.
> *Therefore* I should lock up my property when I go on a journey.

Invoking the essential untrustworthiness argument allows Hobbes to turn a neat rhetorical trick on an objector who says his picture of mankind in the state of nature is too bleak. Hobbes's response is to say: I am not the only one who is condemning mankind. *You* are too, since you behave in a way that only makes sense if you agree with my conclusion.

ACTIVITY

Is it possible to sustain the anarchist position in the face of this rhetorical turn? Is it possible to argue that humankind in the state of nature could live in a cooperative and trustworthy manner, while locking one's front door on the way to the shops or – to put it another way – could one be a cautious and prudent anarchist? (It may help you to answer this question if you recall the argument presented by C.B. Macpherson in Reading 2.1.)

DISCUSSION

Yes, one could hold on to the anarchist position. The careful anarchist could say: 'I don't need such a strong argument to explain my actions. In particular, I don't need the claim in the first premise that people are essentially untrustworthy. In the here and now, because of the corrupting influence of the state, people aren't worthy of trust and are out to get what they can, but there's still a possible organization of human activity in which I could trust people and leave my doors unlocked. I just don't live in such happy circumstances at the moment. But the fact that I don't live in such circumstances now doesn't entail that they might not exist at some time. After all, I don't live in the state of nature. The assumptions that explain my behaviour in the here and now shouldn't be generalized into assumptions about human beings in the state of nature.'

Recall what Macpherson says in Reading 2.1. Writing about man's competitive search for power, he argues that Hobbes's conclusion 'is reached by way of generalizations about men in society ... for it means that Hobbes was using a mental model of society which, whether he was conscious of this or not, corresponds only to a bourgeois market society' (p.104 below). Whether Macpherson is right about Hobbes's account of power or not, the overall point should be clear. The suggestion is that Hobbes is taking particular and *contingent* features of the society in which he lived and illicitly generalizing them into features of man in the state of nature. This was in fact an accusation levelled at Hobbes by Rousseau. Certainly Hobbes seems guilty of such a move in the argument from introspection in Chapter XIII and so open to objection from a careful anarchist. The careful anarchist's argument looks like this:

People are untrustworthy in the current social set up (but not essentially) and will take my property if they can.

I do not want my property to be taken.

Therefore I should lock up my property when I go on a journey.

While the careful anarchist's objection works as an argument, we might want to say that it depends for its power on the success of the anarchist in outlining a picture of the state of nature in which we do not need to lock our doors. Thinkers such as Rousseau and Marx, who are committed – explicitly or otherwise – to this criticism of Hobbes, are going to have to come up with a plausible picture of a non-competitive society themselves.

The argument from the passions

The argument that Hobbes employs is derived from his account of human psychology and the analysis of power that he gave in Chapters X and XI. The remaining plank in the argument is the postulate of equality between men. It is notable here that Hobbes breaks away from any notion of a *natural* hierarchy among human beings: none of us is strong enough or quick enough to dominate over all the others, or even to get out of the way of the others, but each of us is potentially under threat from the confederacy (or conspiracy) of others. Moreover, the weakest is, on his or her own, at least strong enough to kill the strongest. This is a significant break from earlier accounts of political philosophy, in particular, the account given by Aristotle. Aristotle thought that slaves and women were naturally inferior to free men. Hobbes is absolutely clear in his rejection of this hierarchical conception. His acceptance of natural equality between the sexes is indeed radical and has been the starting point for a number of feminist accounts of Hobbes that I shall consider later. But the use Hobbes makes of this point is quite surprising. Hobbes takes a physiological fact about human beings – our natural equality – and uses it to underpin a very unequal balance of power between the sovereign and the subjects.

Hobbes jokes here that we are each roughly as wise as each other, since 'there is not ordinarily a greater sign of the equal distribution of anything than that every man is contented with his share', and none of us will admit to concern that we missed out on our fair share of brains!

The natural equality of ability means that we each have equal expectation of getting what we want. So if you and I desire the same thing, we have an equal chance of getting it. Perhaps, with certain kinds of thing, we could share the object. I can listen to a concert on the radio at the same time as another. But in other cases this will not be possible. I cannot get the same seat at that concert as someone else. In this sort of case, Hobbes thinks, we will naturally become enemies, and try to destroy or subdue one another (Chapter XIII, paragraph 3).

If I plant some crops or build a hut (a 'convenient seat') then at least two things follow. First, according to Hobbes, you will want to take advantage of my hut and my crops. But secondly, you will also know that I will want to keep my crops and I will try to defend them. So you might as well kill me to get them. Knowing this, I might as well take pre-emptive action and kill you first. More generally, I will have to defend my crops and my convenient seat with my life against all comers. Given this knowledge, I will not trust you or any other humans to leave me in peace: the attitude that prevails between us will be one of *diffidence*. (i.e. distrust). The existence of distrust will motivate us into this kind of pre-emptive action, which Hobbes calls 'anticipation' (paragraph 4).

ACTIVITY

Read Jean Hampton's 'Hobbes and Game Theory' (Reading 2.2).

Hampton outlines two sorts of game – a 'one-shot' prisoner's dilemma and a repeated or iterated prisoner's dilemma. There are different outcomes in each case, and there are examples of both sorts of game in *Leviathan*. In the one-shot case, the structure of the prisoner's dilemma means that Hobbes can get to his pessimistic conclusion about the state of war of all against all with somewhat weaker premises than we may have imagined.

It might be thought from the discussion of Hobbes's picture of human nature that it is one of *uniform* greediness. However, in paragraph 4 it is clear that his argument is more persuasive because his assumption is weaker than that. There are two arguments which look similar, but only the second is required for Hobbes's purposes.

(a)   Everyone from pride and desire for glory wants more and more belongings. So there is a natural state of war.

(b)   Some from pride and a desire for glory want more and more belongings. Most would be at ease within modest bounds.

But there is still a natural state of war.

The reasons that Hobbes thinks that argument (b) holds are these. Even if many in the state of nature are happy to live with their own patch of land and in cooperation with others, there will be those who take 'pleasure in contemplating their own power in the acts of conquest, which they pursue farther than their security requires' (paragraph 4). Those who are happy within modest bounds are still under threat from the minority who want increasingly more power. The majority might be happy within modest bounds, but they would not be happy with nothing at all, and so they need to defend themselves. Because attack is sometimes the best form of defence, even the modest majority will need to pre-empt attacks from the inconsiderate few and so enter into a state of war against them.

The point is important because it allows Hobbes to base his theory on a much weaker set of postulates about human nature than the claim that immodest desires are universal, and still deliver the conclusion about the state of nature. It is also an argument that we hear many times from politicians and others, who often say things like: 'It is the mindless minority who spoil things for everyone', when violence breaks out at a football match. Hobbes is pointing to the same kind of mechanism: the immodest appetites of a few which spoil things for everyone. If the mechanism is there, Hobbes does not need such a strong premise about human nature in order for his argument to tell heavily against anarchism.

Natural right and natural law

So far it might seem as if Hobbes is simply giving an anthropological account of human nature, in the sense that he is describing mechanisms that are present and can be observed in people's everyday social interaction but that, in the absence of a coercive power, would tend quickly towards social breakdown. But this would be only a partial picture of Hobbes's intentions. While he is certainly concerned with how we *do* behave and what that behaviour tells us about human nature, he is also interested in how we *ought* to behave. The relationship between these two strands in Hobbes's thought, the descriptive and the prescriptive, is, however, both complex and controversial. The two strands come together in Chapters XIV and XV of *Leviathan*.

ACTIVITY

Read Chapters XIV and XV, and answer the following questions.

1   What is the right of nature?
2   What are the laws of nature?
3   How do these two differ?

Ignore for now the argument of the fool in Chapter XV, paragraphs 4–7 as I shall be dealing with it later.

DISCUSSION

1   The right of nature is, roughly, the freedom to do anything to stay alive.
2   The laws of nature are, roughly, rules which prohibit self destructive behaviour.
3   The right of nature is the absence of moral constraint, whereas laws of nature are themselves moral constraints. The first law of nature – 'to seek peace, and follow it' arises, by reason, from the general exercise of the right of nature.

The right of nature is spelt out at Chapter XIV, paragraph 1. It amounts to the right to do anything we like in the state of nature to secure our self-preservation. You might think that this is so wide a 'right' that it is not sensible to call it a right at all. Hobbes glosses the right of nature as a *liberty* or the absence of a moral constraint and draws a contrast between right, conceived of as a moral freedom, and law, which is a form of moral constraint. This might seem confusing at first: in ordinary language, all sorts of rights – the uncontentious as well as the contentious – seem to involve moral constraints on others. Nevertheless, Hobbes has identified an important feature of our notion of rights. It often helps to analyse a particular right into its component parts: a series of moral relationships between the rights-bearer, the activity concerned, and other moral agents. One basic relationship is the 'liberty right' to the action itself, and this right is the absence of a duty to refrain from that activity. So it might seem that a liberty right to smoke in a particular area would be indicated by a sign saying 'SMOKING PERMITTED'. This sign would mean that I did not have a duty to refrain from smoking the that area.

But Hobbes means more than this when he outlines the right of nature. For the notice saying 'SMOKING PERMITTED' also puts a constraint on other people: it means that they must put up with the smokers in that area. Hobbes's right of nature does not include this constraint on the activity of others. If everyone had full Hobbesian liberty rights, I would be allowed to try to smoke and anyone else would be allowed to try to stop me. What would be missing is any moral constraint on me and others, any sense of not being allowed to do certain things. Hobbes's right of nature is like a sign, hanging up in the state of nature, which says 'ANYTHING AND EVERYTHING PERMITTED'.

It is difficult to think of a sign that promises more freedom. In the state of nature we all seem to have a high level of liberty. But the result is, of course, a war of all against all.

Hobbes believes that, with a little thought, we will realize that 'ANYTHING AND EVERYTHING PERMITTED' is a recipe for disaster. As long as others agree to do so, we should get rid of that policy – 'lay down this right to all things' – and be happy with a much lower level of liberty. We can comfort ourselves with the thought that at least our new lower levels of liberty are equally low. Hobbes sums up this new development in the second law of nature.

Hobbes has a long list of the laws of nature, from fairly abstract and general claims to some quite specific laws covering criminal proceedings. He thinks that these laws of nature are similar to the teachings of Christianity. For example, he says that the second law of nature is equivalent to the biblical golden rule: 'whatsoever you require that others should do to you, that do ye to them' (Chapter XIV, paragraph 5). In paragraph 35, Hobbes cites a version of the golden rule as a *method* of deriving all the other laws of nature. It would look as if the Bible gives a useful rule of thumb guide to the laws of nature.

What, then, is the status of these laws of nature? Hobbes makes a number of different claims. He defines a law of nature in Chapter XIV, paragraph 3 as 'a precept or general rule, found out by reason, by which a man is forbidden to do that which is destructive of his life or taketh away the means of preserving the same, and to omit that by which he thinketh it may be best preserved'. In an intriguing passage at the end of Chapter XV (paragraph 41) he discusses whether or not the dictates of reason that he has been discussing under the title of laws of nature should properly be called 'by the name of laws'. He suggests that this is a mistake, but adds that we can consider the same theorems as delivered in the word of God, and then they are properly called laws. And he has just suggested (paragraph 40) that the laws of nature are the object of inquiry in moral philosophy, suggesting that they are a sort of moral obligation. I shall discuss further the status of the laws of nature later, after outlining the extent of their obligation.

Hobbes also says something interesting about the binding character of these laws of nature. In Chapter XV he says the 'laws of nature oblige *in foro interno*, that is to say, they bind to a desire they should take place; but *in foro externo*, that is, to the putting them in act, not always' (paragraph 36). The Latin phrases translate as 'in the internal forum' and 'in the external forum'. It is perhaps significant that the forum in ancient Rome was the place in which the laws were debated and discussed. The distinction that Hobbes is getting at is similar to the distinction made between 'ideals we can all agree about in the abstract' and 'rules for getting on in the real world'. The laws of nature, suggests Hobbes, are something we assent to in our minds, but they are not guides to action in the state of nature. I think about, weigh up, and give my allegiance to certain rules in the internal forum, but I act on them in the external forum, when I act in situations that are not of my making. So the suggestion is that we are bound to *want* the laws of nature to govern everyone's behaviour, but we are not necessarily bound to *act* on them if nobody else does. The reason for this get-out clause, is that if one person acts according to the laws of nature in a situation where no one else does – such as in the state of nature – he will 'make himself a prey to others, and procure his own certain ruin, contrary to the ground of all laws of nature, which tend to nature's preservation' (Chapter XV, – paragraph 36). Actual obedience to the laws of nature in the state of nature, then, is *self-defeating*: if we try to obey the derivative laws of nature, by keeping our promises and so on, we lay ourselves open to attack, and so infringe the basic law of nature which is to keep alive. So it is clear that the way in which we are bound by the laws of nature varies according to situation. But what is the ground of this obligation? To investigate this it is worth returning to the characterization of laws of nature as 'general rules'.

There are clearly different sorts of general rule. Three different sorts are:

(i) Divine commandments: the word of God, which must be obeyed, just because it comes from God.

(ii) Independent moral obligations: which specify the right and wrong thing to do from a moral point of view.

(ii) The dictates of prudence: which specify what ought to be done to be safe from harm.

We can distinguish between these categories by asking *why* we ought to obey such rules. We ought to obey divine commands because they are the word of God; we ought to obey moral obligations because they tell us what is the right thing to do; and we ought to obey counsels of prudence because that way we will protect our interests. The distinction between these categories is thought to be important because it matters *why* we are being urged to undertake a particular course of action. In the case of Hobbes's theory of the state, is our motive for laying down our rights and being ordered about by an authoritarian ruler just a product of selfish calculation, a matter of looking out for our own interests, or is it a more high-minded matter that entails some sort of formal obligation? The difference can also be put in another way. When I consider what to do, am I thinking only of my own interests, and only derivatively of other peoples interests (in which case I am thinking of what is prudent). Or am I considering everyone's interests impartially (in which case I am thinking of what is morally obligatory)?

Which of these categories do Hobbes's laws of nature fall into? The answer to this question is a highly contentious area of Hobbes studies, with flow and counter-flow of interpretation contending over the last fifty years.[2]

However, there is one line of interpretation which suggests that the parties to the controversy can be brought together. When we read Hobbes, we do not need to decide whether the laws of nature are divine command, independent moral obligations, or prudential guides to our self interest, because all three sources prescribe the same rules.

Suppose we begin with natural laws as independent moral rules. One view of morality argues that the 'good', as 'that which is in accordance with one's nature', is a matter of acting to keep ourselves alive and ensuring that we flourish. Our nature is discoverable by reason, and a body of positive (i.e. man-made) laws can be constructed as a result. Nevertheless, we need to make sure that positive law is in accordance with natural law, since natural law has moral priority over man-made law.

But if natural law produces a form of moral obligation derived from the nature of humankind, why is it thought to be at odds with divine commands on one hand and counsels of prudence on the other? It would be reasonable to think that our nature is a result of God's design, so that the moral obligation to act in accord with nature is an obligation to act in accord with God's design. Presumably God would not be so capricious as to give us a nature according to which we ought to act one way and then command us to act in a different way. So, acting according to God's command and acting according to our nature will coincide. On the other hand, there are also strong reasons for thinking that it is prudent, as well as good, to act in accordance with one's nature. As we shall see, there is plenty of evidence that Hobbes thought that the dictates of morality and the dictates of prudence coincide. By acting prudently – for example, by ensuring that I do not get run over – I live longer and live a more commodious life, just as I flourish if I live according to divine commands. It is possible that the different ways of thinking about Hobbes's laws of nature coincide for practical purposes. We ought to act according to the laws of nature *both* because it is sensible or prudent to do so, *and* because we are morally obliged to do so, *and* because God has told us to do so and has created us such that it is appropriate to do so.

Perhaps Hobbes is working with all of these different conceptions of the laws of nature at the same time. But it would be a mistake to suggest that he was unaware of these different aspects of the question, for it is clear that he is aware when he discusses the example of 'the fool, who says in his heart "there is no justice" '.

The fool, and Hobbes's reply

ACTIVITY

Re-read Chapter XV, paragraphs 4–7 and answer the following questions.

1   What is the argument of the fool?
2   What is Hobbes's response?
3   Is his response adequate?

DISCUSSION

1   The fool is posing a version of a question which has troubled moral and political philosophers for centuries, the question 'Why should I be moral'? The particular version of the question asked by the fool is 'Why should I keep promises when I can gain from breaking them?' 'Why should I keep my part of the bargain when the first performer has already kept his, so that I

have nothing more to gain and plenty to lose?' The fool suggest that, if he breaks his part of the bargain after the first performer has already kept his part, he may gain more than enough to compensate him for the 'dispraise' and antagonistic power of others. The fool can break his promises and get away with it. In the marginal headings that he wrote for *Leviathan*, Hobbes flags up this discussion as 'Justice not contrary to reason'. He needs to show that the dictates of prudence or self-interested rationality coincide with the dictates of morality in order to rebut the argument of the fool.

2   Hobbes has two responses. First, if I act in a way that is likely to cause me harm, but fortunately I get away with it, or even gain from it, that does not mean I have acted prudently. Suppose I cross the road without looking, but luckily, do not get run over, and, because I'm not paying attention to the cars, I have a few more seconds to think about philosophy. I might gain overall, but that would not make my action prudent. It is still foolish to walk into the road so immersed in thought that I do not check whether the road is clear. The argument Hobbes is making can be formalized as follows:

> In most cases unjust action leads to harm to oneself and so is imprudent.
>
> In the few exceptional cases when unjust action seems to lead to some gain, it is still, in fact, imprudent, because it was imprudent to gamble on the result.
>
> The reason it is imprudent to gamble is that, in most cases, unjust action leads to harm to oneself (the first premise above).
>
> *Therefore* it is always imprudent to act unjustly.

The second response that Hobbes makes against the fool is this. An individual in the state of nature who says that she believes it reasonable to break promises will not be admitted into a society for mutual defence. She will be left to her own resources, and will suffer as a consequence. If she is admitted, it can only be because the others in the society have made a mistake, and individuals should not rely on others making mistakes for their own preservation. Those interested in their own preservation cannot then hold the view that it is reasonable to make promises.

Are Hobbes's replies to the fool satisfactory? The success of his first argument depends on the claim that it is imprudent to gamble on an unjust action paying dividends. But is this always the case? It would be difficult to decide without looking at the individual cases. The prudence of any gamble would depend on the odds, the stakes and the possible gains. If the stakes were low, the odds favourable and the possible gains substantial, then perhaps the unjust action would be prudent. It is certainly not the case that Hobbes has a knock-down argument here.

The second argument seems to me either to do too little or too much for Hobbes's programme. If we take Hobbes's argument one way it just does not establish what Hobbes requires. Suppose we take Hobbes's argument narrowly, as advice to someone wondering whether or not to break a contract, then it simply establishes that the person who intends to dishonour a contract should keep quiet about her intention. It does not show that we should not believe 'I should break contracts if I can get away with it'. It shows that *if* we take such a position we should not go around telling anyone about it. What makes the fool a fool is not that he says such wicked things 'in his heart', but that he says them 'sometimes also with his tongue'.

Hobbes's retort is that we cannot rely on such deception, because people have a habit of seeing through it. The fool cannot fool all the people all of the time, as the common phrase goes, so he is better off acting according to the dictates of justice, and prudence and justice coincide. But the other two suggestions of that common phrase are thought to be possible. You *can* perhaps fool some of the people all of the time, and you *can* perhaps also fool all of the people some of the time, particularly if you are good at fooling people. This is all the fool needs to do in order to show that the dictates of justice and the dictates of prudence can diverge. Besides which, whether or not any particular fool has the ability to deceive people successfully over a long period of time is an *empirical* matter, not a conceptual one. Hobbes seems to presume in favour of fools being found out but this presumption needs to be based on an empirically investigation of what happens when people try to deceive one another. Hobbes does not attempt to do this.

But suppose that the empirical evidence did come out on Hobbes's side, and that the presumption in favour of being found out meant that the dictates of prudence and the dictates of justice actually did coincide. His argument, taken in this broader way, then looks more successful. But what would it establish? It shows that the motive of wanting to be trusted seems to be successful in driving individuals to adopt the principles of justice contained in the laws of nature. So it provides a basis for moral behaviour as a condition of admission into society. But, if this is the case, Hobbes has uncovered a motivation towards sociability, self-restraint and cooperation that tells strongly *against* his account of the state of nature. The idea that we will behave well in the state of nature, lest we be thought ill of, and not trusted by others, is a plank in the *anarchist* argument *against* the state and *for* the viability of a non-coercive form of association. If we accept the second reply to the fool we have to reconsider the initial Hobbesian picture of the state of nature as a collection of atomized individuals who only compete and cannot cooperate. We have uncovered a further motivation – the (self-interested) desire to be trusted – that operates as a centripetal force in contrast to the centrifugal forces that are rooted in the three principal sources of quarrel in Chapter XIII: competition, diffidence and glory.

The theory of authorization

Let us, none the less put this objection on one side and grant that Hobbes has shown that a sovereign authority is required. He now needs to show how a sovereign may act. Often, I'm happy for someone to act on my behalf if I have *authorized* them to do so in advance. Hobbes needs a theory of authorization to show when and to what extent the sovereign may act. In providing this theory, Hobbes moves decisively into the realm of politics proper, and away from human nature. Hence the location of Chapter XVI in the work as a whole.

Chapter XVI of *Leviathan* contains a crucial element of Hobbes's theory of the state, which raises two important points for that theory.

ACTIVITY

Read *Leviathan*, Chapter XVI followed by Reading 2.3, 'Hobbes and the purely artificial person of the state' by Quentin Skinner. Then answer the following two questions.

1   What is the relationship between the sovereign and the commonwealth (*civitas* or state)?

2   How does the theory of authorization provide the basis for Hobbes's authoritarianism?

DISCUSSION

1   Skinner poses a general problem for political philosophy. While we often talk of the state as, for example, the real acts of police and politicians, it also seems that the term frequently refers to an abstraction beyond this. What is the connection between the state as an abstraction and the people who execute the state's actions? Hobbes's answer is that the state (*civitas* or commonwealth) is one person, but a 'purely artificial' one, whereas the sovereign is an actual human being who occupies or enacts the purely artificial person of the state. That is, the state is not an actual person but a thing that is represented or 'personated'. The state – which can only act through the sovereign – is immensely powerful simply because it is the recipient of immense rights held by the members of the multitude in the first place. It is because Hobbes's right of nature is so broad that the state's power is so extensive. The sovereign, representing or 'personating' the state which is authorized by the actions of the multitude, has immense but derivative power. Bearing the several rights of nature transferred to the state, the sovereign is entitled to exercise those extensive rights to secure peace. The state consists of the multitude come together and the sovereign represents the state, representing it and – in the literal sense – 'impersonating' it. This is Hobbes's methodological individualism (remember the frontispiece to *Leviathan*). So, for Hobbes, it is a mistake to think of 'the people' versus 'the sovereign' as the parliamentarians did. The multitude are complicit in the actions of the state in a way that grounds the sovereign's power.

2   Skinner carefully reconstructs the theory of authorization in *Leviathan*. It explains how an action can be attributed to me even when it is not physically my action and this provides the basis for Hobbes's authoritarianism. Hobbes claims that subjects voluntarily transfer their rights to a person, who thereby has authority. Authority is held by a person who has received the rights of others. But, importantly, when the transfer has taken place, *it cannot be revoked*. As Skinner puts it, 'Once you have covenanted, you must leave it to your representative, who is now in possession of your right of action, to exercise it at his discretion when acting in your name'. Subjects authorize the sovereign to act on their behalf and so it is contradictory for them to then resist the sovereign or to complain about his or her lawful actions. Once I give away my right of nature, according to Hobbes, the right changes. Recall that the right of nature originally involved no sort of moral constraint on others (see p.84 above). But handing it over *does* involve a constraint. Transferring one's right of nature to another person involves my taking on the moral

constraint not to interfere with that person in the exercise of that right. And this removes the option of disclaiming responsibility for authorized actions. We must 'own up' to the actions of our duly authorized representatives just as we must take responsibility for and own up to our own actions.

If we do this, though, we gain the protection of the state through the person of the sovereign. It is this protection that compensates us for giving up the right of nature, and also grounds the obligation to obey the state. As Hobbes puts it in 'A Review and Conclusion' at the end of *Leviathan*, the book is written 'without other design than to set before men's eyes the mutual relation between protection and obedience, of which the condition of human nature and the laws divine (both natural and positive) require an inviolable observation' (paragraph 17).

Sovereigns and subjects

The theory of authorization, together with the claim that rights are transferred once and for all, provides the basis for Hobbes's distribution of rights between the sovereign and the subject, as well as his fully articulated theory of the state. In Chapters XVIII–XIX and XXI, Hobbes shows how power and rights are distributed between the sovereign and his or her subjects. As might be expected, the sovereign gets the larger share, but Hobbes does leave a crucial right with the subjects.

ACTIVITY

Read *Leviathan*, Chapters XVII–XIX and XXI, and answer the following questions.

1   How do humans differ from ants in terms of their social relationships?
2   Who makes the covenant with whom? What are the implications of your answer?
3   What rights does the subject retain?
4   What is Hobbes's preferred form of government?

DISCUSSION

1   According to Hobbes, ants are inherently sociable, but human beings are not. After reading Hobbes's account of the state of nature this should come as no surprise. Again the target is very likely Aristotle's claim that man is a *zoon politikon* – a political or social animal. It would be useful though to reflect here on Hobbes's case and to see whether it alters the position you took after reading Chapter XIII and Macpherson in Reading 2.1. The issue between Macpherson and Hobbes was whether the competitive behaviour in possessive market society was an outcome of *natural* or *social* properties of humankind.

2   Immediately after the discussion of ants, we get Hobbes's fullest account of the formation of Leviathan 'made by covenant of every man with every man' – social contract (Chapter XVII, paragraph 13). The details of this acount are important. Skinner discusses this passage in Reading 2.3, where

the distinction between the *state*, conceived of as a purely artificial person, and the *sovereign* who bears that person is made clear. Notice the following features of this account. It is an 'as if' account. The pledge given in paragraph 13: 'I authorise and give up my right of governing myself to this man, or to this assembly of men, on this condition, that thou give up thy right to him, and authorize all his actions in like manner', is not an actual pledge. And the 'as if' covenant is made 'of every man with every man', not between subjects and the sovereign. The absolutist nature of the sovereign's powers is thereby reinforced, since if no contract is made with the sovereign, there is nothing he or she can do to break it. The second of the rights of the sovereign (Chapter XVIII, paragraph 4) consists of just this point: sovereign power cannot be forfeited because it is transferred to the sovereign, not loaned to him or her. The list of rights of the sovereign is impressive and provides strong prima facie grounds for suggesting that Hobbes gives an absolutist account. He certainly seems cavalier with those who worry about the threats to liberty that such a sovereign might pose. They should grow up, he effectively suggests, and recognize, through the glasses of moral and civil science, that social breakdown is much worse than the little grievances produced by absolutism.

3   Nevertheless, in Chapter XXI, Hobbes does give an account of the rights of the subject which was sharply criticized in his own time for being much too liberal. Bishop Bramhall, a sparring partner of Hobbes on a variety of issues, called *Leviathan* a 'rebel's catechism' because of the arguments contained in Chapter XXI. A contemporary critique of Hobbes's account, exploring Bramhall's objection is provided by Jean Hampton in Reading 2.4. In this Reading Hampton employs a distinction made earlier in her book *Hobbes and the Social Contract Tradition* (1986) between *alienation* accounts of the social contract and *agency* ones. She spells out the difference thus:

> I shall use the term 'agency social contract' to refer to an argument assuming that political authority is granted by the people to the ruler as a loan, and I shall use the term 'alienation social contract' to refer to an argument assuming that political authority is given as an irrevocable grant. So if political power is handed over once and for all, it is alienated. If it is loaned to the sovereign then he or she is an agent for those who loan the power.
>
> Hampton (1997)

According to Hobbes, then, political power is alienated and so the sovereign cannot break the contract, but he introduces an instability into his account because the subject retains an important right: the right not to endanger his life. Hampton points out that what looks like an argument for a once and for all handover of power in fact collapses into an argument for its temporary loan. The condition of the loan is that the subject's life is not threatened and it is up to the subject to determine whether his or her life is genuinely under threat.

Another point to make about the Hampton extract is that it does not make the subtle distinction between state and sovereign for which Skinner makes such a good case. Skinner's article was published two years after Hampton's book. This does not undermine her critique of Hobbes, but it does show that, even when we are looking at works that have been studied for centuries, advances in scholarship and analysis can still be made.

4 Hobbes identifies three forms of commonwealth: monarchy, democracy and aristocracy. In Chapter XIX he discusses the virtues and 'inconveniences' of each; out of which emerges his favoured form – monarchy.

ACTIVITY

Read Hampton's 'Problems with Hobbes's alienation social contract argument' (Reading 2.4).

Hampton points out that subjects have the right to resist threats to their lives. But they also have the right to decide *when* their life is threatened, so that the power transferred when the right of nature is transferred to the sovereign is not as absolute as it first appears. In fact, humans, being the way they are – creatures that seek pleasure and avoid pain – will always try to preserve their lives against a sovereign who appears to threaten those lives.

We are still left with the question of why Hobbes thought the stronger argument for an irrevocable transfer of rights was necessary. The answer to this question lies back at the beginning of *Leviathan*, in the account of man in the state of nature. If the tendencies towards anarchy and social breakdown are so strong and so essential to our make up, because they are deeply ingrained in our psychological, which means ultimately our physiological, composition, then Hobbes's argument still has some force. We need to hand over our rights, because of the precariousness of our political institutions and the constant pull towards chaos. If, on the other hand, we have a more rosy view of humankind – and Hobbes, in his second reply to the fool provides us with some hints about why we might take such a view – then the form of government we adopt might be rather more limited.

This point might lead us to reflect on our own experiences of political institutions. Have they turned out to be as fragile as Hobbes suggests? Is it the case that allowing for disagreement and debate and limiting the powers of the state only leads to a dramatic collapse of those political institutions back to the state of nature? Of course, the answer will vary according to which set of political institutions we look at, and within which time frame. But the evidence from western Europe and the US does tend to show a degree of resilience among democratic and limited forms of government that tells against Hobbes's position. He would have been surprised that the sort of *institutionalized* competition which marks modern party politics could have gone on in a relatively stable manner for so long. This fact alone is evidence against Hobbes's absolutism. [3]

Hobbes and feminism

You may have noticed that I have referred to the sovereign as 'he or she'. This is because Hobbes explicitly allows that women could be sovereigns. That recognition is one reason why Hobbes's thought is more sexually egalitarian than one might at first expect. Another reason is that his social contract account of the state runs against patriarchal accounts in which legitimate political authority is handed down from fathers to sons. If patriarchal accounts of the *state* are to be rejected, what sort of account should be given of the *family*?

It is perhaps strange that feminist political philosophers should have paid a lot of attention to Hobbes. After all, his political conclusions are, as we have seen, broadly authoritarian ones which aim to establish a very wide and strong obligation to obey the sovereign. This is an argument that seems to leave little space for challenges to male authority. Yet much attention has recently been lavished on Hobbes by theorists who highlight the exclusion of women from the accounts offered by classical political theory up to John Stuart Mill.

ACTIVITY

Read *Leviathan*, Chapter XX. As you read, try work out what Hobbes has in his sights with respect to the traditional account of the family and marriage.

DISCUSSION

Traditional accounts of marriage, patriarchal domination and the family tend to emphasize the naturalness of these arrangements. But Hobbes will have none of this. Natural arrangements would be present in the state of nature, and Hobbes is explicit that there is not a sufficient difference of strength or prudence between the sexes in the state of nature to establish the dominance of men over women and children. In fact, in the state of nature, only women are able to indicate paternity with a degree of confidence, so in the absence of a contract the dominion over children lies with the mother who generates them.

Generalizing from Hobbes's comments in Chapter XX we can get the following Hobbesian position: there is nothing natural or pre-ordained about the domination of men over women, for the same reason that there is nothing natural about the domination of one man over another. Hobbes is consistent in applying his assumption of natural equality to men and women. However, as a matter of fact, 'because for the most part commonwealths have been erected by fathers', men have been able to establish conventional – not natural – domination. The target here is very likely to be Aristotle once again, who claims in *Politics* Book 1 that 'although there may be exceptions to the order of nature, the male is by nature fitter for command than the female, just as the elder and full-grown is superior to the younger and more immature' (Aristotle (1996 edn) 1, 12, 1259b2–5).

Hobbes's decisive break from this notion of a natural hierarchy explains his significance to those who are worried about the exclusion of women from the subject matter of political philosophy.

ACTIVITY

Read Carole Pateman's 'Hobbes and the sexual contract' (Reading 2.5).

Carole Pateman's book *The Sexual Contract* (1988) is an important volume in contemporary political philosophy as well as providing a significant interpretation of the classic texts. Here she gives an account of the importance of Hobbes, pointing out that he breaks with the standard assumption of natural male dominance. Hobbes insists that patriarchal subjection is an example of political right, that is, right established within the institution of political society, not naturally.

In the absence of natural dominance, Pateman needs to construct another story (p.133 below) to explain how men are able to dominate women in political society. Given that *if* women were free to dissent from a pact that subordinated them to men, they *would* dissent, Pateman has to show how women have to have this freedom removed. Women need to be 'taken out of the game' of forming the social contract. Pateman suggests that this is done when giving birth slightly alters the balance in the state of nature, so that women become susceptible to the dominance of men who are then able to defeat women and turn them into families. This means that women lay themselves open to domination when they bear and raise children. But if women – as self-interested and fearful of death as men – recognize this problem, they will abandon their infants, who will consequently die. As a result, the individuals in the state of nature would be the last generation of humankind.

Pateman is working with a rather specific conception of the state of nature here. It does not look like a hypothesized construction, unlike anything that ever happened. It seems instead much more like an anthropological or historical account. Pateman's suggestion, prompted by her investigations into the role played by women in Hobbes's theory, is that Hobbes retreats from a historical account to a thought-experiment account of the state of nature because of the problems posed by the succession of generations. This is an example of a problem that recurs with Hobbes. If the state of nature is so competitive, how can we contract to get out of it? Here Pateman raises the problem – in extremis. If the state of nature is so competitive how can it even reproduce itself? Not only individual lives within the state of nature, but also the existence of humankind – on this historical account – would be short.

Conclusion

This ultra-pessimistic account of the state of nature, in which not only individual human beings but also species existence is under threat, gives one possible outcome of the logic of Hobbes's thought. His account of politics is certainly strongly linked to his account of humankind. If the state of nature were a more attractive prospect, the case for absolution might not be so strong. In John Locke's *Second Treatise of Government* we find just such a coupling: the state of nature is more attractive, allowing for a limited, not absolute, government to enter the lists.

Glossary

absolutism
    A sovereign is absolute if it is the final and supreme human authority over its subjects. Hobbes's theory seems to be absolutist, for example, his sovereign is extremely power-

ful in standing above the laws of the commonwealth. In the sense that no other part of the government was able to limit Hobbes's sovereign, he or she was absolute. Advocates of absolute monarchy welcomed Hobbes's conclusions, if not his method of reaching them. Nevertheless, there is an instability in Hobbes's theory which is introduced by granting subjects the right to preserve their own lives.

anarchy/anarchism

A theory, and advocacy, of a society without state rule. There are two associated claims; the first is that there is no obligation to obey the state: authority can only be rightfully exercised over oneself. A related, but distinct and separable, claim is that human nature is such that stateless societies could be harmonious and cooperative places.

appetites/aversions

The names given to *endeavours* according to their direction. Appetites are endeavours towards objects, aversions are endeavours away from objects.

authoritarianism

A political theory is authoritarian if it prescribes government based on established authority rather than the consent of the governed. Hobbes's account is authoritarian, because he prescribes obedience to existing authority, without inquiring into the legitimacy of its origins.

compatibilism

Compatibilism is a doctrine about the relationship between freedom and determinism. Compatibilists (including Hobbes) believe that we can truthfully be called free even if our actions are determined. This is because the opposite of free action is coerced action, and, in the absence of external constraints, our actions are not coerced. They are causally determined, however, so free action and determined action are compatible.

commonwealth

In the Introduction, Hobbes equates Leviathan with state and commonwealth. The term suggests a common interest among the people who come together to constitute the state, but it is clear that, for Hobbes, the commonwealth is an artificial person, which is represented by the sovereign.

endeavours

These are 'small beginnings of motion within the body of man', before they appear in observable bodily actions.

essential/accidental distinction

This distinction, which comes from Aristotle, allows us to group the properties of a thing which it must have in order to be that thing, and the properties which it need not have. It is essential to me being me that I have the parents that I have: it is not essential that I live in Brighton. 'Accidental' here does not convey the idea of chance or unintendedness that it usually has.

In political philosophy, one of the key disagreements is over which of the properties of human nature are essential and which are accidental and so potentially specific to a space and time. Hobbes wanted to show that self-interested behaviour is essential: marxists and anarchists want to insist that such behaviour is 'accidental' and therefore potentially eliminable.

in foro externo

Literally 'in the external forum'. Essentially, here, Hobbes refers to activities, specifically the execution of the laws of nature. The laws of nature do not always oblige absolutely in this area.

in foro interno

Literally 'in the internal forum'. Essentially, here, Hobbes refers to the mind of a moral agent – an area the laws of nature oblige absolutely.

patriarchy

Literally 'rule by fathers'. However, it is important to distinguish between modern and classical uses of the term. Classical patriarchalism, such as is found in Sir Robert Filmer's *Patriarcha* (1680), is the view that political authority has its roots in the subjection of sons to their fathers. Political authority, therefore, is natural, and does not rely on contract or consent.

sovereign

Hobbes's sovereign is the person who bears the part of the purely artificial person of the state. The sovereign may be a single individual, in the case of a monarchy, or a collection of individuals, in the case of aristocracy or democracy. Hobbes's preference was for monarchy.

Further reading

Gauthier, David P. (1969) *The Logic of Leviathan* (Oxford University Press). This is the standard account of Hobbes interpreted in terms of game theory.

Hampton, Jean (1986) *Hobbes and the Social Contract Tradition* (Cambridge University Press). A more recent account of a game-theoretic approach to Hobbes, expanding on the criticism that his alienation argument reduces to an agency one.

Macpherson, C.B. (1962) *The Political Theory of Possessive Individualism* (Oxford University Press). A contentious but stimulating account of Hobbes, Locke and the Levellers, influenced by a marxist perspective.

Pateman, Carole (1988) *The Sexual Contract* (Polity Press). A sustained critique of the social contract tradition which highlights its exclusion of women.

Skinner, Quentin (1996) *Reason and Rhetoric in the Philosophy of Thomas Hobbes* (Cambridge University Press). A fine example of the Cambridge contextualist school of writing intellectual history with an interesting account of Hobbes's evolving method of argument.

Slomp, Gabriella (2000) *Hobbes* (Macmillan). A recent and controversial analytical account of Hobbes theory of glory in *Leviathan*.

Sorell, Tom (1986) *Hobbes* (Routledge). The best account available of Hobbes's overall philosophy, not just his political theory.

Taylor, A.E. (1938) 'The Ethical Doctrine of Hobbes', *Philosophy*, 13.

Warrender, H. (1957) *The Political Philosophy of Hobbes: his theory of obligation* (Oxford University Press)

Notes

[1] I shall refer to chapters of *Leviathan* by the convention of using their roman numerals, and I will give references to particular paragraphs within chapters by their arabic numbers.

[2] The starting point of this debate is to be found in Taylor (1938).

[3] The argument for absolutism is fleshed out in the remaining chapters of *Leviathan* Part II, which will reward further study. While the basic case is made by the end of Chapter XXI, much of the detail, against limited government, for example, is contained in Chapter XXIX, and Hobbes gives an anti-retributivist account of punishment in Chapter XXVIII.

Readings

'The Theory of Human Nature in Society'

C.B. Macpherson

C.B. Macpherson (1911–87) was for many years professor of Political Science at the University of Toronto. His most famous book is *The Political Theory of Possessive Individualism* (1962), which presented a novel interpretation of early modern English political theory. According to the 'Macpherson thesis' both Hobbes and Locke, articulated political theories that were tied to, and helped to justify, the emergence of capitalist relations of production in seventeenth-century England. This extract presents Macpherson's account of the theory of power and the passions.

At the risk of oversimplification it will be worthwhile to try to set out here the central argument of Hobbes's analysis of the behaviour of men towards each other. This is mostly to be found in Chapters VI to XI of *Leviathan*, though it will be helpful occasionally to look to one of his other works, where a parallel passage sometimes puts a point more clearly. The value of this exercise may be thought to outweigh the risk of distortion if by it we can disengage the main line of his argument clearly enough to see that it requires some assumptions which Hobbes did not make explicit. When these assumptions are brought into the light we may be better able to form a judgement on the validity of his argument and his conclusions.

We may start with the appetites, or desires, as Hobbes also calls them. 'Desires' is in one way the better word to convey his meaning to us, since we are apt to think of appetites as rather animal, whereas Hobbes used the term to cover all sorts of desires, those for the most imaginative and immaterial pleasures as well as those for material gratifications. Yet 'desire' is so vague a term that we may do better to stick to 'appetite', which is more obviously anchored in physiology (which is where Hobbes wanted it to be). Hobbes's first proposition may be stated as 'Men are moved by appetites and aversions'. This proposition itself, of course, sums up and simplifies what Hobbes had said about 'the interiour beginnings of voluntary motions' and the process of deliberation.

If we want to go farther back in Hobbes's chain of reasoning we can say that all voluntary actions are the result of deliberation, which is calculation of the chances that this or that action will gratify one's appetites. But Hobbes himself gives us a short-cut when he says Appetite and Aversion are the names for that 'Endeavour' which is the 'small beginnings of Motion, within the body of Man, before they appear in ... visible actions.'[1] Strictly speaking, these motions within us are responses to some motions from outside: 'that which is really within us, is ... onley Motion, caused by the action of externall objects ...: so, when the action of the same object is continued from the Eyes, Eares, and other organs to the Heart; the reall effect there is nothing but Motion, or Endeavour; which consisteth in Appetite, or Aversion, to, or from the object moving.'[2]

But since external objects are continually acting on man, it is not improper to say (and Hobbes does say) that the appetites and aversions are what determine a man's voluntary actions.

> When in the mind of man, Appetites, and Aversions, Hopes, and Feares, concerning one and the same thing, arise alternately; and divers good and evill consequences of the doing, or omitting the thing propounded, come successively into our thoughts; so that sometimes we have an Appetite to it; sometimes an Aversion from it; sometimes Hope to be able to do it; sometimes Despaire, or Feare to attempt it; the whole summer of Desires, Aversions, Hopes and Fears, continued till the thing be either done, or thought impossible, is that we call DELIBERATION ... In *Deliberation*, the last Appetite, or Aversion, immediately adhering to the action, or to the omission thereof, is that wee call the WILL; the Act, (not the faculty,) of *Willing*.[3]

So we may put as Hobbes's first proposition about human motivation:

1   Men are moved by appetites and aversions.

As soon as the moving force of appetite and aversion has been stated, Hobbes sets out several further propositions about appetites (to which propositions we shall, for convenience of reference, attach our own numbers).

1.1   First, some appetites, 'not many', are innate, as appetite of food: 'The rest, which are Appetites of particular things, proceed from Experience, and traill of their effects ...'[4]

1.2   Second, appetites continually change, and are different in different men: 'And because the constitution of a mans Body, is in continual mutation; it is impossible that all the same things should always cause in him the same Appetites, and Aversions: much lesse can all men consent, in the Desire of almost any one and the same Object.'[5]

1.3   Third, appetites are incessant, that is, they must operate as long as a man is alive: '... Life it selfe is but Motion, and can never be without Desire, nor without Feare, no more than without Sense.'[6] To put this in another way, men desire *felicity*, which is defined as '*Continuall successe* in obtaining those things which a man from time to time desireth'.[7] The point is restated in Chapter XI: 'Nor can a man any more live, whose Desires are at an end, than he, whose Senses and Imaginations are at a stand. Felicity is a continuall progresse of the desire, from one object to another ...'[8]

1.4   Fourth, appetites are of different strengths in different men. Different men have within themselves 'more or lesse Desire of Power, of Riches, of Knowledge, and of Honour'; this 'difference of Passions, proceedeth partly from the different Constitution of the body, and partly from different Education', or, 'not onely from the difference of mens complexions; but also from their difference of customes, and education.'[9]

Putting the third and fourth of these statements together, it follows that all men must seek incessantly to attain satisfaction of their desires but that, since the strength of appetite differs from one man to another, different men will be satisfied with different levels of power, riches, honour, etc.

Having got this far, Hobbes turns to a definition of a man's power:

2   'The POWER *of a Man* (to take it Universally,) is his present means, to obtain some future apparent Good.'[10]

It follows, from this and propositions 1.3 and 1.4, that

3   Every man must always seek to have some power, although not every man is self-impelled to seek as much power as others have, or to seek more than he now has.

Now so far there is nothing very disquieting about Hobbes's propositions. This is because he has said nothing so far about the active relation of one man to other men, or of one man's power to other men's. He introduces this immediately after the definition of a man's power just quoted. And although it involves an important new assumption, he introduces it so inconspicuously that many readers have missed it. He makes a great deal of it three chapters later, in the context of his hypothetical state of nature, where nobody can miss it; but it is of some importance to see that he does introduce it here, where he is clearly talking about men as they are, in going societies. That he does it so inconspicuously is not to be attributed to any desire to conceal his remarkable new assumption, for, as we shall see, in the earliest version of his political theory (the *Elements of Law*) the parallel argument states it quite explicitly. Perhaps he gave it so little emphasis here because he thought by this time that it hardly needed saying.

   The new assumption is stated merely incidentally in his description of the two kinds of power men have: original or natural, and instrumental or acquired.

> *Naturall Power*, is the eminence of the Faculties of Body, or Mind: as extraordinary Strength, Forme, Prudence, Arts, Eloquence, Liberality, Nobility. *Instrumentall* are those Powers, which acquired by these, or by fortune, are means and Instruments to acquire more: as Riches, Reputation, Friends, and the secret working of God, which men called Good Luck.[11]

What is to be noticed here is that a man's natural power is defined *not* as his faculties of body and mind, but as the *eminence* of his faculties compared with those of other men, and that his acquired powers are those he has acquired by means of that eminence. A man's power consists of the amount by which his faculties, riches, reputation, and friends exceed those of other men. We have already been told that a man's power consists of his present means to obtain future apparent good. So Hobbes is saying that a man's present means to obtain future apparent good consists of the amount by which his faculties, riches, reputation, etc. exceed those of other men.

This is not self-evident, nor does it follow from anything earlier in the argument, unless an additional postulate is put in. Hobbes does put it in, explicitly, in the parallel passage in the *Elements of Law*. There he first defines a man's power as the faculties of body and mind plus what further powers he acquires by using them, and then says: 'And because the power of one man resisteth and hindereth the effects of the power of another: power simply is no more, but the excess of the power of one above that of another.'[12] The new postulate is:

4   That every man's power resists and hinders the effects of other men's power. This is asserted to be so universally the case that one man's power may be simply redefined as the excess of his over others'.

Is this self-evident? Hobbes thought it was, to anyone who would take the trouble to look at this own society. Hobbes states it not as a deduction from his physiological postulates, but as a generalization from observation. In the remainder of Chapter X of *Leviathan* he offers an extensive analysis of the power relations of men in society, of the way men actually value and honour each other. In the course of this analysis it is apparent that Hobbes is making another generalization from his observation of society, namely,

5   that all acquired power consists in command over some of the powers of other men.

This is a corollary of proposition 4, in that, since all powers are opposed, the only way you can acquire power is to master the powers opposed to yours. Indeed, 4 and 5, both being generalizations from the same observation of society, might be said to imply each other. Both are summed up in Hobbes's statement: 'The *Value*, or WORTH of a man, is as of all other things, his Price; that is to say, so much as would be given for the use of his Power ...'[13]

By adding propositions 4 and 5, which are based on his observation of society, to the earlier physiologically-based propositions, Hobbes has taken the first step to transforming man's need for power from a harmless to a harmful thing. The desire for power was harmless, or at least neutral, before 4 and 5 were added. True, the earlier proposition 1.4 that some men want more than others, *might* lead to their trying to get it by transferring to themselves some of the powers of others, but it *need* not. And even if it did, it would not necessarily lead to every man engaging in a continual competitive struggle for power in comparison with others and over others, for some men were said to be content with a lower level of gratifications than others. But when 4 and 5 are added, the position is somewhat changed. For then, since by 1.4 some men want more power, which by 4 means more future apparent goods, and since by 5 all acquirable additional power consists of command over some of the powers of other men, it follows that these men will seek to command, that is to transfer to themselves, some of the powers of other men. This would not necessarily in itself lead to every man being pulled into a struggle for power, for that amount of transfer might be consistent with the moderate men enjoying the lower level of gratification which their nature desired. Yet Hobbes asserted that the competitive struggle for power over others was universal. It becomes apparent that Hobbes was making a still further assumption:

6   that some men's desires are without limit.

For if they were limited, some accommodation might be possible between their satisfying their desires and the rest of the people making do with their more moderate level of gratification. It is only if some men's desires are without limit that the other men are necessarily moved to resist having some of their powers transferred (and the only way they can resist is to get into the struggle for power).

Given this further assumption 6, Hobbes's conclusion follows:

7   'So that in the first place, I put for a general inclination of all mankind, a perpetuall and restlesse desire of Power after power, that ceaseth onely in Death. And the cause of this, is not always that a man hopes for a more intensive delight, than he has already attained to; or that he cannot be content with a moderate power: but because he cannot assure the power and means to live well, which he hath present, without the acquisition of more.'[14] Everyone, those with moderate as well as those with immoderate desires, is necessarily pulled into a constant competitive struggle for power over others, or at least to resist his powers being commanded by others. Man's need for power has now become a necessarily harmful thing.

This is the grand conclusion of Hobbes's analysis of human nature. He had only to add to it his postulate about men's innate aversion to death, and a further postulate about men's ability to behave with a clearer view of their own long-run interest than they commonly did, to get his prescription for obedience to an all-powerful sovereign.

Because this conclusion about man's necessarily competitive search for power plays such a large part in the rest of his doctrine, it is worth noticing that it depends on generalizations from his observation of men in society, and not at all on the similar statements he later (in Chapter XIII of *Leviathan*) makes about the necessary behaviour of men in a hypothetical state of nature, in which by hypothesis there would be no political society, no law-enforcing authority. His picture of the way men would necessarily behave in such a condition is so graphic that readers often fail to see that he had really made his whole case already, in considering man in political society. Everything we have seen so far is set out in the first eleven chapters of *Leviathan*, before there is any talk of a state of nature.

The fact that his conclusion about man's competitive search for power is reached by way of generalizations about men in society is significant, for it means that Hobbes was using a mental model of society which, whether he was conscious of this or not, corresponds only to a bourgeois market society. This can readily be seen. The society whose relations he generalizes to get his propositions 4 and 5 is one in which *everyone* can and does *continually* compete for power against others. Every man's power resists and hinders other men's search for power, so pervasively that any man's power is simply the excess of his above others' (proposition 4). Everyone seeks to transfer some of the powers of other men to himself, or to resist the transfer of some of his to others. And he does it not by open force but by a market-like operation which sets every man's value at 'so much as would be given for the use of his Power'.[15]

Even if Hobbes had not told us that a man's value was established in this market manner we could see that it must be so. For it would be impossible to maintain such a universally competitive society as a going concern if everybody in it was constantly seeking to subdue others, or resist being subdued by them, by force. If a society characterized by universal competition for power over others is to remain, for even the shortest length of time, a going society – and that is what Hobbes's model is – it must be one in which there are legal, peaceful ways by which men can transfer some of the powers of others to themselves, and in which everyone is constantly *peacefully* engaged in seeking to get or resist this transfer. It has been demonstrated elsewhere[16] that the capitalist market model is the only one that fits these requirements.

So, even if there were no other evidence that Hobbes was taking for granted a bourgeois model of society ... we may say that he was doing so, and that without so doing he could not have reached his conclusion about the necessary motion of men in society.

Notes

From the introduction to C.B. Macpherson's edition of the *Leviathan*, Penguin Books, 1968, pp.30–9. All references in this Reading are to this edition.

[1] *Leviathan.*, Chapter VI, p.23.

[2] Ibid., p.25

[3] Ibid., p.28.

[4] Ibid., p.24.

[5] Ibid.

[6] Ibid., pp.29–30.

[7] Ibid., p.29.

[8] Ibid., Chapter XI, p.47.

[9] Ibid., Chapter VIII, p.35.

[10] Ibid., Chapter X, p.41.

[11] Ibid.

[12] *Elements of Law*, Part 1, Chapter VIII 8, p.26.

[13] *Leviathan*, Chapter X, p.42.

[14] *Leviathan*, Chapter XI, p.47.

[15] *Leviathan*, Chapter X, p.42.

[16] C.B. Macpherson, *The Political Theory of Possessive Individualism* (Oxford University Press, 1962), Chapter XI, 3.

'Hobbes and Game Theory'

Jean Hampton

The argument that Hobbes presents about the state of nature has recently
been interpreted in game theoretic terms. Game theory looks at human
interaction in a variety of formal ways to show up the mutual
interdependence of our actions and the ways that rational actions can have
consequences quite different from those intended by the actor. Hobbes's
account of the situation in the state of nature has been explained in terms of
one particular element of game theory: the prisoners' dilemma. The
American political philosopher, Jean Hampton, wrote one of the best books
in this area: *Hobbes and the Social Contract Tradition* (1986), which used the
techniques of game theory to investigate the state of nature, and the
possibility of exiting it. This extract is from her last book, *Political Philosophy*.

Hobbes argues that the roughly equal people in such a state of nature would be largely, but not exclusively, self-regarding. They would desire above all else their self-preservation, which would generate in them an interest in many material things. And they would have other powerful desires, in particular the desire for glory. How would people so described behave toward one another?

Not well, says Hobbes. In their attempts to satisfy their largely self-regarding desires, they would inevitably clash, and they would come into conflict with one another so often that the state of nature would inevitably become a state of war 'of every man, against every man'. Hobbes describes the generation of that war in Chapter XIII of *Leviathan*:

> in the nature of man, we find three principal causes of quarrell. First, Competition;
> Secondly, Diffidence; Thirdly, Glory.
> The first, maketh men invade for Gain; the second, for Safety; and the third, for
> Reputation. The first use Violence, to make themselves Masters of other mens
> persons, wives, children and cattell; the second, to defend them; the third, for
> trifles, as a word, a smile, a different opinion, and any other signe of undervalue,
> either direct in their Persons, or by reflexion in their Kindred, their Friends, their
> Nation, their Profession, or their Name.[1]

The result is, eventually, a state of total war in which everyone claims a 'right to all things' on the grounds that there is no object that might not be useful in their struggle for survival against their fellows.

Now initially readers may think Hobbes is being unreasonably pessimistic about people's disposition to engage in war in the natural state. Wouldn't people, even as Hobbes has described them, see the futility of war and the advantages of peace? And wouldn't this mean that they could negotiate some kind of truce among them, producing a cessation of overt violence and perhaps some kind of limited cooperation?

To see why Hobbes would insist that such a truce is not possible in a state of nature and why war would be inevitable no matter how desirable a truce might seem, we must appreciate how the psychology of Hobbesian people is such that it would be *irrational* for them to keep their promise not to attack the others in any truce agreement. The central (albeit not only) problem that Hobbesian people face in the natural state is what is called a *prisoner's dilemma*, or PD (after the example that originally illustrated it), a dilemma that has been much discussed in contemporary social science and philosophy since the 1950s, when it was first explicitly named.[2] A PD is a situation in which the rational actions of rational people lead inevitably to conflict. Figure 1 illustrates the PD faced by two people in a Hobbesian state of nature who have made a truce agreement and are considering whether or not to keep that agreement. The numbers of the matrix correspond to the preferences of each of the agents for the outcome that would occur if each of them performed one of two actions: keep the agreement and refrain from attacking the other, or attack the other. There are four such outcomes, and the numbers rank them (1 is best; 4 is worst). A's preference orderings are on the [right]; B's preference orderings are on the left.

		Agent A	
		Do not attack	Attack
Agent B	Do not attack	2,2	4,1
	Attack	1,4	3,3

Figure 1

Agents who have preference orderings as they are depicted in this PD matrix will find that it is rational for them to attack no matter what the other agent decides to do. To see this, consider how each of them would reason. A notes that if B decides not to attack her, she can either decide to attack him, thereby getting her favorite situation realized, or else she can choose not to attack him, getting only her second favorite situation realized. So if B does not attack her, she concludes she should none the less attack him. She also notes that if B decides to attack her, then she can either refrain from attacking him, in which case she gets her least favorite situation realized, or else attack him, in which case she gets a better (third-place) situation realized. So if B decides to attack her, she should also attack him. But this means no matter which action B chooses, it would be better for A to attack him and not to keep their truce agreement; and since B's preferences are symmetrical, he realizes the same. In a PD situation, even though the cooperative outcome is best for the two of them considered as a collective, it is individually rational for each of them not to cooperate with the other. The irony is, however, that when everyone fails to cooperate, the outcome their actions produce is individually worse for each of them than the outcome that would be produced by universal cooperation!

This dilemma seems to capture the reasons why Hobbesian people in a state of nature persistently fail to cooperate and eventually aggress against one another. The advantages of aggression against (naïve) cooperators (prompting what Hobbes calls 'invasion for gain') and the advantages of aggression as a protective strategy against other aggressors (prompting what Hobbes calls 'invasion from diffidence') make aggression the best action, even though each person in that state would rather be in a state of peace than a state of war. Add to this situation the divisive effects of the desire for glory, and it seems inevitable that the Hobbesian state of nature will eventually be a state of total war.

However, there are other passages in *Leviathan* where Hobbes suggests that PD reasoning is not quite accurate as an account of the way in which Hobbesian people would deliberate in the state of nature. To appreciate what these passages mean, consider how you would reason if you knew there was a good chance that you would be in a *series* of prisoner's dilemmas with another person. Suppose, for example, that you and this other person had neighbouring farms, and in order to harvest all your crops each of you required the other's help. Deciding whether or not to keep an agreement to help one another before any particular harvest places each of you in a prisoner's dilemma, but the failure to keep such an agreement on any particular occasion will also mean that neither of you can count on the other's help in any future harvest because neither of you will unilaterally cooperate. So in a series of PDs, cooperation early in that series can make possible not only the benefits from cooperation in that situation but also benefits from cooperative interactions in future PDs, while the failure to cooperate can foreclose the chance of receiving all future benefits. If those future benefits are factored into your calculations about what to do now, cooperation may often turn out to be rational after all. Depicted in Figure 2 are preferences two individuals would have for cooperating in a prisoner's dilemma that they expect to be only the first of a series of such dilemmas.

In this situation each player's favorite outcome is that produced by joint cooperation, because that outcome will generate the benefits of cooperation in the present situation and make possible benefits from cooperation in future PDs. The favorite outcome in the original PD, in which the agent fails to cooperate but enjoys the other person's cooperation, is not the favorite here, because each agent knows the other agent will never cooperate in the future if he or she reneges now, in which case he or she will never be able to enjoy the cooperative benefits of future PDs.

		Agent A	
		Cooperate	Do not Cooperate
Agent B	Cooperate	1,1	4,2
	Do not cooperate	2,4	3,3

Figure 2

I have been describing what is generally called an *iterated prisoner's dilemma*. If the parties in such a dilemma have preferences as depicted in Figure 2, they will reason as follows: If my partner cooperates, then it will be rational for me to cooperate also. But if my partner fails to cooperate, it would not be rational for me to cooperate (because the outcome of universal non-cooperation is preferred to the outcome in which my partner fails to cooperate but I do). Hence I should cooperate if and only if I have good reason to believe my partner will cooperate also.

There are signs in chapter XV of *Leviathan* that Hobbes believes people in the state of nature are often in iterated PDs, so that Figure 2, and not Figure 1, describes the preferences over cooperation they have in this state. For example, Hobbes says in that chapter that keeping contracts is rational in a state of nature, as long as one can be assured that one's partner is prepared to keep his contract, because such cooperative behavior reassures others that one is the sort of person who can be trusted to keep her side of a bargain in a confederacy contract in which each participant promises to come to the aid of the other if attacked.[3] This is a nice example of the way in which cooperation in one PD makes possible the realization of (even more lucrative) benefits from cooperation in a future PD.

But remember that reasoning in an iterated PD situation results in cooperation only if one concludes that there is good reason to believe one's partner will cooperate. With no assurance that this is so, the rational decision is not to cooperate, forgoing future benefits in order to ensure that one is not harmed by one's partner's folly. So Hobbes's state of nature would still be a state of war, even if most people expected to be in iterated rather than single-play PDs, for as long as they could not get reasonable assurance that their fellows would cooperate. And indeed, it looks as if that assurance would be very hard to get. Hobbes's state of nature is one in which people are disassociated from one another, such that they don't have reliable information about whether their partners in a PD are able to reason well. If you were in such a situation and you believed there was a good chance that your partner was shortsighted or the sort of person whose reasoning was often derailed by passion, then you would worry that she would be unable to appreciate the rationality of cooperation.

So even if many people in Hobbes's state of nature appreciate the rationality of cooperation, many people won't – in particular, those who are bad reasoners or ignorant or shortsighted or greedy for present gain. This leads to trouble, because if you were in that state, when you faced another human being you could not be sure that you were facing someone who appreciated the rationality of cooperation. And you would be a fool to cooperate with someone who might well respond by taking advantage of you – particularly if his doing so was dangerous to your future well-being. Hence 'diffidence' (as Hobbes means the term) requires a defensive, uncooperative posture. Indeed, even if you thought the other person was likely to be a rational cooperator, if that other person feared that *you* were likely an irrational cooperator, then he would be likely to take this defensive posture and thus refuse to cooperate, in which case you would be rational not to cooperate either.

In another place I have used decision theory to try to capture the exact nature of the reasoning process of Hobbesian people in this situation.[4] It is a reasoning process that *can* result in a (rational) decision to cooperate if the reasoner has reasonable assurance that his partner will cooperate also, the gains from mutual cooperation are considerable, and the losses that would be suffered if the reasoner cooperated but his partner did not are not serious. But as the losses increase, then the assurance that each party needs to find cooperation rational must also increase. And in a Hobbesian state of nature the common knowledge that one's partners in PDs are rational is difficult if not impossible to come by, making it difficult to get the assurance one needs in most situations to make cooperation rational. This means that the single-play PD mentality would be the mentality that people in Hobbes's state of nature would feel forced to adopt.

Hobbes's discussion of what he calls 'laws of nature' provides supporting evidence that this assurance problem, faced by people in iterated PD situations, precipitates a state of war. These laws of nature direct people to behave in various cooperative ways, including keeping contracts, refraining from invading or aggressing against another, and so forth. Hobbes calls these laws 'Conclusions, or Theorems concerning what conduceth to the conservation and defence' of people in this situation.[5] Cooperation, he says, breeds a climate of trust and peace that makes possible self-preservation and the exchange of services and benefits necessary for a comfortable and peaceful life. In this way it is behavior that, although other-regarding, is actually in each person's self-interest. Yet despite promulgating these laws, Hobbes does not think they would forestall or in any way provide a remedy for the conflict in his natural state. This is because, on his view, the cooperative actions recommended in these laws of nature are only rational for a person to perform in the state of nature if others in that state are also disposed to perform them:

> For he that should be modest, and tractable, and performe all he promises, in such time, and place, where no man els should do so, should but make himselfe a prey to others, and procure his own certain ruine, contrary to the ground of all Lawes of Nature, which tend to Natures preservation. And again, he that having sufficient Security, that others shall observe the same Lawes towards him, observes them not himselfe, seeketh not Peace, but War; & consequently the destruction of his Nature by Violence.[6]

So each law of nature should really be understood to have attached to it a rider specifying that the cooperative action is directed only if the agent can be assured that the other player(s) will also behave cooperatively. Hence because each of these laws correctly specifies cooperative behavior that in certain circumstances will further our self-preservation, they 'bind to a desire to take place' (as Hobbes puts it in Chapter XV) in that each of us would like to be in a situation where such cooperative action was rational. None the less, in a state of nature, where the rider does not hold, such cooperative behavior could threaten the safety of the one performing it, so that even rational people would find their behavior risky to perform. Hence (for both good and bad reasons) human beings in that state do not follow the laws.

So what is the remedy? To achieve peace, says Hobbes, we need *one* judge with the power to settle any quarrel over anything. That one judge is what Hobbes calls the 'sovereign', who is a political leader with the authority to resolve any issue and the power to enforce any resolution of any issue. Hobbes specifies that a sovereign can be one person or many persons: If it is one person, the government is called a monarchy; if it is many persons, but not all persons, the government is called an aristocracy; if it is all persons, the government is called a democracy. Hobbes believes that monarchy is the best and most effective form of sovereign rule, although he admits that he does not have a decisive argument to prove its superiority.[7]

How is the sovereign created? Hobbes does *not* say that his creation involves the people's conferring authority and power via a contract between them and the sovereign. Indeed, he insists that no such contract should take place, else there will be quarreling between the people and the sovereign about whether or not he has performed according to the terms of the contract. Because there can be no impartial judge to resolve this quarrel, it will likely lead to war and the dissolution of the political society: If the sovereign is designated to resolve such a quarrel, then he will never admit to breaching the agreement, in which case it is useless. And if the people are supposed to resolve the quarrel, then they will likely disagree with one another as well as with the sovereign about whether he has performed well or not. Both sorts of disagreements will lead to conflict and the 'dissolution of the commonwealth'.[8] For this reason, Hobbes says that the sovereign must be created by a process in which the people contract with *one another* about who shall be sovereign and then individually 'authorize' that person in a way that makes them permanently bound to him.

So Hobbes's development of the consent-based theory of political authority does *not* endorse the idea that there is some kind of 'deal' between the ruler and the ruled giving authority and power on condition that she rule 'well'. Instead, Hobbes argues that as a result of determining that the creation of a sovereign is to his or her advantage, each person will decide to agree *with one another* to confer authority so as to create a sovereign, but the actual investiture of authority and power is performed independently and non contractually. Moreover, as I said before, Hobbes uses the language appropriate for an alienation social contract argument because he insists that this investiture is one in which each individual *gives up* his or her power and right to direct his or her own life. He argues from the subject to the ruler because such an understanding of the sovereign's authorization would imply the existence of an agency contract between the sovereign and those she ruled – which Hobbes argues will only precipitate more conflict rather than peace. In the end Hobbes says that peace can be achieved only if people in the state of nature accept the need for a ruler who is quite literally their master.

Hobbes's development of the consent-based theory of authority also differs from the development of that idea in Aristotle's *Politics*. As we've noted, Hobbes is far more egalitarian that Aristotle in that he insists that every human being is the rough equal of every other; in Hobbes's state of nature there are no natural slaves or masters, and women and men are not fundamentally different enough to make the former subordinate to the latter. But according to Hobbes, our equality means that in order to live in peace we must 'invent' a master, that is, we must select a person or group from among us and artificially make him or them master with authority to settle all our disputes.

Notes

From Hampton, Jean (1997) *Political Philosophy*, WestView Press, pp.43–9.

[1] Ibid., Chapter XIII, paragraphs 6 and 7, pp. 61–2.

[2] The game was invented by Merrill Flood and Melvin Dresher; see Flood, 'Some Experimental Games', *Management Science 5* (October 1958): 5–26. It was given its name by A.W. Tucker.

[3] This discussion appears in a passage of *Leviathan* known as the 'Answer to the fool' (Chapter XV, paragraphs 4–5, pp.72–3). I discuss this passage at length in Jean Hampton, *Hobbes and the Social Contract Tradition* (Cambridge University Press, 1986), Chapter 2.

[4] See Hampton, *Hobbes and the Social Contract Tradition*, Chapters 2 and 3.

[5] See *Leviathan*, Chapter XV, 41, p.80.

[6] Ibid., paragraph 36, p.79.

[7] In *Hobbes and the Social Contract Tradition*, pp.105–7, I develop an argument on Hobbes's behalf to support this hypothesis.

[8] Hobbes discusses the causes of the dissolution of the commonwealth in Chapter XXIX of *Leviathan*, but his detailed criticisms of the idea of a contract between ruler and people are in Chapter XVIII, 4, pp. 89–90.

'Hobbes and the Purely Artificial Person of the State'

Quentin Skinner

Quentin Skinner is Regius Professor of Modern History at Cambridge. His
Foundations of Modern Political Thought (1978) is an important work which
helped to establish the 'contextual' approach to reading the classic works of
political thought. In the following paper, he argues that Hobbes distinguishes
between the state and the sovereign in a way that clarifies his account of the
rights and authority of the sovereign.

... [W]e continue to organize our public life around the idea of the sovereign state. But
it seems to me that we do not always understand the theory we have inherited, and
that arguably we have never managed fully to make sense of the proposition that the
person of the state is the seat of sovereignty. This encourages me to hope that an
historical investigation of Hobbes's argument may turn out to be of far more than
purely historical interest.

Hobbes eventually worked out a distinctive and highly influential approach to the
question of how it is possible for a state – or any other abstraction or collectivity – to
perform actions and take responsibility for the consequences. The explanation, he
proposed, depends on making sense of what he describes as the class of attributed
actions. What we need to understand is how actions can be validly attributed to
agents, and genuinely counted as theirs, even when the agent in question did not in
fact perform the action, and perhaps could not in principle have performed it.

Hobbes gives the answer without preamble in Chapter XVI of *Leviathan*, the
chapter entitled *Of Persons, Authors and Things Personated*. His proposed solution
(already implicit in his title) is impressively if deceptively straightforward. It is
possible, he argues, for an action genuinely to be attributed to a collectivity – or to an
abstraction or even a thing – provided that one particular condition is met. The agent
to whom the action is attributed must be represented by another agent who can
validly claim to be 'personating' the first by way of acting on their behalf.[1]
[...]

Hobbes introduces his attempt to analyse attributed action in terms of representation at the start of Chapter XVI of *Leviathan*,[2] where he begins by unveiling his definition of the underlying concept of a person:

> A PERSON, is he, whose words or actions are considered, either as his own, or as representing the words or actions of an other man, or of any other thing to whom they are attributed, whether Truly or by Fiction.[3]

To construe: a general theory of action will not only have to explain how individual persons can represent themselves, so that their words and actions can truly be attributed to them; such a theory will also have to explain how it is possible for one person to represent someone else – or some *thing* else – in such a way that the words or actions of the representative can validly be attributed to the person (or thing) being represented. To put the point in a different way – as Hobbes does later in the chapter – a general theory of action will need to include an account of how it is possible for one person to act in the name of someone else. This is because 'to *Personate*, is to *Act* or *Represent* himselfe, or an other; and he that acteth another, is said to beare his Person, or act in his name'.[4]
[...]

With the introduction of the key concept of an attributed action, Hobbes comes face to face with the principal problem he needs to address. What is to count as the valid representation of one person's words or actions by someone else, such that it will be proper to say of an action performed by a representative that it ought to be attributed to the person – or thing or collectivity – being represented? What, in a word, distinguishes representation from misrepresentation?

Hobbes grappled with this problem in every recension of his civil science, but it was only in *Leviathan* that he arrived at a satisfactory answer, or indeed any answer at all. Once again his solution wears an air of remarkable simplicity, but it constitutes one of the most important theoretical advances he made between the publication of *De Cive* in 1642 and *Leviathan* nearly a decade later, and arguably embodies his most original contribution to the theory of the state.[5] His suggestion is that an action can be validly attributed to one person on the basis of its performance by a representative if and only if the representative has in some way been duly authorized,[6] and hence instructed and commissioned, to perform the action concerned.[7] The crucial concept is accordingly that of authorization[8] and, more specifically, that of being an author and hence in a position to grant authority. These terms make no appearance in *The Elements* or *De Cive*, but in *Leviathan* they furnish the entire theoretical grounding for Hobbes's account of the legitimate state.[9]

The terminology of authors and authorization is introduced at an early stage in Chapter XVI of *Leviathan*. Hobbes first employs these terms when considering the sense in which we can speak of actions, by analogy with possessions, as 'owned' by particular individuals:

> Then the Person is the *Actor*; and he that owneth his words and actions, is the AUTHOR: In which case the Actor acteth by Authority. For that which in speaking of goods and possessions, is called an *Owner*, and in latine *Dominus*, in Greeke kurios, speaking of Actions, is called an Author.[10]

Hobbes is asking what allows an actor – that is, a representative – to claim that he is acting by authority. (I shall sometimes be obliged to follow him in writing as if all such actors are male.) The representative needs to be able to claim that he was duly authorized, in which case the person who granted him authority will count as the author of his action and will have to take responsibility for its consequences. The conclusion is guaranteed by the two stipulations underpinning Hobbes's argument. The first states that anyone who authorizes an action can be identified as its author. The second adds that, when we speak about the authors of actions, we are equivalently speaking about their owners, since we are speaking about those who must 'own up' to whatever is done in their name.[11]

A dramatic implication underlies this analysis, as Hobbes immediately points out:

> From hence it followeth, that when the Actor maketh a Covenant by Authority, he bindeth thereby the Author, no lesse than if he had made it himselfe; and no less subjecteth him to all the consequences of the same.[12]

The implication is brought out still more forthrightly in *De Homine*: 'He is called an author who has declared that he wishes an action to be held as his own which another person has performed.'[13] Hobbes is now prepared unequivocally to state that the reason why authors must 'own up' to the actions they have authorized is that the actions in question will be theirs, not those of anyone else.

The significance of the implication is that it yields the required criterion for judging when an alleged author can validly claim to have been misrepresented. If you are impersonated by a purported representative without having antecedently granted him authority, you are under no obligation to 'own' his actions, since you cannot be said to have authorized their performance. It is only 'when the Authority is evident' that the author is obliged; if, by contrast, 'the Authority is feigned, it obligeth the Actor onely; there being no Author but himselfe'.[14]

To round off his exposition, Hobbes provides an account of the mechanism by which it is possible for one person to receive the kind of authority that enables them validly to represent another and act in their name. He gives his explanation – again by analogy with the ownership of goods – in the same passage of Chapter XVI:

> And as the Right of possession, is called Dominion; so the Right of doing any action, is called AUTHORITY and sometimes *warrant*. So that by Authority, is always understood a Right of doing any act; and *done by Authority*, done by Commission, or License from him whose right it is.[15]

To construe again: to be able to act by authority is to have been granted a commission or license to perform an action by some person or persons who must possess the right to perform it themselves. The grant must take the form of a voluntary transfer of right, since commissioning and licensing are names of voluntary acts. So the receipt of such a commission must be equivalent to the acquisition of the transferred right of performing the action involved.[16] Hobbes later summarizes more clearly in *De Homine*. 'They are said to have authority who do something by the right of someone else',[17] so that 'unless he who is the author himself possesses the right of acting, the actor has no authority to act'.[18]

By signalling acceptance of such a covenant,[19] the authorising agent acquires two contrasting obligations towards his representative. One is the duty to take responsibility for his actions. But the other is a duty of non-interference. This follows from the fact that, whenever an authorising agent voluntarily transfers the right to perform an action, he thereby gives up the right to perform it himself. As Hobbes explains, 'To *lay downe* a mans Right to any thing, is to *devest* himselfe of the *Liberty*, of hindering another of the benefit of his own Right to the same'.[20] He goes on to trace the implications in his most minatory tones:

> When a man hath in either manner abandoned, or granted away his Right; then is he said to be OBLIGED, or BOUND, not to hinder those, to whom such Right is granted, or abandoned, from the benefit of it; and that he *Ought*, and it is his DUTY, not to make voyd that voluntary act of his own: and that such hindrance is INJUSTICE, and INJURY, as being *Sine Jure*; the Right being before renounced, or transferred.[21]

Once you have covenanted, you must leave it to your representative, who is now in possession of your right of action, to exercise it at his discretion when acting in your name.

Before considering how Hobbes applies his general theory, we need to examine one allegedly knock-down objection to his entire line of thought.[22] One commentator who has recently pressed the objection has been Joel Feinberg, who has raised it in discussing Hobbes's example of a master who 'commandeth his servant to give mony to a stranger'.[23] The servant is acting as his master's representative, from which it follows, according to Hobbes, that the act of paying the stranger must be attributed to the master.[24] But according to Feinberg this analysis is dangerously misleading. Although the 'pecuniary consequences' may be the same as if the master had acted himself, 'it is nevertheless true that *he* did not act'; what we have to say is that his servant acted for him.[25] The objection is thus that attributed actions are not actions.

One possible retort[26] would be to insist that, in spite of the obvious difference between attributed actions and actions performed at first hand, the two ought nevertheless to be classified together on the grounds of their numerous family resemblances.[27] But Hobbes makes no attempt to mount this kind of defence, and he surely stands in no need of it. It is true that he likes to speak of attributed actions as if they are genuine instances of action. But it is sufficient for his purposes to defend the much less controversial claim he puts forward about 'ownership': the claim that, when someone acts as an accredited representative, the person being represented must 'own' the consequences of the action as if they had performed it themselves. The action counts as theirs, and is called their action,[28] not because they actually perform it, but because they are under an obligation to take responsibility for its occurrence.[29]

[...]

In Chapter XVII Hobbes goes on to describe the mechanism by which [the transformation of a multitude of men into a single person] takes place. It is as if each individual should agree with everyone else 'to conferre all their power and strength upon one Man, or upon one Assembly of men, that may reduce all their Wills, by plurality of voices, unto one Will'. When they perform this act of mutual covenanting, this is as much as to say that they 'appoint one Man, or Assembly of men, to beare their Person'. So the outcome 'is more than Consent, or Concord; it is a reall Unitie of them all, in one and the same Person', in consequence of which they are now able, through the agency of the person representing them, to act in the manner of a single person with one will and voice.[30]

The name of the artificial person brought into existence when a multitude forms itself into such a unity is the commonwealth or state. As soon as the members of the multitude agree, each with each, 'to appoint one Man, or Assembly of men, to beare their Person', the multitude 'so united in one Person, is called a COMMON-WEALTH, in latine CIVITAS'[31] – the term Hobbes also translates as 'state'.[32] This union or coupling together has the effect of engendering immediate issue in just the manner of a marital union blessed by God – although with one crucial difference later emphasized by Hobbes, namely, that the offspring produced by the union of the multitude has no determinate gender, for 'though *man* be *male* and *female, authority* is not'[33] . As for the name by which Hobbes wishes this figure of authority to be known, he informs us of it in his gravest tones. 'This is the Generation of that great LEVIATHAN, or rather (to speake more reverently) of that *Mortall* God, to which wee owe under the *Immortal God*, our peace and defence'.[34]

We still need to know the name of the person appointed by the members of the multitude to act in their name when they take the decision to be represented. Hobbes replies that the name of this person is the sovereign, who is thereby given authority to 'bear' or 'carry' or act the part of the purely artificial person of the state. The commonwealth or state 'is *One Person*', and 'he that carryeth this Person, is called SOVERAIGNE, and said to have *Soveraigne Power*'.[35] The same distinction is subsequently drawn even more clearly in the Latin version of *Leviathan*. There the holder of *summa potestas* or sovereign power is described, in a phrase closely echoing Cicero's *De Officiis*, as 'he who bears the Person of the State'.[36] The sovereign may in turn be a natural person, as in the case of a monarchy, or an assembly of natural persons, as in the case of an aristocracy or democracy.[37] But in every case the legal standing of the sovereign will be that of 'the absolute Representative of all the subjects'.[38]

It is worth underlining the complexity of Hobbes's argument, if only because so many even of his best commentators have oversimplified it. We are told that the 'civil person' brought into existence by the union of the multitude is the sovereign.[39] As we have seen, however, the name of the person engendered by the transformation of the multitude into one person through their agreement to appoint a representative is not the sovereign but the state. The sovereign is the name of the representative of the multitude united in one person, and is thus the name of the representative of the state.

Armed with this analysis, we can now see how the apparently insubstantial person of the state can nevertheless be the holder of sovereignty and the seat of power. Hobbes concedes of course that all the actions performed by states will in fact be performed by sovereigns acting in their 'politique' capacity.[40] He is always careful to insist, however, that sovereigns are not the proprietors of their sovereignty. They are the holders of offices with duties attached, their fundamental duty being to procure the safety and contentment of the people. Although they are granted the right to exercise complete sovereign power, this power is merely 'placed' and 'resideth' in them by virtue of the office they are asked to discharge.[41] The true status of all lawful sovereigns is thus that they are merely 'the Person representative of all and every one of the Multitude'.[42]

As I have shown, however, the central contention of Hobbes's theory of attributed action is that, whenever a person or collectivity agrees to appoint such a representative, whatever actions are thereafter performed by the representative in their name will be attributable not to the representative but rather to the person or collectivity being represented. Not only will those who appoint the representative be held accountable for the consequences of any actions undertaken on their behalf, but the actions in question will actually count as theirs, not as those of the representative who carries them out. It follows that, whenever our sovereigns exercise their powers in order to procure our safety and contentment, the acts they perform should not be regarded as their own but rather as those of the person whom they are representing, that is, the person of the state. This, then, is how it comes about that we can properly speak – and not by metaphor – of the commonwealth or state as the person who imposes the laws and thereby ensures that our safety and contentment are secured. Although the sovereign is always the legislator, the legislator 'is always the Representative of the Common-wealth'.[43] So 'the name of the person Commanding' is not the sovereign but the person whom the sovereign represents. And the name of that person, as Hobbes eventually declares in a further echo of Cicero, is '*Persona Civitatis*, the Person of the Common-wealth'.[44]

[...]

It remains for Hobbes to distinguish between the representation and misrepresentation of the state's authority. How are we to discriminate between lawful sovereigns and those who merely usurp the powers of the state without enjoying the standing of accredited representatives? To put the question the other way round, who has the right to authorise the actions of the state?

It is not open to Hobbes to reply that sovereigns possess this right. Sovereigns are merely representatives, and all representatives must themselves be authorized. Nor can the actions of the state be authorized by the state itself. If an agent is to authorize its own actions it must be a natural person, capable of exercising its own rights and acting in its own name. But the state is not a natural person; on the contrary, there is a sense in which it more closely resembles a fictitious person such as Agamemnon in Aeschylus's play of that name. Agamemnon has no existence, except as words on a page, until he is brought to life by the skills of an actor who impersonates him and speaks his lines. The state likewise amounts to little more than a verbal entity in the absence of a sovereign to represent it and play its part in the world.

[...]

While the state is not fictional, however, it is undoubtedly a member of the class of persons I have characterized as purely artificial, and bears a close resemblance to such exemplary members of the class as hospitals, bridges and so forth. Like such inanimate objects, the state is unquestionably capable of acting, since it is capable of being represented and of having actions 'truly' attributed to it. Like such objects, however, the state cannot give authority to anyone to represent it, and cannot therefore authorise its own representation. As Hobbes puts it, it has no capacity 'to doe any thing, but by the Representative'.[45] So shadowy, indeed, is its existence that it might be thought to bear a yet closer resemblance to such purely artificial persons as the gods of the heathen. Whereas hospitals and bridges remain things even when they are not being personated, the state in the absence of a sovereign 'is but a word', just as the gods of the heathen are 'nothing' in the absence of a priest to represent them.[46]

Who then is capable of authorising the actions of the state? We already know the answer in general terms from our examination of how it is possible for one person validly to authorize a second to represent a third – as in the case of the owner of a bridge who authorizes an overseer to act on its behalf. As we have seen, two requirements must be met. One is that the natural person or persons authorising the representation must themselves possess the right to undertake whatever actions they intend to authorize. The other is that this right must in turn be owed to the fact that they stand in some appropriate relationship of dominion over the purely artificial person concerned.

According to Hobbes there is only one possible way in which these conditions can be satisfied in the case of the state. The public acts of sovereigns will count as valid acts of the state if and only if the sovereign has been authorized to perform them by each and every member of the multitude. With this contention, Hobbes is finally able to offer his formal definition of a commonwealth or state: it is *'One Person, of whose Acts a great Multitude, by mutuall Covenants one with another, have made themselves every one the Author, to the end he may use the strength and means of them all, as he shall think expedient, for their Peace and Common Defence'*.[47]

Hobbes makes good this central contention by pointing out in the first place that the individual members of the multitude undoubtedly possess the right to perform the actions undertaken by sovereigns as representatives of the state. When Hobbes describes the lines of conduct that sovereigns are authorized to pursue, he always makes it clear that their rights of action are merely those possessed by each one of us in the state of nature. These rights can be summarized as the blameless liberty of using our powers in any way we judge necessary to defend our lives against others and secure ourselves against threats by anticipating them.[48] Because the exercise of these equal rights brings war, we are led by reason to recognize that the best means of attaining peace and other contentments of life will be to transfer our rights to a sovereign who will exercise them on our behalf. When we covenant to appoint such a sovereign, it is accordingly with the specific purpose of providing more effectively for our own peace and contentment. The sovereign is commissioned, in other words, merely to exercise those of our rights which, so long as we exercise them ourselves, will lead to war.[49]

Finally, Hobbes argues in addition that the individual members of the multitude stand – and alone stand – in an appropriate relationship of dominion with respect to the person of the state. The source of their dominion lies in the fact that the union of the multitude brings the state into existence. As a result, the relationship of the multitude to the state is analogous to that of the mother to her infant in the state of nature. Just as the mother brings her child into the world, thereby acquiring dominion over it, so the union of the multitude serves to procreate the state. Hobbes goes to the almost blasphemous extreme of drawing a parallel between this act of engendering and the work of God. 'The *Pacts* and *Covenants*, by which the parts of this Body Politique were at first made, set together, and united, resemble that *Fiat*, or the *Let us make man*, pronounced by God in the Creation'.[50]

What prompted Hobbes to develop this novel and intricate theory of the state? The clue lies, I believe, in attending to what he says at the outset of *Leviathan* about his hopes for the work. He aspires, he says, to pass unwounded between the opposing swords of 'those that contend, on one side for too great liberty, and on the other side for too much Authority'.[51]

[...]

While Hobbes agrees that all lawful government arises from consent, he violently disagrees with the radical implications drawn from this argument by the supporters of Parliament. He seeks instead to demonstrate that these alleged implications embody a peculiarly dangerous plea for too great liberty. As before, moreover, the way in which he mounts his case is by invoking and applying exactly the theory of attributed action on which I have concentrated.

One way in which Hobbes applies his theory is by recurring to his rival account of how it is possible for a multitude to act as 'one person'. A proper understanding of this process, he insists, will wholly defuse the Parliamentarian argument:

> There is little ground for the opinion of them, that say of Soveraign Kings, though they be *singulis majores*, of greater Power than every one of their Subjects, yet they be *Universis minores*, of lesse power than them all together. For if by *all together*, they mean not the collective body as one person, then *all together*, and *every one*, signifie the same; and the speech is absurd. But if by *all together*, they understand them as one Person (which person the Sovereign bears,) then the power of all together, is the same with the Sovereigns power; and so again the speech is absurd.[52]

Hobbes's fiercely polemical message is that, since the people only transform themselves into a collective body by way of instituting a sovereign, it makes no sense to think of them as a collective body setting limits in advance to the exercise of sovereign power.

The main way, however, in which Hobbes applies his theory of attributed action to attack the Parliamentarian cause is by invoking his analysis of what it means to authorize a representative. If we understand this process aright, he insists, we shall see that it is the merest *non sequitur* to suppose that the theory of covenanting commits us to defending the sovereignty of the people. On the contrary, we shall see that the idea of consent as the only source of lawful government is fully compatible with a strong defence of absolute sovereignty and the duty of non-resistance.

As we have seen, Hobbes stipulates that, if an act of authorization is to be validly performed, a transfer of right must take place. Once this covenant has passed, the authorizing agent is left with two specific obligations towards his or her representatives. One is the duty to 'own' their actions and those of any third party for whom they may have been authorized to act. But the other is the duty not to interfere with the execution of their commission, since the right to act as they think best in discharging their task is precisely what has been voluntarily handed over to them.

In Chapter XVII of *Leviathan* Hobbes argues that the covenant by which lawful states are instituted takes exactly this form. When the members of the multitude agree, each with each, to appoint a sovereign representative, theirs is a covenant of authorization embodying a declaration that a body of rights has been transferred.

They covenant 'in such manner, as if every man should say to every man, *I Authorise and give up my Right of Governing my selfe, to this Man, or to this Assembly of men*'.[53] At the same time Hobbes examines the precise character of the covenant involved. What the members of the multitude agree is 'to conferre all their power and strength upon one Man, or upon one Assembly of men'.[54] But as we have seen, this has the effect of producing two immediate consequences. It gives them a single will and voice, thereby converting them into one person, the person of the state. But it also creates a representative of that person in the figure of the sovereign, who is given the job of 'bearing' or 'carrying' the person of the state. To say all this, however, is to say that the members of the multitude remain the authors of all the actions of their sovereign, and at the same time remain the authors of all the actions of the person whom they have authorized their sovereign to represent, namely, the person of the state. Each member of the multitude must now 'acknowledge himselfe to be Author of whatsoever he that so beareth their Person, shall Act, or cause to be Acted, in those things which concerne the Common Peace and Safetie'.[55]

Hobbes lastly turns, in Chapter XVIII, to consider the implications of this political covenant. The members of the multitude have given up their right of using their own discretion to secure their safety and contentment. They have voluntarily handed over their right of self-government to be exercised by their sovereign on their behalf. It follows, according to Hobbes's theory of authorization, that the members of the multitude must now be under an absolute obligation not to interfere with their sovereign in the exercise of the rights they have transferred to him. The sovereign acquires complete discretion and absolute power to decide what should be done to preserve the safety and contentment of every subject under his charge.

Hobbes goes still further. Not only do the members of the multitude have no remaining right to question the actions of their sovereign; they have a positive duty to 'own' whatever actions their sovereign may undertake in seeking their safety and contentment. But this is to say, according to Hobbes's theory of attributed action, that the public acts of the sovereign, and hence of the state, are nothing other than the acts of the individual members of the multitude. So it will not merely be unjust for them to oppose their sovereign; it will actually be self-contradictory, for they will be opposing themselves.

The moral is finally drawn in a powerful summarizing passage in Chapter XVIII:

> Because every Subject is by this Institution Author of all the Actions, and Judgements of the Soveraigne Instituted; it followes, that whatsoever he doth, it can be no injury to any of his Subjects; nor ought he to be by any of them accused of Injustice. For he that doth any thing by authority from another, doth therein no injury to him by whose authority he acteth: But by this Institution of a Common-wealth, every particular man is Author of all the Soveraigne doth; and consequently he that complaineth of injury from his Soveraigne, complaineth of that whereof he himselfe is Author; and therefore ought not to accuse any man but himselfe.[56]

Although Hobbes recurs to this claim with evident satisfaction in a number of later passages, he stands in no need of such uncharacteristic repetitiousness.[57] His account of attributed action already enables him to rest his case against the radical writers of his age. The concept of the political covenant is not a means of limiting the powers of the crown; properly understood, it shows that the powers of the crown have no limits at all. The theory of attributed action lies at the heart of the politics of *Leviathan*.

Notes

From the *Journal of Political Philosophy*, vol. 7, 1, 1999, pp.1–29 (for references, see Bibliography).

[1] Pitkin (1967) rightly stresses that representation is the basic concept. Although I disagree with Pitkin at several points, I am greatly indebted to her classic analysis.

[2] Although Hobbes had already introduced the concept in Chapter XV when discussing the attribution of justice and injustice to actions and to men. See Hobbes (1996 edn), pp.103–4.

[3] Hobbes (1996 edn), p.111.

[4] Ibid., p.112.

[5] As is rightly stressed in Gauthier (1969), p.120 and Zarka (1995), p.197.

[6] Note that 'duly' need not mean 'explicitly': authorization is a possibility for Hobbes.

[7] Hobbes does not say that the representative has to be authorized by the person being represented.

[8] Hobbes (1996 edn), pp.120, 151 explicitly invokes this terminology. On Hobbes's concept of authorization see Copp (1980), pp.582–95, a discussion to which I am particularly indebted.

[9] My discussion is mainly confined to the basic case in which one natural person or body of persons directly authorizes another to act either on their behalf or on behalf of a third party. Hobbes introduces many refinements which I have no space to consider here: conditional authorization (Hobbes (1996 edn), p.115), authorization of assemblies (Hobbes (1996 edn), p.129); and authorization not by mutual covenant but by covenant with a conqueror (Hobbes (1996 edn), p.141). A full analysis of Hobbes's theory would need to take account of these refinements, but in the meantime there are several good reasons for concentrating on the basic case. One is that Hobbes does so himself. Another is that he is not always successful at explaining how the refinements fit on to the basic case. ...[O]ne consequence is that sometimes there is insufficient textual basis for discussing them.

[10] Hobbes (1996 edn), p.112.

[11] I am indebted to the discussion in Pitkin (1967), pp.18–19 on owning and 'owning up'.

[12] Hobbes (1996 edn), p.112

[13] Hobbes (1839 edn), XV.2, p.131: '*Author enim vocatur is, qui actionem quam facit alius pro sua habere se velle declaravit*'.

[14] Hobbes (1996 edn), p.113.

[15] Ibid., p.112.

[16] This is worth underlining, if only because it has sometimes been argued that (as Gauthier (1969), p.124 puts it) although the act of authorization seems to involve 'some translation of right', this is 'evidently not mere renunciation, nor is it transfer, in Hobbes's usual sense'.

[17] Hobbes (1839 edn), XV.2, p.131: 'Itaque authoritatem habere dicuntur, qui quid iure faciunt alieno'.

[18] Ibid., 'Nisi enim is, qui author est, ius habet agendi ipse, actor agendi authoritatem non habet'.

[19] Note that this is the form of the covenant only in what I am calling the basic case – what Hobbes (1996 edn), p.115) calls the case of being 'simply' as opposed to 'conditionally' authorized. Leyden (1982), pp.89–95 discusses the special complexities attaching to conditional authorization.

[20] Hobbes (1996 edn), p.92

[21] Ibid., pp.92–3.

[22] Copp (1980), pp.585–6 offers a more specific objection. I can validly be held accountable for an action performed by someone else if I coerce them into performing it. But coercing is not authorizing; so I can validly be held accountable, pace Hobbes, for actions I have not authorized. Hobbes would not regard this as an objection. For him, coercion and freedom of action are compatible, so that even coercive acts of authorization genuinely authorize. See Skinner (1990) for this aspect of Hobbes's theory of freedom.

[23] Hobbes (1996 edn), p.104; cf. Feinberg (1970), p.227

[24] Ibid., pp.112, 113; cf. also p.156.

[25] Feinberg (1970), p.227.

[26] Copp (1979), pp.177–8 suggests another possible retort: that the question of what it may be misleading to say in the case of the master and his servant depends on what is in question about the episode. Suppose that, although the servant duly hands over the money, a question later arises as to whether the stranger has been paid. What it will be misleading to say in these circumstances is that the master has not paid the stranger. He has paid him – by commanding and thereby causing his servant to make the payment.

[27] Copp (1980), pp.581–2 discusses Feiberg's objection to Hobbes's analysis and proposes this response.

[28] As in *Catiline his Conspiracy* by Ben Jonson (a friend of Hobbes's). See Jonson, B. (1937), *Ben Jonson*, III, 38–9, C.H. Herford and P. Simpson (eds), Oxford University Press, p.469, where Cicero, on his election as Consul, is made to declare: 'For every lapse of mine will, now, be call'd Your error, if you make such ...'

[29] Runciman (1997), p.7. I am much indebted to Runciman's analysis at this point.

[30] Ibid., p.120.

[31] p.120; cf. Polin (1981), p.95 and Tukianinem (1994), p.48

[32] Hobbes's preferred translation of *civitas* is 'Commonwealth'. See, for example, Hobbes (1996 edn), pp.120, 183. But when he uses 'state' as a translation, the word he is translating is almost always *civitas*. For the most striking instance see Hobbes (1996 edn), p.9.

[33] Hobbes (1840 edn), p.434.

[34] Hobbes (1996), p.120.

[35] Ibid., p.121

[36] Hobbes (1668), p.86: 'Is autem qui Civitas Personam gerit, *Summam* habere dicitur *Potestatem*'. Cf. Cicero, M.T. (1913 edn), *De officiis*, I. XXXIV. 124, W. Miller (trans.), Heinemann, p.126 on the office of magistrates: 'se gerere personam civitatis'.

[37] Hobbes (1996 edn), p.129. The question of how assemblies can act as representatives obviously raises further questions, but I am concerned here only with the basic case. So is Hobbes, for he never explains how collectivities can represent the state. According to his general theory, such assemblies assemble, and by what process can they be authorized? Copp (1980), p.599 suggests that Hobbes must regard assemblies as their own representatives, but Hobbes himself never pronounces on this point.

[38] Hobbes (1996 edn), p.156.

[39] See, for example, Baumgold (1988), p.38–9; Burgess (1990), p.678; Fukuda (1997), p.43; Martinich (1997), pp.44–9. But see, by contrast, Jaume (1986), esp. pp.99–100 and Zarka (1995), esp. pp.212, 225.

[40] Hobbes (1996 edn), p.131. See also Hobbes (1996 edn). pp.136, 149,174, 184, 186, 214, 239 and esp. 253 for general claims to the effect that the only way in which the state can act is for the sovereign representative to act in its name.

[41] Hobbes (1996 edn), pp.127, 144, and cf.231. On the sovereign as the holder of an office of trust see Hobbes (1996 edn), pp.126, 143.

[42] Hobbes (1996 edn), p.129. See also Hobbes (1996 edn), pp.121, 155–6, 167, 185, 212, 223 for other references to the fact that the sovereign is merely the representative of the state. It appears to be a shorthand, or perhaps a slip, when Hobbes instead states ((1996 edn), p.187) that the sovereign is 'the person of the Common-wealth' (rather than the representative of that Person).

[43] Hobbes (1996 edn), p.223.

[44] Ibid., p.183; cf. Cicero (1913 edn), I. XXXIV. 124, p.126. Lessay (1992), pp. 159–60 discusses the allusion.

[45] Hobbes (1996 edn), pp.171, 184.

[46] Ibid., pp.245, 114.

[47] Ibid., p.121.

[48] Ibid., pp.87–8, 91.

[49] Ibid., pp.87–9, 124, 131.

[50] Ibid., pp.9–10. But does the artifice created by the multitude more closely resemble a man or a machine? See Tukiainem (1994) and Runciman (1997), pp.16–24 for Hobbes's contrasting structures of imagery at this point.

[51] Hobbes (1996 edn), p.3

[52] Hobbes (1996 edn), p.128; cf. Sommerville (1996), p.262.

[53] Ibid., p.120.

[54] Ibid., p.120.

[55] Ibid., p.120.

[56] Ibid., pp.136, 172; cf. also p.121.

'Problems with Hobbes's Alienation Social Contract Argument'

Jean Hampton

This Reading continues where Reading 2.2 left off.

For generations, readers have found Hobbes's argument powerful. And yet most have thought his logic has gone wrong and have rejected his conclusions. Where is his mistake? As I shall now seek to explain, Hobbes's argument goes wrong in a way that is very important to us given that we seek to understand the best way to formulate a consent-based theory of authority.

Consider what is involved in authorizing the sovereign: According to Hobbes, the state of war prompts every person to claim a right to all things, and these entitlement claims lead to quarreling over everything. Hence he says that the sovereign's creation means every person but the sovereign-designate surrenders this entitlement claim, thereby making the entitlement claim of the sovereign-designate effective. In this way not only effective power but also *authority* is granted to this ruler, as Hobbes makes clear in the following passage from Chapter XVII of *Leviathan*:

> The only way to erect such a Common Power, as may be able to defend them from the invasion of Forraigners, and the injuries of one another, and thereby to secure them in such sort, as that by their owne industrie, and by the fruites of the Earth, they may nourish themselves and live contentedly; is, to conferre all their power and strength upon one Man, or upon one Assembly of men, that may reduce all their Wills, by plurality of voices, unto one Will: which is as much as to say, to appoint one Man, or Assembly of men, to beare their Person; and every one to owne, and acknowledge himselfe to be Author of whatsoever he that so beareth their Person, shall Act, or cause to be Acted, in those things which concerne the Common Peace and Safetie; and therein to submit their Wills, every one to his Will,

and their Judgements, to his Judgement. This is more than Consent, or Concord; it is a reall Unitie of them all, in one and the same Person, made by Covenant of every man with every man, as if every man should say to every man, *I Authorise and give up my Right of Governing my selfe, to this Man, or to this Assembly of men, on this condition, that thou give up thy Right to him, and Authorise all his Actions in like manner.*[1]

So the idea is that this authorization process, in which all agree they will participate with respect to a particular person or assembly, results in the ruler's having power over everyone who participates in the process, as well as the goods each controls. But he holds this power rightfully by virtue of the fact that each person gave up the 'right to govern' herself or himself and bestowed that right on the sovereign. So he can now rightfully command each of them because he now 'owns' these governing rights.

Yet all this talk of 'authorizing' and 'rights' is abstract. What is it that people actually *do* to put the sovereign in this position of authority and power? We shall explore this question at great length in the next chapter, but for now, consider that a sovereign can have legitimacy and power in a society only when he is able to get his people to accept that they *ought* to obey him and when he has the personnel and technology to ensure that he can capture and punish those who do not obey his commands. Hence a sovereign's authority and power depends quite literally on his subjects' obeying him because they take him to be the sole political authority. In particular it is critical that they obey him when he commands them to capture, try, and punish someone who has violated those commands.

But what happens if the sovereign's rule is such that the people believe it is threatening their own lives? Will they persist in thinking that they ought to obey him and accordingly do so, even then? No. Hobbes has described human psychology such that inside or outside the commonwealth each person is concerned to advance his or he own interests, particularly self-preservation. But this means that Hobbes must admit that people in the commonwealth will disobey the sovereign if *they* determine that to obey him means endangering their ability to preserve themselves. And indeed this is exactly what he says: 'The Obligation of Subjects to the Sovereign, is understood to last as long, and no longer, than [*sic*] the power lasteth, by which he is able to protect them ... The end of Obedience is Protection'.[2]

If the people are always going to be concerned to preserve themselves and if the sovereign begins to rule such that their self-preservation is threatened, then their interests are such that they will do what they can to evade his commands, lest their lives be put at risk. Note that *the subjects* decide whether or not the ruler's commands are life-threatening; since it is *their* lives that are at stake, they are the ones who will (and must) make the determination about whether or not they are at risk. (Suppose the ruler decided this issue: He might well proclaim his rules were consistent with the people's well-being when in fact they were not. Only the subjects themselves have the right incentive to determine the preservation value of a sovereign's command because only they run the risk of dying if these commands turn out to be life-threatening.)

Now if only one person concluded that a sovereign's rule is inconsistent with her self-preservation and thus refused to obey one or more of the sovereign's commands, the sovereign's power and authority would not be threatened. But if many or most people make that determination and decide not to obey him, then the sovereign is in trouble. For such a massive refusal to follow his commands would effectively amount to rebellion. Not only would he lose all or most of the support of those parts of the society that enforce his commands (e.g., the police, the court system, the army), but he would also lose the compliance of the population on which any regime relies to function efficiently and cooperatively. Moreover, if all or most of the people decide to start obeying someone else, the sovereign would be effectively deposed, and this new individual would be invested with power and authority.

In the end, it is Hobbes's effectively granting that the people will (and ought to) judge the ruler's performance that is the ruin of his attempt to mount a viable alienation argument. This point was appreciated by some of Hobbes's contemporary critics. For example, one of Hobbes's most vociferous critics, John Bramhall, noted that after claiming subjects must give up their right to all things, Hobbes gives them a bailout clause in Chapter XXI, so that their authorization of the sovereign turns out to be something like: 'I give you, the sovereign, the right to command me in any area, and I will obey you *except* when I decide my life is threatened if I do so.'[3] But, asks Bramhall, who shall judge if a sovereign's commands are threatening to one's self-preservation or not?

> Either it must be left to the soveraign determination, whether the subjects security be sufficiently provided for, And then in vain is any mans sentence expected against himself, or to the discretion of the subject, (as the words themselves [in Chapter XXI] do seem to import,) and then there need no other bellowes to kindle the fire of a civill war, and put a whole commonwealth into a combustion, but this seditious Article.[4]

Bramhall's point is that if each subject judges when he is entitled to disobey the sovereign's commands and when he is not, then to all intents and purposes the sovereign's reign depends upon the judgement of the subjects that his commands are worth obeying, in which case he rules at their pleasure – a situation Bramhall is convinced will result in civil war. Is it any wonder that Bramhall derisively refers to *Leviathan* as a 'rebel's catechism'?[5]

So although Hobbes argues that the people must 'alienate' their right to govern themselves to the sovereign, in fact the only kind of investiture of power and authority that is possible for people as he has described them (and as we know them) is one that is contingent upon their determination that the sovereign is ruling in a way that secures their protection. This means that, in reality, *Leviathan* has two arguments: the 'official' alienation argument and the real but unacknowledged agency argument. The official argument is supposed to end with the conclusion that peace can be achieved only by creating a ruler with absolute power through the alienation of the people's rights to him. But in fact Hobbesian people cannot rationally alienate anything. Although they 'lay down their rights' to the person selected as sovereign when they authorize him, they are prepared to, as it were, pick those rights up again if and when the sovereign's behaviour threatens them. And if enough people refuse to obey him and even take up arms against him if they see him as threatening their lives, then he will be ousted as sovereign. The unofficial 'real' contract argument in *Leviathan* assumes, and must assume, that when the people create a ruler, they do so in a way that makes it possible for them to rescind their grant of authority and power if they believe the ruler is not governing in a way that will advance their interests in security and protection. In a sense, therefore, the assumptions of Hobbes's social contract argument commit him to the view that an 'absolute sovereign' is hired and fired by the people he governs.

But if the sovereign rules at the people's pleasure, then his authority and power are a function of their having loaned him power and authority for as long as doing so is advantageous to them. This is, in fact, the essence of an agency social contract! Hobbes sets out to defend the alienation argument, but his conception of who human beings are and why they want to create government forces him to accept that the creation and maintenance of authoritative rule is something that is always in the hands of those who are subject to it, making the ruler the implicit agent of the people, hired by them and capable of being fired by them if they object to his rule. This implicit agency agreement is the essence of Locke's argument in *Two Treatises of Government*. In a very real sense, Locke needed to look no farther than *Leviathan* for the outlines of his own political theory.

Notes

From Hampton, Jean (1997) *Political Philosophy*, WestView Press, pp.49–52.

[1] Ibid., Chapter XVII, 13, p.87.

[2] Ibid., Chapter XXI, 21, p.114. See also *De Cive*, 'English Works' ii, 6, pp.74–5.

[3] For example, see *Leviathan*, Chapter XXI, 10, p.111.

[4] John Bramhall (bishop of Derry and later of Armagh), 'The Catching of Leviathan or the Great Whale,' appendix to *Castigations of Mr. Hobbes ... Concerning Liberty and Universal Necessity*. Printed by E.T. for John Crooke, at the sign of the ship in Paul's churchyard, 1658.

[5] Ibid., p.515. See Hampton, *Hobbes and the Social Contract Tradition*, pp.199–200, for a discussion of the passages in Leviathan that prompted Bramhall to make this remark. In that work I also discuss the way in which rebellion is none the less difficult because it poses a collective action problem for the disgruntled subjects.

'Hobbes and the Sexual Contract'

Carole Pateman

Originally based in Oxford, Carole Pateman is now Professor of Political Science at UCLA. Amongst her works is *The Problem of Political Obligation: a Critique of 'Liberal Theory'* (1985) which outlines an attack similar to Rousseau's on the liberate account of the social contract. In *The Sexual Contract* (1988), from which this extract is taken, she examines the shifting ways in which social contract theorists either exclude women or assume their subordination in a preceding 'sexual contract'.

For Hobbes, all political power was absolute power, and there was no difference between conquest and contract. Subsequent contract theorists drew a sharp distinction between free agreement and enforced submission and argued that civil political power was limited, constrained by the terms of the original contract, even though the state retained the power of life and death over citizens. Hobbes also saw all contractual relations, including sexual relations, as political, but a fundamental assumption of modern political theory is that sexual relations are not political. Hobbes was too revealing about the civil order to become a founding father of modern patriarchy ... Hobbes differs from the other classic contract theorists in his assumption that there is no natural mastery in the state of nature, not even of men over women; natural individual attributes and capacities are distributed irrespective of sex. There is no difference between men and women in their strength or prudence, and all individuals are isolated and mutually wary of each other. It follows that sexual relations can take place only under two circumstances; either a man and woman mutually agree (contract) to have sexual intercourse, or a man, through some stratagem, is able to overpower a woman and take her by force, though she also has the capacity to retaliate and kill him.

Classic patriarchalism rested on the argument that political right originated naturally in fatherhood. Sons were born subject to their fathers, and political right was paternal right. Hobbes insists that all examples of political right are conventional and that, in the state of nature, political right is maternal not paternal. An infant, necessarily, has two parents ('as to the generation, God hath ordained to man a helper'), but both parents cannot have dominion over the child because no one can obey two masters. In the natural condition the mother, not the father, has political right over the child; 'every woman that bears children, becomes both a *mother* and a *lord*'.[1] At birth, the infant is in the mother's power. She makes the decision whether to expose or to nourish the child. If she decides to 'breed him', the condition on which she does so is that, 'being grown to full age he become not her enemy';[2] that is to say, the infant must contract to obey her. The postulated agreement of the infant is one example of Hobbes's identification of enforced submission with voluntary agreement, one example of his assimilation of conquest and consent. Submission to overwhelming power in return for protection, whether the power is that of the conqueror's sword or the mother's power over her newly born infant, is always a valid sign of agreement for Hobbes: 'preservation of life being the end, for which one man becomes subject to another, every man [or infant] is supposed to promise obedience, to him [or her], in whose power it is to save, or destroy him'.[3] The mother's political right over her child thus originates in contract, and gives her the power of an absolute lord or monarch.

The mother's political power follows from the fact that in Hobbes's state of nature 'there are no matrimonial laws'.[4] Marriage does not exist because marriage is a long-term arrangement, and long-term sexual relationships, like other such relationships, are virtually impossible to establish and maintain in Hobbes's natural condition. His individuals are purely self-interested and, therefore, will always break an agreement, or refuse to play their part in a contract, if it appears in their interest to do so. To enter into a contract or to signify agreement to do so is to leave oneself open to betrayal. Hobbes's natural state suffers from an endemic problem of keeping contracts, of 'performing second'. The only contract that can be entered into safely is one in which agreement and performance take place at the same time. No problem arises if there is a simultaneous exchange of property, including property in the person, as in a single act of coitus. If a child is born as a consequence of the act, the birth occurs a long time later, so the child belongs to the mother. A woman can contract away her right over her child to the father, but there is no reason, given women's natural equality with men, why women should always do this, especially since there is no way of establishing paternity with any certainty. In the absence of matrimonial laws, as Hobbes notes, proof of fatherhood rests on the testimony of the mother.

Hobbes's criticism of the natural basis of father-right suggests that there is only one form of political right in the state of nature: mother-right. There can, it seems, be no dominion of one adult over another because individuals of both sexes are strong enough and have wit enough to kill each other. No one has sufficient reason to enter into a contract for protection. But is this so clear? Even if marriage does not exist, are there families in the natural state? Hobbes has been seen, by Hinton for example, as a patriarchalist not an antipatriarchalist (on the question of paternal right). Hobbes's was 'the strongest patriarchalism because it was based on consent', and he took 'patriarchalism for granted and insert[ed] the act of consent'.[5] Hinton refers to Hobbes's mention of a 'patrimonial kingdom' and to some passages where Hobbes appears to fall back on the traditional patriarchal story of families growing into kingdoms ('cities and kingdoms ... are but greater families'.)[6] The criterion for a 'family-kingdom' is that the family becomes strong enough to protect itself against enemies. Hobbes writes that the family,

> If it grow by multiplication of children, either by generation, or adoption; or of servants, either by generation, conquest, or voluntary submission, to be so great and numerous, as in probability it may protect itself, then is that family called a *patrimonial kingdom*, or monarchy by acquisition, wherein the sovereignty is in one man, as it is in a monarch made by *political institution*. So that whatsoever rights be in the one, the same also be in the other.[7]

Hobbes also writes of 'an *hereditary kingdom*' which differs from a monarchy by institution – that is to say, one established by convention or contract – only in that it is 'acquired by force'.[8]

To see Hobbes as a patriarchalist is to ignore two questions: first, how have fathers gained their power in the state of nature when Hobbes has taken such pains to show that political right is mother-right? Second, why is political right in the family based on force? Certainly, Hobbes is not a patriarchalist in the same sense as Sir Robert Filmer, who claims that paternal right is natural, deriving from procreative capacity or generation, not conquest. Hobbes turns Filmer's social bonds into their opposite: Filmer saw families and kingdoms as homologous and bound together through the natural procreative power of the father; Hobbes saw families and kingdoms as homologous, but as bound together through contract (force). For Hobbes, the powers of a mother in the natural state were of exactly the same kind as those of family heads and sovereigns. Perhaps Hobbes is merely inconsistent when he introduces families into the state of nature. But since he is so ruthlessly consistent in everything else – which is why he is so instructive in a variety of ways about contract theory – this seems an odd lapse. The argument that Hobbes is a patriarchalist rests on the patriarchal view that patriarchy is paternal and familial. If we cease to read Hobbes patriarchally it becomes apparent that his patriarchalism is conjugal not paternal and that there is something very odd about Hobbes's 'family' in the natural condition.

The 'natural' characteristics with which Hobbes endows his individuals mean that long-term relationships are very unlikely in his state of nature. However, Hobbes states in *Leviathan* that in the war of all against all 'there is no man who can hope by his own strength, or wit, to defend himself from destruction, without the help of confederates'.[9] But how can such a protective confederation be formed in the natural condition when there is an acute problem of keeping agreements? The answer is that confederations are formed by conquest, and, once formed, are called 'families'. Hobbes's 'family' is very peculiar and has nothing in common with the families in Filmer's pages, the family as found in the writings of the other classic social contract theorists, or as conventionally understood today. Consider Hobbes's definition of a 'family'. In *Leviathan* he states that a family 'consists of a man and his children; or of a man and his servants; or of a man, and his children, and servants together; wherein the father or master is the sovereign'.[10] In *De Cive* we find, 'a *father* with his *sons* and *servants*, grown into a civil person by virtue of his paternal jurisdiction, is called a *family*'.[11] Only in *Elements of Law* does he write that 'the father or mother of the family is sovereign of the same'.[12] But the sovereign is very unlikely to be the mother, given Hobbes's references to 'man' and 'father' and the necessity of securing patriarchal right in civil society.

If one male individual manages to conquer another in the state of nature the conqueror will have obtained a servant. Hobbes assumes that no one would wilfully give up his life, so, with the conqueror's sword at his breast, the defeated man will make a (valid) contract to obey his victor. Hobbes defines dominion or political right acquired through force as 'the dominion of the master over his servant'.[13] Conqueror and conquered then constitute 'a little body politic, which consisteth of two persons, the one sovereign, which is called the *master*, or lord; the other subject, which is called the *servant*'.[14] Another way of putting the point is that the master and servant are a confederation against the rest, or, according to Hobbes's definition, they are a 'family'. Suppose, however, that a male individual manages to conquer a female individual. To protect her life she will enter into a contract of subjection – and so she, too, becomes the servant of a master, and a 'family' has again been formed, held together by the 'paternal jurisdiction' of the master, which is to say, his sword, now turned into contract. Hobbes's language is misleading here; the jurisdiction of the master is not 'paternal' in the case of either servant. In an earlier discussion, together with Teresa Brennan, of the disappearance of the wife and mother in Hobbes's definition of the family, we rejected the idea that her status was that of a servant.[15] I now think that we were too hasty. If a man is able to defeat a woman in the state of nature and form a little body politic or a 'family', and if that 'family' is able to defend itself and grow, the conquered woman is subsumed under the status of 'servant'. All servants are subject to the political right of the master. The master is then also master of the woman servant's children; he is master of everything that his servant owns. A master's power over all the members of his 'family' is an absolute power.

In the state of nature, free and equal individuals can become subordinates through conquest – which Hobbes calls contract. But in the state of nature there are no 'wives'. Marriage, and thus husbands and wives, appear only in civil society where the civil law includes the law of matrimony. Hobbes assumes that, in civil society, the subjection of women to men is secured through contract; not an enforced 'contract' this time, but a marriage contract. Men have no need forcibly to overpower women when the civil law upholds their patriarchal political right through the marriage contract. Hobbes states that in civil society the husband has dominion 'because for the most part commonwealths have been erected by the fathers, not by the mothers of families'.[16] Or again, 'in all cities, ... constituted of *fathers*, not *mothers*, governing their families, the domestical command belongs to the man; and such a contract, if it be made according to the civil laws, is called matrimony'.[17]

There are two implicit assumptions at work here. First, that husbands are civil masters because men ('fathers') have made the original social contract that brings civil law into being. The men who make the original pact ensure that patriarchal political right is secured in civil society. Second, there is only one way in which women, who have the same status as free and equal individuals in the state of nature as men, can be excluded from participation in the social contract. And they must be excluded if the contract is to be sealed; rational, free and equal women would not agree to a pact that subordinated women to men in civil society. The assumption must necessarily be made that, by the time the social contract is made, all the women in the natural condition have been conquered by men and are now their subjects (servants). If any men have also been subjected and are in servitude, then they, too, will be excluded from the social contract. Only men who stand to each other as free and equal masters of 'families' will take part.

A story can be constructed that is (almost) consistent with Hobbes's general assumption about individuals, to show why it might come about that men are able to conquer women in the natural condition. In order to combat and turn upside-down the argument that political right followed naturally from the father's generative powers, Hobbes had to argue that mother-right, not paternal right, existed in the natural condition and that mother-right originated in contract. So the story might run that, at first, women are able to ensure that sexual relations are consensual. When a woman becomes a mother and decides to raise her child, her position changes; she is put at a slight disadvantage against men, since now she has her infant to defend too. A man is then able to defeat the woman he had initially to treat with as an equal (so he obtains a 'family'). The problem with the story is that, logically, given Hobbes's assumption that all individuals are completely self-interested, there seems no reason why any woman (or man) would contract to become a lord over an infant. Infants would endanger the person who had right over them by giving openings to their enemies in the war of all against all. Thus, all stories of original social contracts and civil society are nonsense because the individuals in the state of nature would be the last generation. The problem of accounting for the survival of infants is part of a general problem in contractarianism... One might speculate that a thinker of Hobbes's brilliance could have been aware of a difficulty here and was thus prompted to make his remark that, in the state of nature, we should think of individuals as springing up like mushrooms, a comment that Filmer dealt with scornfully and swiftly.

Hobbes is unusual in his openness about the character and scope of political domination or political right in civil society. For Hobbes, the distinction between a civil individual or citizen and an individual in subjection to a master is not that the former is free and the latter bound; 'the subjection of them who institute a commonwealth themselves, is no less absolute, than the subjection of servants'. Rather, the difference is that those who subject themselves to Leviathan (the state) do so because they judge that there is good reason for their action, and so they live in 'a state of better hope' than servants. Their 'hope' arises from the fact that an individual 'coming in freely, calleth himself, though in subjection, a *freeman*', and in civil society free men have 'the honour of equality of favour with other subjects', and 'may expect employments of honour, rather than a servant'.[18] Or, as Hobbes puts the point in another formulation, 'free subjects and sons of a family have above servants in every government and family where servants are; that they may both undergo the more honourable offices of the city or family.'[19] In civil society, Leviathan's sword upholds the civil laws that give individuals protection from forcible subjection, but individuals of their own volition can enter into contracts that constitute 'masters' and 'servants'. Or, more accurately, male individuals can.

In the natural state all women become servants, and all women are excluded from the original pact. That is to say, all women are also excluded from becoming civil individuals. No woman is a free subject. All are 'servants' of a peculiar kind in civil society, namely 'wives'. To be sure, women become wives by entering into a contract, and after I shall explore the puzzle of why beings who lack the status of (civil) individuals who can make contracts none the less are required to enter into the marriage contract. The relationship between a husband and wife differs from subjection between men, but it is important to emphasize that Hobbes insists that patriarchal subjection is also an example of *political* right. He stands alone in this. The other classic contract theorists all argue that conjugal right is not, or is not fully, political.

Notes

From Pateman, Carole (1988) *The Sexual Contract*, Polity Press, pp.44–50.

[1] Hobbes, *Leviathan*, in *The English Works of Thomas Hobbes of Malmesbury* (hereafter EW (Germany, Scientia Verlag Aalen, 1966), vol. III, Chapter XX, p.186.

[2] Ibid., Chapter IX, p.116.

[3] Hobbes, *Leviathan*, Chapter XX, p.188.

[4] Ibid., p.187.

[5] R.W.K. Hinton (1968) 'Husbands, Fathers and Conquerors', *Political Studies*, XVI, 1, pp.62, 57.

[6] Hobbes, *Leviathan*, Chapter XVII, p.154

[7] Hobbes, *De Corpore Politico*, or *The Elements of Law*, EW, vol. IV, Chapter IV, pp.158–9.

[8] Hobbes, *Philosophical Rudiments*, Chapter IX, p.122.

[9] Hobbes, *Leviathan*, Chapter XV, p.133.

[10] Ibid., Chapter XX, p.191.

[11] Hobbes, *Philosophical Rudiments*, Chapter IX, p.121.

[12] Hobbes, *De Corpore Politico*, Chapter IV, p.158.

[13] Hobbes, *Leviathan*, Chapter XX, p.189.

[14] Hobbes, *De Corpore Politico*, Chapter III, pp.149–50.

[15] T. Brennan and C. Pateman (1979), '"Mere Auxiliaries to the Common-wealth": Women and the Origins of Liberalism', *Political Studies*, XXVII, 2, pp.189–90. I was prompted to look at this again by J. Zvesper (1985), 'Hobbes' Individualistic Analysis of the Family', *Politics* (UK), 5, 2, pp.28–33; Zvesper, though, sees Hobbes's 'family' in the state of nature as like a 'family' in civil society, despite the absence of 'matrimonial laws'.

[16] Hobbes, *Leviathan*, Chapter XV, p.187.

[17] Hobbes, *Philosophical Rudiments*, Chapter IX, p.118.

[18] Hobbes, *De Corpore Politico*, Chapter IV, pp.157–58.

[19] Hobbes, *Philosophical Rudiments*, Chapter IX, p.121.

CHAPTER 3

John Locke: *Second Treatise of Government*

Jon Pike

By the end of this chapter you should:
- Have read Locke's *Second Treatise of Government* and studied the most important sections in detail.
- Have a good understanding of Locke's political theory.
- Be able to offer some criticism of that theory.
- Have continued and entrenched the discussion of the sources of rightful political authority.
- Be aware of some contemporary interpretations of Locke and of his continuing relevance to political philosophy.
- Have further developed your reading skills.

Introduction

Locke is widely held to be one of the founders of modern liberalism, and his *Second Treatise of Government*, with its clear advocacy of limited government, is one of liberalism's founding documents. There are echoes of the language of the *Second Treatise* in the Constitution of the United States and in the United Nations Universal Declaration of Human Rights. However, the *Second Treatise* was not written in order to 'found liberalism' but to make a contribution to a political debate in England about the limits of a legitimate sovereign.

For some time it was thought that the *Second Treatise* was a *post hoc* justification of the 'Glorious Revolution' of 1688 which deposed James II and put William of Orange on the British throne. But most historians believe that both the first and second treatises were composed between the years 1679 and 1682, and published later in the more favourable political climate after the Glorious Revolution.

The *Two Treatises of Government* were written at a time when Locke's political patron, Anthony Ashley Cooper, Earl of Shaftesbury, and probably Locke himself, were heavily involved in revolutionary politics. Shaftesbury was a leading figure in the Whig attempt to push through an Exclusion Bill (1680) which would prevent Charles II's Roman Catholic brother James from inheriting the throne. For the Whig opponents of James, Catholicism was indissolubly tied to absolutism on the French model. Recent scholarship has shown how far Locke's work reflects the revolutionary pamphlets of the time, and suggests that he was providing 'a political declaration for the revolutionary movement of the 1680s' (Ashcraft (1986), p.576, note 223).

But the revolutionary movement failed, at least in the short term. The exclusion Bill was not enacted and both Shaftesbury and Locke fled to Holland. Their co-thinker, Algernon Sydney was less fortunate, and was executed for writing an attack on the Stuart monarchy. Writing the *Two Treatises* in this period was not just a theoretical exercise, but an intervention in a dangerous political struggle.

In 1688, James II was deposed in the 'Glorious Revolution' and Locke was able to return, and to publish the *Two Treatises*. None the less, he denied their authorship until he was on his deathbed. Because he was on the winning side in 1688, Locke was able to become an establishment figure under the new regime. But this should not blind us to the very real risks he took in writing the *Two Treatises*.

Reading Locke on government

The *First Treatise* is of less importance today than the second; essentially, it clears the decks for the constructive programme of the *Second Treatise*. The *First Treatise* contains Locke's attempted demolition of rival theories to his own, particularly the theory of patriarchal power contained in Sir Robert Filmer's *Patriarcha* (1680).

Before discussing the *Second Treatise* I should point out two problematic aspects of the work. First, there appears to be a striking parallel between the *Second Treatise* and Hobbes's political theory in *Leviathan*. Both Hobbes and Locke use the same political vocabulary. They both discuss the state of nature, the idea of a social contract, and the notion of laws of nature which have moral force. But beware of this similarity. During this chapter I will point out some of the ways in which each author uses these terms in quite different ways. For example, Locke's 'state of nature' clearly has a moral dimension that Hobbes's does not, and his understanding of the relationship between the subjects and the sovereign is very different to that of Hobbes. While both develop propositions about the state from propositions about individuals, it is important to contrast Hobbes's *methodological* individualism (see Chapter 2, p.71 above) with Locke's *moral* individualism.

Another problematic aspect of Locke's *Second Treatise* is the difficulty involved in reading his very long sentences. Locke is a careful and rigorous writer whose theory does not reduce to a set of slogans. He introduces qualifications and supporting arguments to ensure that the reader fully grasps his precise point. He avoids the sort of grammatical construction to be found in party-political discourse nowadays, where rigour and precision of content is often sacrificed to simplicity of form. Locke makes no such sacrifice, so his sentences can be intimidating.

The *Second Treatise of Government* is short enough to read through in two or three sittings. And I recommend that you do this because the structure of the *Second Treatise* is not as clear as Hobbes's *Leviathan*. This should help to get a feel of the whole text before studying specific sections. Fortunately, the nineteen chapters of the *Second Treatise* are structured in short, bite-sized, numbered sections, to which I will refer as I go along.

ACTIVITY

Read completely through Locke's *Second Treatise on Government*.

Locke on the state of nature

A useful way of approaching Locke's political philosophy is to consider what his targets are, namely, the alternative theories of political obligation which he found in Sir Robert Filmer (c.1590–1653) and which he attacked in the *First Treatise of Government*. The first theory is the 'divine right of kings', according to which, kings get their power directly from God, and it is because they have been chosen to be kings by God that we ought to obey them. The second is the theory of patriarchal authority, which holds that political power derives from the power fathers have over their children. The important point to notice is not how strange these theories seem, but that in both these cases, specifically *political* authority comes from another, *non-political*, source: in the first case from God and in the second from fathers. Political authority is not a separate kind of authority but a derivative one.

The derivative nature of political authority is common ground between Locke and Filmer. But whereas for Filmer, political authority is a form of natural authority extended into the political realm, for Locke, political authority is not natural but conventional. He illustrates the twists and turns taken by the theory of patriarchal power in the *First Treatise*. It is in that treatise that Locke believes that he has disposed of the 'divine right of kings argument' and the 'patriarchal power argument'. He is working by a process of elimination. It is clear then that he either has to come up with another theory to replace these or accept, as he says in §1 'that men live together by no other rules but that of beasts'. So Locke's programme is first destructive and then constructive.

To get the alternative theory of political authority going, Locke needs to show that the state of nature – and the entire absence of political authority – is not a viable option. He needs to identify, then, what we owe to political structures, and what it is that precedes them.

ACTIVITY

Read the Preface and Chapters I–III (§§1–21) and then answer the following questions.

1   What is Locke's state of nature?

2   How does Locke's state of nature differ from the account offered by Hobbes?

3   What, according to Locke, is the difference between the state of nature and the state of war?

DISCUSSION

1   For Locke, the state of nature is a pre-political condition in which all humankind is equal and independent but governed by the law of nature which is disclosed to them by God-given reason.

> 2   Locke's state of nature has much more *moral content* to it, in contrast to the picture painted by Hobbes, which was, morally speaking, quite bare. This is because Hobbes's main objective was to work out how we would *behave* in the state of nature, whereas Locke wants to show what rights and obligations we have in the state of nature.

Section 6 gives us the clearest account of this.

1   There is a prohibition on destroying oneself.

2   All are equal and independent.

3   No one ought to harm another in his life, health, liberty or possessions, unless it is in order to do justice to an offender, by taking away the other's life, liberty, health, limb, or goods.

4   Everyone is bound to preserve himself and also to preserve the rest of mankind.

It is important to notice, too, that these obligations on each of us have corresponding rights. If a person is bound not to harm another, it makes sense to think that he has a right not to be harmed by another.

Later on, Locke modifies these principles and introduces further ones. For example, in §12 Locke gives a consequentialist account of punishment; and there is another moral principle introduced in §16: 'when all cannot be preserved, the safety of the innocent is to be preferred'. So overall Locke's state of nature has a good deal of moral content.

I suggest you think of Locke's individuals in the state of nature as ones with moral boundaries already in place, which determines their rights and their legitimate moral powers. These particular rights are not constructions of an organized society, or a matter of convention, but exist before conventions are created. For this reason they are called *natural* rights. The idea that individuals have rights prior to the construction of political society is an extremely important one for contemporary debates about *human* rights. One of the central arguments in such debates is that recognition of human rights is recognition of something more 'basic' than those created by the particular laws passed by individual nation states. This is one reason why *international* declarations of human rights are thought to be particularly important. Their property of being international corresponds very roughly to Locke's notion that these rights are natural. Both the property of being international and of being natural appeal to the 'objectivity' of rights, beyond the conventions of particular states. As such, human rights are morally prior to such particular laws. This is because someone possesses human rights just because he is human, whether or not these rights are recognized by a particular state. A person's moral status as a human is more basic than his status as a citizen of any particular nation state. So nation states can be justly condemned if they infringe such rights.

One of these natural rights is called by Locke, rather confusingly, a power. It is the executive power of the law of nature: that is, the right to punish offenders against the law of nature. This right exist because the preservation of mankind is threatened by the actions of those who offend against the law of nature. So the right to punish is derived from a principle that is the moral 'bottom line' for Lockean individuals: the duty to preserve mankind. The derivation requires the principle that if I have a duty to do X, I have a right to do what is necessary in order to do X (as you have seen in Reading 1.4, 'Dirty Hands', this is a contentious principle).

There are no close parallels to the executive power of the law of nature. It is somewhat similar to the common notion of making a citizen's arrest, though the executive power of the law of nature goes beyond this in that it includes the power to punish as well as the power to arrest. The right includes the right to punish a crime against the law of nature, and the right to take reparation. Locke lays out a plausible case for the relations between these rights (§§8–11). Now this sounds as if the executive power of the law of nature is something like a right to take the law into your own hands; but this would misrepresent Locke's view because the individual who exercises the executive power of the law of nature in the state of nature does not *take* the law from anywhere else: the law *starts* with this right. That is, there is a foundational role for natural justice in Locke's theory. Moreover, the justice has its source in self-governing individuals, historically as well as theoretically: Locke's model was probably the accusatory system of justice which existed in Europe in the twelfth and thirteenth centuries. Under this system charges were made by private individuals rather than state functionaries, and the courts were a much more ad hoc affair then than they later became (Tully (1993), pp.21–3).

Where do natural rights and duties come from? A common objection to theories of rights is that they assume the existence of the very things that they theorize. But Locke's account is not open to the objection of circularity. He makes it clear in §6 that God is the source of the rights and duties that we have in the state of nature. God creates us and puts us on the earth, and we are therefore 'his property'. This has been called the 'workmanship model' (Tully, 1980) of rights and obligations. According to this model, the creator of a thing has rights over it, and the moral relationship between the creator and the created thing derives from the 'workmanship' of the creator. The same model is used by Locke to explain both the relationship between God and human beings and the relationship between human beings and the objects on which they labour. Since we are God's property, we are obliged not to commit suicide – or, as Locke puts it, 'to quit our station wilfully'. Suicide is presumptuous: it is for God, not his creations, to decide when their time on earth has come to an end. But if I am not permitted to kill myself, because my life is owed to God, then I am not permitted to kill others whose lives, likewise, are owed to God. Moreover, Locke says, I am positively obliged to preserve the rest of mankind.

At the foundation of Locke's account is a profoundly theological conception of humankind. Because this conception that is not widely held today, it creates a problem for our reception of Locke. His political positions – on liberalism, human rights, the right to oust an oppressive regime, the politics of consent and so on – are now the dominant ones of the day, but his theoretical underpinning of that position is not. Whether a secular account of a Lockean political philosophy can be produced is very much in question. [1]

Justice starts with, and is derived from, the rights of the individual in the state of nature. But what then is the status of these rights and powers? It is clear that they are specified by the Law of Nature. This key notion is one that we encountered in Hobbes's *Leviathan* (Chapter 2, pp.85–7 above). In §12 Locke claims that the Law of

Nature is more easily recognized than positive law. Positive law – the actually codified and written down law of a particular country – is 'right' insofar as it is grounded on natural law. Locke is critical of the 'fancies and intricate contrivances of men' who express their own, partial, interests in 'the municipal laws of countries'. The idea that natural law trumps or overcomes positive law is going to be crucial for Locke's justification of our rights to oust a government. (Think of those who resisted the anti-Jewish laws in Hitler's Germany. They might have said about those laws: 'They may well be laws, but they are not right! They offend against natural justice!')

Locke's account of the state of nature provides the basis for the two important claims in the *Second Treatise*. It provides the backdrop for his opposition to absolutism. A consistent claim of Locke's is that the absolutist monarch is in a relationship with his subjects that is not *morally* different from the relationship between individuals in the state of nature and, in fact, in §13 he suggests that there are practical reasons for preferring the state of nature to absolutism. It also contains the moral apparatus – in contrast to Hobbes – required to establish exclusive property rights (see pp.153–7 below).

In §19 Locke makes a clear distinction between the state of nature and the state of war and there seems a fairly clear allusion to Hobbes and Hobbesians ('which however some men have confused'). The key difference between Locke and Hobbes is this: if individuals in the state of nature behave rationally – that is, according to the law of nature – then it will be a state of peace. But unfortunately they do not behave rationally and the state of peace falls apart. For Hobbes the state of war was not a product of irrational action, but of rational, pre-emptive behaviour.

On Locke's account, irrational people, who harm others for their own gain or fail to get the proportions right when they use the executive power of the law of nature, resort to force contrary to the law of nature. And it is the use of force contrary to the law of nature that transforms the state of nature into the state of war. None the less, for Locke, that use of force, though it might be likely, is not inevitable. However, he is perhaps ambivalent in his account of the state of war, and it is easy to see why. He is pulled towards giving an optimistic account of life in the state of nature, by the need to defend only limited, not absolute government. But he is also pulled towards a pessimistic account, because if the picture is too rosy, then there is no incentive to leave the state of nature.

For Locke then, we are faced with a series of 'inconveniences' in the state of nature. He specifies these later in the *Second Treatise*, §§124– 6. I have skipped a large section of the *Second Treatise* to get to the 'inconveniences' of the state of nature. This is because Locke's structure is not always as logical as it could be.

ACTIVITY

Read §§124–6, and do the following exercise. How do the three 'inconveniences' of the state of nature suggest a structure of government to resolve them?

DISCUSSION

The 'inconveniences' match up to the standard three-way division of the functions of government into legislative, judicial and executive branches. [2] Locke justifies the three branches in a particularly neat manner.

I have shown that Locke's account of the state of nature differs in important ways from the Hobbesian model. But which of these differences is most important? Iain Hampsher-Monk offers a useful guideline:

> whilst tempting, it is most misleading to think of Locke's state of nature in the same terms as Hobbes's: to suggest for example that the essential difference between the two thinkers lies simply in the degree of unpleasantness to be found in their respective states of nature, and to argue that Hobbes disallows rebellion whilst Locke can defend both it and limited government simply because the more pleasant state of nature makes the consequences of a return to it less disastrous. To think in this way is to miss most of the importance of Locke, for it is to miss the essentially moral status of Locke's conception of natural man and of the state of nature.'

> (Hampsher-Monk (1992), p.84)

So the key distinction is one of moral status: Hobbes and Locke use their conceptions of the state of nature to do different sorts of things, and to play a different role in the account of political authority: it is not just a matter of the degree of unpleasantness that one finds in the alternative pictures. I have summarized the distinctive positions in the table below. However, please handle the summary with care: it is an unambiguous abstraction from quite layered and ambiguous texts. (For example, there is *some* discussion of morality in Hobbes's state of nature, and Locke does make *some* claims about behaviour.)

Hobbes and Locke on the state of nature

	Hobbes	**Locke**
Principal message	Anarchic tendencies of humankind, and the consequent precariousness of political institutions	Pre-political, moral foundations of politics
Theoretical status	Behavioural: tells us how we would behave	Moral: tells us what rights and duties we would have
State of nature vis-à-vis state of war	These are identical	These are opposites (though Locke is equivocal)
Rights/obligations in the state of nature	The right of nature: no duties not to do X	Specified natural rights
Natural law in the state of nature	Binds only *in foro interno*, not *in foro externo*	Binds, and is accompanied by, 'executive power'

The beginnings of political societies

How does Locke move on from his hypothesis about the state of nature to a consideration of government? His account here is justly famous, and has been the target of much criticism.

ACTIVITY

Read Locke's *Second Treatise*, §§87–131 (from Chapters VII–IX) and answer the following questions.

1 What is Locke's central objection to absolutism (§§90–3)?
2 What are the two objections that Locke foresees and tries to reply to?

DISCUSSION

1 Locke wants to deny (§93) that 'men are so foolish that they take care to avoid what mischiefs may be done them by pole-cats, or foxes; but are content, nay, think it safety, to be devoured by lions'. Locke's case is that it is not rational to hand all one's power over to one individual if what one fears most is the misuse of power against oneself. This argument probably sounds plausible to us, because we have recent memories of the use of power against individual citizens and who understand, from recent examples of totalitarian states such as Hitler's Germany or the Soviet Union, the concerns about an authoritarian state. The case would seem less plausible to mid-seventeenth-century writers who understood, from their own contemporary examples, the dangers of anarchy. Such an argument would identify a central flaw in Hobbes's account and it does seem likely that the sections here were directed specifically against the theory of *Leviathan* (Chapter XVIII). Hobbes fails to show why being ruled by an absolute sovereign would be, either in fact or morally speaking, preferable to being in the state of nature. So he fails to provide reasons for us quitting the state of nature for something that, according to Locke might be even worse.

2 The first objection to Locke's account is that the contracts to set up government never actually took place. The second objection is that, because we are all born under government, there are no free individuals around to enter into these contracts.

ACTIVITY

Sections 95–9 contain Locke's statement of the original contract. Read these and answer the questions below.

1 Locke emphasizes the 'bareness' – the simplicity and transparency – of the original contract. Is he right to do so?
2 Does the contract create the government?

DISCUSSION

1 No. The apparently simple contract involves a number of implicit commitments.

> **2   No. The contract forms a community which then entrusts the government with power.**

As for Hobbes, the individuals who become subjects contract not with the sovereign but with each other. Locke says that in so doing they form a community. This community goes on to entrust the government with power.

Locke is somewhat misleading about the simplicity of the contract. It is true that Locke says that 'barely agreeing to unite into one political society ... is all the compact that is, or needs be, between the individuals, that ... make up a commonwealth' (§99). But the previous sentence contains an important principle: 'Whosoever therefore out of a state of nature unite into a community, must be understood to give up all the power, necessary to the ends for which they unite into society to the majority of the community'. The thought behind this principle is: if I will a particular end, and a certain means is necessary to that end, it can reasonably be taken that I will the means to that end. If I make a contract, it can be reasonably expected that I agree to whatever is foreseeably necessary to fulfil the contract.

Suppose I promise to collect my partner from her office at five o'clock. But when five o'clock arrives, I fail to appear. Eventually she telephones me, and I explain that, while I promised to collect her from her office, I later decided that I didn't want to drive today. Having made this decision, I couldn't collect her. Her response would be something like this: 'That's absurd; you know that driving is a necessary part of collecting me from the office. So when you promised that, the promise entailed an implicit commitment to driving the car, and you can't back out of the implicit commitment and still pretend that you made the promise. It isn't just that you're fickle and unreliable; you can't have meant it when you said you would promise to collect me in the first place.' And she would be right.

Locke is making a similar sort of point. If I agree to A, but B, C, and D are a set of foreseeable and necessary conditions for A, then when I agree to A it can be taken that I agree to B, C, and D. For Locke, agreeing to unite into one political society is not an act bare and simple but carries with it many implicit commitments: for example, giving up the executive power of the law of nature and agreeing that the community be directed by the will of the majority (or the will of more than a simple majority, if that is what is agreed).

So, underpinning Locke's view is a specific criterion of rationality. That is, a rational person who has a particular end, is someone who agrees to, or does, what can be foreseen as necessary for attaining that end, and rejects measures which thwart that end. Locke thinks that with this criterion of rationality and some claims about what conditions necessarily accompany what goals, he can establish a contract that carries with it substantial commitments.

Finally, what does the contract establish? It brings about the community which decides, by majority agreement, the preferred form of the state. The power that is held by the community is now entrusted under certain conditions to the government. It is important to see exactly what the two-stage nature of this process is. In stage one, individuals consent to unite into one political society. This carries with it an implicit, and simultaneous, commitment to the majority choice of governmental system. It is a mistake to see the contract to unite into one community and the controlling of that community by majority consent as a separate stages: it is only one stage.

The second stage is the one in which the community entrusts its power to a government, sometimes called the 'entrustment stage'. §136 states it particularly clearly: 'men give up all their natural power to the society which they enter into, and the community put the legislative power into such hands as they think fit, with this trust, that they shall be governed by declared laws, or else their peace, quiet, and property will still be at the same uncertainty, as it was in the state of nature'.

Criticisms of Locke on the original contract

The first objection: the status of the original contract

The classical expression of the criticism of Locke on the hypothetical contract was articulated by the Scottish philosopher David Hume (1711–76) in his essay 'Of the Original Contract', published in 1748.

ACTIVITY

Read Locke's *Second Treatise*, §§100–12, followed by Reading 3.1, Hume's 'Of the Original Contract', part 1. Then answer the four questions below.

1   What is Hume's objection to Locke's account?
2   What is Locke's reply to an earlier form of this objection?
3   Who do you think wins this particular dispute?
4   What could the loser do to strengthen his position?

DISCUSSION

1   There is no historical record to support Locke's account.
2   Governments are antecedent to records.
3   I think Hume wins on the historical point.
4   Locke could say that the historical account is not the main point; what is important is how societies ought to be formed.

Hume's central point is that, as a matter of fact, political obligation doesn't come about in the way that Locke suggests that it does. In fact, it is a much less consensual and much more coercive story than Locke suggests. Historically, although, there might have been an original contract ages ago, this was never formal, and certainly it is not the main source of political authority now. Instead, political authority is much more a matter of acquiescence in the rule of those who have achieved their position, often by conquest. This acquiescence arises from a process by which people become accustomed to a certain form of rule, and so eventually learn to go along with it.

Locke, in his historical account, wants to insist that there is a consensual historical root to political obligation, although in §112 he concedes that his understanding is only probable. He places a lot of emphasis on explanations for there being so few records of the supposed contract.

On the factual question – the actual existence of a series of contracts, which establish legitimate governments – Locke surely has to concede Hume's point. Locke's arguments certainly do not do all he wants them to do, in this respect, and we have seen that he recognizes that they are not watertight. But there's another answer to the question of who wins this exchange, that is, no one does, because Locke and Hume are not talking about the same thing. While Hume is giving an account of how governments actually come into being, and gain the acquiescence of their subjects, Locke is talking about something else altogether. He is concerned with the *rightful* origin of government, not with how it actually happens. So Hume is providing a broadly *descriptive* account, telling an historical story. It is really a piece of political sociology, whereas Locke's account is *normative* or *prescriptive*. It is about what ought to happen if we want to set up a legitimate government with authority over us. So the two philosophers are aiming at different targets and therefore neither really lands any telling blows.

This answer is adequate up to a point but it needs pursuing. First it doesn't seem likely that this is how Locke understood what he was doing. In the passage you have just read, he does try to give some historical support for his argument. He does try to tell a descriptive story. What is more, he does believe that most governments are legitimate. But Locke wouldn't be the first philosopher to have misunderstood the implications of his own theory. If so, then there are two directions we can take to construct a Lockean (but not Locke's) theory.

First, a Lockean could say 'it's true that no actual contracts were made; but my theory is not interested in a descriptive claim. I can "bite the bullet" and say that these governments which were not established by contract just are not legitimate. It's just the case that very few, if any, governments are legitimate'.

Secondly, a Lockean could defend governmental legitimacy on a different basis, by suggesting that the theory is not an account of a *process* by which governments become legitimate, but an account of the *criteria* by which we judge whether a government is legitimate or not. It is necessary and sufficient for a government to be legitimate that it *would* command our consent *if* we were to be asked. In other words, the consent that we owe to the government stems from a hypothetical contract and not an actual one. The notion of 'hypothetical contract' is a very fertile notion and it has been central in the revival of liberal political philosophy in the second half of the twentieth century, especially in the work of John Rawls (Rawls (1971) and (1993)).

However, it is difficult to read §§100–12 and suggest that this second Lockean construction is what Locke actually intended. But it is a useful way of advancing a Lockean theory while remaining sensitive to the way that Hume's critique seems somehow to miss the point.

The second objection: tacit consent

ACTIVITY

Read Locke's *Second Treatise*, §§113–22 and try to extract Locke's argument for political obligation.

Locke's argument for political obligation says that members of a community ought to obey the government because they have consented to it.

The argument goes like this. In the beginning, political power belongs to each individual separately. The members of the community are owners and masters of themselves individually and each is equal in this respect to all others. The power of governments then can only come from the individuals who possess the power in the first place. We say something like 'I give you permission to tell me what to do, and what not to do'.

On Locke's account it is absolutely crucial that the institution that makes the laws has our consent. One aspect that political philosophers often want to emphasize about this account is its *voluntarism*. A theory of political obligation is a sort of voluntarism if it involves the voluntary handing over or loan of power from a subject to a sovereign, rather than the seizure of power.

This all sounds plausible. It suggests an answer to the question 'Why should I obey the law?' that goes like this: 'You should obey the law because you agreed to. By your own consent you handed over the power of governing yourself to the state.' In order to get a full theory it is necessary to supplement the theory with a series of reasons about why I would hand over this power. For Locke, as we have seen, these are reasons to do with the 'incommodious' (unpleasant) quality of the state of nature. But the significant emphasis remains on the voluntary nature of political power. Political power is held by the state, the police and so on *with my consent*, and because of that I should obey them.

Voluntarism under strain: the anarchist objection

There is an obvious objection to the voluntarist account. The anarchist, or anyone else who wants to, can say 'I never did consent! No one asked me, and if they had asked me, I would have said "no". As it is, now that you have explained why I ought to obey the law, I want to withdraw my consent.'

The anarchist raises the following problem for Locke's theory: it is too easy for individuals to evade political authority, since they can do so by withholding any expression of allegiance. What you would end up with is a situation in which some citizens would be under an obligation to obey the law since they had given their assent to the state and others would not be under such an obligation. But that would be an absurd way to establish a state. What we require is a universal source of political obligation, one that applies to everyone. This demand for explicit consent looks like a dead end, and Locke amends his theory to take account of this problem.

ACTIVITY

Read Locke's *Second Treatise*, §§119–22.

The thought Locke expresses is something like the rhetorical charge hurled at left-wing demonstrators in Britain and America during the Cold War: such protesters were told that they should 'Go back to Russia'. A charitable reconstruction of that thought would be 'If you don't like the government you live under, or its policies, you can leave. If you chose not to leave, it can be taken as a sign that you do accept that government. So it is contradictory for you to complain about that government or its policies.' Today someone might employ a slightly different form of the same argument, and say that when you vote or when you accept state benefits you consent to the state and so incur obligations to it. Locke's argument is that when you do a certain thing or series of things you in fact consent to have obligations placed upon you. *Express* consent is given by saying, for example, 'I agree to obey the government'. *Tacit* consent is given when I take some action which in some way entails, or is equivalent to, saying 'I agree to obey the government'. In particular, Locke thinks that by quietly enjoying the protection of the state you give it your tacit consent.

Tacit consent is not the same as another notion – a derivation of political obligation that looks at first quite similar – that we should obey the government because it is *fair* to do so. In the case of tacit consent, the putative subject of the government acts such that the act entails or is equivalent to consent to the government. On the fairness account, something received by the putative subject entails that he owes obedience to the government. There is no intermediate step where doing something is held to entail consent. So, on the fairness account, one might want to suggest that receipt of state benefits places you under an obligation to obey the government because it would be fair to do so. But one need not say that consent was given at the same time as the benefits were received. On the tacit consent account, a disobedient individual is doing something contradictory, whereas on a fairness account a disobedient individual is ungrateful.

In summary, consent can be given either *actually*, or *hypothetically*. If given actually, it can be given *explicitly* (expressly) or *tacitly*. Then there's another basis of obligation: from *fairness*, which doesn't depend on consent at all.

ACTIVITY

The political philosopher Jean Hampton is sympathetic to the aim of developing a contract theory of government, but perceives serious problems if it is grounded on tacit or hypothetical consent.

Read Hampton's 'Do People Actually Consent to Political Authority?' (Reading 3.2), and then, bearing this in mind along with my account of fairness, look at the following accounts of an individual's supposed obligation to obey the law. In each case identify the best explanation of the source of the supposed obligation.

1   Tom moves from Britain to Los Angeles and eventually becomes a naturalized citizen of the United States. What best characterizes the source of the obligation he has to obey the law?

2   Gerry receives state benefits and uses the NHS. Sam says "Gerry, you clearly go along with the government in accepting these things, so you ought not to break the law". What is the basis of Sam's idea of obligation?

3   In the pub, Sally and Anne each get a round of drinks; then it is my turn. What is the basis of my obligation to buy a round?

4   John wonders whether he should obey a particular law. He imagines a community of rational citizens, who know nothing of their own life situations, and decides whether they would make such a law. If they would, he concludes, then he is under an obligation to obey it. What is the source of this obligation?

   Express consent

   Tacit consent

   Hypothetical consent

   Fairness

   Not decidable

DISCUSSION

1   Express consent: naturalized citizens explicitly swear allegiance to the flag, government and constitution of the USA.

2   Tacit consent: the claim is that Gerry goes along with – consents to – the government, by doing something else (accepting welfare benefit and health care). (Someone might say that Gerry is also obliged by a fairness principle, but that is not what Sam's claim involves.)

3   Undecidable. The most plausible answer, I think, is that I owe Sally and Anne a drink from fairness, but it could be argued that I had tacitly agreed to the convention of round buying, and hence to buy my round, by accepting the first two drinks.

4   This is a form of hypothetical consent. My consent, given *if* a certain set of arrangements were in place, is translated across into an obligation to obey the law now.

The avoidability of tacit consent

The notion of tacit consent relies on the relationship between two things: the giving of consent and the act that stands silently in its place. If this action is to stand in for express consent, then it must have the same morally relevant properties as express consent. What then are those properties? What is it that we actually do when we consent to something, and under what circumstances would it be wrong to say we consent? The logical content of Hume's objection is that the action that Locke has in mind does not have the same morally relevant properties as consent.

ACTIVITY

Read part 2 of Hume's 'Of the Original Contract' (Reading 3.1).

Try to reconstruct Hume's objection to the Lockean account of tacit consent in your own words?

DISCUSSION

It is very hard to leave one's country (i.e. to avoid doing that which is said to constitute tacit consent).

If it is very hard to avoid doing that which is said to constitute tacit consent, then the consent is not free.

Consent must be free if it is to be binding.

You might have said that Hume's objection was that consent was forced, whereas it needed to be freely given. This would not be quite correct, as the answer would be too black and white. Rather than seeing 'being forced' and 'being free' as two categories into which we can divide human actions, it is often better to see them as poles on a scale, and to situate human action on that scale according to the alternatives available to the agent at the time. Coercion, then, is a matter of degree, and that is made clear by talking about an option being very hard to take. Locke was sure, and argues in §189, that 'he has no lawfull authority, whilst force, and not choice, compels them to submission'. So, if he was being consistent, he cannot have thought that the equating of tacit consent with residence was a mater of forcing consent out of an individual.

The background fairness objection

So Hume's objection is about the difficulty of taking certain alternative courses of action, which means that tacit consent is not fully free. And, though Hume himself did not do so, his point can be extended to encompass concerns over the wide social and economic disparity that exists between individuals, which weakens their ability to give straightforward consent. The thought here is captured in the claim that we are all free to dine at the Ritz. Of course, for some of us, dining at the Ritz may be an everyday activity, for others it may be a once-in-a-lifetime extravagance, and for others, it is never going to happen. But, still, since there are no racial or sex bans, or other formal restrictions, we are all free to dine! Of course, what is suggested by the example is that the freedom that we all have to dine is only formal and not substantial, since it is restricted by economic inequality.

And what is true of my ability to dine at the Ritz is also true of my ability to enter into a wide series of agreements. I may be formally free to enter into them, but background conditions of social and economic inequality mean that freedom is not real. Some of the best philosophers in the social contract tradition have accepted this, and stipulated a background justice condition which needs to be satisfied if consent is to be freely given. John Rawls puts it like this:

> we need an account of when agreements are free and the social circumstances under which they are reached are fair ... The role of the institutions that belong to the basic structure is to secure just background conditions against which the actions of individuals and associations take place. Unless this structure is appropriately regulated and adjusted, an initially just social process will eventually cease to be just, however free and fair particular transactions may look when viewed by themselves.

(Rawls (1993), p.266)

So unless the background institutions are in place that secure the conditions for free agreement, Locke's voluntarism doesn't merit its name.

The intention qualification

According to Locke's account, 'barely walking down the King's highway' is enough to generate tacit consent. But this seems odd. I certainly do not think of myself as consenting to anything when I walk down the road. And one would normally want to say that if I am taken to be promising to do something, I should at least understand, and perhaps intend, that my actions can be taken that way. The idea that I make a promise without intending to promise is incoherent. But for Locke, acts that I neither understand nor intend as giving consent can properly be taken that way. If we accept this view of how I can place myself under an obligation, then Locke has certainly managed to rescue his theory of obligation from the anarchist objection. The anarchist may say that she never consented, but the Lockean has an answer: you consented every time you walked down the road to go to the shops. But this answer is only achieved at considerable cost. If we accept this account of consent, we lose all that was attractive about Locke's voluntarism in the first place. If I tacitly consent, when I neither understand that I consent, intend to consent, nor can easily avoid consent, then Locke's notion of consent is a very weak one indeed.

It looks as if Locke's notion of tacit consent is in a bad way, and many contemporary philosophers agree that there is no sound core to the idea of consenting tacitly. Either consent is a form of express consent, though given in a rather odd way (as, for example, when the chairman of a board-meeting asks the members of a committee whether there are any objections to meeting at the same time next week: here, not raising objections is a way of consenting, but, arguably, it is a way of expressing consent by not saying anything; and the 'not saying anything' is an explicit response to an actual question) or it is not a form of consent at all.

But even if the details of Locke's consent argument are liable to unravel, this should not blind us to its initial plausibility: the notion that it is up to me to decide how I am governed remains an attractive one even though Locke may not have shown clearly how we *give* our consent, for a Lockean could argue none the less that when we *withdraw* our consent, governments lose their legitimacy. In other words, the consent-based account of political obligation can help us to see that governments can lose their right to govern. It is this possibility that makes the *Second Treatise of Government* a revolutionary tract.

The right to oust an oppressive government

It is a crucial claim of Locke's *Second Treatise* that the people have the right to disobey and to oust from power an oppressive government. This is perhaps his most enduring political legacy, albeit based on an unsystematic discussion that runs throughout the second half of the treatise.

ACTIVITY

Read from Chapter XII to the end of the *Second Treatise* paying particular attention to §§135, 149, 160, 202, 212, 221, 226–8, while considering the following question.

Some of Locke's contemporaries saw Locke as advocating a right to rebel. Why would they be wrong?

DISCUSSION

They would be wrong because, for Locke, the word 'rebellion' clearly has a negative import, since it is a matter of going against the natural or reasonable order of things. But it is the oppressive government, not the people, who go against the natural order of things.

What is distinctive about his position is the account he gives of the natural or reasonable order, in which whatever powers a government has derives from the people. This differs radically from those who saw patriarchal forms of power as the model for the state. In §135, Locke makes it clear that the law of nature governs legislators as well as individual members of the community. Because the law of nature is the will of God 'no human sanction can be good or valid against it'. It is unfortunately quite easy to identify concrete and recent examples of this same situation. The Holocaust, and other state-backed genocidal practices during the twentieth century are clear cases in which regimes have acted against the law of nature.

Locke's reasonable case is that the infringement of that law of nature dissolves a person's ties of obedience to the government. But it is not just in the case of clear infringements of natural law that governments can lose the trust of the people; it is lost if they fail to fulfil their purpose of furthering the common good. Locke's argument that government is limited to the furtherance of the common good is most clearly outlined in §131, where it is presented as the outcome of an argument about what rational people would do. Since 'no rational creature can be supposed to change his condition with an intention to be worse', then a rational creature who undertakes to be governed does so with the intention that their position be improved. Invoking this principle of rationality, Locke suggests that there are psychological, as well as moral limits to what a government may do. The whole end of government is an amalgamation of all these individual intentions, 'the peace, safety, and public good of the people'.

Importantly, the collecting of these intentions together changes matters somewhat. Locke is explicit that this purpose can justify the infringement of other valuable objects such as the defence of property rights. The best illustration of his position comes in §160 where Locke outlines a view that we can identify as *consequentialist*: in principle, the rights of the individual may be infringed in pursuit of beneficial consequences for the people as a whole. You will recognize this position from the discussion of Machiavelli in Chapter 1, but may be surprised to find it resurfacing in the work of Locke. A ruler may diverge from a 'strict and rigid observation of the laws' (§159) protecting property rights for example, by pulling down a house to stop the spread of a fire (this drastic step was taken during the Great Fire of London in 1666).

Locke's account in Chapter XIV of the ruler's prerogative power does two things. It shows up an implicit tension between his account of natural rights, including property rights, and the goal of pursuing the common good. The resolution of this tension in favour of wielding the prerogative power in the defence of the primary law of nature ought to lead us to qualify our understanding of Locke as an archetypal liberal. At the same time, however, it is clear that the prerogative power of the government is harnessed to and directed at the common good.

A government that infringes natural law can be ousted but so can one that infringes positive law. He makes this clear particularly in §202 'whosoever in authority exceeds the power given him by the law ... ceases in that to be a magistrate; and, acting without authority, may be opposed'. The reason for this is straightforward: 'wherever law ends, tyranny begins' (§202).

Locke is progressively narrowing the scope for a government to act legitimately. First, governments may not infringe natural law. Then they must further the public good, and may be opposed if they do not. Finally, they must act within the legal framework that has already been established. If we leave aside the tensions in Chapter XIV, which rather undermine Locke's consistency, the structure of a strong case for limited government can clearly be made out.

The import of these limits to governmental power – established through moral claims about natural law and psychological claims about the actions of rational individuals – is that no government can have absolute arbitrary power. A government that legislates or acts outwith these limits need not be obeyed (§221). The limitations are contained in the notion that the government is entrusted with its power on certain conditions. To use Hampton's terms, introduced in Chapter 2 (Reading 2.4), Locke sees the government as a temporary agent of the people, which has their power on loan, not as an institution to whom power is alienated or handed over once and for all. A government that breaks the conditions on which the trust was bestowed in the first place, abuses the trust invested in it.

This theory faces two lines of criticism, both of which could be thought of as inspired by Hobbesian considerations. First, suppose we accept that trust can break down. Why doesn't this dissolve the civil society, the community, as well as the government? After all, civil society is an artificial creation by a contract between individuals.

A second, and related, criticism is: is not Locke laying down a basis for continual disruption and discord, even if there is no fundamental reversion back to the state of nature?

ACTIVITY

How might Locke answer these two criticisms? The most helpful paragraphs are at §§243 and 224–30.

DISCUSSION

While Locke is sometimes ambiguous, the claims made in §243 are the ones that tend to reinforce his overall theory. The notion of the community, working at an intermediate level between government and individual, stops any reversion to the state of nature when a government is replaced. This institution is more stable because the power that every individual hands over to the community stays with that community, while the trust which the community places in a ruler is conditional and straightforwardly revocable.

Locke's answer to the claim that he is laying down a basis for rebellion works in three different ways. First he makes an empirically rooted claim: 'such revolutions happen not upon every little mismanagement in public affairs' (§225). Second, he pricks the claims of rulers to automatic obedience, cutting them down to size by unflattering comparison (§227) – legislators can be rebels. Thirdly, in §228, he bites the bullet. Locke compares the challenge to him to the suggestion that honest men may not oppose robbers or pirates because this may cause bloodshed or disorder. But, says Locke, honest men may oppose robbers or pirates *even if* this may occasion bloodshed or disorder. Rousseau uses a similar example to make the same point in the *Social Contract* (Chapter iii). By Locke's own analogy, then, honest men may oppose unjust rulers who have forfeited their trust, *even if* doing so may lay a foundation for rebellion and civil wars. This shocking and revolutionary conclusion – the sharpest contrast to Hobbes's view – goes a long way to establish Locke's originality and place in the canon of political philosophy. Interestingly, though, it is combined in the *Second Treatise* with a sustained and markedly unrevolutionary defence of individual property rights.

Locke's theory enjoins governments to act in pursuit of the common good in accordance with both natural and positive law. A government needs to act, then, in such a way as to protect the natural rights of its citizens. For Locke, private property is just such a natural right, and it is the task of legitimate government to protect it.

Locke on property

We are surrounded by things owned. None the less, from my desk, I can just about see the beach at Brighton, which is composed of pebbles. Let us suppose that those pebbles are not owned by anyone in particular. Suppose I were to go down on to the beach, pick up a pebble and bring it home. Would I thereby own it? As for my desk, I myself bought it, but at some point, it must have been made from wood which came from trees. How was ownership established over those trees? What makes it right that one particular person and not another particular person owns that tree? These are the sort of fundamental questions about ownership that Locke tackles in Chapter V. There are also more directly political concerns at stake. We have seen that Locke wanted to insist on the limited nature of legitimate governmental power. One of those limits concerned the right of governments to appropriate the possessions of its subjects without their consent. The issue of forced appropriation was a live one in seventeenth-century England. Locke was concerned to defend property from arbitrary monarchical power, although his argument has also been used to defend the notion of specifically private property against those who question its moral basis (see, for example, Nozick (1974) for a Lockean defence of private property).

ACTIVITY

Read the *Second Treatise*, Chapter V, §§25–51.

Chapter V is full of puzzles and theories. It is a good example of Locke's 'over-determined' style of argument. That is to say, Locke gives us many different reasons for agreeing with the same conclusions. If we manage to reject one argument, another pops up to defend the same conclusion. This is like someone saying, I can show you it is Sunday today, because the church bells are ringing, *and* the Sunday papers are on sale, *and* the radio announcer has just said it is Sunday. I will discuss only one, famous, puzzle in Locke's account of property: the so-called 'mixing argument'. In doing so, I want to show how some modern philosophers go about using the raw materials provided by Locke.

In Chapter V Locke presents an account of the *natural* basis of *initial* property rights. The two qualifications here are important: the right Locke wants is first *natural* as opposed to *conventional*. We could agree a convention whereby acting in a specific way was understood to give limited property rights. One example of this sort of convention is the practice of reserving sun beds at the beach by putting a towel on them. This practice depends on agreement on a rule: if someone puts their towel on a sun bed, they have rights over that sun bed for a day. But note the very limited nature of the convention. I do not normally gain even temporary property rights over most things by putting a towel on them. According to the convention I do gain temporary property rights over a sun bed by putting a towel on it. Locke's account is different and more general. Property rights do not necessarily depend on any agreement on a convention.

Locke's account is also importantly one of *initial* property rights. One readily understood way to gain property rights in many things – providing you have the money – would be to buy the thing from the previous owner. But Locke is not so interested in property rights gained like this. Recall that the right to private property is one of the natural rights that it is the point of government to defend. So Locke needs a natural right to private property that is prior to government and the law. He needs to justify the property rights that are established over what is initially unowned.

So Locke's task is to establish what could give someone unimpeachable property rights over something unowned, such as a section of the surface of the moon, or a part of Antarctica, or a pebble from Brighton beach. Locke argues in §27 that it is a person's labour, an active relationship to the object, that establishes ownership.

ACTIVITY

What would give someone unimpeachable property rights over something unowned, such as a section of the surface of the moon, or a pebble on Brighton beach? (Remember, you are not allowed to introduce into the account any clauses about agreement with other people.)

DISCUSSION

This is a difficult task, but some important elements of an account might be that the person was the first to get to the object, or that he or she, and no one else, picked it out and started to use it.

ACTIVITY

Read the *Second Treatise*, §27 again, carefully, then put Locke's paragraph into your own words.

DISCUSSION

1   Every man owns himself, and that includes his labour.
2   So when he mixes his labour with something, he makes that thing his property, because he mixed something he owned with something he did not own.
3   So he has established specific property rights in that thing.
4   All this is true as long as there is enough, and as good, left in common for others.

ACTIVITY

Is this argument plausible? Leaving aside for now the important proviso 'enough, and as good', make a note of any flaws in the argument before reading on.

A modern political philosopher, Jeremy Waldron, has presented a critique of the argument in §27.

ACTIVITY

Read Waldron's 'Two Worries about Mixing One's Labour' (Reading 3.3).

As you read, ask yourself 'what are the two worries?'

DISCUSSION

1   *The incoherent recipe worry*

I can understand the recipe for mixing ingredients together to make a cake. But what is the recipe for mixing one's labour? Unlike flour or sugar, one's labour can't be something separate from the mixing. The notion of 'mixing one's labour' does not fit with the logical form of straightforward propositions about mixing. There is just no other substance separate from the activity of mixing, that is mixed with the object.

2   *The lost sandwich worry*

The second worry is this: the individual is taken to own the object with which he mixes his labour, because that is the only way of ensuring that he still owns the labour. Waldron insists though, that:

> once the mixing takes place, the labour is to all intents and purposes, lost in the object. There is no longer a question of protecting anyone's entitlement to it since the labour, *qua* labour, no longer exists.

(Reading 3.3, p.177 below)

> This is like dropping a sandwich into a vat of cement which nobody in particular owns. Once the sandwich is in the cement it ceases to exist as a sandwich and so it doesn't belong to anyone at all.

Note the usefully explicit structure of Waldron's argument in his paper. He says, for example, 'Even if this difficulty did not exist, there would be another grave problem in Locke's idea of mixing one's labour.' So, like Locke's argument that I pointed to earlier, Waldron's is over-determined: that is, he has two good reasons for rejecting Locke's argument. If we manage to defeat one, he has another argument that defends the same position. Waldron's arguments seem decisive against the mixing argument that Locke employs in §27. It does not seem reasonable to regard labour as something that can be mixed with something else in order to generate property rights.

But recall my original example of picking up a pebble from Brighton beach. If I gained property rights in that pebble, they did seem to come from something I did to it, even though all I did was to pick it up. I didn't change the pebble in any way. Perhaps I just picked it up because I thought it would look good on my mantelpiece. And that *thought* is important. In picking it up I had a purpose: it wasn't just a random act. That idea of purpose is going to be useful for a reconstruction of Locke's argument. A. John Simmons does preserve the essentials of the Lockean account in his reply to Waldron and several other philosophers who have made similar points about §27.

ACTIVITY

Read Simmons's 'The Lockean Theory of Rights' (Reading 3.4). How does Simmons respond to Waldron's worries?

DISCUSSION

He suggests that both arguments of Waldron attack a conception of labour as a kind of substance to be literally mixed or blended with an object. It is this notion of labour that Simmons wants to reject. Instead he comes up with an account of labour 'as a purposive activity aimed at satisfying needs or supplying the conveniences of life' (Reading 3.4, p.181). Simmons notes that the idea of labour here has similarities with the 'process of objectifying oneself in the world by making concrete what was abstract – as Hegelian or Marxist views of labour or property sometimes suggest' (see Chapter 5 on the idea of labour as objectification).

So my labour in picking up a pebble can be analysed like this. I have an idea, let us say, to find a pebble with a hollow in it that I can use as a candlestick. I pick up the pebble, with this idea, this purpose, in mind. In so doing, I bring the object within my life and plans. As Simmons puts it, 'What I "add" to the thing on which I labour is its role in my purposive activities and the consequent right over it that I acquire' (ibid., p.182).

How does this account help to answer the objections that Waldron had to Locke's first account? Well, the first worry was that the idea of mixing one's labour is incoherent, since there is nothing separate from the mixing that goes on that can be identified as labour. But on Simmons's reconstruction, the pebble is mixed with my labour as it is brought into the realm of my purposive action. The second worry was that once the mixing takes place, the labour is lost in the object. So mixing A, which I own, can't give me rights in B into which I have mixed A, since the action of mixing destroys A 'to all intents and purposes'. But on the labour-as-objectification model, this isn't a problem. My purposive projects continue: the pebble continues to be part of my plan to scavenge a candlestick, until I decide that pebble candlesticks are aesthetically displeasing, and throw it away. The activity doesn't disappear after it is carried out, because what makes the activity *that* particular activity, rather than a random act, is the purpose with which it is done, and that purpose depends on a plan. So Simmons's strategy is to replace the notion of labour as a simple substance with a richer notion of realizing a plan, or purpose. By doing this he is able to defuse Waldron's objections to the 'mixing one's labour' argument of §27.

You will have to decide whether you think that Simmons has come up with a reasonable reconstruction of the meaning of §27. Perhaps your judgement is that Waldron has still done irreparable damage to Locke's account. But it is not open to you to reject Simmons's conclusion on the basis that he is misleading about Locke's words. Simmons is clear about this: 'Locke, of course, says none of this explicitly, but it helps to make better sense of what he does say' (ibid.). So Simmons is reconstructing Locke, but also going beyond what Locke himself actually says.

There is much more to say about Locke's account of individual property rights. We noticed one Lockean proviso above; that the appropriation of property is justified as long as there is 'enough, and as good left ... for others'. Locke also thinks that we cannot appropriate property which we will simply waste, since this would go against God's intentions in providing for us. However, the institution of money makes a huge difference: we can overcome the non-spoilage restriction by using money to exchange for perishable goods. It is not entirely clear how the 'enough, and as good' constraint is supposed to operate in a market economy, and commentators have come up with both egalitarian and inegalitarian accounts of Locke's views (Tully (1980); Macpherson (1962)). Notwithstanding such disputes, the account of property in Chapter V is the classic account in the liberal tradition, and its fertility is clear. We have examined one part of that account, and seen how two political philosophers go about criticizing and reconstructing it.

This is a useful point to reflect on conceptions of political philosophy with Locke's *Second Treatise* in mind. This book considers some of the most famous texts of political philosophy, but in the case of the *Second Treatise* it is not unusual to come away with the sense that, if we are harsh and strict critics, little in terms of its substantial theses are sustainable. The theory of tacit consent in particular seems to be so problematical that one might conclude that it merely serves these days as target practice for students of political philosophy. At the same time, we may often believe that Locke really is on to something important, and the deep penetration of broadly Lockean notions into contemporary political discourse – talk of universal human rights and the idea of 'people power', for example – emphasizes that they are still ideologically potent. In this context of apparent analytical collapse and ideological potency, the reconstructive strategy of philosophers like Simmons shows that there is still much to engage with in Locke.

Glossary

accusatory system of justice

A system of natural jurisprudence in which accusations were made by private individuals rather than state prosecutors. The accuser would swear an oath to the truth of his charge, and seek support from other private individuals. The Court of Appeal was an ad hoc affair with no permanent or paid officials. The accusatory system of justice was banned by papal decree in 1215 (Tully (1993), pp.21–3).

community

For Locke, the community is what emerges from the state of nature. The community entrusts its interests to a government and it is the job of the government to serve the interests of the community. Communities are relatively stable, according to Locke, so that a change of government does not mean that the crisis of political power will lead to a reversion to an antagonistic state of nature.

express consent

Express consent is consent given explicitly by a promise to obey the government and laws of a state. An example of express consent is the ceremony which naturalized citizens of the USA undergo when they become such citizens. Tacit consent is the supposed giving of consent by some other means than an explicit promise.

natural law/positive law

Natural law is the moral law that governs the state of nature. In Locke's view, it is discoverable by human reason. Positive law, on the other hand, is the law created by actual legislatures. For Locke, natural law trumps positive law if and when the two conflict.

natural rights/conventional rights

Natural rights are the set of rights possessed by individuals in the state of nature. Conventional rights are rights that are established by social conventions. An example of such a convention is the practice of reserving rights over the use of, say, a chair by being the first person to say 'bags I have that chair'.

normative/descriptive

An account is normative if it prescribes conduct – if it tells us what we ought to do by laying down norms. An account is descriptive if it simply describes a process or series of events. Most philosophers agree, following Hume, that descriptive accounts do not entail normative conclusions: how things are does not determine how they should be.

voluntarism

In political philosophy, an account of legitimate government and our obligation to obey the law which rests on voluntary action. On a voluntaristic theory, obligations arise from actions freely taken by those who become obligated.

This understanding of voluntarism should not be confused with the use of the term 'voluntarism', often by Marxists, to denote and criticize accounts which overplay the importance of the human will and down play, for example, economic constraints. These sorts of charges concern the best explanation of events and processes, and are thus descriptive; whereas voluntarism in the theory of political obligation has normative content.

workmanship model

A model of morality and rights which rests on an analogy between God and human beings to show that property arises from maker's rights. The supposed fact that we are God's workmanship – has implications for our moral status. For example, we are prohibited from committing suicide. Equally, the fact that I have worked on a particular piece of wood to make a chair has implications for the moral status of the chair. It is my workmanship, and belongs to me and I may prevent others from using it (Tully (1980); but see Simmons (1992), pp.256 – 64.

Further reading

Iain Hampsher-Monk's *A History of Modern Political Thought* (Blackwell, 1992) is an important survey of the history of political thought.

John Horton and Susan Mendus (eds), *John Locke: A Letter Concerning Toleration in Focus* (Routledge, 1991). Locke's *Letter* (1689) is his other great political work. It is available in many editions; this one is accompanied by some useful secondary material.

Robert Nozick's *Anarchy, State and Utopia* (Basic Books, 1974)is a highly entertaining classic of modern political philosophy. It owes much to Locke, but also goes far beyond the *Second Treatise* to provide a radical argument against an extensive state.

A. John Simmons's *The Lockean Theory of Rights* (Princeton University Press, 1992) gives a clear, careful and analytical account of the theory of rights in the *Second Treatise*.

D.A. Lloyd Thomas's *Locke on Government* (Routledge, 1995) is a reliable guide to the *Second Treatise*.

James Tully's *A Discourse on Property* (Cambridge University Press, 1980) contains his contested reading of Locke on property. Tully is the leading 'contextualist' Locke scholar whose views are to be found in a valuable and fascinating collection of papers, *An Approach to Political Philosophy: Locke in Contexts* (Cambridge University Press, 1993).

Notes

[1] See, for example, Nozick (1974).

[2] It is commonly thought that there are three functions which government must fulfil and, consequently, three 'arms' of government: the legislature makes the law; the executive branch cthe executive – implements the law; the judicial branch – the judiciary – judges if and when the law is broken. Locke justifies the three branches in a particularly neat manner.

Readings

'Of the Original Contract'

David Hume

David Hume (1711–76) is perhaps the most important philosopher of the eighteenth century, and his contribution to political philosophy is fertile. In these extracts from his essay (published 1748), Hume criticizes those such as Locke who explain our allegiance to a political society in terms of a contract. Hume's critique is at least in part historical, but also contains a famous thought experiment in which he compares residence in a country to remaining on a ship. In neither case, he suggests, can legitimate authority be deduced from the fact that the individual remains in the same place.

1

When we consider how nearly equal all men are in their bodily force, and even in their mental powers and faculties, till cultivated by education; we must necessarily allow, that nothing but their own consent could, at first, associate them together, and subject them to any authority. The people, if we trace government to its first origin in the woods and deserts, are the source of all power and jurisdiction, and voluntarily, for the sake of peace and order, abandoned their native liberty, and received laws from their equal and companion. The conditions, upon which they were willing to submit, were either expressed, or were so clear and obvious, that it might well be esteemed superfluous to express them. If this, then, be meant by the *original contract*, it cannot be denied, that all government is, at first, founded on a contract, and that the most ancient rude combinations of mankind were formed chiefly by that principle. In vain, are we asked in what records this charter of our liberties is registered. It was not written on parchment, nor yet on leaves or barks of trees. It preceded the use of writing and all the other civilized arts of life. But we trace it plainly in the nature of man, and in the equality, or something approaching equality, which we find in all the individuals of that species. The force, which now prevails, and which is founded on fleets and armies, is plainly political, and derived from authority, the effect of established government. A man's natural force consists only in the vigour of his limbs, and the firmness of his courage; which could never subject multitudes to the command of one. Nothing but their own consent, and their sense of the advantages resulting from peace and order, could have had that influence.

Yet even this consent was long very imperfect, and could not be the basis of a regular administration. The chieftain, who had probably acquired his influence during the continuance of war, ruled more by persuasion than command; and till he could employ force to reduce the refractory and disobedient, the society could scarcely be said to have attained a state of civil government. No compact or agreement, it is evident, was expressly formed for general submission; an idea far beyond the comprehension of savages: Each exertion of authority in the chieftain must have been particular, and called forth by the present exigencies of the case: The sensible utility, resulting from his interposition, made these exertions become daily more frequent; and their frequency gradually produced an habitual, and, if you please to call it so, a voluntary, and therefore precarious, acquiescence in the people.

But philosophers, who have embraced a party (if that be not a contradiction in terms) are not contented with these concessions. They assert, not only that government in its earliest infancy arose from consent or rather the voluntary acquiescence of the people; but also, that, even at present, when it has attained full maturity, it rests on no other foundation. They affirm, that all men are still born equal, and owe allegiance to no prince or government, unless bound by the obligation and sanction of a *promise*. And as no man, without some equivalent, would forego the advantages of his native liberty, and subject himself to the will of another; this promise is always understood to be conditional, and imposes on him no obligation, unless he meet with justice and protection from his sovereign. These advantages the sovereign promises him in return; and if he fail in the execution, he has broken, on his part, the articles of engagement, and has thereby freed his subject from all obligations to allegiance. Such, according to these philosophers, is the foundation of authority in every government; and such the right of resistance, possessed by every subject.

But would these reasoners look abroad into the world, they would meet with nothing that, in the least, corresponds to their ideas, or can warrant so refined and philosophical a system. On the contrary, we find, every where, princes, who claim their subjects as their property, and assert their independent right of sovereignty, from conquest or succession. We find also, every where, subjects, who acknowledge this right in their prince, and suppose themselves born under obligations of obedience to a certain sovereign, as much as under the ties of reverence and duty to certain parents. These connexions are always conceived to be equally independent of our consent, in Persia and China; in France and Spain; and even in Holland and England, wherever the doctrines above-mentioned have not been carefully inculcated. Obedience or subjection becomes so familiar, that most men never make any enquiry about its origin or cause, more than about the principle of gravity, resistance, or the most universal laws of nature. Or if curiosity ever move them; as soon as they learn, that they themselves and their ancestors have, for several ages, or from time immemorial, been subject to such a form of government or such a family; they immediately acquiesce, and acknowledge their obligation to allegiance. Were you to preach, in most parts of the world, that political connexions are founded altogether on voluntary consent or a mutual promise, the magistrate would soon imprison you, as seditious, for loosening the ties of obedience; if your friends did not before shut you up as delirious, for advancing such absurdities. It is strange, that an act of the mind, which every individual is supposed to have formed, and after he came to the use of reason too, otherwise it could have no authority; that this act, I say, should be so much unknown to all of them, that, over the face of the whole earth, there scarcely remain any traces or memory of it.

But the contract, on which government is founded, is said to be the *original contract*; and consequently may be supposed too old to fall under the knowledge of the present generation. If the agreement, by which savage men first associated and conjoined their force, be here meant, this is acknowledged to be real; but being so ancient, and being obliterated by a thousand changes of government and princes, it cannot now be supposed to retain any authority. If we would say any thing to the purpose, we must assert, that every particular government, which is lawful, and which imposes any duty of allegiance on the subject, was, at first, founded on consent and a voluntary compact. But besides that this supposes the consent of the fathers to bind the children, even to the most remote generations, (which republican writers will never allow) besides this, I say, it is not justified by history or experience, in any age or country of the world.

Almost all the governments, which exist at present, or of which there remains any record in story, have been founded originally, either on usurpation or conquest, or both, without any presence of a fair consent, or voluntary subjection of the people. When an artful and bold man is placed at the head of an army or faction, it is often easy for him, by employing, sometimes violence, sometimes false pretences, to establish his dominion over a people a hundred times more numerous than his partizans. He allows no such open communication, that his enemies can know, with certainty, their number or force. He gives them no leisure to assemble together in a body to oppose him. Even all those, who are the instruments of his usurpation, may wish his fall; but their ignorance of each other's intention keeps them in awe, and is the sole cause of his security. By such arts as these, many governments have been established; and this is all the *original contract*, which they have to boast of.

The face of the earth is continually changing, by the encrease of small kingdoms into great empires, by the dissolution of great empires into smaller kingdoms, by the planting of colonies, by the migration of tribes. Is there any thing discoverable in all these events, but force and violence? Where is the mutual agreement or voluntary association so much talked of?

Even the smoothest way, by which a nation may receive a foreign master, by marriage or a will, is not extremely honourable for the people; but supposes them to be disposed of, like a dowry or a legacy, according to the pleasure or interest of their rulers.

But where no force interposes, and election takes place; what is this election so highly vaunted? It is either the combination of a few great men, who decide for the whole, and will allow of no opposition: Or it is the fury of a multitude, that follow a seditious ringleader, who is not known, perhaps, to a dozen among them, and who owes his advancement merely to his own impudence, or to the momentary caprice of his fellows.

Are these disorderly elections, which are rare too, of such mighty authority, as to be the only lawful foundation of all government and allegiance?

In reality, there is not a more terrible event, than a total dissolution of government, which gives liberty to the multitude, and makes the determination or choice of a new establishment depend upon a number, which nearly approaches to that of the body of the people: For it never comes entirely to the whole body of them. Every wise man, then, wishes to see, at the head of a powerful and obedient army, a general, who may speedily seize the prize, and give to the people a master, which they are so unfit to chuse for themselves. So little correspondent is fact and reality to those philosophical notions.

Let not the establishment at the *Revolution* deceive us, or make us so much in love with a philosophical origin to government, as to imagine all others monstrous and irregular. Even that event was far from corresponding to these refined ideas. It was only the succession, and that only in the regal part of the government, which was then changed: And it was only the majority of seven hundred, who determined that change for near ten millions. I doubt not, indeed, but the bulk of those ten millions acquiesced willingly in the determination: But was the matter left, in the least, to their choice? Was it not justly supposed to be, from that moment, decided, and every man punished, who refused to submit to the new sovereign? How otherwise could the matter have ever been brought to any issue or conclusion?

The republic of Athens was, I believe, the most extensive democracy, that we read of in history: Yet if we make the requisite allowances for the women, the slaves, and the strangers, we shall find, that that establishment was not, at first, made, not any law ever voted, by a tenth part of those who were bound to pay obedience to it: Not to mention the islands and foreign dominions, which the Athenians claimed as theirs by right of conquest. And as it is well known, that popular assemblies in that city were always full of licence and disorder, notwithstanding the institutions and laws by which they were checked: How much more disorderly must they prove, where they form not the established constitution, but meet tumultuously on the dissolution of the ancient government, in order to give rise to a new one? How chimerical must it be to talk of a choice in such circumstances?

The Acheans enjoyed the freest and most perfect democracy of all antiquity; yet they employed force to oblige some cities to enter into their league, as we learn from Polybius.

Harry the IVth and Harry the VIIth of England, had really no title to the throne but a parliamentary election; yet they never would acknowledge it, lest they should thereby weaken their authority. Strange, if the only real foundation of all authority be consent and promise!

It is in vain to say, that all governments are or should be, at first, founded on popular consent, as much as the necessity of human affairs will admit. This favours entirely my pretension. I maintain, that human affairs will never admit of this consent; seldom of the appearance of it. But that conquest or usurpation, that is, in plain terms, force, by dissolving the ancient governments, is the origin of almost all the new ones, which were ever established in the world. And that in the few cases, where consent may seem to have taken place, it was commonly so irregular, so confined, or so much intermixed either with fraud or violence, that it cannot have any great authority.

My intention here is not to exclude the consent of the people from being one just foundation of government where it has place. It is surely the best and most sacred of any. I only pretend, that it has very seldom had place in any degree, and never almost in its full extent. And that therefore some other foundation of government must also be admitted.

Were all men possessed of so inflexible a regard to justice, that, of themselves, they would totally abstain from the properties of others; they had for ever remained in a state of absolute liberty, without subjection to any magistrate or political society: But this is a state of perfection, of which human nature is justly deemed incapable. Again; were all men possessed of so perfect an understanding, as always to know their own interests, no form of government had ever been submitted to, but what was established on consent, and was fully canvassed by every member of the society: But this state of perfection is likewise much superior to human nature. Reason, history, and experience show us, that all political societies have had an origin much less accurate and regular; and were one to choose a period of time, when the people's consent was the least regarded in public transactions, it would be precisely on the establishment of a new government. In a settled constitution, their inclinations are often consulted; but during the fury of revolutions, conquests, and public convulsions, military force or political craft usually decides the controversy.

When a new government is established, by whatever means, the people are commonly dissatisfied with it, and pay obedience more from fear and necessity, than from any idea of allegiance or of moral obligation. The prince is watchful and jealous, and must carefully guard against every beginning or appearance of insurrection. Time, by degrees, removes all these difficulties, and accustoms the nation to regard, as their lawful or native princes, that family, which, at first, they considered as usurpers or foreign conquerors. In order to found this opinion, they have no recourse to any notion of voluntary consent or promise, which, they know, never was, in this case, either expected or demanded. The original establishment was formed by violence, and submitted to from necessity. The subsequent administration is also supported by power, and acquiesced in by the people, not as a matter of choice, but of obligation. They imagine not, that their consent gives their prince a title: But they willingly consent, because they think, that, from long possession, he has acquired a title, independent of their choice or inclination.

2

Should it be said, that, by living under the dominion of a prince, which one might leave, every individual has given a *tacit* consent to his authority, and promised him obedience; it may be answered, that such an implied consent can only have place, where a man imagines, that the matter depends on his choice. But where he thinks (as all mankind do who are born under established governments) that by his birth he owes allegiance to a certain prince or certain form of government; it would be absurd to infer a consent or choice, which he expressly, in this case, renounces and disclaims.

Can we seriously say, that a poor peasant or artizan has a free choice to leave his country, when he knows no foreign language or manners, and lives from day to day, by the small wages which he acquires? We may as well assert, that a man, by remaining in a vessel, freely consents to the dominion of the master; though he was carried on board while asleep, and must leap into the ocean, and perish, the moment he leaves her.

What if the prince forbid his subjects to quit his dominions; as in Tiberius's time, it was regarded as a crime in a Roman knight that he had attempted to fly to the Parthians, in order to escape the tyranny of that emperor? [1]

A company of men, who should leave their native country, in order to people some uninhabited region, might dream of recovering their native freedom; but they would soon find, that their prince still laid claim to them, and called them his subjects, even in their new settlement. And in this he would but act conformably to the common ideas of mankind.

Notes

From Hume, David (1748) 'Of the Original Contract', in *Essays Moral, Political and Literacy*, Oxford University Press, 1963, pp.454–63.

[1] Tacit. Ann. vi. cap. 14. Or as the ancient Muscovites prohibited all travelling under pain of death? And did a prince observe, that many of his subjects were seized with the frenzy of migrating to foreign countries, he would doubtless, with great reason and justice, restrain them, in order to prevent the depopulation of his own kingdom. Would he forfeit the allegiance of all his subjects, by so wise and reasonable a law? Yet the freedom of their choice is surely, in that case, ravished from them.

'Do People Actually Consent to Political Authority?'

Jean Hampton

In this extract, Jean Hampton spells out some of the problems with the notion of tacit consent, and with its contemporary rendering by John Rawls and others in terms of hypothetical consent. She suggests that this latter notion implies a 'Platonic conception of political authority'. This is a reference to the theory contained in the *Republic* in which Plato advocates rule by specially moral and virtuous Philosopher Kings.

The ... most serious [problem] challenges the way in which the argument derives authority from individual consent. The philosopher most famous for questioning the success of the contractarian derivation of authority from consent is the eighteenth-century Scottish philosopher David Hume. A social contract argument says that in the same way my doctor has authority to take out my appendix if we have contractually agreed that she should do so, my state has authority to dictate how I should behave in certain areas if we have contractually agreed that it should do so. Both the patient and the subject in these contracts confer authority to the doctor or the state in exchange for certain services. So on such a view the state has authority over me only if I have given it that authority. And just when, asks Hume, have most of the world's population undertaken this contractual obligation? People, he notes, generally obey the state because they think they are 'born to it', not because they have promised to do so. As Hume wryly observes:

> Were you to ask the far greatest part of the nation, whether they ever had consented to the authority of their rulers, or promis'd to obey them, they wou'd be inclin'd to think very strangely of you; and wou'd certainly reply, that the affair depended not on their consent, but that they were born to such obedience. [1]

Proponents of contract arguments have defended their argument against Hume's criticisms by insisting that it isn't meant as a *history* of the creation of states but only as an account of the nature of political authority. Hence any objection to the effect that the argument is historically inaccurate is beside the point.

But so stated, this defence doesn't work. Locke's contract argument presumes that states are both explained and justified by the way they are created by the people who are subject to them. Hence if the argument is right, it must be possible to develop a historically accurate account of how states come into existence by the people's consenting activity (and indeed Locke himself tries to give such a history in §§100–22 of the *Second Treatise*). If it turns out that throughout history states have been created in ways that have not involved subjects' consent and people have taken themselves to be subject to political authority for reasons other than that they have consented to such authority, then the consent that the contract argument requires in order to explain and legitimate that authority has simply not occurred – and the contract argument would have failed to locate the source of political authority.

Now we see why the historical implausibility of the contract argument is so worrisome. The contract tradition has been persistently ridiculed for failing to provide evidence that anything like the kind of explicit agreement analogous to the agreement that authorizes my doctor to treat me has ever occurred in a political context. And appealing to consent when it simply hasn't occurred fails to explain the fact of political authority.

In response supporters of the contractarian methodology have often insisted that the consent and the contracts in their arguments are only 'hypothetical' occurrences and not historical events: The contract theorist is, on this view, using the contract talk not to give any dubious history lessons but merely to justify the state in terms of what people *could agree to* in an equal and impartial setting. Insofar as a state is the sort of institution that we believe people could have agreed to, then it is authoritative; otherwise it is not.

But one modern philosopher, Ronald Dworkin, has the appropriate rejoinder: 'A hypothetical contract is not simply a pale form of an actual contract; it is no contract at all'. [2] No one takes it that any of us is obliged by make-believe contracts but only by real ones. Hence whatever excellent use a hypothetical contract has in helping to illuminate the nature of justice ... a contract that was never really made cannot explain real authority. To paraphrase movie mogul Samuel Goldwyn, hypothetical consent is not worth the paper it's not written on. [3]

Moreover, an appeal to hypothetical consent may be nothing more than covert reliance on a Platonic conception of political authority. Consider that if I say that a government is authoritative over you because you would have consented to it in ideal conditions, I'm implicitly saying that your ideal, hypothetical consent is deserved by virtue of the merits of this government. This sort of appeal therefore bases our political obligation to an authoritative political regime not on actual consent but on whether that regime is just or in some way good or desirable on moral grounds. [4] It must be these moral grounds that deliver the regime's authority, and talking about the consent any of us *would* give it in ideal conditions is simply a way of eliciting the judgement that the regime is sufficiently morally satisfactory to be considered authoritative. So authority is being derived from the morality of the regime, which in turn explains why it would be consented to by the right people; in contrast, a genuine consent-based theory makes the authority derive from the real consent itself – perhaps even in situations where the regime consented to cannot survive moral scrutiny. (So a real consent theory has to hold it out as possible that a political regime has authority even in situations where people in ideal circumstances would *not* consent to it, because in this world real people have consented to it.)

So what about the notion of tacit consent? Perhaps we can understand this form of consent as the source of political authority and successfully locate it in the historical actions of real people. If this is possible, then the consenting behaviour of people could be taken, contra Hume, as the source of the political authorities throughout history after all.

However, it is difficult to know how to understand the notion of tacit consent such that it is both successful in authorizing someone to have the kind of control over human beings that governments are supposed to have and also present in history. Suppose, for example, that tacit consent is understood to be granted (as Plato suggests) when one remains in a society and enjoys its benefits. Yet the mere acceptance and enjoyment of benefits is usually not taken to obligate us in any way to our benefactor if we have not previously agreed to give that obligation in exchange for those benefits (it certainly wouldn't do so normally in a court of law – acceptance of benefits rarely if ever counts as making a promise). [5] And as Locke notes, it is hard to see how acceptance of benefits makes us *members* of the state – it certainly doesn't oblige any foreign traveller who enjoys the benefits of the state while she is here. So it seems we must have a beefier conception of consent to explain the fact of political authority. But the more we interpret consent as explicitly made or explicitly promisorial, the more difficult it becomes to argue that all or even most citizens of regimes around the world have ever given it.

I take this to be an extremely serious problem with the social contract argument's attempt to develop a consent-based theory of political authority, which will have to be resolved if the argument is to be plausible... Suffice it to say here that unless a consent-based theory can develop a way of formulating a notion of consent that is both authority-giving and historically plausible, this approach to political authority is just not viable.

In view of these problems, it is fair to say that despite the enormous popularity of Lockean contract theory since publication of the *Two Treatises of Government*, his social contract argument is an unsatisfactory development of the idea that the political authority of a ruler is derived from the consent of those people who are subject to him. Can we come up with a better development of that idea? We had better be able to do so if we want to answer the anarchist... Unless we can come up with a new, successful account of political authority, anarchism is the only justifiable position with respect to the state.

Notes

From Hampton, Jean (1997) *Political Philosophy*, WestView Press, pp.64–7.

[1] David Hume, *A Treatise of Human Nature*, ed. L.A. Selby-Bigge, rev. P.H. Nidditch (Oxford: Clarendon Press, 1978), Book III, part ii, sec. viii, p.548.

[2] Ronald Dworkin, 'The Original Contract', in Norman Daniels, ed., *Reading Rawls* (New York: Basic Books, 1974), p.17.

[3] Popular legend has it that Goldwyn's original remark was, 'A verbal contract isn't worth the paper it's written on'. The paraphrase I give is often attributed to Robert Nozick.

[4] See A.J. Simmons, *On the Edge of Anarchy: Locke, Consent and the Limits of Society* (Princeton University Press, 1993), p.78.

[5] To quote Nozick, 'The fact that we partially are "social products" in that we benefit from current patterns and forms created by the multitudinous actions of a long string of long forgotten people ... does not create in us a floating debt which the current society can collect and use as it will.' From *Anarchy, State and Utopia* (New York: Basic Books, 1974), p.95.

'Two Worries About Mixing One's Labour'

Jeremy Waldron

Jeremy Waldron, Professor of Law at Columbia University, is a contemporary political philosopher whose recent writings include *The Dignity of Legislation* (1999) and *Law and Disagreement* (1999). He is also the author of a number of important papers on Locke. In 'Two Worries' he considers one issue in Locke's theory of property and subjects it to detailed, and critical, scrutiny.

I

Does the idea of *mixing one's labour* provide the basis for a plausible account of the genesis of property rights in Locke's state of nature? [1] Or is it merely a dramatic and rhetorical way of expressing the force of other arguments based ultimately on, say, utility or desert? In this paper I will argue that the idea of the mixing of labour is fundamentally incoherent and that therefore it can add nothing at all, apart from an oddly worded metaphor, to whatever other arguments Locke wants to put forward for the proposition that individuals working on goods owned in common in the state of nature are entitled to the products of their labour.

The considerations that Locke puts forward for this proposition fall into at least four main groups. First, dominating the whole account in the *Two Treatises*, there is an argument based on a principle of *need*. Unilateral acquisition of entitlements by individual labour is presented as the only sensible way of allocating material resources to human needs in the state of nature. The idea is that, if unilateral appropriation were not permissible, people would be obliged to perish in the meantime while more consensual arrangements were being set up.[2] Secondly, and complementing this, there are considerations of efficiency. In a society where private property can be acquired by labour, everyone is better off, even the non-proprietors. As Locke puts it: 'a King of a large fruitful Territory' where original communism still prevails 'feeds, lodges, and is clad worse than a day Labourer in England'.[3] Thirdly, there is an argument based on something like a *labour theory of value*. Locke suggests that in the case of many important resources, the labour that has been expended on them is the source of so much of the value they possess that the labourer is entitled to the resource in roughly the same way that a creator is entitled to his creation. [4] Fourthly, we seem at times to catch sight of a strand of argument based on a principle of *desert*. God has commanded men to labour; so 'the Industrious and the Rational' are entitled to the products of their labour inasmuch as they have shown by their initiative that they are people of more merit than 'the quarrelsom and Contentious' who complain about private appropriation. [5]

In addition to these four considerations, we have what appears to be an independent line of argument based on the idea that a labourer mixes his labour with the object on which he works. This is presented in a very well-known passage which I shall quote in full:

> Though the Earth and all inferior Creatures be common to all Men, yet every Man has a Property in his own Person. This no Body has any Right to but himself. The Labour of his Body, and the Work of his Hands, we may say, are properly his. Whatsoever then he removes out of the State that Nature hath provided, and left it in, he hath mixed his Labour with, and joyned to it something that is his own, and thereby makes it his Property. It being by him removed from the common state Nature placed it in, hath by this labour something annexed to it, that excludes the common right of other Men. For this Labour being the unquestionable Property of the Labourer, no man but he can have a right to what that is once joyned to, at least where there is enough, and as good left in common for others. [6]

There is no mention here – at least, no explicit mention – of any considerations of need, efficiency, value or desert. The argument looks as though it is meant to stand up on its own. In what follows I am going to consider it as such, and I shall leave aside the (interesting) exegetical question of whether Locke really intended this as an independent line of argument. It is sufficient, I think, that many interpreters have taken it as such.

There are good reasons for adopting this approach. It is well known that none of the four arguments I mentioned provides a watertight case for private property. Two of them at least – the argument based on the labour theory of value and the argument based on desert – appear equally capable of being adapted to socialist conclusions: anything said about the desert of, or the value added by, an independent Lockean appropriator seems equally applicable to the case of an employee working industriously on resources already appropriated by someone else.[7] But, although each of the arguments is incomplete, perhaps they complement each other and together make up a convincing case for private property. If this is how we want to interpret them, then at some stage each strand of argument has to be examined on its own, to see how valid it is in itself, and what support it is capable of lending to the others. One of my conclusions in this paper will be that the argument involving the mixing of labour is, by itself, incapable of establishing anything at all, and so cannot help any of the others. Its appearance as part of the complex Lockean case for property is a distraction: it makes that case look more substantial than it really is.

An additional reason for examining the argument about the mixing of labour is that it has become important once again in political philosophy. In *Anarchy, State and Utopia*, Robert Nozick insists that any adequate conception of economic justice must have a place for a principle of justice in acquisition – a principle which specifies the ways in which individuals may appropriate previously unowned resources. Nozick did not think it necessary to spell out the details of such a principle himself, but he alluded to the Lockean principle of mixing one's labour, and offered a number of criticisms of it. [8] Those criticisms have provided the inspiration for the present paper. But I think they indicate, not merely that the argument based on mixing labour is incomplete or that it needs to be spelled out in more detail, but rather that it is defective to the point of incoherence, and cannot operate as a principle of justice in acquisition.

II

If there *is* a line of argument in the passage I quoted above, it must go something like this:

1   A Person who labours on an object mixes his labour with that object.

2   But that person owns the labour which he mixes with the object.

3   So the object which has been laboured on contains something which the labourer owns.

4   To take the object out of the labourer's control without his consent would violate the entitlement mentioned in 2 and 3.

5   Therefore, no one may take the object out of the labourer's control without his consent.

6   But this amounts to an entitlement in the labourer over the object.

7   Thus, a person who has laboured on an object is entitled to that object.

In this way, an entitlement to an object is seen to be generated out of the prior entitlement to one's labour, on the basis that recognising the former is the only way to uphold and maintain respect for the latter once the labour has become mixed with the object.

So the idea that labour is literally *mixed with* an object is clearly crucial. Without it there would be no way of transferring the force of the entitlement to labour to the object which has been laboured on. Let us consider the idea of mixing one's labour, then, in a literal way, to see whether it makes sense. On the face of it, the proposition,

(P) Individual *A* mixes his labour with object *O*

seems to involve some sort of category mistake.[9] Surely the only things that can be *mixed* with objects are other objects. But labour consists of *actions* not objects. How can a series of actions be mixed with a physical object? Admittedly, from time to time, for various reasons, philosophers have purported to quantify over actions and events, treating them, in some contexts at least, as entities in their own right.[10] But I do not think that disposes of the difficulty in the present case.

We can see this if we compare (P) with a more straightforward proposition about mixing:

(Q) The cook mixes the egg with the batter.

In (Q), there seem to be three objects referred to – the cook, the egg, and the batter. There is also, if you like, the action of mixing the egg into the batter. Now we may treat this action as an entity or we may not. What matters for my criticism is that, entity or not, the action is certainly not identical with any of the other entities involved. It is distinct from the egg and the batter and the cook. That seems quite straightforward.

Let us try a similar analysis of (P). Again, we may say that there are at least three entities referred to:

(P1) the labourer, A, who is the analogue of the cook;

(P2) the labour of A, which, like the egg, is (supposedly) the subject matter of the mixing; and (P3) the object, O, the analogue of the batter, into which the labour is being mixed.

So far so good. But where is the fourth element, the analogue of the action of mixing? Perhaps it is the labour of A; after all, the Lockean claim is that *by labouring* the producer mixes his labour with the product. But A's labour features *already* in the account we have given, as the ingredient, (P2), which is being mixed in. So instead of the four distinct elements which we had in the straightforward case of (Q), we have now at most only three. There is the mixer, the thing being mixed in, and the thing into which it is being mixed; *but there is no distinct action of mixing*. Or, if you like, we can put it the other way round. There is the mixer, the action of mixing, and the object into which something is being mixed; *but there is nothing which is being mixed in*. We have ingredient and mixture but no mixing, or mixing and mixture but no ingredient. Either way, the ordinary notion of mixing seems quite inappropriate to the case that Locke is describing. The situation lacks the requisite plurality. [11]

Our original hunch about a category mistake has led us to discover a much deeper flaw. It is not just that the idea of mixing one's labour treats labour as a *thing* which can be mixed with other things. It is rather that the phrase 'mixing one's labour' is shown to have the logical form of 'mixing one's mixing'. And that just seems defective.

Is there any way in which Locke's argument can be rescued from this apparently devastating criticism? An attempt may be made along the following lines. Perhaps (P) is being used by Locke in the first premise of the argument in a way which distinguishes it, in terms of its logical form, from (Q). If this is the case, then the fact that (P) does not conform to the logic of (Q) no more makes (P) ill-formed than the difference between, say, 'A has a pain in his foot' and 'A has a growth in his foot' makes the first of these ill-formed. In other words, it may be objected, on behalf of the Lockean argument, that we are interpreting the idea of mixing one's labour too literally. There may be some other perfectly legitimate sense for (P) which does not require the plurality of elements which (Q) requires.

There are two things to say about this objection. First, it is not at all clear that one *can* come up with an interpretation of (P) which will *both* avoid my attack *and* do the work in the argument which Locke seems to want the notion of mixing one's labour to do. Remember that the mixing of labour with an object is supposed to *explain and justify* the principle of labourers' entitlements. It is no good suggesting, for instance, that (P) is just a fancy or rhetorical way of saying '*A* labours on *Q*'. For that leaves premise 1 of the Lockean argument saying redundantly that a person who labours on an object labours on an object. The notion implicit in 3 – that the object thereby comes to *contain* the person's labour – is left completely mysterious. The question would still remain open: why does labouring on an object generate an entitlement for the labourer over the object in question? If the argument we are considering has any independent force at all, the Locke is using (P) to *answer*, not to beg, this question. Any reinterpretation of (P), then, has to be able to fill that role.

Secondly, the criticism I have made is not only of the expression 'mixing one's labour' but also of some of the other expressions used by Locke in the section quoted: labour is said to be joyned and annexed to objects by the labourer. These expressions, in their ordinary sense, all share the logical form of (Q): that is, they all involve the idea of someone's brining one thing into relation with another. So they are equally open to the criticism that, in the case of labouring on an object, there are *not* two things to be brought into relation with one another but only one thing and an action that is performed on it. Just as we do not ordinarily talk of *mixing* actions with objects, so we do not ordinarily talk of *joining* or *annexing* them to objects, and my criticism explains why.

III

Even if this difficulty did not exist, there would be another grave problem in Locke's idea of mixing one's labour which prevents it doing the job in argument that he wants it to do.

The argument, as we saw, depends on the claim that if something to which I am entitled (e.g., my labour) becomes mixed with some other object, then the only way to safeguard and maintain my entitlement to the former is to entitle me to the latter object in which it has become embedded. In the literature, this claim has been attacked on a number of grounds. Robert Nozick raises the question whether deliberately mixing something one owns with something one does not own should not be regarded as a way of losing the former rather than as a way of gaining the latter. [12] Other critics have suggested that, even if labour does become irretrievably embedded in an object so that it cannot afterwards be disentangled from what was not the producer's property in the first place, nevertheless we need not concede that the producer is entitled to the product in full. Our available devices of ownership are subtle enough to allow us to confer on him a more modest entitlement, more in keeping with the proportion between his contribution and the naturally given raw material. So he may be allowed, for instance, a limited degree of control over and benefit from the product, or he may be entitled to *other* goods which have exactly the value of the improvements he made to the objects he worked on. [13] Even if this is not possible in Locke's state of nature, it is certainly possible now in civil society. So it is difficult to see how property entitlements generated initially by Lockean entitlements to the *whole* product of labour (value added plus raw materials) can operate today as moral side constraints on the pursuit of the economic and distributive goals of civil society.

But the second objection that I want to develop is more fundamental than this. I dispute whether entitling the producer to the whole product of his labour can even be regarded as *a way* of protecting his entitlement to the labour, let alone as the only way of doing so. Even if we assume, for the moment, that the idea of mixing labour makes sense, still, once the mixing takes place, the labour is to all intents and purposes lost in the object. There is no longer a question of protecting anyone's entitlement to *it*, since the labour, *qua*[14] labour, no longer exists.

Once again, a straightforward analogy can assist us. Suppose there is a vat of wet cement lying about which belongs to nobody in particular, and I drop my ham sandwich into it. Before I can retrieve the sandwich, the cement hardens into a concrete block. (Or, better still: as in Locke's case, the cement is lying about and I *intend* to drop my sandwich into it, not wanting to retrieve it.) Can I now claim the concrete block in order to protect my entitlement to the sandwich? Can I object, when someone takes the block out of my control, that he is violating my entitlement to the sandwich? Surely that would be regarded as some sort of joke. My ham sandwich has gone; whatever the justice of my claim to the concrete block, it has nothing to do with my claim still to be the owner of the sandwich. An entitlement to an object consists in the right to use, control and dispose of that object. But even if I am allowed to use, control or dispose of the concrete block, I can do none of these things with regard to the sandwich.

Of course, things would be different if there were any possibility of recovering the sandwich from the block, but sandwiches do not usually survive such experiences. And, anyway, to put the case on all fours with the one Locke is describing, we have to conceive of the mixture of concrete and sandwich as irreversible. (Otherwise Locke has no answer to the point that the producer is entitled, at most, to be given back his labour.) So the sandwich as such is as good as lost, despite the fact that we know where it is. As something which can be the subject-matter of an on-going entitlement, generating other entitlements by its attachment to other things, it no longer exists for us.

No doubt the concrete block is different from what it would have been if the sandwich had not been dropped into the cement; presumably it is a little larger and its internal structure is slightly different. But the question raised by the alteration is just this: 'Who is to have the concrete block, altered in this way by the insertion of the sandwich?' That may be an important question. But what has transpired makes the question 'Who is to have the sandwich?' irrelevant to that.

Similarly, in the case of an object with which labour has been 'mixed'. The fact that the object has been laboured on certainly makes a difference to it. But the question is now: 'Who is to have the object, given that labour has made this difference to it?' In finding the answer to this question, or, more important, in finding a justification for the obvious answer, the further question, 'Who is to have the labour which made the difference?' is no use at all.

This becomes even clearer when we approach the troubled question of what it is to own, or be entitled to, one's labour. The notion that labour is, in any plausible sense, the *property* of the labourer has been severely criticized in the literature. [15] If it means anything at all, it means, presumably, that the labourer has a right to liberty. Nobody else has any such right over the labourer's actions as would entitle him to dispose of those actions without the labourer's consent. But ownership in this sense has no relevance *now* to labour that has freely been expended in the past. There is no intelligible question of my liberty *now* in respect of actions I performed freely *yesterday*. The idea of the ownership of labour, understood in this libertarian sense, cannot do any work once the actions which constitute the labour have taken place.

In *A Discourse on Property*, James Tully suggests that by 'owning one's labour', Locke simply means being the conscious agent (initiator, creator) of the actions concerned. [16] If so, then Locke can make *some* sense of the idea that one continues to own one's labour after it has been 'mixed' with an object: it continues to be the case that one was the agent of those actions. But he can do this only at the expense of severing the link between *ownership of* labour and *entitlement or right to* labour. Any right-related notion of ownership is going to be inapplicable to labour once it has been irretrievably mixed with or annexed to an object.

It has to be emphasized that these considerations are not intended to show that producers are *not* entitled to the products of their labour. Surely the fact that a labourer has made such a difference to an object is of considerable importance in determining the just way to dispose of the product. The problem for political philosophers is to explain *why* this is so. Here what I have shown is that one strand of argument in the famous explanation tendered by John Locke is defective to the point of incoherence. But nothing has been said against the other components of the Lockean case. [17]

Notes

Waldron, Jeremy (1983) 'Two Worries about Mixing One's Labour', *The Philosophical Quarterly*, vol. 33, no 130, pp.37–44.

[1] John Locke, *Two Treatises of Government*, edited by Peter Laslett (Cambridge, 1960), II, Chapter Five.

[2] Ibid., I, §86, II, §28.

[3] Ibid., II, §41.

[4] Ibid., II, §§40–4.

[5] Ibid., II, §§32 and 34.

[6] Ibid., II, §27.

[7] I owe this point to David Miller's paper, 'Justice and Property', *Ratio*, 22 (1980), p.7.

[8] Robert Nozick, *Anarchy, State and Utopia* (Oxford, 1974), pp.150, 160, 174–5, and 202–3.

[9] [A *category mistake* is made when a term belonging in one particular category is mistakenly transferred across to another, inappropriate, category. So if I ask 'what colour is Sunday?' I make a category mistake. Colour is not the sort of term that applies to days of the week.]

[10] Cf. Donald Davidson, 'The Logical Form of Action Sentences', in *Actions and Events* (Oxford, 1980).

[11] This view seems to be shared by Karl Olivecrona, 'Locke's Theory of Appropriation', *Philosophical Quarterly* 24 (1974), p.226, where he remarks: 'It would be absurd to contend that the "labour" of killing a deer or picking an acorn from the ground is, in the exact sense of the expression, "mixed" with the deer or the acorn respectively. Locke cannot have meant it so'. But that is what Locke writes. Olivecrona does not indicate why he thinks the contention absurd.

[12] Nozick, op. cit., pp.174–5.

[13] This objection is particularly important in the case of land: see Lawrence Becker, *Property Rights: Philosophic Foundations* (London: 1977), p.34, and James Tully, A Discourse on Property: Locke and his Adversaries (Cambridge, 1980), pp.117–19.

[14] [The Latin for 'as', *qua* is a term that philosophers use to emphasize the specific meaning of the term they are using. When Waldron writes that 'the labour qua labour, no longer exists', what he means is that the labour, conceived of as labour, no longer exists, though it may exist conceived of as something else.]

[15] See, especially, J.P. Day, 'Locke on Property', *Philosophical Quarterly* 16 (1966), p.207.

[16] Tully, op. cit., pp.106–10.

[17] The idea that human labour comes to be 'contained' in a product as a result of the process of production is, of course, heavily relied on by Marx, in *Capital* and elsewhere. It is worth considering whether similar criticisms apply to his account. I am inclined to think that they do not, inasmuch as Marx is not relying on the labour-mixing idea as a basis for entitlement, but rather for his theories of value and alienation. But that would be a subject for a separate paper.

'Reconstructing Locke on Property'

A. John Simmons

A. John Simmons is Professor of Philosophy at the University of Virginia and is the author of important works on Locke, including *On the Edge of Anarchy: Locke, Consent and the Limits of Society* (1993) and *The Lockean Theory of Rights* (1992). In this extract from the latter book, Simmons attempts to reconstruct Locke's account of the origins of property rights, in the face of criticisms such as Waldron's in Reading 3.3. He does so by asking us to think of labour not as a substance but as the practice of bringing external objects into line with our particular plans and intentions.

... A plausible reconstruction of Locke's mixing argument must begin by specifying more carefully just what 'labour' is. What, to take the first step, did Locke mean by 'labour'? The examples of labour used by Locke involve a wide variety of free actions, such as gathering, hunting, cultivating, and reaping, and Locke seems in places to equate 'the actions or labour of' a person (*Second Treatise*, §44). Many of these actions (such as picking up acorns) involve no hard work (strenuous or demanding labour), so labour is not confined to what we might normally describe as 'toil.' [1] Nor is mere physical exertion, even if it is strenuous, sufficient to count as labour, since then animals (or perhaps machines) could labour and make property. [2] It is our 'intellectual nature' that makes us 'capable of dominion' (*First Treatise*, §30); the labourer must be acting freely and intentionally, not merely behaving. Labour for Locke, then, is action that is free and intentional, [3] aimed or purposive (in the sense of intending to produce a result of use to self or others). [4]

Not all free, intentional, purposive action can count as labour for Locke, however, for he seems to want to contrast labour at least with play or recreation. [5] One can make property *for* play, it seems (e.g., carve a bat from wood, or make a ball from hide and sawdust), but not *by* playing. Labour must be aimed at satisfying human needs or making human life more comfortable or convenient, in a way which play typically is not. I cannot make property in land merely by playing ball on it (although perhaps I might make property in the land by clearing and marking out part of my fair share of land to serve as a baseball diamond). Nor can I make a property in land by simply walking over or occupying the land, unless I add to that occupation my labour on the land. [6] Labour must be aimed at a useful result.

But while labour must thus be intentional and purposive, labour cannot consist simply in *having* the intention to use a thing or a purpose for it. Intending to take X, thinking of X, declaring X one's own, wanting X, pointing at X, and seeing X first are all ways of *not* labouring on X. Labour must show enough seriousness of purpose to 'overbalance' the community of things. In situations of competitive liberties (e.g., where anyone may make property in a thing by labour), the Lockean rule is 'first come, first served.' But to count as 'first comer,' an appropriate act must be performed; and for things of use the appropriate act for claiming them is to use them (i.e., labour on them to produce a result of use). One's labour need not be completed to 'begin a property,' but it must (to abuse legal language) constitute a real 'attempt' and not 'mere preparation.' The hunter who chases the hare 'has employed so much labour ... as to find and pursue her' and 'has thereby removed her from the state of nature, wherein she was common, and hath begun a property' (*Second Treatise*, §30). Although the hare has not yet been caught, the hunter has invested sufficient labour in the hunt that another's taking it would constitute an injury, robbing the hunter of his labour. [7]

Some labour, it may be objected, constitutes such a small investment that it is hard to see how it is more of an injury to deprive a labourer of his product than, say, a planner of the object of his plan. One might easily spend more time and effort planning how to use the acorns in front of one than in actually gathering them. Why should 'picking up' give title to a thing, but not 'figuring out how to use' (or even 'pointing to')? Locke's answer must be, I think, that picking up (and other kinds of labour) brings things within the immediate range of *use* for our purposes, in a way that thinking of or pointing to does not. Labour gives property because when we labour on a thing 'we are so situated with respect to it, as to have it in our power to use it.' [8] Physical *touching* may not be necessary (I can own the water in my pail, or the gold nuggets just uncovered in my mine); but one must have begun the physical process of making deliberate, productive use of one's property (body, labour) by altering nature. And to use a thing is to actually incorporate it into one's ongoing projects and pursuits. [9]

Let us try to think of labour in Locke's texts, then, not as a kind of substance, to be literally mixed or blended with an object, but as a kind of purposive activity aimed at satisfying needs or supplying the conveniences of life. [10] Labour in this sense can include (be mixed with) external things in a fairly straightforward way. As we think about, choose, or carry out various aspects of our life plans (our projects and pursuits), external things are often central to them. Indeed, control over certain external goods is a prerequisite for almost any typical life plan. We may first labour 'internally' to produce a plan, idea, theory, or invention; but we must eventually labour on what nature provided to realize the plan (merely having the plan at most gives us property in the plan, not in the physical stuff necessary to realize it). We bring things within our purposive activities ('mixing our labour' with them) when we gather them, hunt them, enclose them, and use them in other productive ways. Grazing my cattle on a pasture counts as mixing my labour with it, for by doing so I bring it within the scope of a legitimate plan for use. This is why Locke can say that 'the grass my horse has bit' is 'my property,' in the grass (*Second Treatise*, §28). Labour and its product is thus not only an expression of and necessary condition for individual autonomy,[11] but a process of 'objectifying' oneself in the world by making concrete what was abstract (as Hegelian and Marxist views of labour or property sometimes suggest).[12] 'Mixing labour' in this way need not, of course, bring about any physical change in the object on which one labours. Gathering and catching mix labour and give property, but often don't change their objects. The object is changed only in the sense of being brought within my life and plans, by being made 'a part of me,' by being brought within the protective sphere of my property (rights).[13] What I 'add' to the thing on which I labour (*Second Treatise*, §28) is its role in my purposive activities and the consequent right over it that I acquire.

Locke, of course, says none of this explicitly, but it helps to make better sense of what he *does* say. As we have seen, where the argument from human needs and God's intentions affirms a natural right of self-preservation, Locke's mixing argument begins with a broader right of self-government (control over one's body and labour), which is, of course, in part just a right of non-interference with respect to other persons. This emphasis on self-government, including control over one's plans and projects, is explicitly in Locke's texts. And property is an indispensable condition of self-government. Property does not, then, just insure survival; it is also the security for our freedom, protecting us against dependence on the will of others and the subservience to them that this creates (*First Treatise*, §41). Our 'intellectual nature' makes us 'capable of dominion' precisely because each is naturally free and the equal of any other; property secures that freedom and equality. Those who emphasize that property is essential to choice, freedom, or agency, then, capture an important part of the spirit of Locke's theory of property. [14]

Understanding labour as a kind of purposive activity, and the mixing of labour with an object as bringing the object within the activity, allows the Lockean to better respond to the attacks on the mixing argument ... While the mixing metaphor may not be the most felicitous way to express the idea, the *literal* mixing of labour that seemed so problematic ... is now replaced with a perfectly intelligible notion of 'mixing labour.' And mixing our labour cannot be a way of losing what we own, rather than acquiring what we do not ... because what we own (our labour) is never 'separated' from us. Our plans and projects, insofar as they continue, include those natural resources in which we have 'invested our labour.' Our purposive activities are inseparable from us. But why does only the *first* labour ground property, not subsequent labour on things already taken by another ...? Because the right of self-government, from which property in external things is derived, is a right shared equally with all other persons. It is, as a result, a right only to such freedom as is compatible with the equal freedom of others. To try to control for one's own projects external goods that have already been incorporated into the legitimate plans of others, would be to deny to others that equal right. We may make property with our labour only in what is not already fairly taken as 'part of the labour' of another.

Notes

From Simmons, A. John (1992) *The Lockean Theory of Rights*, Princeton University Press, pp.271–5.

[1] Olivecrona, K. (1994) 'Appropriation in the State of Nature: Locke on the Origins of Property', *Journal of the History of Ideas*, 224, and 'Locke's Theory of Appropriation', *Philosophical Quarterly*, 226; Christman, J. (1986) 'Can Ownership Be Justified by Natural Rights?', *Philosophy and Public Affairs*, 172; Cohen, G.A. (1985) 'Self-Ownership, World Ownership, and Equality', in Lucash, F.S. (ed.) (1986) *Justice and Equality Here and Now*, Cornell University Press, p.122.

[2] Rapaczynski, A. (1987) *Nature and Politics*, Cornell University Press, pp.186–7; (1981) 'Locke's Conception of Property', *Journal of the History of Ideas*, 307.

[3] Labour must be chosen, and choice is only a possibility for rational ('intellectual') beings. This does not mean that the idea of 'forced' or 'coerced' labour is unintelligible. Coercion is consistent with freedom in this sense (the robbery victim may *choose* to hand over his money, even though the choice is made at gunpoint), but physical manipulation and compulsion (which produce bodily movement but *not* action) are not.

[4] Movements of my body caused by disease or the actions of others, say, or accidental conduct could thus not count as labour. See Becker, L. (1976) 'Labor Theory of Property Acquisition', *Journal of Philosophy*, 654.

[5] In Locke's letters to Grenville, this contrast is clear. See Tully's discussion of this point (Tully, J. (1980) *A Discourse on Property*, Cambridge University Press, p.109).

[6] See Olivecrona, ibid., p.225; and Ryan, A. (1984) *Property and Political Theory*, Basil Blackwell, p.33. Ashcraft notes that Locke's refusal to accept mere occupancy as a ground of property was also a rejection of the claims of idle, aristocratic holders of large estates (Ashcraft, R. (1986) *Revolutionary Politics and Locke's Two Treatises of Government*, Princeton University Press, pp.281–2).

[7] Compare Locke's view with that of the Supreme Court of New York concerning the fox in Pierson v. Post (see Becker, L. and Kipnis, K. (eds) (1984) *Property: Cases, Concepts, Critiques*, Prentice-Hall, pp.28–32).

[8] Hume, D. (1978 edn) *A Treatise of Human Nature*, L.A. Selby-Bigge (ed.), Oxford Univeristy Press, 3.2.3.

[9] McNally, 'Locke, Levellers', 30; Fressola, 'Liberty and Property', 320–1.

[10] Becker, L. (1977) *Property Rights*, Routledge 4; Scanlon, T. (unpublished) 'Thoughts about Rights in a State of Nature', 10. The account sketched below follows Scanlon's in many important respects.

[11] Rapaczynski, for instance, emphasizes that property is not just for consumption in Locke, but for self-sufficiency and autonomy (op. cit., pp.172–5). See also Polin, R. (1963) 'Justice in Locke's Philosophy', in Friedrich, C. and Chapman, J. (eds) (1963) *Nomos VI: Justice*, p.269.

[12] See Wood, A. (1990) *Hegel's Ethical Thought*, Cambridge University Press, p.106.

[13] Here the ideas of 'mixing labour' and 'incorporation' can be seen to come together. I have both invested my labour in the object (moved myself 'outward') and brought the object within my own realm (moved it 'inward'). The full variety of ways in which one can usefully employ nature is perhaps not adequately suggested by Locke's examples. I may use a tree, for instance, not only as lumber to build with, or as a source of nuts, but as an elabourately carved monument to my love for Claudette Colbert, as shade for my yard, as a model for my painting, and so on. All of these ways of 'mixing labour' might give property, provided the use continues and others are not in need of the tree. That you could make better use of it than I am doing is simply irrelevant, unless you need it and it is surplus for me. It may seem that my examples involve 'recreation,' not labour. But if I may create a property in the baseball bat I carve (from unneeded wood) for use in recreation (as Locke would surely admit), then other work I do to make life more convenient or comfortable should create property as well.

[14] See, for example, Plamenatz, J. (1963) *Man and Society*, vol. 1, Longman, p.249; Hospers, J. (1973) 'Property', *Personalist*, 271; Machan, T. (1989) *Individuals and Their Rights*, Open Court, pp.142–6; Wheeler, S.C. III (1987) 'Natural Property Rights as Body Rights', in Machan, T. (ed.) *The Main Debate: Communism versus Capitalism*, Random House, pp.284–6; Gould, C.C. (1986) 'Contemporary Legal Conceptions of Property and their Implications for Democracy', in Werhane, P., Gini, A. and Ozar, D. (eds) *Philosophical Issues in Human Rights*, Random House, pp.231–2.

CHAPTER 4

Jean-Jacques Rousseau: *The Social Contract*

Derek Matravers

By the end of this chapter you should:
- Have read most of *The Social Contract* through at least twice.
- Have understood the nature of the problem Rousseau was attempting to solve.
- Have understood the nature of his solution, including the role of the general will, and why individuals should subscribe to the general will.
- Have understood the difference between the sovereign authority and the government.
- Have understood the difference between negative and positive liberty, and why Rousseau has been taken to be an advocate of positive liberty.
- Appreciate there are conflicting interpretations of the scope of the general will.

Introduction

The first person who, having enclosed a plot of land, took it into his head to say this is mine and found people simple enough to believe him, was the true founder of civil society. What crimes, wars, murders, what miseries and horrors would the human race have been spared, had some one pulled up the stakes or filled in the ditch and cried out to his fellow men: 'Do not listen to this impostor. You are lost if you forget that the fruits of the earth belong to all and the earth to no one!'

(Rousseau (1987 edn) *Discourse*, p.60)

The Social Contract is, depending on who you believe, a passionate denunciation of tyranny, or a work that paved the way for Hitler and Stalin. The French revolutionaries in the eighteenth century and the Cuban revolutionaries in the twentieth claimed it as a textbook. The fact that it is called *The Social Contract* suggests it is in the tradition of liberals such as Locke; on the other hand, non-liberals such as Marx considered himself in Rousseau's debt (Marx (1844), p.20).

The Social Contract was, Rousseau says in his Foreword, taken from a larger work 'now long abandoned'. This was a work on political institutions, which he began to write in 1755, the year after he completed the *Discourse on the Origin of Inequality* (hereafter I shall refer to this as 'the *Discourse*').[1] In the discussion of *The Social*

Contract, I shall refer to the *Discourse* to illuminate the argument. There are two reasons for looking at the *Discourse* in this introduction. First, its explicit concerns indicate the problems that were in Rousseau's mind when he began thinking about what became *The Social Contract*. Second, both works make use of a 'social contract'. The role of the contract is different in each case, however. The *Discourse* culminates in a specious social contract, which enshrines inequality; in *The Social Contract*, however, it endeavours to provide the foundations of a just society.

Discourse on the Origin of Inequality

The *Discourse* was written in response to a question set by the Dijon academy: 'What is the origin of inequality among men, and is it authorized by natural law?' In his reply Rousseau contrasted two conceptions of 'man': man in the 'state of nature' is contrasted with man in the 'civil state'. I should start by saying something about Rousseau's use of the masculine pronoun. It is indubitable that, both in the *Discourse* and *The Social Contract*, Rousseau meant 'man' to apply only to men. I shall follow the widespread practice of revising Rousseau, and taking 'man' to refer to all people: that is, assuming the arguments in *The Social Contract* apply equally to men and women. This poses at least two problems: first, that there are elements of Rousseau's philosophy (particularly those I discuss later on pages 194–5) that make the extension to women difficult (Canovan (1987)); second, some people claim that political theorists in the social contract tradition (including Rousseau) offer a gendered account of citizenship, slanted to the male (Pateman (1980); Marion Young (1989)). Both approaches are worthy of consideration; however, before they can be evaluated one would need to have read and understood *The Social Contract*, and that prior task is the concern of this chapter.

The contrast between the *state of nature* and the *civil state* is used frequently in political philosophy; it occurs in Hobbes and Locke. In neither the *Discourse* nor *The Social Contract* is Rousseau intending to describe an actual historical period; we are supposed to take the state of nature as a thought experiment (cf. *Discourse*, pp.34, 38–9).[2] In both works Rousseau seeks to weigh the benefits of civil life against its drawbacks. He reveals what we derive from civil life by contrasting it with the life we would have had, had no civil society existed.

Hence, it is crucial that when we imagine the state of nature for purposes of comparison, no feature we derive from civil life slips into the picture. In thinking about the state of nature, Rousseau presents a picture of men who are tranquil and content; unencumbered by responsibility, and self-sufficient in a world of plenty. Everything natural man should need is available to him, and all his desires can be easily satisfied.

In a misunderstanding that appeared even while he was alive, Rousseau is sometimes said to exalt 'the noble savage'. That is, he is taken to advocate the superiority of 'natural man', and even a return to that state. This is doubly mistaken. First, people who live in the state of nature can no more be noble than ignoble. Those kinds of qualities only make sense within the context of a civil state. Second, a return to the state of nature is impossible. The tranquillity of natural man is a result of having only desires that can be satisfied. Society has destroyed that option for us; it would not be a matter of taking off our tailored clothes, but of a demolition of our minds (*Discourse*, p.94). From our perspective, the state of nature is not only unattainable, it is not desirable: 'since savage man desires only the things he knows, and knows only those things whose possession is in his power or easily acquired, nothing should be so tranquil as his soul and nothing so limited as his mind' (*Discourse*, p.101).

So, on the one hand we have 'natural man' with his tranquil but limited mind. On the other hand, what has civil society to offer by way of a contrast, and is it better or worse? The picture of civil society in the *Discourse* is pessimistic. The state of nature, Rousseau speculates, ceases when 'men multiplied to the point where the natural productions were no longer sufficient to nourish them' (*Discourse*, p.47). They are forced to live together and cooperate in their hunting and their agriculture. This in itself is not bad, and, indeed, before things go wrong, man goes through its 'happiest and most durable epoch' (*Discourse*, p.65). So what does go wrong? In brief, inequalities start to matter.

According to Rousseau, those in the state of nature possess *amour de soi* (love of self). This directs them to pursue their basic health and physical functioning. Once circumstances have forced them into the company of others, they also develop *amour-propre* (variously translated; self-aggrandizement is probably as good as any). The interpretation of this notion is controversial, but most agree that there is a form of *amour-propre* which is the pursuit of one's own benefits for the purposes of differentiating oneself from others. In other words, those suffering from excessive *amour-propre* can only obtain their satisfactions by noting that others are less well off than they are. Rousseau sees this as inevitable once people begin to form societies.

> People become accustomed to consider different objects and to make comparisons. Imperceptibly they acquire ideas of merit and beauty which produce feelings of preference ... Each one began to look at the others and to want to be looked at himself, and the public esteem had a value. The one who sang or danced the best, the handsomest, the strongest, the most adroit or the most eloquent became the most highly regarded. And this was the first step toward inequality and, at the same time, towards vice.

(*Discourse*, pp.63–4)

Rousseau's conception of *amour-propre* is similar to Hobbes's conception of eminence (cf. Chapter 2, p.76 above). Both conceptions involve an individual's feeling of the need to make more of themselves than others. There is a crucial difference, however: Hobbes ascribes the 'sense of honour' arising from eminence to human nature in general, while, for Rousseau, *amour-propre* is a distortion brought about by socialization. This is part of the crucial presupposition that runs through all Rousseau's political work. Human nature is not a given; it is moulded by external (especially political) circumstances. Rousseau sums this up succinctly in his autobiography, *The Confessions*: 'I had seen that everything is rooted in politics and that, whatever may be attempted, no people would ever be other than the nature of their government made them' (Cohen (1953), p.377; cf. O'Hagan (1999), pp.11ff.). Despite the bleak picture of the social situation painted in the *Discourse*, Rousseau's view allows the possibility that such bleakness is not inevitable; it is not built into human nature. It is possible that there might be some way of structuring society, some form of politics, where the effects on individuals are positive and beneficial. As we shall see, in *The Social Contract* Rousseau attempts to describe such a form.

With socialization comes decline. The strongest and the most adroit work to improve their own lot at the expense of others, and so natural inequalities are compounded by social inequalities. Soon there are enormous differences of wealth and power. Even then, Rousseau thinks, if people had paused and reflected they might have taken steps to revert to their happier condition (*Discourse*, p.68) were it not for the advent of private property.

Rousseau's account of private property reflects his reading of Locke (cf. Chapter 3, pp.153–7 above). A person's labour gives the cultivator the right to the produce of the soil he has tilled. Consequently, this gives him the right to that field, at least until harvest. As this continues from year to year, this is 'easily transformed into property' (*Discourse*, p.67). Once again, Rousseau's view differs from that of his predecessors. Recall the conclusion of Locke's argument: 'for this labour being the unquestionable property of the labourer, no man but he can have a right to what that is once joined to ...' (*Second Treatise of Government*, V, 27). For Rousseau, however, the transformation is not a matter of right, but merely a matter of fact. Rather than having a right to the property, the labourer merely owns it; the ownership is not legitimate. This does not matter, of course, unless another person challenges the labourer about their ownership, as will happen when there is no longer sufficient property to satisfy everyone. As the ownership is a fact and not a right, the facts can be changed. New arrivals can take advantage of this; rather than starve or become paid labourers, they can change the facts by taking fields by force.

> There arose between the right of the strongest and the right of the first occupant a perpetual conflict that ended only in fights and murders. Emerging society gave way to the most horrible state of war; since the human race, vilified and desolated, was no longer able to retrace its steps or give up the unfortunate acquisitions it had made ...

> (*Discourse*, p.68)

Despite the differences in view, the situation Rousseau arrives at is that which Hobbes feared. Everybody's position is worse than it was in the state of nature. The wealthy live in perpetual fear of murder and of having their land seized, the poor of starvation. There is, according to Rousseau, a solution. One of the wealthy,

> ... having shown his neighbours the horror of a situation which armed them all against each other and made their possessions as burdensome as their needs, and in which no one could find safety in either poverty or wealth ... invented specious reasons to lead them to his goal. 'Let us unite,' he says to them, 'in order to protect the weak from oppression, restrain the ambitious, and assure everyone of possessing what belongs to him. Let us institute rules of justice and peace to which all will be obliged to conform, which will make special exceptions for no one, and which will in some way compensate for the caprices of good fortune by subjecting the strong and the weak to mutual obligations. In short, instead of turning our forces against ourselves, let us gather them into one supreme power that governs us according to wise laws, that protect and defends all the members of the association, repulses common enemies and maintains us in an eternal concord'.

> (*Discourse*, p.69)

This 'specious social contract' (O'Hagan (1999), p.53) introduces law and changes fact into right. With the advent of law, everyone is obliged to respect the ownership claims of those who have acquired their property by violence. This is the origin of inequality.

> Such was, or should have been, the origin of society and laws, which gave new fetters to the weak and new forces to the rich, irretrievably destroyed natural liberty, established forever the law of property and of inequality, changed adroit usurpation into an irrevocable right, and for the profit of a few ambitious men henceforth subjected the entire human race to labour, servitude and misery.

> (*Discourse*, p.70)

The enshrining of inequalities in law has meant that societies persist in a state of 'labour, servitude and misery'. Rousseau goes on to speculate about a different social contract: one that will be fair, rather than one that speciously legitimates misery. Indeed, he suggests a solution akin to that which he will develop in *The Social Contract*, although, at this stage he is pessimistic about its chances of success. The seed was there, however, for a different approach to the fundamental organization of society. Rousseau must have taken this idea, worked with it and, when he eventually published it, produced the most optimistic defence of the legitimacy of society prior to Marx.

Reading *The Social Contract*

The Social Contract is divided into four books, and each book is divided into short chapters. I shall refer to the text by citing the number of the book, then the chapter and then the paragraph in the chapter. The paragraphs are not numbered in the text.

In reading *The Social Contract* there are three potential sources of confusion. The first is that, although Rousseau's primary interest is in the principles behind a just state, he is also interested in the practical matter of implementing those principles. This is evident from the very first sentence: 'I intend to examine whether, in the ordering of society, there can be any reliable and legitimate rule of administration, *taking men as they are and laws as they can be*' (I, preamble, p.45, [1]; my italics). That is, whatever laws philosophy finds as the foundations for a legitimate administration have to be laws that could be applied to a society of people with all their inevitable imperfections. Unfortunately, he does not always make it clear whether he is discussing what could be done in principle or what can be done in practice, with the result that there are times when he appears to contradict himself.

Second, in addition to the principles that underlie a legitimate society and how people can be motivated to act according to those principles, Rousseau also discusses the best form of government for it. The legitimacy of a society is built into its very foundations; how a society is governed is a question that can be addressed only after the foundations have been laid.

Third, the title of the book, *The Social Contract*, might lead you to expect an account similar to that of Hobbes and Locke. All three philosophers include, at some stage of their accounts, an agreement by which individuals bind themselves into a collective body (cf. Chapter 2, pp.92ff. and Chapter 3, pp.142ff. above). The difference between Rousseau and his two predecessors is that Hobbes and Locke go on to argue that the resultant body transfers its rights to some further entity. For Hobbes it is an individual or assembly, and for Locke it is a government. For Rousseau, the rights remain with the collective body itself. Government does have a role to play, but only as a servant of the collective body; there is no transfer of rights to it (or indeed to anything else).

On Rousseau's account, therefore, the term 'social contract' is limited to the agreement individuals make among themselves. Rousseau himself occasionally seems unhappy with the term, sometimes referring to the agreement as a 'pact' (I, vi, p.73). He is not, however, totally at odds with eighteenth-century usage. Then, the term referred broadly to those theories that argued for the legitimacy of authority on the basis of the consent of the ruled. This contrasted with theories that attempted to find some other basis, such as the divine right of some individual to rule (Gourevitch (1997), p.xv). On this usage, Hobbes, Locke and Rousseau are all social contract theorists.

Book I of *The Social Contract* considers the principles that underlie a legitimate society. It opens with what is probably the most famous sentence in political philosophy: 'Man was born free, and everywhere he is in chains'. Rousseau once more begins his discussion with the state of nature, before returning to one of the key points also discussed in the *Discourse*: that force is quite different from right (compare the discussion here with Hobbes's discussion in *Leviathan*, Chapter 18; cf. Chapter 2, p.92 above). The 'fundamental problem' Rousseau intends to solve is described in I, vi, which also introduces his solution: the general will. Then, in I, vii, he describes the 'moral and collective body', the legitimate state which emerges from this solution.

Book II continues to describe the elements of the state. It also introduces the figure of 'the legislator'; a problematic figure introduced to solve a particular problem. Rousseau brings out the kind of society which could be governed according to the general will, demonstrating the consequences for equality in II, xi.

Book III concerns the strengths of various forms of government. It is important to realize, when you read this, that this is a different issue from the fundamentals which are the concern of Books I and II. The government is a body that serves the people in putting these fundamentals into action. The nature of government is a secondary matter; to be sorted out only after the fundamentals are in place. Hence, the concerns of Book III are different from, and secondary to, the concerns of Books I and II.

Book IV is largely concerned to describe a society governed roughly according to the principles Rousseau advocates: ancient Rome. Rousseau's detailed account is not central to our concerns, so I would advise you to skip Chapters iv, v and vi and return to them later in your own time. The other chapters in Book IV are important; dealing with questions such as how we discover the general will and the role of religion in Rousseau's society.

ACTIVITY

Read the whole of *The Social Contract* (pp.45–168), omitting IV, iv–vi. Do not worry if you cannot fathom every detail; we shall consider the important points presently. Pay careful attention to the chapter titles as a guide to what is being discussed.

The problem

> ... instead of destroying natural equality, the fundamental contract substitutes
> moral and legal equality for whatever degree of physical inequality nature has put
> among men; they may be unequal in strength or intelligence, but all become equal
> through agreed convention and by right.
>
> (I, ix, p.62, [8])

By the end of the *Discourse* Rousseau has shown how inequalities have become
enshrined in law. In *The Social Contract* he is not interested in how inequalities have
come about, but in giving an account of a society which preserves that which is
important in the state of nature, namely, freedom. To understand this account, we
need to grasp exactly what he takes the problem to be.

ACTIVITY

Read I, i (pp.45–6) and the first four paragraphs of I, vi (pp.54–5) and do the
following exercise. *The Social Contract* opens with the most famous sentence
Rousseau penned. What do you think Rousseau means when he talks about
man being in chains? Considering the earlier discussion of the *Discourse* might
help.

DISCUSSION

The chains are those imposed by living in societies in which injustice is
enshrined in the laws (all existing societies, according to Rousseau). Man is
born a free individual, yet he is living in the chains of civil society. We cannot
simply break those chains; we have seen that Rousseau does not believe there
is a route back to the natural state. Instead, Rousseau is going to investigate
whether there is a way of organizing civil society that does not constrain
('chain') the natural freedom of its citizens.

The rest of I, i is rather opaque. The important point is again one that was made in the
Discourse: there is no law in the state of nature, only force. All law springs from the
social order, which is not natural but created.

What Rousseau himself calls 'the fundamental problem' is stated in I, vi (p.55).
There are two important features of the problem that make it difficult to solve. First, a
'form of association' needs to be found in which individuals are able to participate but
in which they are as free as they would be outside the association. This has a
paradoxical air: how can an individual be in a state, and obtain all the benefits of
living in a state, and yet remain as free as they were outside the state? Second, this
must apply to *each and every person*. There can be no compromise solutions or
following the will of the majority; the state must not override the will of *any* of its
members. How can there be laws that obligate individuals, but which do not impinge
on that individual's freedom? How can a society be run if every law needs to be agreed
to by every member? Unless these conditions are met, however, the problem explored
in the *Discourse* will not be solved.

The general will

Rousseau's solution to the problem involves his greatest contribution to political philosophy: his notion of the general will. To understand his discussion of the general will in I, vi, recall the point made on page 190 above: Rousseau's use of 'social contract' refers only to the idea that a people are governed by their own consent. Rousseau's description of the general will in I, vi has two steps. First, there is the 'the complete transfer of each associate, with all his rights, to the whole community' (p.55). Instead of each of us pursuing our individual interests (as described in the *Discourse*), we each hand over all our rights to the community. As the community consists only of ourselves, this is not the abnegation of control it seems. Second, this community is then thought of something like a person: a 'moral and collective body' with a will of its own (the general will). What that body would will is what is good for the community as a whole.

This chapter is only part of the story. The overall shape of Rousseau's solution is that it is in each individual's best interests to act according to the general will. Hence, when individuals are acting in their own best interests, they will be acting in a way that is best for society. As a result, nobody will need to be coerced and there will be no diminution of freedom. (I will address the question of why it is in each individual's best interests to act according to the general will presently.)

ACTIVITY

Read the whole of I, vi (pp.54–6) followed by Reading 4.1, 'The General Will' by John C. Hall. When you have completed the reading, do the following exercises.

1 Write brief descriptions (no more than a couple of lines) of (a) an individual's particular will, and (b) the general will.

2 Read the following passage and answer the questions below:

'If the soccer team won the cup final, they would earn enough money to build the changing rooms they need. They would only win if they had their best player as captain. Jack badly wanted to be captain, but was probably not their best player.'

(i) What is Jack's particular will?

(ii) Give one example of the team's general will.

(iii) If Jack were the best player, would the object of his particular will also be the object of the general will?

DISCUSSION

1 (a) An individual's particular will are those things he or she wants. (b) The general will 'may be defined as the desire ... which every member of a community may be presumed to share, to promote what is in the common interest of all the members of that community' (Reading 4.1, p.222).

2(i) To be captain of the team.

(ii)   Three are possible: to win the cup final, to build the changing rooms, to have their best player as captain.

(iii) Yes, it would.

There is an apparent ambiguity in the term 'the general will'. It could refer to what is *in fact* in the best interest of the group, whether the group knows it or not (what Hall calls 'the common interest'). Alternatively, it could refer to what the group *decides*, through the right procedures, is in its best interest (the nature of such procedures will be considered later (pp.196–9)). For example, consider a circumstance in which the 'moral and collective body' (the state) needs to decide a fundamental matter, such as whether or not to dissolve the government. Let us further assume that, as a matter of fact, dissolving the government would not be in the state's best interest, and yet the decision of the state, arrived at through the right procedures, is that the government should be dissolved. Which is the general will of the state?

There are two points to make in response to this. The first is to point out that, provided people decide what is in fact in the state's best interest, the two meanings will stay together. Although, as we shall see, Rousseau has reason to think the right procedures will reliably discover the correct answer, it remains possible that what is decided is not what is in fact in the state's best interest. This will become clear in IV, i. Second, as I say above, the ambiguity may be more apparent than real. Rousseau's fundamental problem is to preserve the freedom of *each* individual, and this places limits on what the general will could be. For example, it might be in the state's best interest to enslave some section of the population; this could not be part of the general will as it unfairly burdens those people. We shall see later (pp.196–9), that the procedures for discovering the general will ensures that burdens are spread fairly.

I, vi, 10 introduces many terms which will become clearer as you proceed, but you can keep track of them by consulting this chapter's glossary. One of these terms, 'the sovereign' refers to the supreme authority in the body politic. For Rousseau, it is the 'moral and collective body' which has the general will. Because each individual has subscribed totally to this body, the interests of the sovereign and that of the individual necessarily coincide. This is why the sovereign 'does not need to give any form of guarantee to its subjects' (I, vii, 5). 'Sovereign' and 'state' both refer to the same entity; the former when it is active, the latter when it is passive. The same distinction might be marked by the terms 'leader' and 'head'. We might call someone the leader of a party when they are doing something and the head of the party when we are just drawing attention to the position they occupy – the same person is picked out in each case. Rousseau's point is that whether we think of ourselves as private individuals or as members of the state, we are not in relation to something external to us. We are in a relation of part (the individual) to whole (the sovereign). Furthermore, provided we take the general will as our own, it is a whole that necessarily acts in our best interests.

Rousseau's problem was to show how individuals could obey the will of the state, and yet remain as free as before. His solution is to (a) identify the will of the state as the general will and (b) claim that if all individuals freely adopt the general will, then in obeying the will of the state they will only be obeying themselves. This solution will work only if individuals freely adopt the general will. But why does Rousseau think they should?

The 'remarkable change'

I, viii fills in the missing part of Rousseau's argument. So far in *The Social Contract,* the only two advantages we have been given for subscribing to the general will have been the rewards of cooperation and mutual assistance. Perhaps, as a matter of fact, we are forced into cooperation by circumstance, but force does not make right. Hence, the question remains as to why cooperating with others is justified, and not simply a fact we have to endure. One answer would be if the general will always provided us with a better option than any other available. However, that does not seem plausible; there always seems an alternative to cooperation that would benefit the particular individual. This is known as the problem of 'free-riding'; it is in any particular individual's interest to ride for free, provided the system as a whole is sustained by everyone else buying tickets. Free-riding is good for that individual, but unfair on all those who keep the system going and effectively subsidize the free-rider.

This section gives Rousseau's argument for why it is in the interests of each and every individual to join the moral collective. The argument draws on the arguments in the *Discourse*. Recall, in the *Discourse,* for a man in the state of nature 'nothing should be so tranquil as his soul and nothing so limited as his mind'. Here we have the full balance sheet, and we find that the state of nature is devoid of everything it takes to be 'an intelligent being and a man'. Even the initial attractions of natural liberty and possession start to pale when we realize that these would have to be maintained by force.

The argument is that each of us has an interest in possessing the attributes we would acquire by participating in the civil state: being part of the moral collective. Rousseau argues for the benefits of subscribing to the general will both by indicating the drawbacks of the state of nature, and the benefits of the civil state. In the state of nature we are motivated not by reason but by appetite; we are a slave to it. In the civil state we undergo a 'remarkable change'; we actually become different in that properties absent in the state of nature (reason, morality) become part of us.

ACTIVITY

Read I, viii (pp.79–81) and complete a 'balance sheet' of benefits gained in the civil state against benefits lost from the state of nature. Here is an example of one entry below:

Civil state	State of nature
justice	instinct

My version of the 'balance sheet' is shown in note 3(p.213).

DISCUSSION

It is clear from the 'balance of gains and losses' that the 'remarkable change' has a number of relevant features. The genuine social contract, like the specious social contract of the *Discourse*, makes property a matter of right, rather than something one needs to keep hold of by force. However, unlike the specious social contract, it has other features that will, eventually, ensure that people's freedom is preserved. An important feature is 'moral liberty', which, in I, viii, is contrasted with 'natural liberty'. Natural liberty is that enjoyed in the state of nature: it is the freedom from obstacles that might stand between an individual and the satisfaction of his or her desires (this was described on page 186 above). Civil society takes this away from us. In what sense, then, is our changed state one of *liberty*? The argument is in the claim that 'to obey a law which we have imposed on ourselves is freedom'. In the state of nature we are free to act; but we act from our desires, and our desires are not freely chosen, which is why Rousseau describes being driven by appetites as 'slavery'. We have true freedom ('moral liberty') if our actions are the result of laws we have freely chosen; that is, the prescriptions of the general will. Consider the following analogy. A rich and well-connected drug addict might be free to satisfy all her desires; she has perfect natural liberty. The problem is that her desire is overwhelming, and is ruining her health and her life. Is she free or is she a slave to her desires? Would she not be *truly* free if she could be persuaded to choose desires more conducive to a worthwhile life?

There are two steps, therefore, to acquiring moral liberty. First, people's characters need to be altered so they choose to pursue the right goals. Second, liberty is identified with the pursuit of those goals. The standard criticism of the pursuit of moral liberty (from within liberal political philosophy) is directed at the notion of 'the right goals'. Liberals find something sinister in the idea that the state should attempt to alter the desires people happen to have, in favour of some abstract conception of the desires they ought to have. This is debate to which we shall return on pages 208–10.

The general will: its nature, how we discover it and its limits

The nature of the general will

The version of *The Social Contract* we have is, as I have said, taken from a larger work. There is evidence that it was put together from a number of different sources (Hall (1973), pp.52–65). It is clear that Rousseau was concerned with at least two different strands of thought: (a) the principles behind the legitimate state and (b) its actual workings in practice. In Book II it becomes necessary to sort these two strands out.

Rousseau distinguishes between the legislature and the executive: those who make the laws and those who implement them (III, i). The former is the sovereign, whose will is the general will– the basic acts of the general will are called the law (II, vi, 6). The latter is the government (also called 'the ruler' or 'the prince'): 'an intermediate body set up between subjects and sovereign to ensure their mutual correspondence, and is entrusted with the execution of laws and with the maintenance of liberty, both social and political' (III, i, 5). In short, the government is the body that governs the state according to the general will. The government does not make the law; it merely applies it in particular instances. For example, the law might be that there should be an army commanded by officers. It will be the task of the government to decide the nature of the army, and the identity of the officers. Rousseau calls such decisions 'acts of magistracy' or 'decrees'.

ACTIVITY

Read II, i and ii (pp.63–5; ignore the final paragraph of ii). Write a short paragraph explaining the two points Rousseau makes in these two chapters about the nature of the sovereign. Be guided by the chapters' titles.

DISCUSSION

First, II, i: the authority of the sovereign (the moral and collective body that is the people) cannot be transferred to a sub-group of the whole, or a particular person. The reason given is that the particular will of the person chosen cannot be guaranteed to be in accord with the general will. This is obviously a rejection of Hobbes's account of legitimacy: that the people should transfer sovereign power to a single person or to an assembly. Second, II, ii: the sovereign remains indivisible from the people. It cannot be alienated; that is, it cannot be *given* away, to the government or to anything else. This means that all other bodies (governments, magistrates, etc.) do not have any sovereign power at all. They are always mere servants of the people. (The footnote, that the vote need not be unanimous, is eventually explained at IV, ii.)

As is clear from II, ii, Rousseau claims that the day-to-day running of the state is not a matter of the general will, but requires a government to put the general will into action in particular circumstances. Rousseau says in II, i, that a 'chief's orders' can pass for the general will, provided the sovereign does not actively oppose them. Hence, although 'the chiefs' are technically servants of the sovereign they can take silence to mean consent. This is a dangerous principle in practical politics. However, Rousseau says, he 'will explain this at greater length'.

How we discover it

ACTIVITY

Read II, iii (pp.66–7).

As we have seen, the general will is that which promotes the common interest of the state. Rousseau assumes that there is only one course of action which corresponds to the general will: there is only one course of action which, within the constraints of the will having to preserve the interests of each individual, will *optimize* the common interest of the state. He points out in the first paragraph that it is one thing for there to be a general will, it is quite another for us to know what it is. It does not make sense to talk of the general will going wrong, however 'the people' might go wrong in trying to discover it. Rousseau describes how the general will is discovered in two separate discussions: in II, iii, 2 and in IV, i and ii.

Unfortunately, the first passage in which the problem is discussed is unclear. Most agree that the procedure comes in stages. First, all the particular wills of the individuals are collected. Then the 'excesses and insufficiencies' of these are taken away; a procedure which looks as if it is aimed at finding what all the particular wills have in common. Some translations maintain this is all there is to it; 'the common element remaining...' is the general will (e.g. Betts (1994)). Others maintain that there is a final stage: the differences between the particular wills are summed, and it is the 'sum of the differences' that is the general will (e.g. Cole (1973)).

This seems to be a case in which translation depends upon interpretation. Identifying the general will as the common element across all particular wills makes some sense, but identifying it as the combination of what is *different* in everybody's desires does not. Furthermore, the latter interpretation is straightforwardly inconsistent with what Rousseau goes on to say in his more extended discussion of how we find the general will in Book IV.

In this discussion, Rousseau makes it clear that although what people think can change, what is in fact in a state's interest is 'constant, unalterable, and pure' (IV, i, [6]). The discussion of peasant societies indicates that Rousseau thinks that provided the state is small enough, and the people honest enough, discovering the general will should be easy and unanimity will reign. However, once people no longer think of themselves primarily as members of a collective body, they will put forward their private interests and dissent will break out. How, in such circumstances, is the general will to be discovered? In IV, ii Rousseau argues that a vote should be taken, and the view of the majority should be followed. This is, initially at least, a surprising claim. Recall Rousseau's statement of the 'fundamental problem': the freedom of *each and every* person must be preserved. How is this compatible with the demand that the minority follows the will of the majority?

ACTIVITY

Read IV, i and ii (pp.91–9) and answer the following questions.

1   What, for Rousseau, is the point of taking a vote?

2   What does Rousseau mean when he claims that 'if my particular will had prevailed... I should not have been free' (IV, ii, [8])? Think about the discussion of 'moral liberty' (pp.194–5 above).

DISCUSSION

1   The discussion of this occurs in IV, ii, 8. Rousseau contrasts his use of voting with the use of the vote in a democratic referendum. In Rousseau's state, people are not asked whether or not they approve of a proposition (which is what they would be asked in a referendum) but whether they think the proposition in fact expresses the general will. If the majority thinks the proposition is in accord with the general will, this is taken to be the case (this will be explained below).

2   We know that obeying the general will is (according to Rousseau) the way of becoming free. We also know that the decision of the majority is the general will. Hence, only if an individual follows the will of the majority (rather than there own will, if it differs) will they be free. Here is an analogy

(based on Hall (1973), pp.106–7). Fred wants to buy a Picasso. He goes to an auction and bids for a picture he believes to be a Picasso. Jane, who has a method of discovering whether pictures are Picassos or fakes, finds that the picture Fred is bidding for is a fake and sabotages the bid. On the one hand Fred does not get what he wants because he does not get the picture he bid for. On the other hand there is a clear sense in which if he had got the picture he would not have got what he wanted, because he wanted a Picasso and the picture is a fake. In the same way, if I want to obey the general will, being forced to follow the will of the majority does not deprive me of what I want. For, whatever I might think, the view of the majority tells us what the general will is, and is thus what I *really* want.

Why does Rousseau think that the opinion of the majority is, in fact, the general will? This question is one that is considered in Reading 4.2, 'The Public Interest' by Brian Barry. In this paper Barry attempts to apply Rousseau's ideas to a modern context.

ACTIVITY

Read Reading 4.2 and answer the following questions.

1   Rousseau claims that people should not be allowed to form 'partial associations', or if they do so, such groups should be many and small. Why is this? (Look at the presuppositions Rousseau needs to make in order that voting will be an effective method of discovering the general will.)

2   In the paragraph following the quotation from II, iv, Barry appears to move from the claim that the general will is 'equally in the interests of the all members of the group' to the claim that the 'policies ... will effect everyone in the same way'. Why does Barry think he can make this move?

DISCUSSION

1   The two presuppositions Rousseau needs are that everyone should ask himself 'the right question' (that is, what is the general will) and that everyone has an equal, better than even chance of getting the right answer. If people form groups, then they will be influenced by what is good for the particular group they are in (that is, the general will *for that group*). Hence, they will not be asking themselves the right question, and, as they are not even asking the right question, they will (obviously) not have an even, or better than even chance of getting the right answer. For example, imagine that a sizeable number of people in a state belong to a trade union, and imagine further that a vote is being taken to ascertain the general will on whether to unify with another state. The union, fearful of an influx of cheap labour, instructs all its members to vote against, as that is *the general will of the union*. Those votes will not be a help in discovering the general will of the state (although, of course, the general will of the union and the general will of the state could coincide; however, this would happen by chance). The ban on partial associations (or the insistence that there are so many that their biases cancel each other out) might be thought to provide evidence of the totalitarian nature of Rousseau's thought. However, we can see that Rousseau had good reason for it; it was a necessary part of his method for discovering the general will.

> 2   Finding the general will is finding a law that applies to everyone. Each individual has a vote, and no individual will vote for a law that places an unfair burden on him or herself. As a result the only laws that will be voted for are ones that apply to everyone equally.

Although the general will applies to everyone equally, this does not mean that it will affect everyone in the same way. For example, it may be the general will of a sports team to have their best player as captain. This applies to everyone equally, in that no one is excluded from the reckoning as to who is the best player. However, the outcome will not be the same for everyone; the effect on the best player (whoever that might be) will be greater than the effect on the others. We will consider this further in the next section.

The existence of partial associations is not the only matter that needs sorting out prior to the settling of the general will. If the citizens of the state hold vastly different amounts of wealth and power, then the kind of reciprocity which the general will presupposes will be impossible. The vote may well be skewed if some are rich enough to buy others, and others are so poor they need to sell themselves. Hence, in II, xi, 2 Rousseau proposes a rough equality of wealth and power. I said at the outset that Rousseau was fundamentally concerned with freedom, and this is evident here. Equality is advocated, but only for the purpose of a greater good; to facilitate the general will to maintain the freedom of everyone.

The limits of the general will

II, iv argues for two important limitations on the power of the sovereign: first, that the sovereign can only concern itself with matters that are 'important for the community to use' and second that the general will must be general 'not only in essence but also in respect of its object'.

ACTIVITY

Read II, iv (pp.67–70) taking note of these two points.

The first point appears to contradict the 'complete transfer of each associate, with all his rights, to the whole community' of I, vi, 6. This is not necessarily so. Recall that Rousseau is aiming for a state in which nobody is subject to a will that is not their own. Desires we have which are not going to impinge on the freedom of other people are not a threat to anyone's freedom, hence are of no concern to Rousseau (or the general will). In the state of nature there is no need to divide our desires into two sorts: those which are purely private and those in the public sphere. In I, iv Rousseau claims that when we join the moral community, we alienate all our individual *rights* to the general will. Unlike the public sphere, the private sphere is not a matter of rights (as it is only the individual involved). So the upshot is that we are not allowed to pursue our particular wills in the public sphere when we join the moral community; in this sphere, we are subordinate to the general will.

The separation of the public and private is characteristic of liberal political philosophy; you will have met it in Locke and will meet it again in Mill. For Locke, the private sphere was defined in terms of the rights the individual possesses in the state of nature. For Mill, we are in the private sphere provided our actions do no harm to others. In both these cases this boundary acts so as to protect the individual from the state; the power of the state ought not to cross into the private sphere. For Rousseau, however, the sovereign body is supreme. So, although there is a boundary between the public and private sphere ('what is important for the community to use'), 'the sovereign authority alone judges the degree of importance' (II, iv, 3). Hence, the liberal check on the power of the state, the boundary between public and private, is itself a matter of the sovereign's decision. Hence, lacking this safeguard, it becomes even more important to show that the general will cannot discriminate against individuals.

As we have seen, the general will is what is in fact in the best interests of the state. It is, however, more than that. In order that the freedom of each individual is preserved, the general will should be acceptable to each person. Each person is taken into account in framing it, and each person should subscribe to it; 'it must issue from everyone in order that it should apply to everyone'. As we saw in the discussion of Brian Barry's paper, the consequence is that the general will applies to everyone equally. No particular individuals are allocated disproportionate burden or benefit.

Do not be confused by Rousseau's terminology; by a 'law' he means a specific deliverance of the general will. Hence, laws never select particular individuals; they apply to everyone equally. We have already seen that applying to everyone equally is not the same as having an equal effect on everyone. A law stated in general terms might apply only to a particular individual. Consider, for example, a society in which there is only one millionaire: Mr Jones. There could be a law, 'all millionaires are to pay twice as much tax as everyone else'. Although Mr Jones is the only person affected by this law, it applies to everyone equally. Anyone who was a millionaire would be affected; it happens that Mr Jones is the only millionaire. As such a law is the general will, we know that such a tax system is in the best interest of the state.

I said above that the moral and collective body fixes the boundary between the private and the public spheres. However, beyond indicating that the general will covers matters of importance, Rousseau does not specify the principles on which the decision to fix the boundary would be based. What is the province of the general will? Should it, as my example suggests, include general principles of taxation? Or should its concerns be more fundamental than that?

The answer to this question is controversial. On the one hand, Rousseau argues that laws 'are no more than a society's conditions of association' (II, vi, [10]); that is the basic conditions determining the foundation of the state. This suggests the province of the general will is very narrow. On the other hand, in III, xii–xiv he claims that it 'is not sufficient for the people to have assembled once in order to settle the constitution of a state by giving its sanction to a body of law' (III, xiii, 1). There should be periodic assemblies of the sovereign body, and, while they will not be performing tasks properly done by government, they will be deciding something. This suggests a broader province for the general will. We will return to this point later (pp.209ff.), when we discuss Rousseau and totalitarianism.

II, v considers the question of whether the sovereign has the right to take the life of a citizen. This question was considered by both Hobbes and Locke (in *Leviathan*, Chapter XXI and *Second Treatise of Government*, Chapter IV, 23 respectively). The problem is that subscribing to the state is supposed to be in the individual's interest. If this is true, how can the state ever be justified in taking an individual's life? For it cannot be in any person's interest to be killed.

ACTIVITY

Read II, v (pp.71–2) and describe the two solutions Rousseau gives to this problem.

DISCUSSION

1   'Whoever wills the end wills the means'. In other words, committing oneself to live in a state according to the general will involves committing oneself to everything necessary to create and sustain such a state. If this involves putting those who are a danger to the state to death, then each of us is committed to that (even if it is one of us that is put to death).

2   In violating the general will individuals cease to be a member of the state; rather, they become individuals who are at war with the state. Hence, the state is no longer under any obligation to consider their interests; indeed, 'the right of war is to kill the vanquished'.

Notice that condemning a criminal (a particular act) cannot be an act of the sovereign but of the government. Notice also that Rousseau thought the death penalty should be restricted to extreme cases: there is 'nobody so wicked that he cannot be made useful in some respect'. Hobbes and Locke favoured the second of Rousseau's two solutions. That is, capital punishment is legitimate because there is of a state of war between the individual and the state. Neither took Rousseau's more radical suggestion that, having willed the end and so the means for the preservation of the state, a condemned person has consented to their own execution.

We have seen that the sovereign cannot hand over its powers, nor can it divide itself up, without destroying itself. The general will cannot err, as it is just what tends to public welfare. However, the people's view of the general will might be wrong. Rousseau gives a method for discovering the general will; by taking a vote under some specific conditions. The acts of the general will are laws. Specific acts, which deal with particulars, are decrees and are acts of government (the ruler or prince) rather than the sovereign.

The final paragraph of II, vi takes us on to our next discussion. Rousseau now has to face a circularity in his argument. He has argued that the application of reason to human affairs comes about as a result of forming a moral and collective body acting according to the general will. Hence, what is needed to set up such a body (a group of laws) can only be formulated by an exercise of the general will. But the general will only comes into existence when the body has been set up. So it cannot get started. 'This' says Rousseau, 'is why it is necessary to have a legislator' (II, vi, 9).

The legislator

ACTIVITY

Read II, vii (pp.76–9) followed by Reading 4.3, 'The Legislator' by N.J.H. Dent. Dent thinks 'the preconditions that make the appeal to reason in public affairs possible' are often non-rational. Explain briefly why he thinks this and find an apposite quotation from II, vii that supports the case.

DISCUSSION

The legislator is a genius who sets up the state and gives it its laws. These are then endorsed and added to by the people (once they have formed a state and are able to act according to the general will). The legislator cannot *force* people to become a state (that would be wrong) and he cannot *reason* with them (prior to forming a state, people are not governed by reason). Hence, he will need to resort to non-rational methods of persuasion: in particular, pretending to have divine authority and persuading people to form a state by claiming that to do so is the will of the gods.

A number of quotations would serve to support the argument, although the most apposite has as its conclusion a view explicitly endorsed by Dent (pp.229 below).

> In order that a people in the process of formation should be capable of appreciating the principles of sound policy and follow the fundamental rules of reasons of state, it would be necessary for the effect to become the cause; the spirit of community, which should be the result of the constitution, would have to have guided the constitution itself; before the existence of laws, men would have to be what the laws have made them. Thus the legislator is unable to employ either force or argument, and has to have recourse to another order of authority, which can compel without violence and win assent without arguing.
>
> (II, vii, [9])

The idea of a genius from outside creating the conditions under which people are able to form a state might sound strange to us. However, Rousseau does refer to historical precedent: he refers explicitly to Calvin, but also alludes to Moses, Muhammad and Numa. Rousseau himself was twice invited to write the constitution of a state: for Corsica and for Poland. As Dent says, Rousseau invokes the legislator to solve a problem that is still with us. Individuals cannot form themselves into a people until they can consult their reason. However, they can only do this after becoming a people. Hence, the need for a legislator who can provide them with the laws to form them into a people.

Government

We saw on page 195 above that Rousseau distinguishes between the sovereign and the government. The nature of government is the principal concern of Book III. This is less concerned with principle, and more with the practical problems of running a state.

The reasons for government

ACTIVITY

Read III, i and ii and do the following exercises.

1 Find two reasons in the first five paragraphs of III, i why states need a sovereign *and* a government.

2 Explain Rousseau's claim that 'the act by which a people submits to the authority of chiefs is not a contract'.

3 List the three different wills Rousseau claims influence a member of the government (a magistrate).

4 What, according to Rousseau, is the advantage and what the disadvantage of having a government by a single person?

DISCUSSION

1(i) The sovereign decides on the general will: laws that apply equally to everyone. However, running a state also involves acting on a will that applies to particular people. The government is needed to do this. This is the distinction Rousseau makes between 'force' and 'will'.

(ii) The government is needed for 'mutual correspondence' between subjects and sovereign. That is, a body is needed to make sure that the people act upon the laws they make for themselves.

2 The government has no authority of its own; it is the servant of the sovereign which delegates power to it. As it has no authority, it has no bargaining position – hence it cannot make a contract. The people do not promise to obey the government; the government is the servant of the people.

3(i) The magistrate's private will. This is what is in the interests of the individual magistrate.

(ii) The corporate will of the government. This is what is in the best interests of the government. The corporate will is the general will *of the government,* but a particular will with respect to the state.

(iii) The general will of the state.

4 Rousseau claims that, in any single individual, the particular will is strongest, followed by the will of the group to which he belongs (the corporate will) followed by the general will. Hence, in government by a single person, the corporate will and the particular will of that individual will be identical and hence will be very strong. So an advantage is that the government will be 'vigorous'. The disadvantage is that the particular will of an individual is furthermost from the general will.

This makes intuitive sense. Running associations by committee can be time-consuming and inefficient, but putting all the power into the hands of one individual does leave the association at the mercy of their particular ways of doing things.

What Rousseau says here looks inconsistent with his claims in Book I in which he maintains that, in the mind of the decent citizen, it is the general will that is the strongest. What is in his mind here is the threat to sovereignty by the government. Because they have the power, members of the government are able to act on their particular wills and this will be a great temptation ('power corrupts ...'). So in their position, one needs to recognize that their particular wills are likely to be strongest (cf. Levine (1976), pp.127–8).

The forms of government

Having established the need for the sovereign to institute a government to enact particular laws in conformity with the general will, the question then arises as to what sort of government would be best. The answer to this question, according to Rousseau, depends partly on the nature of the country to be governed. These chapters examine the different sorts of government. They also contain some fairly wild speculations and generalizations linking particular attributes of a country with the nature of its inhabitants. Amongst the oddest of the assertions, is the claim (in III, ix) that *the* sign of good government is how readily its citizens multiply.

ACTIVITY

Read III, iii–ix. Which form of government does Rousseau think best overall, and why does he come to that decision?

DISCUSSION

In III, v Rousseau claims the best form of government is an elective aristocracy. By 'aristocracy', Rousseau means government by a group which is less numerous than the sovereign, but larger than one. The advantage with electing members of the group is that the public will choose those people who are most able to govern (those who have probity, enlightenment, experience and so on). A small group means that meetings can be conveniently held and business discussed in an orderly and diligent manner. They will also be able to build relationships with authorities abroad.

The decline of the state

ACTIVITY

Read the final eight chapters of Book III which concern reasons for the decline of the state, and some of Rousseau's ideas about how this can be prevented.

III, x and xi exhibit Rousseau's pessimism about human institutions, and are interesting in the way in which they prefigure Marx. The main point is made in III, xi, 2: 'the political body, like the human, begins to die as soon as it is born, and carries within it the causes of its own destruction'. Affirming that 'the principle of political life lies in the sovereign authority', Rousseau then turns to how this authority can be maintained. His proposed solution, to form an assembly of the people is, as he admits, only practical for small states. An expedient, for a large state, is to hold several assemblies in different parts of the state.

With the advance of communications technology, the idea of periodic consultation of the sovereign faces fewer practical problems, so it might be thought that Rousseau's popular sovereignty could now be put in place. The difference between the role of the government and that of the sovereign needs to be observed. If all the people were consulted over issues that were properly the concern of government, that would simply be a democratic government. What is as issue here is something different: the people coming together as the sovereign, the moral and collective body, to decide the general will. The sovereign would not concern itself with particular matters but with matters of law (a point stressed in III, xviii).

It was an important part of the message of Book I that people will act according to the general will only if they see themselves as part of a moral and collective body, rather than as self-seeking individuals (see I, viii). As we have seen, Rousseau argues that it is in each person's interests to act according to the general will. This prompts the further question, however, of how to motivate people to act according to their best interests. This is an important question for Rousseau (see Gourevitch (1997), p.xiii), and in III, xv, he begins to discuss the means by which people can be made to do so (this will be discussed on pp.206–8).

ACTIVITY

Read III, xv (pp.126–9). Find five features of a state which Rousseau takes as symptoms of decline.

DISCUSSION

1   Defending the state by use of a professional army, rather than it being the duty of each citizen.
2   Allowing deputies to represent citizens in the sovereign assembly.
3   Using a part of one's wages (taxes) to fund other people to perform one's duties as a citizen.
4   Not attending, or not caring about, the assemblies.
5   'The weakening love of country, the energy spent on private interests, the immense size of the state, conquests and the abuse of government': Rousseau claims these have been cited as the cause of (2).

Rousseau's principal point is that made in II, i: sovereignty cannot be represented. The whole project of *The Social Contract* is to describe a state in which the liberty of each individual is preserved. This is done by each individual contracting to obey only himself or herself, by obeying the general will. Obviously, if individuals then send delegates to decide the general will for them, the sense in which the general will is their own will is lost, and they will no longer be free.

You might have wondered about Rousseau's attack on 'the people of England' (III, xv, [5]). This is because in England, it is claimed that Parliament is the supreme law-making body (in other words, Parliament is sovereign). This would require the sovereignty of the people to be *represented* by Parliament, which Rousseau claims is impossible. However, Rousseau would not have minded if the English system were that the people remained sovereign, and Parliament was simply the English form of government.

III, xvi–xviii make three separate points. First, III, xvi reaffirms the claim that the sovereign does not contract itself to obey the government. Rousseau provides four separate arguments of the claim (finding these I will leave as an exercise for the reader). Second, in III, xviii Rousseau rescues himself from apparent contradiction. The appointment of the government is a particular act, it names particular people. Hence, it cannot issue from the general will (which only deals with matters that 'apply to everyone'); it must issue from the government. Obviously, a government cannot appoint itself before it exists. The solution to this conundrum is for the sovereign assembly to think of itself as its own democratic government, consisting of all the people. Under this identity, it is able to issue a particular act to set up the government it wishes. It then reverts to being a sovereign. Rousseau points out that the British House of Commons can do this when an issue comes before it which it is inappropriate for Parliament to discuss, but all right for a committee of Parliament to discuss. It merely thinks of itself as a large committee, discusses the point, and then reports to itself afterwards. Third, III, xviii reaffirms the point that government has no power of its own; all its power is derived from the sovereign which appoints it. Rousseau repeats the suggestion (originally made in III, xiii) that there be periodic assemblies to consider how the government is doing. In essence, this is what happens in a British general election, with two vital differences. First, an election only changes the personnel, not the form of government, and second, an election delegates sovereignty to Parliament (rather than merely electing a government) – something which Rousseau does not think possible.

To sum up. Rousseau argues that government is needed because a state cannot be run by the general will alone. An elective aristocracy (which is roughly our representative democracy) is generally his favoured form of government, although different governments suit different circumstances. However, government brings with it a clash of wills, and all states contain within them the seeds of their own decline.

Persuasion and coercion

Persuasion

I have argued that the fundamental good Rousseau aims to preserve is freedom. Freedom is threatened when people are not equal: that is, when one person has power over another. As people are not equal in nature, they need to be made equal by convention, and that convention is obedience to the general will. I, viii argues that each person has reason to obey the general will; in doing so, they fulfil their better natures. However, Rousseau is aware from the beginning that he needs to write for 'men as they are, and laws as they can be' (I, preamble). Men, being what they are, will need more than an appeal to their better natures to enlist them in 'the moral and collective body' (I, vi). The relevant texts here are II, xii and IV, vii and viii.

> ## ACTIVITY
>
> Read II, xii and IV, vii and viii (pp.88–90, 156–68)

At II, xii, 5 Rousseau speaks of the law 'graven... in citizens' hearts... the true constitution of the state': namely, that which refers 'to moral standards, to custom and above all to public opinion'. Rousseau's term, here translated as 'moral standards', is *moeurs*. This has no precise English equivalent. It refers to standards at work in a society (including moral standards) as well as tastes and customs. In IV, vii and viii Rousseau makes some suggestions about how these things can be safeguarded, in order that the general will be preserved as the arbiter of the fundamental laws. First, he suggests the re-establishment of the Roman office of censor; an official position which is independent of the government. The task of the censor is to strengthen moral standards and opinion, and use them to support the state by applying them in particular cases. Moral standards are created by the way the state is constituted, and, when the state degenerates, so do these standards. The censor cannot recreate them once they have degenerated. However, while the state is healthy it can vocalize public opinion in particular instances for good effect and Rousseau gives two amusing examples of this.

Rousseau's second suggestion is to motivate people to act according to the general will by enlisting the persuasive power of religion. On its publication *The Social Contract* was condemned in both Geneva and France, principally for the contents of IV, viii. At the time, the nature of the relation between church and state was a vexed question much considered by philosophers. For example, it occupied two of the four books of Hobbes's *Leviathan*.

> ## ACTIVITY
>
> In IV, viii (pp.158–68) Rousseau describes three 'kinds' of relation between religion and society and finds them wanting. What are these, and what is wrong with them? What kind of religion does he advocate as a replacement, and what do you think people found objectionable about it?

> ### DISCUSSION
>
> The three kinds of religion, and what is wrong with them, are:
>
> 1   A religion 'with no temples, no alter, no ritual', devoted to worshipping God and 'the external duties of morality'. Although Rousseau subscribes to this (it resembles the Calvanism of his native Geneva), it suffers from a fatal flaw in that it 'has no particular relationship to the body politic'. In other words, it can play no role in reinforcing individuals' respect of the law and their thinking of themselves as citizens.
>
> 2   A sort of unity of church and state. The gods are the gods of the state, and law prescribes the rites. This is good in that it harnesses the power of religion in the service of preserving the state. However, it suffers from two defects. First, it is based on 'error and lies' (true religion is just not like that). Second, it makes people 'bloodthirsty and intolerant'. If you see all

your enemies not only as subjects of another state, but as infidels, it is easier to kill them.

3   A system in which people are asked to have a twin allegiance; both to the state and to religion, an authority above the state. Thus Catholics are supposed to owe allegiance to the state and to the Church of Rome. This is worse than not harnessing religion to support the state – religion is actively working against it: 'Anything that breaks up the unity of society is worthless; all institutions that put man in contradiction with himself are worthless'.

Rousseau's idea of a replacement is given in the following quotation: 'There is therefore a purely civil profession of faith, the articles of which it is the business of the sovereign to determine; not exactly as religious dogmas, but as sentiments of sociability, without which it is impossible to be either a good citizen or a loyal subject'. It looks as if Rousseau is advocating that the 'articles of religion' should not be the word of God, but should be established by the sovereign for the purposes of encouraging sociability. Thus religion should not be encouraged in a state because it is true, but because it helps preserve the state. This will obviously be objectionable to those who think religion is the word of God.

The thoughts on religion in this chapter are more explicit than anything else Rousseau wrote on the subject. They deal specifically with the social role of religion. His proposals on individual religious belief and the nature of God can be found in 'The Creed of the Savoyard Vicar', in Book IV of *Emile*. Although this ranges more widely, containing discussions of the nature of God and the nature of his relations with us, it also contains an attack on the credentials of the Catholic Church, and a plea for religious toleration.

Coercion

'Its first-fruits in practice were the reign of Robespierre; the dictatorships of Russia and Germany (especially the latter) are in part and outcome of Rousseau's teaching' (Russell (1945), p.674). This was written by Bertrand Russell when Hitler had been defeated, and Stalin was a major power in the world. How could a philosophy dedicated to the preservation of freedom have drawn such a condemnation?

The claims that Rousseau's philosophy points towards totalitarianism goes back at least to Burke, in his *Reflections on the Revolution in France* (1790). It is not something Rousseau discusses in any particular section of *The Social Contract*; rather it emerges out of the theory as a whole. However, crucial pieces of evidence arise in IV, viii, [32] and I, vii, [7–8]. We have already seen that Rousseau's apparently intolerant view that 'partial associations' should be banned (II, iii), can be justified (within his account) on grounds of fairness (p.198).

The controversy centres on Rousseau's claim that people can be 'forced to be free' (I, vii, [8]). The paradoxical way in which the point is put obscures its obvious reading. We have seen that, for Rousseau, true freedom consists in being free from the slavery of appetite and the will of others. Both of these are achieved by participation by everyone in the sovereign, governed by the general will. Hence, in being forced to obey the general will, individuals are being forced to be free.

The claim that forcing people to obey the general will is contributing to their freedom is made more sinister by the discussion in IV, viii, [32]: to 'lie before the laws' is to be punished by death. This penalty is not imposed for atheism (Rousseau advocates religious tolerance) but for acting in such a way as to undermine the moral and collective body. The impression is of a state in which citizens are free only to follow the official line, on pain of death.

This interpretation, however, is contested. Recall the discussion on pages 200ff. in which two possible views of the province of the general will were canvassed. Either it is narrow, concerning only 'a society's conditions of association' (II, vi, [10]), or the sovereign assemblies issue more detailed laws.

The 'conditions of association' will be such matters as the form of government, and the limits of state power. If we put this together with the thought that the general will should not impose an undue burden on any particular individuals (which we found in Brian Barry's discussion in Reading 4.2), we can conclude that the conditions of association do not place an undue burden on individuals. Indeed, it has been argued that what emerges are the just foundation for a liberal state (Dent (1988); cf. Rawls (1973), p.140). However, if we interpret the general will as having a broader province, there will be more detailed proposals individuals will be obliged to accept. The kind of state that would result from trying to realize this position would tend towards intolerance.

Whichever way we interpret the text, it is common ground that, between the *Discourse* and *The Social Contract*, Rousseau's notion of freedom changes from that of being able to act on one's 'appetites', to that of acting according to the general will. *The Social Contract* describes a political system where people's natures will be changed from what they were in the state of nature, to being the kind of person who will freely choose the general will. The first of the two interpretations of the general will described above attempts to show that this change is compatible with liberalism: that the change is from a person who resorts to force, to a person who respects others. However, it is characteristic of liberalism to find the project of changing people according to some abstract ideal suspicious. If we take the second interpretation of the general will, we might find the change is from people with the desires that they happen to have, to people who adopt a different set of desires. For example, they might sublimate their own desires for some 'greater' good; perhaps the greater good of the state.

This liberal suspicion of the manipulation of people's desires forms the basis of one of the most celebrated essays in modern political philosophy: Isaiah Berlin's 'Two Concepts of Liberty'.

ACTIVITY

Read Reading 4.4, 'Two Concepts of Liberty' by Isaiah Berlin and answer the following questions.

1   Which concept of freedom does Rousseau take to be characteristic of the state of nature, and which of the civil state? You might want to look back at pages 194–5.

2   Does Rousseau commit the 'monstrous impersonation' Berlin mentions with respect to positive freedom? You might want to look at I, vii.

DISCUSSION

1   Berlin says of negative freedom: 'Political liberty in this sense is simply the area within which a man can act unobstructed by others'. On page 195, I characterized freedom in the state of nature as 'the freedom from obstacles that might stand between an individual and the satisfaction of his or her desires'. This looks a good match. The characterization of positive freedom Berlin gives includes: 'to be moved by reasons, by conscious purposes, which are my own, not by causes which affect me, as it were, from the outside'. This looks very like Rousseau's description of the 'moral liberty' of the civil society: 'to obey a law which we have imposed on ourselves is freedom' (I, viii).

2   The 'monstrous impersonation' is equating knowing what is best for a person (even if they do not) with claiming that what is known is what the person *really* wants (even if they deny it). Rousseau does seem open to this charge. He claims that it is in each individual's best interest to pursue the general will. In imposing this 'best interest' on people we are not infringing on their freedom but giving them what they really want: 'forcing them to be free'. How much this matters will depend on where you think the limits of the general will should be drawn (although, for Berlin, any constraint on behaviour by other people, no matter how justified, will be a constraint on negative freedom).

The same tension between negative and positive freedom appears in the work discussed in the next chapter: Karl Marx and Frederick Engels's *The German Ideology*.

Glossary

censor

An official of the state, independent of government, entrusted with the task of shaping and strengthening moral standards and opinions, and supporting the state by applying them in particular cases.

civil religion

A religious system which consolidates and perpetuates the bonds of union between all the members of the civil society.

civil state

Also referred to as the 'civil society'. The 'moral and collective body', comprised of a group of individuals, and under the direction of the general will.

corporate will

A term Rousseau uses to describe the general will *of the government* (III, ii).

executive

The body (i.e. the government, ruler or prince) which acts with the derived authority of the general will, putting its deliverances into effect in particular cases.

free-rider

Term used to describe a person who derives benefits from a system that is supported by the contributions of its users, but who does not make any contributions himself or herself.

freedom

A central concept in Rousseau's political thought. See *positive liberty*, *negative liberty* and *moral liberty*.

general will

The general will of a group is what is in the best interests of that group. Applied to the 'moral collective', that is, Rousseau's sovereign, it is what is in the best interests of the state. Because it 'issues from everyone in order that it should apply to everyone' (II, iv), it should not place an unfair burden on any individual in particular.

government

The executive of the state. Also sometimes called 'the prince', or 'the ruler' (depending on translation). Members of the government are called 'magistrates', and the deliverance of government are called 'decrees'.

legislator

A figure who persuades a disparate collection of people to form a state. The legislator is not part of the state, and plays no further role once the people have bound together as a sovereign body.

moral liberty

The liberty acquired in the move from the state of nature to the civil state. A form of *positive liberty*, which consists of being part of a moral and collective body and obeying the general will, rather than pursuing one's appetites.

negative liberty

A term introduced by Isaiah Berlin to describe the condition in which a person can act unobstructed by others (the kind of liberty prized by liberals; also the kind of liberty found in the state of nature).

partial associations

A group within the state, which has its own interests. Rousseau would like either to ban partial associations, or have so many of them their influence is cancelled out. The problem is that if individuals pursue the will of the particular association to which they belong, they will not be pursuing the general will of the state.

particular will

The desire each individual has to advance his or her personal advantage.

positive liberty

A term introduced by Isaiah Berlin to describe the freedom that consists of being under one's own rational control. This includes being free from pursuing the desires one simply happens to have (as opposed to pursuing goals one has chosen).

social contract

An agreement in which each individual transfers all his force and rights to the whole community. This creates a moral and collective body, under the supreme authority of the general will.

sovereign

The bearer of supreme and final authority in the state. For Rousseau, the sovereign consists of the moral and collective body formed by all adult members of the civil association.

specious social contract

A term used in the text to refer to the social contract described in the *Discourse on Inequality*. The contract is a pact between the rich and the poor for mutual advantage, but legitimates all the injustice brought about by the use of force.

state of nature

A term Rousseau uses to describe a hypothetical state, prior to the establishment of the civil state. Rousseau stresses that not only do people's circumstances differ in the state of nature and the civil state, but their actual nature and character do as well.

will of all

The will of all of a group is the sum of all the particular wills of members of the group.

Further reading

Rousseau, J.-J. (1987 edn) *Discourse on the Origins of Inequality*, trans. D.A. Cress, Hackett.

Canovan, M. (1987) 'Rousseau's Two Concepts of Citizenship' in Kennedy and Mendus (1987), pp.78–105. An interesting and provocative feminist view of Rousseau's arguments.

Dent, N.J.H. (1988) *Rousseau*, Blackwell. An interpretation of Rousseau which defends him against the charge of totalitarianism.

Dent, N.J.H. (1992) *A Rousseau Dictionary*, Blackwell. A useful and balanced reference book.

Hall, J.C. (1973) *Rousseau*, Macmillan. A slightly old-fashioned, but none the less interesting, overview of Rousseau's political philosophy.

O'Hagan, T. (1999) *Rousseau*, Routledge. A major study, looking at all aspects of Rousseau's work.

Pateman, Carole (1980) 'The Fraternal Social Contract' in Goodin and Pettit (1993), pp.45–59. An interesting argument to the effect that the social contract does not result in a universal conception of citizenship, but rather one slanted towards the male.

Plamenatz, J. (1963) *Man and Society*, 2 vols, Longman. A comprehensive study of all the theorists included in this book.

Wokler, R. (1995) *Rousseau*, Oxford University Press. An excellent little book which sets Rousseau and his thought in context.

Notes

[1] This is the second of three 'discourses' written by Rousseau. The other two are *The Discourse on the Sciences and the Arts* and *The Discourse on Political Economy*.

[2] For an argument to the contrary, see Hall (1973) pp.29–30.

[3]

Civil state	**State of nature**
Justice	Instinct
duty	physical impulse
right	appetite
reason	inclinations
intelligent being and a man	limited and stupid animal
civil freedom	natural freedom
proprietary ownership	right to anything that tempts him
moral liberty	appetitive slavery
moral quality to actions	
faculties exercised and improved	
ideas are amplified	
feelings ennobled	
soul is elevated	

Readings

'The General Will'

John C. Hall

This extract describes the features of the general will, and draws out the similarities and differences between Rousseau and Hobbes. Hall reminds us that by 'freedom', Rousseau sometimes means the ordinary notion that contrasts with such states as slavery. The distinctively Rousseauean notion of 'moral freedom', which Hall also mentions, I discuss on pages 194–5 above. Another point to note is Hall's claim that the particular will and the general will do not refer to different desires. That is, if I want something (perhaps to live in a democracy) that is a particular will of mine. The very same want might also be the general will if, as a matter of fact, living in a democracy is in the best interest of the state.

Introduction

The central idea of Rousseau's theory of political right is the general will. Around this idea are clustered others – words like *sovereign*, *state*, and *law*, which play big parts in the exposition of his theory, and are found to be definable in terms of each other and of the general will – but these other words are borrowed from his predecessors, even though he gives them all a new meaning. The expression 'general will', on the other hand, is his own. No one had used it as a technical term of political philosophy before the appearance, in 1755, of vol. V of the *Encyclopédie*. Nor was it just the expression that was new: the idea that the expression was coined to express was also new. Furthermore, whatever is new in the way Rousseau uses the other words of the group will be found to originate in this same central idea. For example, when we look at the things he says about the sovereign, we can divide them into two clearly distinct classes: (a) what could equally well have been said by Hobbes – e.g. that sovereignty is indivisible, that the sovereign alone is the source of law, and that it cannot make laws that bind itself; (b) what is peculiar to Rousseau, and, to someone who understands by *sovereign* what Hobbes understood, inexplicable – e.g. that the sovereign cannot hurt anyone in particular, and that the power to condemn a criminal is one that the sovereign can confer but cannot exercise. When we look more closely at the statements of the second class in their context, we find that they follow from the premiss that the sovereign, by definition, exercises the general will.

It is therefore most important that before attempting to interpret Rousseau's theory in detail we should discover what the expression 'general will' means. Failure to do this is certain to result in comprehensive misunderstanding.

The will of a corporate person

Now the idea that a body composed of many people might in some sense have one will was not at all new – in fact it was a commonplace of the political and legal thinking of the time. It is a feature both of Continental legal systems and of English law that such bodies of people as partnerships, companies, town councils, etc., should count for some legal purposes as if they were each a single person. They can, for example, own property, be guilty of crimes, enter into contracts, and issue instructions to their servants. To indicate that they have these powers, they are known as 'legal persons', 'corporate persons' or (by some Continental legal writers, including Pufendorf) 'moral persons'. Now if we want to determine whether a person (in the literal sense of 'person') has entered into a contract or issued an instruction, we need to make sure that he has done something *voluntarily*; it is not enough that he should have uttered certain words in his sleep or under threat from a gunman. To put it in more old-fashioned language, there must have been a *will* to make this contract or issue this instruction before we can rightly impute the contract or the instruction to the person in question. The same is true of corporate persons. For the town council to issue an instruction to its dustmen to collect refuse from such-and-such a place, there must be a voluntary action on the part of someone. But of course not every member of the council needs to take part in this action in person. It is enough for one person – the person authorised to do so – to sign the relevant paper or utter the relevant words. In Hobbes's language (*Leviathan*, chap. XVI), he is the 'actor' who 'bears the person' of all the other members. In this way a voluntary action by one man *counts* as a voluntary action of the whole body; and so one can speak of the whole body, though it has many members, as having one will.

This terminology and the corresponding way of regarding authority was transferred, by Hobbes, Pufendorf, Locke and others, from corporate bodies within the community to the community itself. According to all of them certain acts of an authorised person (or, it might be, the resolutions passed under a certain procedure at some kind of meeting) count as expressions of the will of the whole community, just as certain decisions of the managing director of a company and certain majority votes at an annual general meeting can count as decisions or acts of the whole company. This theory had a twofold explanatory effect, as can be seen very clearly in Hobbes's version of it in *Leviathan*, chapters XVI and XVII. First, it is explained how those in authority come to have power to control the actions of others. They are obeyed because their commands are not regarded as expressions of their own will, but as expressions of the will of the whole community. It is as if the whole community were issuing the command, and backing it with the intention to enforce it. Secondly, it is explained how the individual is implicated in the actions of those in authority, sharing the responsibility for them, just as he takes responsibility for his own voluntary actions. This is the case because the individual is presumed to have authorised all the actions of the ruler, to have given him as it were a blank cheque which will count as the individual's own voluntary instruction however the ruler may fill it in.

Now this theory, that the will of one or more individuals can be counted as being the will of the whole community, is explicitly rejected by Rousseau, in *Social Contract*, II, i and III, xv, and even more clearly in *Gen* I, 4 ([The Geneva manuscript] an earlier and clear version of *Social Contract*, II, i). Nevertheless, his own theory grew out of the Hobbesian one. The question that Hobbes had answered with his theory of authorisation was a question that posed itself also for Rousseau, viz. 'How is it that a crowd of different individuals, all wanting different things, can nevertheless form a single community capable of united action and having a common claim on the individual's loyalty?' Both Hobbes and Rousseau were struck by the analogy between the concerted action of a community in pursuit of some common end and the voluntary action of an individual in pursuit of an end of his own. Both therefore sought to find in the community something that would function like the *will* of an individual, i.e. his capacity to engage in voluntary actions. Hobbes found that the legal conception of a corporate person acting through its authorised representative provided an adequate solution to the problem of where such a common will could be found. Rousseau rejected this solution and provided an entirely different one of his own, which yet retained some of the terminology of the solution he rejected.

To appreciate Rousseau's solution we must look back at his opinions about human nature, as stated in *Origins of Inequality*, Part I... I [have] summarized these in the form of three propositions, asserting respectively that man was by nature (a) solitary, (b) governed by self-interest and pity (pity disappears from view in the final version of *Social Contract* – when establishing the theory of the general will Rousseau always assumes that man is wholly motivated by self-interest),[1] (c) distinguished from other animals by free will and the capacity for self-improvement. From these three propositions Rousseau inferred man's natural innocence, and from the last of them he inferred his capacity to progress from mere innocence to virtue. Two further propositions must now be added, which are assumed rather than stated in *Origins of Inequality*, but certainly form an essential part of Rousseau's view of man, which any theory of political right must, in his view, take account of. These are (d) that freedom is an essential part of human happiness, and that it can therefore never be in a man's interest to lose his freedom, and (e) that virtue is a necessary condition of happiness, vice a sufficient condition of unhappiness. Each of these propositions needs further comment.

In Book V of *Émile* (p.567) and more briefly in *Social Contract*, I, viii, last paragraph (a passage which is not in *Gen*, and which, because of its reference to *Émile*, must belong to the final revision), Rousseau puts forward a theory of what is commonly called 'moral freedom', according to which that man only is truly free who is master of himself and not the slave of his own passions. In this sense only the virtuous man is free; only he is free to achieve what his rational, as opposed to his impulsive, self wants. I mention this theory (which Rousseau derived from the Stoics and from Plato) because the fact that he held it is often mentioned by commentators. For our purposes it is more important to notice that it is *not* this 'moral freedom' that he usually means when he speaks of freedom as a constituent of happiness. Usually he is referring to freedom of a much more ordinary kind – such things as the freedom to walk in the woods, freedom from having to make polite conversation, and in general the freedom to do whatever one wants, restricted only by the nature of things. The opposite of freedom is slavery – to be obliged to do what someone else wants rather than what one wants to do oneself. That freedom in this ordinary sense is good and essential to happiness is a view that pervades all Rousseau's works,[2] and in particular *Émile* itself. That slavery is in itself bad and destructive of the happiness of those that are subject to it is at all times axiomatic to Rousseau, and by *slavery* in almost all contexts he means, not subjection to one's own passions, but subjection to the will of another human being. This is as true of *Social Contract* as of other works. The famous opening sentence 'Man was born free, but everywhere he is in chains' sets the keynote of the work. The chains referred to here are social, as the following denunciations of Grotius show. Rousseau does, it is true, go on to speak of showing how man's loss of freedom can be made legitimate, but this claim is intentionally paradoxical, and the solution to the paradox is, as we shall see, that in a legitimate society man does not in fact lose his freedom, but merely changes the field in which it is exercised.

That virtue is a necessary constituent of happiness is maintained by Rousseau in many places, above all in *La Nouvelle Héloïse*, which can be seen as a treatise in fictional form designed to prove just this proposition. The natural man of *Origins of Inequality*, Part I, is not, it is true, in the strict sense virtuous, having no positive moral qualities, good or bad; but neither is he happy, being too stupid to enjoy the delights of the natural state (*Gen* I, 2). As we have seen, virtue arises, in Rousseau's view, from man's exercise of his own capacity for self-improvement. It cannot be imposed by a master and therefore presupposes freedom. Conversely, slavery depraves man, not merely inhibiting the acquisition of virtue but destroying natural innocence, as has been shown in *Origins of Inequality*, Part II. Proposition (e) therefore reinforces proposition (d). Each implies that freedom is essential to human happiness.

Conditions to be satisfied in any legitimate social system

Rousseau is setting out to justify social bonds of a certain kind as legitimate (*Social Contract*, I, i = *Gen* I, 3). *Legitimate* normally means 'according to law', but that cannot be exactly the meaning here, since law itself is one of the things that is to be justified as legitimate. The word must be used analogically. There must be, in his view, some rational principle or principles by which an entire political system, including law itself, can be justified in the same way that other human institutions and activities within any society are justified by the laws of that society. The traditional natural law theory had of course claimed to derive from the nature of man and the universe not only such rational principles, but a whole code of morality, applicable to nations and to individuals. Rousseau ... rejected the traditional theory; but that is not to say that he rejected the appeal to nature as the source of justifying principles in morals and politics. Far from it – the whole of *Origins of Inequality* is in effect an appeal to nature in order to justify his own rejection of established political and social conventions. What he rejected in the traditional theory was the attempt to derive directly from nature detailed social institutions and rules. The origin of such rules must, he thinks, be sought in conventions. But these conventions in their turn must be justified or condemned in so far as they accord with or outrage the requirements of human nature.

So, in the last pages of *Origins of Inequality*, existing inequalities stand condemned as unnatural.

Now Rousseau does not say in so many words that when he speaks of social bonds being *legitimate* he means by *legitimate* 'in accordance with the requirements of human nature'. But when we look at the arguments he gives in *Social Contract*, I, i and vi–viii (=*Gen* I, 3) to establish why we need to institute such bonds, and why, to be legitimate, they must take a certain form, we find that it is in fact the requirements of human nature (as he understood them) that are being appealed to.

The first reason given is that there comes a point in human history at which association is necessary for the preservation of the human species, which 'would perish if it did not change its manner of existence'. That this point is reached is a fact of nature.[3] Rousseau does not here go into details, but he had done so in *Origins of Inequality*, Part II. The conjunction of two features of man's nature, his self-love and his capacity for self-improvement, produces in the course of time a situation such as Hobbes had described as a war of all against all. Being, by this time at least, rational, men decided that their own interest required them to associate, i.e. to act in concert with others instead of acting purely as individuals. Association in itself entails some restrictions on what a man may do; and so, since the reasons that made men associate originally still apply, this argument is enough to prove that *some* form of social bond is legitimate as being a consequence of man's nature as a being motivated by rational self-interest.

So far Rousseau agrees with Hobbes; but now they part company. There is more to human nature than motivation by self-interest. We must also take account of the propositions (c), (d), and (e) set out on p.218 above. The social bond must be of a kind that it takes account of man's perfectibility, of his need for freedom and of his need for opportunity to exercise virtue. The type of association recommended by Hobbes, in which men become subjects of an absolute ruler whose commands, however arbitrary, they are obliged to obey, takes no account of these. A man who is subject to the arbitrary will of another man is not free; human nature being what it is, it can never be reasonable for a man to give up his freedom; a Hobbesian society, therefore, can never be legitimate.

If this point had been made to Hobbes, he would no doubt have replied on such lines as these: the commands of the sovereign do not cover in detail the whole of every individual's life. They simply set limits within which the individual is free to make his own choices (*Leviathan*, chapter XXI). Indeed, he will have more freedom than in the state of nature, since only now can he be confident that his neighbours will not be able to frustrate everything he attempts to do, and that he will therefore be free to undertake long-term projects with some hope of completing them.

Such a counter-argument will only convince those who believe, with Hobbes, that submission to the arbitrary will of an absolute ruler is the *only* way by which one can escape from the war of all against all. Rousseau did not believe this. He believed that human beings could associate with each other without anyone needing to submit to the arbitrary will of anyone else; i.e. without anyone having to do anything that he did not himself want to do. The problem that he believes that he has solved is, in his own words, 'to find a form of association...by which each, while uniting himself with all, nevertheless obeys only himself and remains as free as before' (*Social Contract*, I, vi).[4]

Such an association would be legitimate, by comparison with that recommended by Hobbes, in that not only were men made secure, but their freedom was also fully preserved. If, in addition, it were found to promote human virtue and self-improvement it would be legitimate absolutely.

How can men associate with each other without losing their freedom? This can be done, thinks Rousseau, if each individual voluntarily does what is in the interest of all, instead of doing what is in his own particular interest without reference to the interest of others. 'Of course', we are tempted to reply, 'but if men were willing to respect others' interests there would be no problem. The problem arises because, in Rousseau's view, men are motivated primarily by self-interest, and therefore do not respect one another's interests unless forced to do so.' But this reply misses the important point: it is not the interests of *others* that we are to follow, but the interest of *all*. *All* includes *us*. If any action is in fact in the interest of all, then every one of us may be presumed, if rational, to want it to be done. Any one of us, therefore, if he does this action himself, is doing something that he himself wants to do.

'General will'[5] is the name Rousseau gives to this rational desire, which we may all be presumed to have, that what is in the common interest of all should be done. It is an abstraction, in that there is no one who wants *only* what is in the interest of all. If you examine what any particular individual wants at any one time, you will find that he wants a number of things that it would be against some other people's interest that he should have. But there will be some things that he wants to happen as being in his own interest that coincide with what every other person (in so far as he is rational and correctly informed) wants to happen as being in *his* interest. Now we are exercising the general will just in so far as we are wanting this latter class of thing to happen. Otherwise we are exercising what Rousseau calls our *particular will*.

Now it is important to realise that this distinction between general and particular wills is not a distinction between two kinds of mental event whose occurrence might be recorded and counted by introspection. It is not the case that we have at one time good desires for what is in the common interest and at other times perverse desires for what is in our own exclusive interest. Rather, all our desires are alike, Rousseau thinks, in being for what is in our own interest, but as a matter of objective fact some of what we desire happens to be also in the interest of everyone. To discover whether in any particular case our own will coincides with the general will and if so how far, we need to look not at our own mental processes but at the thing we want to bring about, and to discover whether it is in fact in everyone's interest. If it is, then our will is the general will. If what we want is partly but not wholly in everyone's interest, then our will is the general will in so far as we are wanting the part that is in everyone's interest, but is a particular will in so far as we are wanting the part that is not in everyone's interest. So what is from the introspective psychologist's point of view a single desire may for Rousseau be a mixture of the general will and a particular will.

A simplified example will illustrate this point. Suppose that the community in question is a family of two children. Their father has an afternoon off and has offered to spend it by taking them both for a treat. One of them wants to be taken to the pantomime, the other to the zoo. However, each of them would rather go on the treat preferred by the other than go on no treat at all. Let us suppose that the two possibilities exhaust the field of possible treats and exclude each other – either both children go to the pantomime or both to the zoo; it is not possible for one to go to one and one to the other, or for either to go to both. The desires of the two children are thus in conflict. But they are not wholly in conflict, since each child wants to be taken on a treat rather than to have nothing at all, even if that were to mean accepting the choice of the other. To be taken on a treat is in the interest of both members of the community, and each child, in so far as he wants that, shares in the general will, which has the common interest as its object. In so far as the respective desires of the two children are in conflict, this is to be attributed (if we follow Rousseau's terminology) to their particular wills. But this is not to say that each child engages in two distinct mental operations – wanting there to be a treat, on the one hand, and wanting it to be the one of his own choice on the other. Rather, each child has a single desire – to go to the pantomime in one case, to the zoo in the other – but the object of this desire can be analysed into an element common to both and an element peculiar to each. No introspective expertise is needed to carry out this analysis; all one needs to know is what is in the interest of each, which in turn we can decide (within the limits of this artificial example, at least) if we know what each of them would choose in different circumstances.

The connection between the general will and anyone's occurrent desires (i.e. with his desires as mental occurrences taking place at a particular time) is therefore a tenuous one, or even non-existent. If it is in everyone's interest that a certain state of affairs (say peace) should obtain, then everyone who knows this to be so may be presumed to desire that state of affairs, in some sense of 'desire'. But this is not to say that a conscious mental process of desiring peace is occurring in everyone's mind simultaneously. Rather we have here another use of the word 'desire' – the *dispositional* use, according to which someone can always be truly said to desire or want peace if, whenever the question arises whether he wants peace or not, his choice (in whatever way he may make it, whether by a thought, in words or images, or by a spoken answer, or by an action) is for peace. So in my example of the two children, each could be said to desire (in the dispositional sense) that a treat of some sort should take place, in that each would choose to have the treat preferred by the other rather than to have no treat at all.

The general will may be defined therefore as the desire (in the dispositional sense), which every member of a community may be presumed to share, to promote what is in the common interest of all the members of that community. If we want to give content to the general will, i.e. if we want to determine what specific course of action it requires, we must first determine what is in fact in the common interest. But if this is so, what is the point of introducing the notion of the general will? Since we need the notion of the common interest in order to explain that of the general will, why does Rousseau not simply speak of the common interest and drop all talk of the general will? It would seem as easy to speak of people pursuing the common interest above private interests as to speak, as Rousseau does, of them putting themselves under the direction of the general will; and yet the latter expression says no more than the former. Since the former is also simpler and more intelligible, why does Rousseau not use it? The answer can be found if we remember that Rousseau's initial problem was to find a form of association which would leave man at least as free as he was in his pre-political state. Now for everyone to pursue the common interest does not on the face of it solve this problem. Are we to be *made* to pursue the common interest? If not, how will this form of association be effective? If we are, have we not lost our freedom? The point of the formulation in terms of the general will is that it suggests the answer to these questions. In a legitimate society we all pursue the common interest because we want to, because it is an interest we all share. In this sense the general will 'comes from all' (*Social Contract*, II, iv = *Gen* I, 6); to obey it is therefore no loss of freedom, since we are only obeying ourselves. [...]

Bibliography

Rousseau, J.-J. (1911 edn) *Émile*, trans. Barbara Foxley, Dent, Everyman's Library.
Rousseau, J.-J. (1913 edn) *The Social Contract and Discourses*, trans. G.D.H. Cole, Dent, Everyman's Library.

Notes

From Hall, John C. (1973) *Rousseau: An Introduction to his Political Philosophy*, Macmillan, pp.66–76.

[1] In *Gen* II 4, in some paragraphs later omitted, he allows pity to be part of the motivation of private morality, but explicitly rejects the idea that it could be the source of the concept of justice, which is founded, by way of the general will, on self-interest.

[2] It might be thought that the happy servants depicted in *La Nouvelle Héloïse* (in the part [Bk iv, letter 10] where he describes the ideal country estate managed by Julie and her husband) are exceptions; but as Rousseau in fact points out that they want nothing better than to serve their virtuous mistress, they are, though servants, still free to do what they want to do.

[3] I do not mean that it is a fact of nature that man necessarily reaches a certain stage of social and technological development. To say that would be to make Rousseau out to be a historicist, which ... he was not. But it is a fact of nature that *if* he reaches such a stage of development then the species 'would perish if it did not change its manner of existence'.

[4] This passage does not occur in *Gen*, but the thought is not new to the final version. It is found, though expressed more diffusely, in *Political Economy* (1913 edn), pp.239–40.

[5] The interpretation given in this section is based on *Political Economy*, and on *Social Contract*, I, vii (particularly the penultimate paragraph), II, i (first paragraph), and II, iv, *Gen* I, 4 and 6.

'The Public Interest'

Brian Barry

The paper from which this extract comes did much to renew interest in Rousseau's work, as it showed that notions such as 'the general will' were not impossibly abstract notions, but had practical application. The interpretation of Rousseau offered here reflects Barry's liberal outlook. That is, Barry interprets the general will as protecting the interests of each and every individual.

A convenient way of examining some of the ramifications of this theory is to work over some of the things Rousseau says in the *Social Contract* about the 'General Will'. Judging from critiques in which Rousseau figures as a charlatan whose philosophical emptiness is disguised by his superficial rhetoric, it is hard to see why we should waste time reading him, except perhaps on account of his supposedly malign influence on Robespierre. I doubt the fairness of this estimate, and I am also inclined to deprecate the tendency (often though not always combined with the other) to look on Rousseau through Hegelian spectacles. We need to dismantle the implausible psychological and metaphysical theories (e.g., 'compulsory rational freedom' and 'group mind') which have been foisted on Rousseau by taking certain phrases and sentences (e.g., 'forced to be free' and 'moral person') out of context. As a small contribution to this process of demythologizing Rousseau I want to suggest here that what he says about 'the general will' forms a coherent and ingenious unity if it is understood as a treatment of the theme of common interests.

Rousseau's starting point, which he frequently makes use of, is that any group will have a will that is general in relation to its constituent members, but particular with respect to groups in which it in turn is included. Translating this into talk about interests it means that any policy which is equally favourable to all the members of a given group will be less favourable to member A than the policy most favourable to A, less favourable to member B than the policy most favourable to B, and so on; but it will be more favourable to each of the members of the group than any policy which has to be equally beneficial to an even larger number of people. Suppose, for example, that a fixed sum – say a million pounds – is available for wage increases in a certain industry. If each kind of employee had a separate trade union one might expect as many incompatible claims as there were unions, each seeking to appropriate most of the increase for its own members. If for example there were a hundred unions with a thousand members apiece each employee might have a thousand pounds (a thousandth of the total) claimed on his behalf, and the total claims would add up to a hundred million pounds. At the other extreme if there were only one union, there would be no point in its putting in a claim totalling more than a million pounds (we assume for convenience that the union accepts the unalterability of this amount) and if it made an equal claim on behalf of each of its members this would come to only ten pounds a head. Intermediate numbers of unions would produce intermediate results.

Rousseau's distinction between the 'will of all' and the 'general will' now fits in neatly. The 'will of all' is simply shorthand for 'the policy most in A's interests, taking A in isolation; the policy most in B's interests, taking B in isolation; and so on'. (These will of course normally be different policies for A, B and the rest.) The 'general will' is a *single* policy which is equally in the interests of all the members of the group. It will usually be different from any of the policies mentioned before, and less beneficial to anyone than the policy most beneficial to himself alone.

We can throw light on some of the other things Rousseau says in the one-page chapter II.iii. of *The Social Contract* by returning to the trade union example. Suppose now that the leaders of the hundred trade unions are told that the money will be forthcoming only if a majority of them can reach agreement on a way of dividing it up. A possible method would be for each leader to write down his preferred solution on a slip of paper, and for these to be compared, the process continuing until a requisite number of papers have the same proposal written on them. If each started by writing down his maximum demand there would be as many proposals as leaders – the total result would be the 'will of all'. This is obviously a dead end, and if no discussion is allowed among the leaders, there is a good chance that they would all propose, as a second best, an equal division of the money. (There is some experimental evidence for this, presented in Chapter 3 of Thomas Schelling's *The Strategy of Conflict*.)[1] Such a solution would be in accordance with the 'general will' and represents a sort of highest common factor of agreement. As Rousseau puts it, it arises when the pluses and minuses of the conflicting first choices are cancelled out.

If instead of these arrangements communication is allowed, and even more if the groups are fewer and some leaders control large block votes, it becomes less likely that an equal solution will be everyone's second choice. It will be possible for some leaders to agree together to support a proposal which is less favourable to any of their members than each leader's first choice was to his own members, but still more favourable than any solution equally beneficial to all the participants. Thus, as Rousseau says, a 'less general will' prevails.

In II.iii. Rousseau suggests that this should be prevented by not allowing groups to form or, if they do form, by seeing that they are many and small. In the less optimistic mood of IV.i., when he returns to the question, he places less faith in mechanical methods and more in widespread civic virtue. He now says that the real answer is for everyone to ask himself 'the right question', i.e., 'What measure will benefit me in common with everyone else, rather than me at the expense of everyone else?' (I have never seen attention drawn to the fact that this famous doctrine is something of an afterthought whose first and only occurrence in the *Social Contract* is towards the end.) However, this is a difference only about the most effective means of getting a majority to vote for what is in the common interest of all. The essential point remains the same: that only where all are equally affected by the policy adopted can an equitable solution be expected.

> The undertakings which bind us to the social body are obligatory only because they are mutual; and their nature is such that in fulfilling them we cannot work for others without working for ourselves ... What makes the will general is less the number of voters than the common interest uniting them; for, under this system, each necessarily submits to the conditions he imposes on others: and this admirable agreement between interest and justice gives to the common deliberations an equitable character which at once vanishes when any particular question is discussed, in the absence of a common interest to unite and identify the ruling of the judge with that of the party.
>
> (II.iv. Cole's translation) [2]

Provided this condition is met, nobody will deliberately vote for a burdensome law because it will be burdensome to him too: this is why no *specific* limitations on 'the general will' are needed. Disagreements can then be due only to conflicts of opinion – not to conflicts of interest. Among the various policies which would affect everyone in the same way, each person has to decide which would benefit himself most – and, since everyone else is similarly circumstanced, he is automatically deciding at the same time which would benefit everyone else most. Thus, to go back to our example of a law prohibiting assault: disagreement will arise, if at all, because some think they (in common with everyone else) would make a net gain of opportunities from the absence of any law against assault, while others think the opposite. This is, in principle, a dispute with a right and a wrong answer; and everyone benefits from the right answer's being reached rather than the wrong one. Rousseau claims that a majority is more likely to be right than any given voter, so that someone in the minority will in fact gain from the majority's decision carrying the day. This has often been regarded as sophistical or paradoxical, but it is quite reasonable once one allows Rousseau his definition of the situation as one in which everyone is co-operating to find a mutually beneficial answer, for so long as everyone is taken as having an equal, better than even chance of giving the right answer, the majority view will (in the long run) be right more often than that of any given voter. (Of course, the same thing applies in reverse: if each one has on average a *less* than even chance of being right, the majority will be *wrong* more often than any given voter.) The formula for this was discovered by Condorcet and has been presented by Duncan Black on page 164 of his *Theory of Committees and Elections*.[3] To illustrate its power, here is an example: if we have a voting body of a thousand, each member of which is right on average fifty-one per cent of the time, what is the probability in any particular instance that a fifty-one per cent majority has the right answer? The answer, rather surprisingly perhaps, is: better than two to one (69%). Moreover, if the required majority is kept at fifty-one per cent and the number of voters raised to ten thousand, or if the number of voters stays at one thousand and the required majority is raised to sixty per cent, the probability that the majority (5100 to 4900 in the first case or 600 to 400 in the second) has the right answer rises virtually to unity (99.97%). None of this, of course, shows that 'Rousseau was right' but it does suggest that he was no simpleton.

To sum up, Rousseau calls for the citizen's deliberations to comprise two elements: (a) the decision to forgo (either as unattainable or as immoral) policies which would be in one's own personal interest alone, or in the common interest of a group smaller than the whole, and (b) the attempt to calculate which, of the various lines of policy that would affect oneself equally with all others, is best for him (and, since others are like him, for others).

Notes

From Barry, Brian (1964) 'The Public Interest', *Proceedings of The Aristotelian Society, Supp. Vol.* xxxviii, 1–18.

[1] Schelling, Thomas (1960) *The Strategy of Conflict*, Harvard University Press.

[2] Rousseau, J.-J. (1973 edn) *The Social Contract and Discourses*, G.D.H. Cole (trans. and ed.), revised and augmented J.H. Brumfitt and J.C. Hall, Dent.

[3] Black, Duncan (1958) *Theory of Committees and Elections*, Cambridge University Press.

'Legislator'

N.J.H. Dent

This is an entry from Nicholas Dent's *A Rousseau Dictionary*. Dent is a Rousseau scholar who has published much, giving his own interpretation of the philosopher (see Dent (1988)). His reference book gives more straightforward expositions of various of Rousseau's ideas.

The figure, or function of the 'legislator' in Rousseau's political theory strikes many people as one of its most curious, and unconvincing, elements. But in introducing this quasi-divine creature, he was addressing a central issue for all political theory.

In Rousseau's view, the most urgent issue facing any prospective civil state is that of devising the most just and most beneficial fundamental laws that will comprise the basic terms of association for each member of that institution: 'The people, being subject to the laws, ought to be their author; the conditions of the society ought to be regulated by those who come together to form it' (*The Social Contract*, II, ch. 6, 193; *Œuvres Complètes*, III, 380). If and when 'the people' do instigate and authorize the law, they are all alike members of the sovereign body, and their legislative will is the general will.

But having established how things ought to be, Rousseau goes on to raise difficulties for himself:

> But how are they to regulate them? Is it to be by common agreement, by a sudden inspiration? Has the body politic an organ to declare its will? Who can give it the foresight to formulate and announce its acts in advance? ... How can a blind multitude ... carry out for itself so great and difficult an enterprise as a system of legislation? Of itself the people always wills the good, but of itself it by no means always sees it. The general will is always upright, but the judgement which guides it is not always enlightened.

> (*The Social Contract*, II, ch. 6, 193; *Œuvres Complètes*, III, 380)

It is these and other allied problems which '[make] a legislator necessary'.

The legislator is said to be a semi-divine or divinely inspired person of 'superior intelligence beholding all the passions of men without experiencing any of them', whose 'happiness would have to be independent of us and yet ready to occupy itself with ours' (all quotations in the entry are drawn from *The Social Contract*, II, ch. 7; *Œuvres Complètes*, III, 381: 'The Legislator'). He is neither governor nor, strictly, sovereign; for although he may propose laws he cannot enact or authorize them, and once he has completed his work he either leaves or returns to the status of a common citizen. But somehow – by his superhuman intelligence, his sympathetic impartiality, his extraordinary foresight – he can not merely devise an appropriate body of fundamental laws, but also prevail upon the 'blind multitude' to exercise their sovereign authority by enacting this very code. He is unable to appeal either to force (since he has none) or to reason (since the multitude is 'blind'); so he 'must have recourse to an authority of a different order, capable of constraining without violence and persuading without convincing' (that is, without producing reasons capable of affording complete rational conviction).

What authority is this? It is divine authority, speaking in the name of God (or of the gods) and thereby making people think that the same God-originated decrees that bind each person in conscience are also to be found in the laws of the state. But invoking divine authority is notoriously the recourse of every trickster and fraud. What will show that wisdom, not trumped-up nothings, is being offered?

Rousseau has identified an important issue, but he appears to be setting himself an impossible problem here. When he says that 'the people always wills the good, but ... by no means always sees it' he formulates the issue in a somewhat misleading way, appearing to suggest that although there is, here, a well intentioned body of people eager to do the right thing, it is somehow unable to hit on the right thing. The legislator helps them with this. But if we ask just why they are unable to hit on the right thing, we see that this formulation of the problem misrepresents its true nature.

In Rousseau's view, what makes it hard for the right rule (law) to be identified is that people neither see nor feel that their own individual good is, and must be, tied in with everyone else's good if a just and beneficial social state for any of them is to result. A mere multitude, in which each is concerned with his own separate affairs, cannot see how the common interest is, and must be, their own best interest. This is not so much because they intend to distort or subvert the general will to their own advantage (so that it becomes, in effect, only a sectional will in place of the general will) – though this can happen. It is rather that no one has any sense of the way in which the good of each and the good of all stand or fall together. Each 'finds it difficult to realize the advantages he might hope to draw from the privations good laws impose'.

The legislator's task, then, is in essence that of creating a sense of common loyalty, common destiny, to unite these unconnected persons so that the 'yoke of public happiness' is experienced by each as the condition for his own happiness. Isolated persons lose, or overcome, their separateness to a degree, and share each other's needs and good as their own. The very achievement of this sense of common life gives people the 'vision' they require to see the good. It is not a question of a cognitive act that is separate from the volitional act. The right orientation of the will, towards the common good of all, is at the same time the overcoming of the obstacles to understanding what is the right thing to do.

It is Rousseau's view that it will take some special inspiration or motivation to make persons used to considering their advantage from the viewpoint of solitary, independent beings alone, enlarge their sense of the demands that life rightly makes on them to take on board a concern for the common good of all. It is that inspiration which the legislator attempts to provide by claiming to speak in God's name.

When Rousseau allows that this claim can be fraudulent he is merely acknowledging that not all such appeals can create and sustain an adequate bond of common union. The legislator cannot, by himself, and unaided by other facilitating conditions (which Rousseau discusses at length in *The Social Contract*, II, chs 8–10, all of which concern the 'fitness of the people' to receive laws), create an enduring social spirit. At most, he can open the way to the possibility of it, by bringing people to think of themselves as 'one people' with a shared destiny. Many other factors will contribute to the survival (or disappearance) of that spirit.

We are ourselves now so accustomed to living under common laws that we forget that it took many centuries for any sense of common dependence, let alone common union, to emerge in England or America (to the extent that it has emerged, or survives, anyway). Civil wars, for example, occurred during the process. Rousseau makes his concerns seem more problematic than they are by speaking as if the 'birth of a nation' could be brought about after just a short gestation. In fact, the pangs of delivery may take hundreds of years, but a major part of what is going on during that time is what Rousseau is describing – that is, the formulation and consolidation of such a sense of shared life and cause that it is possible for laws that honour each person alike to be formulated and accepted by all alike, rather than seen as an outrageous imposition, as embodying the requirements of a common good and as such to be resented or hated, because no such good was believed in.

Throughout his political writings Rousseau stresses the need for bonds of shared sentiment, if people are to concern themselves with their fellows. This is what the legislator is endeavouring to introduce. Given our modern wariness of rampant nationalism, which this emphasis can lead to – and of which Rousseau too was well aware – it is all too easy to overlook the fables and heroic events that sustain a country's sense of identity, and that make citizens do things for their fellows that reason unaided might fail to direct them to do. Liberalism is perpetually embarrassed by the often non-rational preconditions that make the appeal to reason in public affairs possible, and sometimes effective. Rousseau is not so shame-faced.

Notes

From Dent, N.J.H. (1992) *A Rousseau Dictionary*, Blackwell, pp.144–7.

'Two Concepts of Liberty'

Isaiah Berlin

Isaiah Berlin was Professor of Social and Political Theory at Oxford. Until his death he was probably the foremost theoretician, and defender, of the liberal position in political philosophy. His writings have been widely influential. In particular, the distinction drawn in this essay between negative freedom and positive freedom has inspired much debate.

I

To coerce a man is to deprive him of freedom – freedom from what? Almost every moralist in human history has praised freedom. Like happiness and goodness, like nature and reality, it is a term whose meaning is so porous that there is little interpretation that it seems able to resist. I do not propose to discuss either the history of this protean word or the more than two hundred senses of it recorded by historians of ideas. I propose to examine no more than two of these senses – but they are central ones, with a great deal of human history behind them, and, I dare say, still to come. The first of these political senses of freedom or liberty (I shall use both words to mean the same), which (following much precedent) I shall call the 'negative' sense, is involved in the answer to the question 'What is the area within which the subject – a person or group of persons – is or should be left to do or be what he is able to do or be, without interference by other persons?' The second, which I shall call the 'positive' sense, is involved in the answer to the question 'What, or who, is the source of control or interference that can determine someone to do, or be, this rather than that?' The two questions are clearly different, even though the answers to them may overlap.

The notion of negative freedom

I am normally said to be free to the degree to which no man or body of men interferes with my activity. Political liberty in this sense is simply the area within which a man can act unobstructed by others. If I am prevented by others from doing what I could otherwise do, I am to that degree unfree; and if this area is contracted by other men beyond a certain minimum, I can be described as being coerced, or, it may be, enslaved. Coercion is not, however, a term that covers every form of inability. If I say that I am unable to jump more than ten feet in the air, or cannot read because I am blind, or cannot understand the darker pages of Hegel, it would be eccentric to say that I am to that degree enslaved or coerced. Coercion implies the deliberate interference of other human beings within the area in which I could otherwise act. You lack political liberty or freedom only if you are prevented from attaining a goal by human beings.[1] Mere incapacity to attain a goal is not lack of political freedom.[2] This is brought out by the use of such modern expressions as 'economic freedom' and its counterpart, 'economic slavery'. It is argued, very plausibly, that if a man is too poor to afford something on which there is no legal ban – a loaf of bread, a journey round the world, recourse to the law courts – he is as little free to have it as he would be if it were forbidden him by law. If my poverty were a kind of disease which prevented me from buying bread, or paying for the journey round the world or getting my case heard, as lameness prevents me from running, this inability would not naturally be described as a lack of freedom, least of all political freedom. It is only because I believe that my inability to get a given thing is due to the fact that other human beings have made arrangements whereby I am, whereas others are not, prevented from having enough money with which to pay for it, that I think myself a victim of coercion or slavery. In other words, this use of the term depends on a particular social and economic theory about the causes of my poverty or weakness. If my lack of material means is due to my lack of mental or physical capacity, then I begin to speak of being deprived of freedom (and not simply about poverty) only if I accept the theory.[3] If, in addition, I believe that I am being kept in want by a specific arrangement which I consider unjust or unfair, I speak of economic slavery or oppression. The nature of things does not madden us, only ill will does, said Rousseau.[4] The criterion of oppression is the part that I believe to be played by other human beings, directly or indirectly, with or without the intention of doing so, in frustrating my wishes. By being free in this sense I mean not being interfered with by others. The wider the area of non-interference the wider my freedom.

This is what the classical English political philosophers meant when they used this word.[5] They disagreed about how wide the area could or should be. They supposed that it could not, as things were, be unlimited, because if it were, it would entail a state in which all men could boundlessly interfere with all other men; and this kind of 'natural' freedom would lead to social chaos in which men's minimum needs would not be satisfied; or else the liberties of the weak would be suppressed by the strong. Because they perceived that human purposes and activities do not automatically harmonize with one another, and because (whatever their official doctrines) they put high value on other goals, such as justice, or happiness, or culture, or security, or varying degrees of equality, they were prepared to curtail freedom in the interests of other values and, indeed, of freedom itself. For, without this, it was impossible to create the kind of association that they thought desirable. Consequently, it is assumed by these thinkers that the area of men's free action must be limited by law. But equally it is assumed, especially by such libertarians as Locke and Mill in England, and Constant and Tocqueville in France, that there ought to exist a certain minimum area of personal freedom which must on no account be violated; for if it is overstepped, the individual will find himself in an area too narrow for even that minimum development of his natural faculties which alone makes it possible to pursue, and even to conceive, the various ends which men hold good or right or sacred. It follows that a frontier must be drawn between the area of private life and that of public authority. Where it is to be drawn is a matter of argument, indeed of haggling. Men are largely interdependent, and no man's activity is so completely private as never to obstruct the lives of others in any way. 'Freedom for the pike is death for the minnows';[6] the liberty of some must depend on the restraint of others. Freedom for an Oxford don, others have been known to add, is a very different thing from freedom for an Egyptian peasant.

This proposition derives its force from something that is both true and important, but the phrase itself remains a piece of political claptrap. It is true that to offer political rights, or safeguards against intervention by the State, to men who are half-naked, illiterate, underfed and diseased is to mock their condition; they need medical help or education before they can understand, or make use of, an increase in their freedom. What is freedom to those who cannot make use of it? Without adequate conditions for the use of freedom, what is the value of freedom? First things come first: there are situations in which – to use a saying satirically attributed to the nihilists by Dostoevsky – boots are superior to Pushkin; individual freedom is not everyone's primary need. For freedom is not the mere absence of frustration of whatever kind; this would inflate the meaning of the word until it meant too much or too little. The Egyptian peasant needs clothes or medicine before, and more than, personal liberty, but the minimum freedom that he needs today, and the greater degree of freedom that he may need tomorrow, is not some species of freedom peculiar to him, but identical with that of professors, artists and millionaires.

What troubles the consciences of Western liberals is, I think, the belief, not that the freedom that men seek differs according to their social or economic conditions, but that the minority who possess it have gained it by exploiting, or, at least, averting their gaze from, the vast majority who do not. They believe, with good reason, that if individual liberty is an ultimate end for human beings, none should be deprived of it by others; least of all that some should enjoy it at the expense of others. Equality of liberty; not to treat others as I should not wish them to treat me; repayment of my debt to those who alone have made possible my liberty or prosperity or enlightenment; justice, in its simplest and most universal sense – these are the foundations of liberal morality. Liberty is not the only goal of men. I can, like the Russian critic Belinsky, say that if others are to be deprived of it – if my brothers are to remain in poverty, squalor and chains – then I do not want it for myself, I reject it with both hands and infinitely prefer to share their fate. But nothing is gained by a confusion of terms. To avoid glaring inequality or widespread misery I am ready to sacrifice some, or all, of my freedom: I may do so willingly and freely; but it is freedom that I am giving up for the sake of justice or equality or the love of my fellow men. I should be guilt-stricken, and rightly so, if I were not, in some circumstances, ready to make this sacrifice. But a sacrifice is not an increase in what is being sacrificed, namely freedom, however great the moral need or the compensation for it. Everything is what it is: liberty is liberty, not equality or fairness or justice or culture, or human happiness or a quiet conscience. If the liberty of myself or my class or nation depends on the misery of a number of other human beings, the system which promotes this is unjust and immoral. But if I curtail or lose my freedom in order to lessen the shame of such inequality, and do not thereby materially increase the individual liberty of others, an absolute loss of liberty occurs. This may be compensated for by a gain in justice or in happiness or in peace, but the loss remains, and it is a confusion of values to say that although my 'liberal', individual freedom may go by the board, some other kind of freedom – 'social' or 'economic' – is increased. Yet it remains true that the freedom of some must at times be curtailed to secure the freedom of others. Upon what principle should this be done? If freedom is sacred, untouchable value, there can be no such principle. One or other of these conflicting rules or principles must, at any rate in practice, yield: not always for reasons which can be clearly stated, let along generalized into rules or universal maxims. Still, a practical compromise has to be found.

Philosophers with an optimistic view of human nature and a better belief in the possibility of harmonizing human interest, such as Locke or Adam Smith or, in some moods, Mill, believed that social harmony and progress were compatible with reserving a large area for private life over which neither the State nor any other authority must be allowed to trespass. Hobbes, and those who agreed with him, especially conservative or reactionary thinkers, argued that if men were to be prevented from destroying one another and making social life a jungle or a wilderness, greater safeguards must be instituted to keep them in their places; he wished correspondingly to increase the area of centralized control and decrease that of the individual. But both sides agreed that some portion of human existence must remain independent of the sphere of social control. To invade that preserve, however small, would be despotism. The most eloquent of all defenders of freedom and privacy, Benjamin Constant, who had not forgotten the Jacobin dictatorship, declared that at the very least the liberty of religion, opinion, expression, property must be guaranteed against arbitrary invasion. Jefferson, Burke, Paine, Mill compiled different catalogues of individual liberties, but the argument for keeping authority at bay is always substantially the same. We must preserve a minimum area of personal freedom if we are not to 'degrade or deny our nature'. [7] We cannot remain absolutely free, and must give up some of our liberty to preserve the rest. But total self-surrender is self-defeating. What then must the minimum be? That which a man cannot give up without offending against the essence of his human nature. What is this essence? What are the standards which it entails? This has been, and perhaps always will be, a matter of infinite debate. But whatever the principle in terms of which the area of non-interference is to be drawn, whether it is that of natural law or natural rights, or of utility, or the pronouncements of a categorical imperative, or the sanctity of the social contract, or any other concept with which men have sought to clarify and justify their convictions, liberty in this sense means liberty *from*; absence of interference beyond the shifting, but always recognizable, frontier. 'The only freedom which deserves the name, is that of pursuing our own good in our own way', said the most celebrated of its champions. [8] If this is so, is compulsion ever justified? Mill had no doubt that it was. Since justice demands that all individuals be entitled to a minimum of freedom, all other individuals were of necessity to be restrained, if need be by force, from depriving anyone of it. Indeed, the whole function of law was the prevention of just such collisions: the State was reduced to what Lassalle contemptuously described as the functions of a night-watchman or traffic policeman.

II

The notion of positive freedom

The 'positive' sense of the word 'liberty' derives from the wish on the part of the individual to be his own master. I wish my life and decisions to depend on myself, not on external forces of whatever kind. I wish to be the instrument of my own, not of other men's, acts of will. I wish to be a subject, not an object; to be moved by reasons, by conscious purposes, which are my own, not by causes which affect me, as it were, from outside. I wish to be somebody, not nobody; a doer – deciding, not being decided for, self-directed and not acted upon by external nature or by other men as if I were a thing, or an animal, or a slave incapable of playing a human role, that is, of conceiving goals and policies of my own and realizing them. This is at least part of what I mean when I say that I am rational, and that it is my reason that distinguishes me as a human being from the rest of the world. I wish, above all, to be conscious of myself as a thinking, willing, active being, bearing responsibility for my choices and able to explain them by reference to my own ideas and purposes. I feel free to the degree that I believe this to be true, and enslaved to the degree that I am made to realize that it is not.

The freedom which consists in being one's own master, and the freedom which consists in not being prevented from choosing as I do by other men, may, on the face of it, seem concepts at no great logical distance from each other – no more than negative and positive ways of saying much the same thing. Yet the 'positive' and 'negative' notions of freedom historically developed in divergent directions, not always by logically reputable steps, until, in the end, they came into direct conflict with each other.

One way of making this clear is in terms of the independent momentum which the, initially perhaps quite harmless, metaphor of self-mastery acquired. 'I am my own master'; 'I am slave to no man'; but may I not (as Platonists or Hegelians tend to say) be a slave to nature? Or to my own 'unbridled' passions? Are these not so many species of the identical genus 'slave' – some political or legal, others moral or spiritual? Have not men had the experience of liberating themselves from spiritual slavery, or slavery to nature, and do they not in the course of it become aware, on the one hand, of a self which dominates, and, on the other, of something in them which is brought to heel? This dominant self is then variously identified with reason, with my 'higher nature', with the self which calculates and aims at what will satisfy it in the long run, with my 'real', or 'ideal', or 'autonomous' self, or with my self 'at its best'; which is then contrasted with irrational impulse, uncontrolled desires, my 'lower' nature, the pursuit of immediate pleasures, my 'empirical' or 'heteronomous' self, swept by every gust of desire and passion, needing to be rigidly disciplined if it is ever to rise to the full height of its 'real' nature. Presently the two selves may be represented as divided by an even larger gap; the real self may be conceived as something wider than the individual (as the term is normally understood), as a social 'whole' of which the individual is an element or aspect: a tribe, a race, a Church, a State, the great society of the living and the dead and the yet unborn. This entity is then identified as being the 'true' self which, by imposing its collective, or 'organic', single will upon its recalcitrant 'members', achieves its own, and therefore their, 'higher' freedom. The perils of using organic metaphors to justify the coercion of some men by others in order to raise them to a 'higher' level of freedom have often been pointed out. But what gives such plausibility as it has to this kind of language is that we recognise that it is possible, and at times justifiable, to coerce men in the name of some goal (let us say, justice or public health) which they would, if they were more enlightened, themselves pursue, but do not, because they are blind or ignorant or corrupt. This renders it easy for me to conceive of myself as coercing others for their own sake, in their, not my, interest. I am then claiming that I know what they truly need better than they know it themselves. What, at most, this entails is that they would not resist me if they were rational and as wise as I and understood their interests as I do. But I may go on to claim a good deal more than this. I may declare that they are actually aiming at what in their benighted state they consciously resist, because there exists within them an occult entity – their latent rational will, or their 'true' purpose – and that this entity, although it is belied by all that they overtly feel and do and say, is their 'real' self, of which the poor empirical self in space and time may know nothing or little; and that this inner spirit is the only self that deserves to have its wishes taken into account. [9] Once I take this view, I am in a position to ignore the actual wishes of men or societies, to bully, oppress, torture them in the name, and on behalf, of their 'real' selves, in the secure knowledge that whatever is the true goal of man (happiness, performance of duty, wisdom, a just society, self-fulfilment) must be identical with his freedom – the free choice of his 'true', albeit often submerged and inarticulate, self.

This paradox has been often exposed. It is one thing to say that I know what is good for X, while he himself does not; and even to ignore his wishes for its – and his – sake; and a very different one to say that he has *eo ipso* chosen it, not indeed consciously, not as he seems in everyday life, but in his role as a rational self which his empirical self may now know – the 'real' self which discerns the good, and cannot help choosing it once it is revealed. This monstrous impersonation, which consists in equating what X would choose if he were something he is not, or at least not yet, with what X actually seeks and chooses, is at the heart of all political theories of self-realization. It is one thing to say that I may be coerced for my own good, which I am too blind to see: this may, on occasion, be for my benefit; indeed it may enlarge the scope of my liberty. It is another to say that if it is my good, then I am not being coerced, for I have willed it, whether I know this or not, and am free (or 'truly' free) even while my poor earthly body and foolish mind bitterly reject it, and struggle with the greatest desperation against those who seek, however benevolently, to impose it.

This magical transformation, or sleight of hand (for which William James so justly mocked the Hegelians), can no doubt be perpetrated just as easily with the 'negative' concept of freedom, where the self that should not be interfered with is no longer the individual with his actual wishes and needs as they are normally conceived, but the 'real' man within, identified with the pursuit of some ideal purpose not dreamed of by his empirical self. And, as in the case of the 'positively' free self, this entity may be inflated into some super-personal entity – a State, a class, a nation, or the march of history itself, regarded as a more 'real' subject of attributes than the empirical self. But the 'positive' conception of freedom as self-mastery, with its suggestion of a man divided against himself, has in fact, and as a matter of history, of doctrine and of practice, lent itself more easily to this splitting of personality into two: the transcendent, dominant controller, and the empirical bundle of desires and passions to be disciplined and brought to heel. It is this historical fact that has been influential. This demonstrates (if demonstration of so obvious a truth is needed) that conceptions of freedom directly derive from views of what constitutes a self, a person, a man. Enough manipulation of the definition of man, and freedom can be made to mean whatever the manipulator wishes. Recent history has made it only too clear that the issue is not merely academic.

The consequences of distinguishing between two selves will become even clearer if one considers the two major forms which the desire to be self-directed – directed by one's 'true' self – has historically taken: the first, that of self-abnegation in order to attain independence; the second, that of self-realization, or total self-identification with a specific principle or ideal in order to attain the selfsame end.

Notes

This version of the essay is from Berlin, Isaiah (1998) *The Proper Study of Mankind*, Pimlico, pp.191–206.

[1] I do not, of course, mean to imply the truth of the converse.

[2] Helvétius made this point very clearly: 'The free man is the man who is not in irons, not imprisoned in a gaol, nor terrorized like a slave by the fear of punishment.' It is not lack of freedom not to fly like an eagle or swim like a whale. *De l'esprit*, first discourse, chapter 4.

[3] The Marxist conception of social laws is, of course, the best-known version of this theory, but it forms a large element in some Christian and utilitarian, and all socialist, doctrines.

[4] *Émile*, Book 2, p.320 in *Oeuvres complètes*, ed. Bernard Gagnebin and others (Paris, 1959–), vol. 4.

[5] 'A free man', said Hobbes, 'is he that ... is not hindered to do what he has a will to.' *Leviathan*, chapter 21, p.146 in Richard Tuck's edition (Cambridge, 1991). Law is always a fetter, even if it protects you from being bound in chains that are heavier than those of the law, say some more repressive law or custom, or arbitrary despotism or chaos. Bentham says much the same.

[6] R.H. Tawney, *Equality* (1931), 3rd edn (London, 1938), chapter 5, section 2, 'Equality and Liberty', p.208 (not in previous editions).

[7] Constant, *Principes de politique*, chapter 1, p.275 in Benjamin Constant, *De la liberté chez les modernes: écrits politiques*, ed. Marcel Gauchet ([Paris], 1980).

[8] J.S. Mill, *On Liberty*, chapter 1, p.226 in *Collected Works of John Stuart Mill*, ed. J.M. Robson (Toronto/London, 1981–), vol. 18.

[9] 'The ideal of true freedom is the maximum of power for all members of human society alike to make the best of themselves', said T.H. Green in 1881. *Lecture on Liberal Legislation and Freedom of Contract*: p.200 in T.H. Green, *Lectures on the Principles of Political Obligation and Other Writings*, ed. Paul Harris and John Morrow (Cambridge, 1986). Apart from the confusion of freedom with equality, this entails that if a man chose some immediate pleasure – which (in whose view?) would not enable him to make the best of himself (what self?) – what he was exercising was not 'true' freedom: and if deprived of it, he would not lose anything that mattered. Green was a genuine liberal: but many a tyrant could use this formula to justify his worst acts of oppression.

CHAPTER 5

Karl Marx and Frederick Engels: *The German Ideology* (Part 1)

Derek Matravers

By the end of this chapter you should:

- Have read *The German Ideology* (Part 1) through at least twice and 'On the Jewish Question' at least once.
- Have an understanding of the intellectual context in which they were written.
- Understand the concepts of alienation, the division of labour and private property and the relations between them.
- Understand Marx and Engels's hostility to the state as a further form of alienation.
- Understand Marx and Engels's account of historical change, and understood and appreciated the significance of G.A. Cohen's account of functional explanation.
- Understand Marx and Engels's account of ideology.
- Understand the role of revolution, and the role of the proletariat in the transition to communism.
- Grasp one liberal argument against communism.

Introduction

Karl Marx's ideas have given rise to a political system that has had a direct practical effect on the lives of many millions of people. It is understandable, therefore, that people should think of Marx in terms of the politics of countries such as China or the Soviet Union. Marx needs to be read with a fresh eye, free from assumptions made on the basis of Marxist politics. Like Rousseau, Marx was motivated by deeply humanitarian impulses. He thought that people were made less than human by the forces acting on them in the social and political environment. Freedom could be attained by becoming aware of these forces, and then doing something to change them. In some ways, he did for society what Freud did for the mind – he stripped away the appearance and showed us what was at work underneath. He illuminated every subject he wrote about, which included philosophy, sociology, history, economics and politics.

This chapter concentrates on one central text: Part 1 of *The German Ideology*. I shall refer to section divisions introduced by C.J. Arthur (Arthur (1974)). Arthur divides the text into four major sections, each with subsections the title of which gives some indication of its content. References to the text will be made by citing the letter of the major section, the number of the subsection, followed by the number of the paragraph (page references will also be to the Arthur edition). So A3:2 is the second paragraph of the third subsection of section A. Marx and Engels's manuscript, on which the various editions of *The German Ideology* are based, was damaged and pages were lost. Hence, editions of the book do vary in content.[1] I will also be discussing an early essay by Marx: 'On the Jewish Question'. This will illuminate some of the criticisms of the state made in *The German Ideology* (Part 1), as well as being an important criticism of liberalism.

First, I will comment on the relation between my exposition here and recent Marxist criticism, then, say something about Hegel's influence on Marx and Engels and his followers, and finally, in this introduction, I shall place the composition of the work in the broader context of Marx's life and thought.

Many people have written (and continue to write) on Marx, and there is considerable variation in both the interpretation and evaluation of his work. An important book on the fundamentals of Marxism is G.A. Cohen's *Karl Marx's Theory of History: a Defence* (1978). Cohen claimed to write according to two constraints: 'on the one hand, what Marx wrote, and, on the other, those standards of clarity and rigour which distinguish twentieth-century analytical philosophy' (ibid., p.ix). The view of Marx presented here is closer to Cohen's and the (so-called) 'analytical Marxists' than to other traditions.[2]

Looking back on the composition of *The German Ideology* (1845–6), Marx wrote: 'we decided to set forth together our conception as opposed to the ideological one of German Philosophy, in fact to settle accounts with our former philosophical conscience' (Marx (1859), p.212). Although I am not going to concentrate on this settling of accounts with his early Hegelianism, it is something you will need to understand a little about if you are to understand *The German Ideology*, and also if you are to grasp the central tenets of Marxian philosophy.[3]

Marx is here referring to a stage of his life during which he was a follower of the German philosopher, G.W.F. Hegel (1770–1831). Hegel taught at the university in Berlin where Marx studied, and several important Marxian concepts (including alienation) have their origin in his writing. Hegel left a large body of work, which included a theory of historical development. One of his key ideas is that the history of the world is not just a matter of things happening one after another, but is something that has meaning and significance. The point can be put by analogy with the development of a person. An individual consciousness develops from that of a new-born to the full self-consciousness of an adult. Think of the world as a 'super-being', called by Hegel the 'subject' or 'idea'. The claim is that this too is unfolding in self-consciousness. The subject (like a person) is developing into full self-consciousness. That is, everything that happens is part of a general process that the subject has to pass through in its drive to self-consciousness. In other words, things do not simply happen by accident; they make sense as part of a grand scheme. Looking at how history has developed will, therefore, tell us about the grand scheme. In addition, once we have grasped the outlines of the grand scheme we will be able to appreciate the significance of what has happened in history. To sum up, historical events do not happen by chance, their happening is part of some grand rational process. We could put the point in an epigram: what is real (history) is also rational, and what is rational (the grand scheme) is also real.

Marx and Engels did not want to 'settle accounts' with Hegel himself, but with a group of German philosophers with whom Marx had previously been associated, the so-called 'Young Hegelians'. (Those referred to by name in *The German Ideology* are Ludwig Feuerbach, David Strauss, Max Stirner and Bruno Bauer.) Hegel's followers divided into two camps. Both sides accepted the equivalence between the rational and the real. For the conservatives (The 'Old' or 'Right' Hegelians), this meant that what was real was therefore rational: that which had reached the latest and therefore highest state of development. In particular, German culture (or even more particularly, the Prussian state) was supremely rational and to criticize, or seek to alter, it was both irrational and immoral. The Young Hegelians thought that only the rational was *truly* real; lots of things (including the Prussian state), although *apparently* real, were full of anachronisms and inconsistencies. Reality needed to form a consistent whole and radical measures might be needed to achieve this. Furthermore, and this is what earned the contempt of Marx and Engels, the principal forum for such revolutionary updating was the realm of thought. This accounts for the bitterly sarcastic opening of *The German Ideology*. It should be noted that, despite Marx and Engels's accusations, Hegel did not hold that human history was the history of mind. His notion of the subject embraced both of what we would call 'mind' and 'the world' (Wood (1993), pp.427–8).

Before leaving the Hegelians, something should be said about Ludwig Feuerbach (1804–72), whose name Marx and Engels used as the title of the first part of *The German Ideology*. Two of Feuerbach's claims in particular influenced Marx and Engels. First, he argued that talk of the Hegelian 'subject' and 'idea' needed to be reinterpreted as talk about actual material conditions. The motor of history was not the spiritual unfolding of the subject's self-consciousness, but the sum of material conditions which caused people to act as they did. Furthermore, talk about the transcendental (anything beyond what it is possible to experience, for example, God) was something indulged in by people as a distraction from the miseries of their actual lives. This belief is reflected in Marx's pithy comment, 'Religion ... is the opium of the people' (Marx (1843–4), p.28). Such systems of thought keep people from a true awareness of the actual causes of their problems.

Marx had left university in Berlin in 1842. Over the next couple of years, writing for radical journals, he worked out some of the basics which bore full fruit in his later writings. During this period he wrote a number of essays, including 'On the Jewish Question'. Expelled from Germany, he moved first to Paris (where he met Engels) and then Brussels. Here, in 1845–6, they wrote *The German Ideology*. This takes the ideas on which Marx had been working (specifically, on the state, on alienation and on the theory of history) and combines them in a single outlook (Arthur (1974), p.21). Although the book lacks the detailed accounts of history and economics Marx was to master in his later writings, it is important, both as a stage from which the later writings can be understood, and a statement of a distinctive Marxian[4] philosophy in its own right.

Reading *The German Ideology*

The German Ideology (Part 1) is only about sixty pages long. It is not, however, a particularly easy read. There are two main reasons for this. First, its authors never polished it for publication. Themes are introduced, briefly discussed, and then dropped only to be taken up later. (C.J. Arthur, in his edition, has introduced headings and sub-headings that give an idea of the content of each section and sub-section.)

Second, Marx and Engels sometimes break off polemically to attack the Young Hegelians. The details of this need not worry us. This principally occurs in the Preface; A1; some of B1 and B2; the second half of B3; some of D1 and D4.

Even when not being polemical, Marx and Engels are lively writers who are exciting to read. They were keenly aware that capitalism enabled some to live in comfort at the expense of keeping others in misery. Although officially they were producing, amongst other things, an objective analysis of capitalism, a fierce sense of moral indignation at this unfairness shines through their prose. Also, because they were analysing historical processes, they tie their abstract points down to concrete historical changes. This use of examples often helps to keep track of the argument. Above all, you can sense in their writing the development of a system that attempts to make sense of the human world: its history and our experience of it. It is this final point that has, for many people, made reading Marx and Engels an experience that has changed their life.

In their writings, Marx and Engels continually speak of 'man'. As with the other authors in this book this raises a number of complicated issues. The status of women was an important part of the communist programme (see Marx and Engels (1848), p.173). Furthermore, there are substantial questions about the relation between *Marxism* and women. As these issues do not arise explicitly in *The German Ideology* (Part 1), I am going to ignore them. In analysing Marx and Engels's arguments, the term 'man' shall be taken to refer to both men and women.

ACTIVITY

Read all of *The German Ideology* (Part 1). In common with other first readings of the texts studied in this book, do not try to grasp the arguments in all their detail. Rather, try to get an overview; an impression of what Marx and Engels were trying to achieve.

Alienation, the division of labour and private property

Alienation, the division of labour and private property are three of several important ideas discussed in *The German Ideology* (Part 1). Here, I am going to examine how they are used in A2, A3, A4 and C2. Do not expect a sustained discussion; rather, these passages contain points that put together, give us Marx and Engels's view.

Alienation

Marx's thoughts on alienation originate in Hegel; more particularly, in the Young Hegelians' critique of religion (this is discussed in Reading 5.1). Marx wrote an essay entitled 'Alienated Labour' shortly before writing *The German Ideology* in which he claimed the following. The labour of the worker results in the creation of objects. These objects appear hostile and alien to him or her. Furthermore, it is not only that workers are alienated from the product of their labour, the actual productive process becomes alien. This is unfortunate, as humans are essentially producers. Hence, they are alienated from the process and the product of their essential selves. Marx ends with the bold claim that 'the whole of human servitude is involved in the relation of worker to production' (Marx (1844), p.67).

ACTIVITY

Read the first four paragraphs of A2 and C2 (particularly the final three paragraphs) and then read Jonathan Wolff's 'Playthings of Alien Forces: Karl Marx and the Rejection of the Market Economy' (Reading 5.1). This Reading covers several of the notions we will be considering: historical materialism, alienation and communism.

When you have completed the reading, summarize in three short paragraphs the three claims about alienated labour Wolff considers (in the section headed 'Alienated Labour').

DISCUSSION

1   Under capitalism people perform a form of labour unworthy of human beings. That is, productive labour, which should be a pleasurable and fulfilling task, becomes something the worker has to do in order to make money to survive. (As Marx put it elsewhere, '[the worker] is at home when he is not working, and when he is working he is not at home' (Marx (1844), p.62)).

2   Capitalism itself is an alienated product of human activity. This has two aspects. First, human beings cease to feel 'at home' in the world. Second, our products come to control and dominate us. In particular, we are dominated by the workings of market forces which are outside our control. Wolff gives some examples of this on page 276. This is a point that runs through all of Marx's work: to be free is not simply to be free from coercion from other people, it is to be free of the blind forces of the capitalist market as well.

3   Mankind does not recognize its 'communal essence'. Under capitalism it is appropriate to exploit advantage we have over others for profit, rather than to relate to them as a fellow human beings.

Notice that 1 and 3 are partly psychological claims, about what it is like to live in a capitalist society. This contrasts with 2, the claim that, whatever we might think, we are the 'playthings of alien forces'. Alienation does have these two sides to it. Psychologically, capitalism makes us alienated, in that we lack a sense of life as meaningful. Economically, all our lives are dominated by forces we cannot control: namely, the large market relations all our little transactions help create. This is the root of Marx and Engels's criticism of what Berlin later called 'negative liberty' (see Reading 4.4). The consequence of negative liberty in the economic sphere is a system that oppresses us all.

C2 contains a vivid sketch of alienation in the psychological sense. Because of competition, individuals 'have to strain their energy to the utmost'; we each spend more time and energy on alienated labour. Everything noble 'religion, morality, etc.' is destroyed. This is because big business takes it over and puts a price on it, or because there is no longer the time or space for it (cf. Marx and Engels (1848), p.161). Furthermore, all natural relationships: relationships to our communities or to each other are transformed into 'money relationships'.

The division of labour

ACTIVITY

Now read the rest of A2, and all of A3 and A4.

In A4:6–8 the division of labour is held responsible for individuals being at the mercy of market forces, and so responsible for the second of the two senses of alienation described above. This claim by Marx and Engels is, however, problematic. In A:2 and A:3 Marx and Engels give the following sense to 'division of labour': as the economy develops, different tasks are identified and different people are allocated to these tasks. What matters in a capitalist market economy is that the product is produced efficiently. If this means separating the various tasks that go into producing it, and dividing the labour so that each person just gets one of those tasks (as on a production line) then that is what the market will force the capitalist to do. The worker bears no relation to the product as something he or she has produced, and is certainly alienated from it in our first sense. This sense is supposed to be responsible for the second sense: the individual being at the mercy of market forces (that is, capitalism). However, production lines seem no more characteristic of a capitalist economy than they are of a communist economy, in which the market forces *are* under conscious control (Arthur (1986), p.163; Elster (1986), pp.50–1). So it is unclear why Marx and Engels think communism would abolish the division of labour. If one adds to this the claim that communism would abolish alienation, then it becomes unclear what the relation between the division of labour and alienation is. To answer this we need to dig further into the text.

ACTIVITY

Answer the following questions.

1   Find a second sense of 'division of labour' (look at A4:5).
2   What presuppositions are necessary for the implementation of communism and why?

DISCUSSION

1 At A4:5 Marx and Engels claim that 'as soon as the division of labour comes into being, each man has a particular, exclusive sphere of activity forced upon him and from which he cannot escape'. That is, labour is divided into different specialisms and each of us is a specialist. If all this meant was that we were forced into specialist tasks on the production line this would only be the first sense identified above. However, Marx and Engels take it that the division of labour would force us into different vocations: hunter, fisherman, herdsman or cultural critic.

2 The first is that alienation must become an 'intolerable power' against which a sufficient number of people would be willing to join a revolution. That is, the system must appear to produce great wealth for the few, and a miserable, alienated life for the many. The second is that the productive forces must be developed. If not, then, when the revolution comes, there will not be the abundance needed for communism to succeed and all that will happen is that unfulfilled desires ('wants') will become more generalized (cf. Marx and Engels (1848), p.183). Later Marxists have been sceptical about the probability of these two presuppositions occurring at the same time. For obvious reasons, people are more likely to be miserable and alienated at times of scarcity than in times of abundance. As Trotsky remarked, 'societies are not so rational in building that the dates for a proletarian dictatorship arrive exactly at that time when the economic and cultural conditions are ripe for socialism [communism]' (quoted in Elster (1986), p.160).

The claim to abundance provides the means for the abolition of alienation. In a communist, and therefore abundant, society people will not need to work on production lines, but will be able to do the jobs they want. Hence, communism will abolish alienation in all its senses.

There are grounds here for scepticism. As Jonathan Wolff argues, it is at least plausible that communist regulation will get these relations 'under our control again'. It is more difficult to see how communist regulation would overcome the other senses of alienation. We will see an argument for abundance later (pp.255–6), but even if we grant that some resources may be abundant, other resources (such as living space and raw materials) are inherently limited (Kymlicka (1990), p.166). Furthermore, the sense individuals may have that their lives lack meaning may have other complex causes: the nature of industrial work under any system, biological facts about human beings or inherent problems in the co-ordination of complex activities (Elster (1986), p.54). The advent of communism is unlikely to do away with such causes. I will examine a reply to some of this by Marx and Engels below (p.258).

Private property

ACTIVITY

It is clear that Marx and Engels think the division of labour and alienation are bound up with each other. What is not so clear is why, in A4:1 they claim that 'division of labour and private property are ... identical expressions'. Read this passage carefully, and try to work out the argument.

DISCUSSION

Let us take Marx and Engels's own analogy, and think of two ways in which a family could be organized. First, the traditional family in which authority rests with the father. He works for a living and controls the finances. The mother (who we can assume has some money of her own, whether given by her husband or not) looks after the house, and the children contribute in ways which the father dictates. All have their own sphere of work, with money allocated to running that sphere. In other words, with the division of labour comes the need to ensure that people spend only the money allocated to them (private property). Furthermore, the family will need to find some way of 'punishing' those who spend more than they own, or who do not do their jobs properly.

Second, in a family in which there is no division of labour, nobody has a specific job; everyone simply does what needs to be done. Here there would be no point in dividing up the money so that each person got a share; as nobody has a specific task, nobody needs a specific budget. It would be much better for everyone to contribute what they could to the communal pot, and take what they need out of it.

This answers the question about the link between the division of labour and private property. Without a division of labour, everything can be held communally and there need be no private property. It is worth noticing that the second model of the family (which is in some respects analogous to the communist state) could only work at the level of society given the two presuppositions described above. First, that there is abundance (money is not scarce). If there is very little in the communal pot, and we are all allowed free access to it, then my buying my dinner might deprive my sister of hers. Second, that people are free of alienation; they are honest and community-minded. If I am alienated from others, I will continually raid the communal pot (that is, others' contributions) to support my lavish lifestyle.

Given the other aspects of Marx and Engels's thought, one can see why they thought the individuals in the second model of the family would not be alienated. They would not have work imposed upon them, they would do only what they needed to do in order to support the community. Hence, they would not need to work to survive and they would not be exploited.

The picture that emerges from *The German Ideology* (Part 1) is this. In a clear sense, individual transactions give rise to market forces. These return to dominate individuals, by distorting the way they work, which in turn has distorting effects on their psychologies. When communism dawns, and market forces are brought under conscious control, alienation in this sense will disappear. Furthermore, people will not be forced to work to create more private property for others. Hence, they will be able to find fulfilment in satisfying labour which they choose to do.

Civil society and the state

Marx and Engels continue their analysis of, and their indictment of, capitalism by looking at the form it takes politically. In liberal political thought (this comes out particularly in Locke's *Second Treatise of Government*, especially Chapter XI) the state and civil society are distinct. The responsibilities of the state include making and enforcing laws and ensuring basic political rights. In a liberal state everyone, no matter how poor or wealthy, is *politically* equal in being a citizen of the same state. In principle, everyone will have the same basic rights and be equal before the law. Civil society comprises all those relations between people that involve industry and trade, and various informal associations. Such society is 'governed' by the morality which emerges from it: basic principles of fairness and decency.

This independence of state from society gives Locke an answer to the following question. The laws (given by the state) formulate what is allowed and disallowed; they codify what we think is right and wrong. If, in addition, morality emerges from the state rather than from civil society, then morality and law have the same basis. If this were the case, how could we ever argue that the state has passed an unjust law? We have seen that Rousseau did not separate civil society from the state. Hence, for him, the general will 'is always right' (Rousseau, *The Social Contract*, II, iii). As long as the state is regulated by the general will the question of an unjust law never arises.

The liberal's view is that morality emerges in civil society, and it is one task of the state to pass laws that reflect that morality. So each of us can judge how well or badly the state has done from our standpoint in the civil society. This relies on two assumptions. First, that civil society is in fact independent of the state (otherwise it will not be a source of independent criticism) and second, that the inhabitants of the civil society are rational, autonomous individuals (otherwise they will not be capable of passing judgement on the state) (cf. Hindess (1993), pp.316–17).

Marx formulated his position on the relation between the state and civil society in an early essay, 'On the Jewish Question' (1843). This he considered an attack on liberalism. That is, it is an attack on the characteristically liberal project of limiting politics to the creation of a regime of rights to politics, liberty, security and property (what Marx refers to as 'political emancipation') (cf. Wolff (1996), p.143).

I will refer to 'On the Jewish Question' by paragraph numbers, 1–94 (be aware of the single line paragraphs). The essay begins with an extended recapitulation of Bauer's argument (paragraphs 1–23), before Marx gives his own views. Some important points are as follows:

(i)   'Political emancipation is not the completed consistent form of religious emancipation because political emancipation is not the completed and consistent form of human emancipation' (26).

(ii)   '[T]he political annulment of private property has not only not abolished private property, it actually presupposes it' (30).

(iii)   'Political emancipation is of course a great progress' (35).

(iv)   'Thus none of the so-called rights of man goes beyond egoistic man, man as he is in civil society, namely an individual withdrawn behind his private interests and whims and separated from community' (79).

ACTIVITY

Read the first part of 'On the Jewish Question' and then answer the following questions. Ignore paragraphs 39–48, which is a detailed discussion of the Christian state that does not introduce anything new that is germane to our concerns. Then read 'Marx's Early Critique of Liberalism' by Jon Pike (Reading 5.2) and answer the following questions.

1   What is Marx's argument for (ii) above?

2   Why does he claim (iii)?

3   (i) What, according to Pike, is Marx's criticism of liberal rights in 'On the Jewish Question'? (ii) From Pike's discussion, how do you think a liberal might reply?

DISCUSSION

1   The argument comes in the rest of paragraph 30. The state declares such things as 'birth, class, education and profession' to be 'unpolitical differences'. For example, the state would not permit such differences to disallow a person from voting. There is only a point in doing this – there is only a point in the state existing – if there are differences to declare politically irrelevant. Similarly, the state can only declare private property politically irrelevant; this action only makes sense if private property will continue to flourish in civil society.

2   Political emancipation is an advance over the hierarchical and oppressive situation that preceded it. This is characteristic of Marx's historical perspective. The state characterizes a period of history (capitalism). It emerges from one situation in which there was no state (feudalism) and will disappear into another (communism). The historical nature of the state is stressed in *The German Ideology* (Part 1).

3   (i) According to Pike, liberal rights are 'a particular limited construct' that has the appearance of 'an immutable truth'. Pike shows that talk of rights only makes sense in conditions where the activities defended by those rights are under threat. So, 'those who universalize rights and regard them as foundational for human political morality, thereby universalize threats and regard threats as foundational for human morality'. This is not necessary; there is an alternative to morality founded on threats and that is, in Pike's words, a 'society of universal friendliness'.

(ii) Pike discusses two conditions which, he says, makes threats likely and therefore rights important. The first is scarcity of resources. There is (currently) no shortage of oxygen, so nobody talks of there being a right to oxygen. There is a shortage of private land, so the people have a right to control over their land. The second is the absence of altruism. People cannot be counted on to pay attention to the concerns and interests of others. If both of these conditions obtain, it looks as if we need talk of rights. The liberal can reply that both of these conditions do obtain and so we do need talk of rights. There is scarcity of resources, and, however many decent people there are about, it is insanely optimistic to think that people can be counted on always to be altruistic. As we shall see, Marx did have replies to these points (which will be considered later).

As part of sense 2 of 'alienation' (p.242 above), I claimed that 'capitalism itself is an alienated product of human activity'. This is an idea Marx took from Feuerbach's discussion of religion (which was mentioned in the Introduction). In Reading 5.1, Jonathan Wolff put Feuerbach's ideas as follows:

> The central thought is that man makes God in his own image. Protagoras said, 'If triangles had a God, it would have three sides'. Feuerbach agrees. Everything human beings have said about God is a mystified expression of things true of themselves. Human beings project their own powers and attributes on to an abstract, non-existent entity. Instead of enjoying and glorying in these powers, man 'alienates them', raises them to an infinite level, and worships them. Marx says that 'religion is a devious acknowledgement of man, through an intermediary'.

(Wolff, Reading 5.1, p.274 below)

Man, unhappy in the world, conjures up an external entity (God) and escapes this unhappiness by finding release in worshipping this entity. 'On the Jewish Question' describes an analogous situation. Man, unhappy in the world, conjures up an external entity (the state) and escapes this unhappiness by finding he is free and equal in this entity. The state (and its corollary, capitalism) is as much an alienated product of human activity as religion. This is what Marx says in 'On the Jewish Question':

> When the political state has achieved its true completion, man leads a double life, a heavenly one and an earthly one, not only in thought and consciousness but in reality, in life. He has a life both in the political community, where he is valued as a communal being, and in civil society, where he is active as a private individual, treats other man as means, degrades himself to a means, and becomes the plaything of alien powers. The political state has just as spiritual an attitude to civil society as heaven has to earth.

(paragraph 31)

The only way people can escape from such alienation is by full human emancipation, rather than mere political emancipation.

ACTIVITY

Now read A4 (again) and B1. B1:2 in particular stresses the historical nature of the state. It is clear that Marx and Engels disagree with liberalism's two presuppositions concerning the relation between state and society described above. First, the forces of production (the materialistic basis) are fundamental, and explain both society and the state so they cannot be independent of each other (this will be discussed below, pages 252–6). Second, we cannot step outside our circumstances and make a rational autonomous judgement about them. Our consciousness, as much as our situation, is a product of the forces of production: 'circumstances make men just as much as men make circumstances' (B1:4).

Also read C3 and D1 (especially D1:5) where the state is explicitly discussed.

The main thread of Marx and Engels's argument considering the relation of state and law to property is that the ruling class have 'purchased' the state through taxation and loans. The state, however, gives the appearance of responding to the will of the citizens. Despite the appearance of the state being the product of free choice, however, it is in fact created to fit the demands of the forces of production.

In the section Arthur entitles 'The Relation of State and Law to Property' (C3:5, p.81) Marx and Engels present a particularly vivid case of what is being talked about. If you own a piece of private property, you will believe you can do with it what you will. Marx and Engels point out that this is an illusion. It depends on a large background over which you have no control. If you are a shopkeeper, you might think you can do what you like with your shop. However, if a supermarket opened next door this would reveal your thought to be an illusion. The only thing you could do would be to cease trading. Once again, we are 'playthings of alien forces'. This, according to Marx and Engels, is the unspoken outcome of liberal theories of private property such as that of John Locke.

D1 (pp.82–6), which principally concerns the proletariat and the revolution, will be fully discussed on pp.259–62 below. What is of particular interest here is the claim that capitalism gives us an idea of ourselves as free individuals, independent of any particular role. For Marx and Engels this is a dangerous bourgeois illusion. We are not free; in the 'war of all against all' we are 'more subjected to the violence of things'. The serf had a particular place in the world and had to fulfil the duties attached to such a place. However, he also enjoyed various protections; for example, a plot of land and protection from attack. The capitalist state makes us free citizens. However, in society big business, unlike the nobles, has no obligation to protect us. We can simply be tossed aside if we no longer contribute to the making of profit. Even though Marx and Engels claim that political emancipation is a step forward from feudalism, the state only provides an illusion of freedom and equality.

Historical materialism

'Historical materialism' was not a term used by Marx or Engels. They preferred to think of their approach as a method rather than a worked out system of ideas (McLellan (1980), p.135). However, the term has become standard so it is the term I shall use. *The German Ideology* (Part 1) contains the longest exposition of Marx and Engels's thoughts in this area, as usual distributed throughout the book. The account is sketchy, and devoid of the detailed historical knowledge Marx acquired later in his life (specifically during the 1850s and 60s, while writing *Capital*, his final great work on economics and human freedom).

Hegel believed that history was not simply a matter of successive events (see pp.239–40 above); some story could be told which gave it a unity. Marx and Engels took over this belief. But, unlike Hegel, the pattern is not a rational working out of self-consciousness, rather it is the inexorable expansion of the productive forces. The productive forces are anything necessary for making things: the machines, the raw material and the labour power (cf. Cohen (1978), p.32). People, even to the extent of their consciousness and sense of who they are, are products of these changes (this is dealt with in the section entitled 'The philosophy of historical materialism' in Jonathan Wolff's Reading 5.1, pp.271–3 below).

Thirteen years after he and Engels wrote *The German Ideology*, Marx presented what he called 'the guiding principles of my studies', which included a clear and concise statement of historical materialism.

> In the social production of their existence, men inevitably enter into definite relations, which are independent of their will, namely relations of production, appropriate to a given stage in the development of their material forces of production. The totality of these relations of production constitutes the economic structure of society, the real foundation, on which arises a legal and political superstructure and to which correspond definite forms of social consciousness. The mode of production of material life conditions the general process of social, political and intellectual life. It is not the consciousness of men that determines their existence, but their existence that determines their consciousness.
>
> (Marx (1859), p.211)

How does labour drive the development of history? Marx and Engels separate the productive forces, the relations of production and the superstructure. The productive forces are specified above. The relations of production are the social arrangements: importantly, who owns what property. Finally, the superstructure consists of such things as the legal and political aspects of a society. The key idea is that the relation between the productive forces and the relations of production is not stable; it changes with time. At some times the relations of production stimulate the productive forces, at other times they 'fetter' (inhibit) them. Marx and Engels call the circumstance in which the relations of production fetter the productive forces 'a contradiction'. Such contradictions provide the grounds for a revolution, which moves society on to a different set of relations of production; ones that stimulate the productive forces.

At the time at which they wrote *The German Ideology*, Marx and Engels had not settled on a terminology for describing what I will refer to as 'the forces of production', the relations of production and the superstructure. Alternative terms for the relations of production are 'form of intercourse', 'mode of intercourse' and 'relations (or conditions) of intercourse' (see Arthur (1974), n.1, pp.42–3). The context usually makes it clear what is being talked about; I will, however, point out the variations in terminology when appropriate.

ACTIVITY

Read A2 where these ideas are first discussed. Notice how Marx and Engels explain various things (the separation of town and country, the division of labour) by the need for the productive forces to develop. This will give you a taste of the sort of explanations that are to come.

List the three forms of ownership Marx and Engels consider, and write a short paragraph describing the social structure characteristic of each.

DISCUSSION

1   Tribal ownership. The social structure is based on the patriarchal family: chieftains, members of the tribe and then slaves. (Note that slavery develops when an economic need for slaves arises; that is, increase in population and a growth of wants.)

2   State association. This is less clear. The members of the tribe have become citizens (who own private property) and there are slaves. Marx and Engels also mention the 'small peasantry' (who are presumably not slaves, but who do not own much or any property) being transformed into the proletariat. The proletariat (which I will discuss below) are defined by Engels as 'the class of modern wage labourers who, having no means of production of their own, are reduced to selling their labour power in order to live' (Marx and Engels (1848), p.158). In other words, those who have to make a living by working for a wage.

3   Feudal property. There is a nobility who use force to keep not slaves, but serfs. That is, people who are allowed to farm their own plot of land provided they pay their dues to their local noble. The equivalent in the towns was the guilds, in which a craftsman (the noble) employed journeymen and apprentices (the serfs). The nobles themselves form an association under the monarch.

In each case Marx and Engels claim that these social arrangements are caused by an expansion in the forces of production.

The principal discussion of historical materialism occurs in C (pp.68ff.). Unfortunately four pages of the manuscript at the beginning of this section are missing. What we have picks up on what must have been a discussion of two different forms of association.

Natural association (the country). People united by familial tribal bonds, using their labour to extract a living from the natural locality in which they find themselves. There is no division of labour.

Civilized association (the town). A group of independent people, brought together, who live by making money and using that to buy food. This leads to the division of labour and the accumulation of capital.

ACTIVITY

Read all of C (pp.68–81). Note in particular the crucial changes that take us from one period to the next, and the character of the periods which followed these changes.

The first change was the serfs moving from the country to the town. The serfs found the work they could do dictated by the existing guilds (the guilds in the cities were analogous to the nobles in the country). They either had a skill, in which case they worked for the guild, or they became 'day-labourers', and part of the 'rabble'. The rabble is separate from the workers in the guilds. The rabble is made up of individuals who entered the town separately, and who thus have never had the chance to 'organize'. Marx and Engels mention two further facts. First, medieval craftsmen performed all the tasks associated with making their product; there was no division of labour (in the first sense described on page 243). Thus the craftsman had a 'contented slavish relationship' with his work which is contrasted with the alienated indifference of the modern workman. Second, capital only exists in the form of items that are of use, such as tools ('estate capital'). These are then passed down 'from father to son'.

The second change was the separation of production and commerce. One group of people make goods and another group sells them. An immediate effect was the division of labour. One can imagine that a merchant noticed that the wheels made by A were better than those made by B, but the blade of the plough made by B was better than that made by A. So wheels were bought from A, blades from B and put together by C. People became distanced – alienated – from the product of their labour. Furthermore, some medium of exchange was needed to 'pay' for the component parts. So, money ('moveable capital') developed and capitalism was well on its way.

C2 continues the story from the middle ages. It divides subsequent history into three periods: (a) from mediaeval times until the mid seventeenth century; (b) from then until the mid eighteenth century; (c) from then up to, and including, the industrial revolution. The bourgeoisie are the dominant class of capitalism. They own the means of production in which they employ others. They are able to live on the profits, and so have no need to work. The petty bourgeoisie own their means of production, but not on a scale that enables them to live without labouring (shopkeepers and so on) (cf. Cohen (1978), p.86). Once big business is dominant, people begin to lead the kinds of alienated lives I considered above (p.243).

The forces of production tend to expand throughout history; G.A. Cohen calls this 'the development thesis' (cf. Cohen (1988, p.21). Historical materialism, is the view that the development thesis explains historical change. For example, it was the development of the technology of weaving which, because it could be carried out by individuals without much skill, caused the break-up of the guilds (C2:3). A development in the productive forces (better weaving technology) explains a change in the relations of production (the break-up of the guilds).

If all the explanations were that simple, there would be no problem. However, it sometimes looks as if facts about the productive forces and the superstructure explain changes in the productive forces. This appears to be what is going on at D1:1: it looks as if the burghers (a role that belongs to the sphere of productive relations) are creating the conditions (the break-up of the feudal system) which will lead to an expansion of the productive forces (the rise of manufacturing). There appears to be a logical contradiction here (not a contradiction in the Marxian sense (see p.250) According to historical materialism, expansion of productive forces should cause the changes in productive relations. Here, it is a change in the productive relations that appears to cause the change in productive forces. The productive forces are being explained by that which they are supposed to be explaining, which is impossible.

ACTIVITY

G.A. Cohen shows the contradiction is only apparent by giving a careful analysis of the way in which the forces of production are the fundamental explanation.

He does this in a paper in which he has summarised his main findings on historical materialism, and where he provides a commentary on them. An extract from this paper constitutes Reading 5.3; read this and answer the following questions.

I   What precise definitions does Cohen give of the 'three ensembles' mentioned in the Preface to A Contribution to the Critique of Political Economy: the productive forces, the relations of production and the superstructure?

2   What relations does Cohen identify as holding between the 'three ensembles'?

3   Cohen gives three different versions of functional explanation:

(i)   e occurred because f occurred

(ii) e occurred because it caused f

(iii) e occurred because the situation was such that an event like e would cause an event like f.

Why does Cohen reject (i) and (ii) and accept (iii)?

4   What point does Cohen make in his discussion of the hollow bones of birds towards the end of the Reading (p.293)? [5]

5   Which stands to Cohen's vision in the way the relations of production stand to the forces of production, the bridge of his nose or his right eye?

DISCUSSION

I   'The productive forces are those facilities and devices which are used to productive effect in the process of production: means of production on the one hand and labour power on the other' (p.288). Cohen then goes on to define 'means of production' and 'labour power'.

'Relations of production are relations of economic power, of the economic power people enjoy or lack over labour power and means of production' (p.289).

Cohen claims that the superstructure 'includes the legal and state institutions of society, or at least some of them' (p.290). However, because the point is controversial, in the Reading he discusses property law only.

2   Cohen says: 'the level of development of the productive forces explains the nature of productive relations, and ... they in turn explain the nature of the character of the superstructure co-present with them' (p.290). It is a fact about explanation that if A explains B, and B explains C, then A explains C. If my ringing a bell explains the noise, and the noise explains you being woken up, then my ringing the bell explains you being woken up. So Cohen is here claiming that the development of the productive forces (A) explains both the productive relations and the superstructure (B and C). The relation between the three ensembles is illustrated in the following diagram.

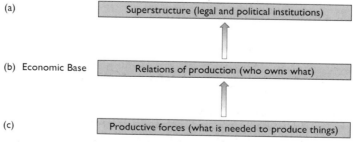

Figure 1   (c) explains the nature of (b), and (b) explains the nature of (a); the specific nature of (a) and (b) is explained by their capacity to enable the expansion of (c).

3   The key point here is that an event can only be explained by something that came before it, not something that came after it. For example, in order for the alarm ringing to be the explanation of what woke Fred up, the alarm would need to have started ringing before Fred woke up. If Fred woke up before the alarm started ringing, there must have been some other explanation. An event cannot be explained by its effects (because they come after the event) only by its causes (because they come before the event).

As Cohen says, (i) explains a later occurrence in terms of an earlier one. It makes no more sense than it would to say 'the alarm started ringing because Fred woke up'.

The same applies to (ii). The equivalent this time would be 'the alarm started ringing because it caused Fred to wake up'.

Having eliminated the other two candidates, Cohen 'elects' what he takes to be the only other option, that is, (iii). This is equivalent to: 'the alarm started ringing because the situation was such that an event like the alarm ringing would cause an event like Fred waking up'. This does make sense. What caused the alarm to ring was Fred setting it. What caused Fred to set it was that he knows that events like the alarm ringing would wake him up, and he wants to wake up. So he sets the alarm, it rings and he wakes up. What explains the alarm ringing is the fact that, in such situations, alarms ringing have a tendency to wake people up. It is this fact that causes people to set them, which causes them to go off. So the sequence of events is as follows. Notice that each event is earlier than the one it explains.

Events like alarms ringing wake people up.

Fred is aware of this fact, which caused him to set the alarm.

The alarm started to ring because it was set to go off.

Fred woke up.

So although it is not true that the alarm started ringing because Fred woke up (option (i) that was rejected), the alarm started ringing because, as a matter of fact, events like alarms ringing cause events like Fred waking up.

The case is analogous to that which we are trying to explain. The forces of production have an inexorable tendency to expand. It is a fact that a certain change in the relations of production will cause an expansion in the productive forces. However, the change in the relations of production cannot be explained by its effects. It can, however, be explained by the fact that changes like the one we are talking about in the relations of production have a tendency to cause an expansion of the productive forces.

4   Darwin's theory of evolution explains how the fact that a change tends to bring about an effect can make that change happen. As Cohen points out, 'no one has given good answers to the similar questions ... about historical materialism'. In the case of the alarm clock it was not simply the fact that events like alarms ringing wake people up that caused the alarm to ring. Fred needed to be aware of this fact and that awareness cause him to set the alarm. Even if it is a fact that changes like the one we have been talking

about in the relations of production have a tendency to cause an expansion in the productive forces, how does that fact bring about the change in the productive forces? Take an example from C.2: the decline of the guilds. It may be a fact that events like guilds declining bring about the expansion of the productive forces. However, this makes it look as if the guilds somehow knew that self-destructing was going to help make the productive forces expand. How did they know? One explanation would be similar to Fred knowing about alarm clocks' tendency to wake people up. Someone could know that destroying the guilds would cause an expansion in the productive forces, and, like Fred setting the alarm clock, destroy the guilds. Although possible, it is not very plausible either that people act for such esoteric motives or that single individuals can have such large effects. Finding how these things happen on a large social scale is more analogous to finding out how nature managed to bring about the change in birds' wings that would enable them to fly.

5   It is Cohen's right eye that stands to his vision in the way the relations of production stand to the forces of production. It is a fact that the structure of the eye is as it is, because it aids vision. This mechanics of this are explained by Darwin's theory of evolution. Although the bridge of his nose aids his vision (by supporting his glasses), there is no mechanism connecting this fact with the structure of the bridge of his nose. So some things can be functional for others, even if it is false that they are as they are because they are functional for others.

We can now see that why the example from D:1 (the existence of the burghers apparently explaining the expansion of manufacture) is not a problem. Let us grant Marx and Engels's claim that the serfs becoming burghers would lead to the break-up of feudalism and an increase in the forces of production. It is this fact that explains the creation of burghers. There is no contradiction: it is the fact that it will bring about changes in the forces of production that explains the appearance of burghers, and it is just that appearance that brings about the change.

Finally, look at a passage in C:2, 16:

> [Its development] produced a mass of productive forces, for which private [property] became just as much a fetter as the guild had been for manufacture and the small, rural workshop for the developing craft. These productive forces received under the system of private property a one-sided development only, and became for the majority destructive forces; moreover, a great multitude of such forces could find no application at all within this system.

This conclusion, drawn from the argument of *The German Ideology* (Part 1), supports Rousseau's claim that 'The body politic, like the human body, begins to die from the very moment of its birth, and carries within itself the causes of its destruction' (Rousseau, *The Social Contract*, III, XI, 2). Marx and Engels claim that, in the same way as the guilds had to go because they were a fetter on the development of manufacturing, private property has to go because it is a fetter on the expansion of the forces of production. People are unable to utilize their potential for production if they do not have the means to do it. In a capitalist system, the means of production are in the hands of the few. So private property is hampering the potential for production. This fettering of the forces of production is a necessary factor in the end of capitalism and its replacement by communism. Contrary to predictions, however, capitalism continues to be dominant. This will be further examined below (pp.258ff.).

In summary, according to Marx and Engels, change occurs when the relations of production are a fetter on the forces of production. The claim that the occurrence of an event is explained by the desirability of its effects is only apparent; such explanations are not incompatible with, indeed they presuppose, explanation in terms of causes. Because capitalism is a fetter on production forces, it contains within itself the seeds of its own destruction.

Ideology

In addition to the theory of history, and the work on alienation, the other prominent Marxian theme in *The German Ideology* (Part 1) is ideology. An ideology is a set of ideas, and the dominant ideology is that set of ideas which dominates the civil society at the time. So the dominant ideology of the bourgeoisie (the dominant ideology of capitalism) is that people should have the freedom to trade, employ others, make money and so on, and should be politically emancipated.

ACTIVITY

The two sections through which I will explore Marx and Engels's thoughts on ideology are A2 and B3 (pp.42–8, 64–8). Read these sections (but concentrate on the second half of A2:16–20, pp.46–8).

In A2:17 (p.47) Marx and Engels use the metaphor of a 'camera obscura'. Just as, in that apparatus, the image on the screen appears inverted, so in ideology, people and their circumstances appear upside down. This metaphor can be taken in two ways. Like Feuerbach's idea of God, it might be that what is in fact our own creation is inverted; it is seen as external to us and dominating (Elster (1986), pp.180–1). Alternatively, it might allude to our thinking our decisions spring from our own free will, unconditioned by the world, but really that relation runs in the opposite direction. 'Life is not determined by consciousness, but consciousness by life' (A2:18, p.47). Marx and Engels look to be proposing productive forces as the fundamental explanation of changes in what we think and who we think we are. Hence, the fundamental question when evaluating someone's thought is 'what is it about their society that made them think like that?'. We cannot start with philosophy and explain the actions of people. We have to start with people and how they live, and show how philosophy will emerge from that.

It is implausible to think that our consciousness is wholly determined by our social and economic circumstances. If this were so, then all aspects of consciousness would be identical for everyone in the same social and economic circumstances, which is demonstrably untrue (Cohen (1988), pp.155–79). However, we can take Marx and Engels to be making a more plausible claim: namely, that that part of people's consciousness which is part of the superstructure will be determined by the productive relations (which are, in turn, determined by productive forces). This, after all, is what historical materialism claims. The superstructure includes, according to Cohen's definition 'the legal and state institutions of society, or at least some of them'

(Reading 5.3, p.290). So the kinds of belief that Marx and Engels take to be determined are those which are about property laws, the way to run the state, and the correct way to run an economy.

ACTIVITY

Read the first half of B3 again (pp.64–6) and answer the following questions. For Marx and Engels:

1   Whose ideas are dominant in society?
2   How do these ideas get established?

DISCUSSION

1   It is there in the first sentence of this section: 'The ideas of the ruling class are in every epoch the ruling ideas' (p.64). That is, those ideas which suit the economic position of the ruling classes are the ones that are accepted as eternal truths. Marx and Engels give us some examples: in feudal times the concepts of honour and loyalty were dominant, in bourgeois times concepts of freedom and equality. It was honour and loyalty to the local noble that kept the serfs in their place, and freedom and equality that allow the bourgeois to run a 'free market' based around private property. (In *The Communist Manifesto*, Marx and Engels define explicitly the freedom they want to abolish: 'By freedom is meant, under the present bourgeois conditions of production, free trade, free selling and buying' (Marx and Engels (1848), p.171)).

2   I would say that there are two parts to this answer. First, there are the basic mechanics. The ruling class have the power to 'regulate the production and distribution of the ideas of their age'. To put it crudely, they control the newspapers (and nowadays television). Second, when a new class takes over, they need to get society as a whole behind them. So, they need to represent their own class interests in general terms – as being in the interests of everyone. In other words, they have to represent their ideas as applying universally: 'it has to give its ideas the form of universality, and represent them as the only rational, universally valid ones' (p.66).

These two explanations are interestingly different. In 1, the explanation is a functional one: the ideas of the ruling class are dominant because they serve the interests of that class. Cohen's account (pp.252–5 above) can be used to make sense of this apparent explanation of a phenomenon in terms of its effects. The explanation in 2, concerns the mechanics of the mechanism by which the ideas of the ruling class become dominant.

According to Marx and Engels, the dominant ideology has the following two characteristics. First, it does not appear to those who hold it as simply a passing set of ideas caused by the economic system, it appears as part of the way the world is. So, for us, it seems freedom and equality are more than the product of the current structuring of the forces of production, they seem fundamental human rights (or 'external law' as Marx and Engels put it). This, according to Marx and Engels, only goes to show how steeped in the ideology we are. Second, the dominant ideology serves to prop up the ruling class, and keep the other classes down. So, while the proletariat appear to be free, they are not free at all. They are forced to sell their labour to live, and in doing so make more money for capitalists who are then better able to secure their position as dominant. Both these points were made in 'On the Jewish Question'. The liberal rights of the capitalist state, solemnly proclaimed as eternal truths in the various versions of the 'Declaration of the Rights of Man', actually serve as a 'justification of egoistic man separated from his fellow men and the community' (79). There is even, at the end of 80, an early version of the metaphor of the camera obscura.

We can put together thoughts about alienation and ideology here to form an answer to the charge, frequently made against Marxism, that it does not reward initiative and ignores the fact that people are motivated by profit. This is a variety of the claim (which I made on p.244 above) that communism will not overcome alienation, because there are certain problems inherent in human nature which will persist. That people are motivated by profit is a widespread belief about human nature. However, it is a belief one would expect to be central to the ideology of a capitalist society; it serves the interests of the ruling class. This does not mean that in a properly communist society such a belief would survive. Without ideological support, we could come to see the belief as false and find that people might be motivated by their commitment to the common good.

There are at least two other places in this book where the same, or a similar point, is made. In Chapter 2 on Hobbes, you read C.B. Macpherson's claim that, in his views on power, Hobbes mistook ideological beliefs for natural beliefs: 'Hobbes was using a mental model of society which, whether he was conscious of this or not, corresponds only to a bourgeois market society' (p.104). In Chapter 6 (p.322), you will see that Mill, although he did not have the substantial theoretical support provided by Marx and Engels, makes the same point with respect to the perceived natural inferiority of women: 'But was there ever any domination which did not appear natural to those who possessed it?' he asks, rhetorically (Mill (1988 edn), p.12).

For Marxist theoreticians, changes in the economic structure are the 'real content' of historical changes; for example: 'The French Revolution... was fought under the slogan "Liberty, Equality and Fraternity". But the development of a market economy and the rise of the bourgeois class was the real content of the crisis, and its outcome was to clear the path for a capitalist mode of production to flourish' (Arthur (1986), p.154). Such explanations are plausible only if supported by a credible account of how the effects (the rise of the bourgeois class) produced the cause (a revolution driven by noble ideals). Functional explanations are only as plausible as the mechanisms on which they rely. As was said above (p.254), Marx generally does not provide sufficiently detailed accounts for us to evaluate the mechanisms).

Should we accept that liberal rights are not eternal, but rather local phenomena which serve the purposes of the bourgeoisie? This claim can come in two forms. The first is that the members of the ruling class consciously conspire, through their ownership of the media, to perpetuate these ideas with the purpose of keeping themselves on top. There is not much to be said for such a view. A weaker and more plausible form does not require us to believe in a conscious conspiracy. In much the same way that animals evolved to suit the environment without there being any deliberate intention behind it, so ideas can evolve and only those which suit the social environment survive. At the moment, bourgeois ideas survive in, and serve to support, a bourgeois environment (cf. Cohen (1978), Chapter IX).

Even this weaker claim has been questioned. Substantial arguments would be needed to show (of a widespread set of beliefs) that (a) they are held because they serve the interests of the ruling class and (b) they work against the interests of many if not most of those who believe them (cf. Rosen (1997) and Wolff (1996)). Marx and Engels do not provide such arguments. In particular, the fact that the interests of the bourgeoisie *are* served by such a set of beliefs is no such argument. As Cohen says, the fact that the bridge of his nose is functional for his vision (because it supports his glasses) is no evidence for the claim that it exists *because* it is functional for his vision (Reading 5.3, p.294; cf. p.255 above).

In conclusion, an ideology is a set of ideas, and the dominant ideology is that set of ideas which dominates the civil society at the time. Uncovering the ideological basis for an idea might reveal its 'true content'. In the absence of detailed arguments it is impossible to substantiate either of these claims.

The Proletariat, the revolution and communism

The key passages for this topicare B3:3 and D.

ACTIVITY

Read these passages now (pp.65–6, 82–95). Note that the term 'forms of intercourse' is, as indicated earlier, what has been referred to as 'relations of production'. Section D contains the detailed discussion of the progress to communism; sandwiched in the middle of this discussion is a discussion of circumstances in which the development of history can be altered, or even short-circuited.

D1:1 discusses the notion of class: 'separate individuals form a class only insofar as they have to carry on a common battle against another class; otherwise they are on hostile terms with each other as competitors' (p.82). Despite the fact that the bourgeoisie have to compete against each other as capitalists, Marx and Engels suggest they form a class because they have a common interest (in this case fighting a common enemy). From elsewhere in their writings, it seems Marx and Engels held that a group needs to meet two criteria in order to be a class: to share a particular role in the prevailing relations of production, and be conscious of themselves as a class (McLellan (1980), p.182). They claim that there are 'class interests'; which are the interests of the group rather than the interests of the individual members of that group. This should put you in mind of Rousseau's account of the general will: the group has interests which are not necessarily identical to the particular will of any member of the group (see p.192 above).

We have seen that the development of history is driven through the resolution of contradictions between the relations of production and the productive forces. The ruling class, those who benefit from the relations of production, will be threatened when the relations of production are threatened. Following the revolution, the relations of production will be organized in the interests of the new ruling class. For example, the landowners and feudalism were replaced by the bourgeoisie and capitalism. What is needed to create a free society is a class which has nothing, and therefore no class interests to pursue. A revolution by them will result in a society which is not governed for the sake of class interests; indeed, separate classes will disappear.

The proletariat is in a unique position. Freedom for them could only be freedom from private property. Hence, following the revolution against capitalism, all property will be held in common. There will be no 'have-nots', nobody will be forced to work for others (work will be 'self-activity'), and relations will be between 'individuals as such'. In a revolution, the new ruling class need to represent their interests as the universal interest in order to carry the population with them. Because they have no specific class interests, the proletariat's claim to represent the universal interest will actually be true. This is the historical mission of the proletariat.

Various themes we have considered already reappear in this discussion of the transition to communism. It should be clear from D1:4 why the proletarian revolution is directed against the state: Marx and Engels argue that the state forms 'an illusory community'; it gives the appearance of freedom, but really enshrines the inequalities of capitalism. Freedom, equality and the cultivation of abilities will only be possible in an authentic community.

There is also a discussion of identity, formed through ideology, which is reminiscent of the discussion in 'On the Jewish Question'. In that essay, it was claimed that individuals who had enjoyed political emancipation were free as citizens of the state (they were, of course, still oppressed as members of civil society). For Marx and Engels the state (the 'illusory community') is itself a form of alienation and encourages other forms of alienation produced by private property and the division of labour. Marx and Engels contrast it with the freedom available in 'the community'. That is, the communist society in which all alienation will have been abolished (cf. p.244).

The problem, once again, arises because of the division of labour. Instead of being themselves, people are forced to identify with being bus drivers, artists or whatever. In one way this could be seen as a benefit capitalism brings to the individual. Prior to the emergence of capitalism, our split identities are 'concealed' (D1:5). A person seemed to have only one role: they were a noble or a commoner and thought of themselves as a noble or as a commoner. In capitalism individuals can think of themselves as someone who just *happens* to be a bus driver or an artist; they could have been something else if they had so chosen. This is what Marx and Engels mean by 'accidental'; it is not that we are bus drivers (or whatever) by accident, it is rather that being a bus driver is not something we have to be in order to be ourselves. This apparent freedom is a dangerous bourgeois illusion (see above, p.249); in reality, people are dominated by capitalism and so 'more subjected to the violence of things' (D1:5, p.84). To be free from domination by capitalism, or by our jobs, we need to be free from alienation in a rationally organized communist community.

The argument is similar to that of Rousseau's *The Social Contract*. It might appear that people are more free in the state of nature because they can do as they like. However, in the state of nature, individuals are at the mercy of superior force. Hence, it is only by living according to the general will that we are truly free, both from our appetites and the possibility of our subjugation by others.

The proletarian is keenly aware of the difference between his or her individuality and role as a worker. Unlike the serf, to whom moving to town seemed a step towards freedom, the only option open to the proletariat is to overthrow the condition that makes them workers. Once this is achieved, people will have a unified identity once more; they will be people, rather than each split into a person aspect and a worker aspect. What will emerge from this is an authentic community in which people can be free. We have met the claim before, however, both in Marx and Rousseau: we cannot be free if we are the 'playthings of alien forces'; that is, if we are subject to forces over which we have no conscious control. Hence, we need to be conscious of our production of social relations, and this can only take place at the level of community cooperation (cf. Wood (1981), p.52).

The similarity of approach might make the disparaging reference to Rousseau in D1:8 (p.85) surprising. Marx and Engels initially appear to misread Rousseau; to claim he was describing a community of individuals who simply *happened* to come together. Rousseau, like Marx and Engels, saw an individuals' identities as constituted by their place in a community. However, it could be that Marx and Engels meant that Rousseau's community started from a position in which people held private property. This would inevitably be a society characterized by alienation, rather than an authentic community.

In D2 there is also more detail of the mechanics of change which underlie historical materialism; that is, the change in which one form of intercourse (set of relations of production) are replaced by another. Marx and Engels sum up their view thus: 'all collisions in history have their origin ... in the contradiction between the productive forces and the form of intercourse' (D2:6, p.9).

Note the final point made in *The German Ideology* (Part 1): Rousseau had argued that in order to create a non-oppressive civil society, there needed to be 'a remarkable change in man' (Rousseau, *The Social Contract*, I, VIII, 1). We have seen that one of the presuppositions of a communist society is similar: that people will cease to be ruthlessly competitive, and become cooperative; 'the alteration of men on a mass scale is necessary' (D4:10, pp.94–5). This will come about through revolution; only a revolution will rid society of 'the muck of ages'. This suggests a violent revolution is necessary in the transition to communism (a point Marx reconsidered in his later life).

Marx and Engels consider an alternative to the slow progress of history in a passage which runs from D2:4 through to the end of D3 (pp.88–90). D2:4 lists three ways in which the development of a country can be speeded up, or even 'short-circuited'. First, new countries (such as North America) in which settlement is by the most advanced individuals from the old countries. Second, by conquering countries (such as the Normans conquering England) so that a new form of intercourse can be imposed. Third, by countries being forced to modernize because of international competition (such as Germany in competition with England).

The principal alternative to Marx and Engels's view is that history is driven by conquest. D3 begins by describing this view of history, and discusses why Italy did not involve itself in conquest (it had no expanding population). Marx and Engels then give four reasons why conquest could not be a sufficient explanation of history.

Read D3 (pp.89–90) and list the different circumstances where explanations in terms of conquest fall short, and economic explanations take over.

DISCUSSION

Conquest cannot be the whole explanation, because an explanation would still be required concerning the nature of the conquered economy, and conditions necessary for the conquerors to make use of what they find. Any explanation in terms of conquest must be supplemented, therefore, by an explanation in terms of historical materialism. Marx and Engels provide three specific instances.

1   Some objects (for example, a bank account) cannot be taken without the whole economic system being adopted as well.

2   The same is true of 'modern industrial capital' (there is no sense in taking a light-bulb back to a non-electrified economy).

3   Taking must stop somewhere. When it does, production starts from the state of productive forces the takers found in existence.

In summary, the proletariat do not have class interests; their interests are universal. Therefore they are the only class which can take us to communism: an authentic community characterized by abundance, an absence of alienation and freedom. This transition will happen through revolution.

The liberal critique of Marxism

> The charges against Communism made from a religious, a philosophical, and, generally, from an ideological standpoint are not deserving of serious examination.

(Marx and Engels (1848), p.171)

The German Ideology (Part 1) is an argument that capitalism will, and should, be replaced by communism. There are undoubtedly gaps in the argument. The mechanisms underlying historical materialism are unclear. Marx provides no reason to think that any alternative to capitalism will expand the forces of production more than capitalism (indeed, the experience of rational economic planning over the last century suggests otherwise). There is no reason to believe a communist society, characterized by abundance and devoid of alienation, is possible. However, the critique of capitalism – that it alienates us from each other and ourselves – appears to have great force. The kind of regime favoured by liberalism, a political emancipation in the form of a state that gives us equality, liberty, security and the right to property, is an illusory community that is itself a form of alienation (cf. p.248). In this final section, I will consider an extract from a book by Will Kymlicka, which criticizes Marx's concept of alienation.

ACTIVITY

Read Will Kymlicka's on 'Alienation' (Reading 5.4) and do the following exercise:

1 What is meant by the claim that Marx is a 'perfectionist'?

2 Write a short paragraph stating Kymlicka's argument against Marx on alienation.

DISCUSSION

1 Kymlicka says that perfectionist arguments say that resources should be distributed in such a way as to encourage the realization of distinctively human potentialities and excellencies, and to discourage ways of life which lack these excellencies (Reading 5.4, p.297). In other words, communism will give us the resources to live a full human life (of unalienated labour) and capitalism will deprive us of the resources to live a full human life (by giving us alienated labour).

2 Kymlicka's argument is that unalienated labour is not the only value that gives us a perfect life, there are others. Amongst those he mentions are: playing tennis, raising children, having good stereo equipment, friendship, love and art. In planning our lives, we may want to 'do a trade'; that is, accept unalienated labour in exchange for more of these other goods. In short, there does not seem any reason to organize a society around giving everyone unalienated labour, rather than organizing it (as the liberal would prefer), in such a way that people can pursue their own conceptions of the good.

This can be seen as another instance of the conflict between negative and positive freedom (see Reading 4.4). Rousseau advocated the general will as the single goal society ought to pursue. Marx and Engels advocate the elimination of alienation. Both of these are a form of positive freedom. The alternative Berlin describes is to grant people negative freedom: the freedom to act unobstructed by others. For Rousseau that would be a society rife with self-interest and domination. For Marx and Engels, it is the civil society they described in 'On the Jewish Question'. The debate still goes on as to who is right.

Conclusion

Our reading of *The German Ideology* (Part 1) has followed two threads of argument. One is Marx and Engels's account of historical change. Change happens because the prevailing relations of production inhibit the expansion of the productive forces. This leads to class conflict and revolution. The other is the changing way in which individuals live their lives under the different relations of production. Specifically, people live alienated lives under capitalism. The two threads come together in the thought that, because the capitalist relations of production are a fetter on the productive forces, a revolution will come. As a class that has no specific class interest to pursue will conduct this revolution, the outcome will be in the interests of everyone. The result will be a communist society, from which alienation will be absent. Finally, we have seen reason to doubt whether the pursuit of the single goal of eliminating alienation is a project we ought to pursue.

Appendix: headings and sub-headings to the Arthur edition

Preface
'Hitherto men have constantly made up for themselves false conceptions ...'

I Feuerbach. Opposition of the Materialist and Idealist Outlook

A. Idealism and Materialism
A1 The Illusions of German Ideology
'As we hear from German ideologists ...'
A2 First Premises of Materialist Method
'The premises from which we begin are not arbitrary ones ...'
A3 History: Fundamental Conditions
'Since we are dealing with Germans ...'
A4 Private Property and Communism
'With the division of labour, in which all these contradictions are implicit ...'

B. The Illusion of the Epoch
B1 Civil Society – and the Conception of History
'The form of intercourse determined by the existing productive forces ...'
B2 Feuerbach: Philosophic, and Real, Liberation
'It is also clear from these arguments how grossly Feuerbach is deceiving himself ...'
B3 Ruling Class and Ruling Ideas
'The ideas of the ruling class are in every epoch the ruling ideas ...'

C. The Real Basis of Ideology
C1 Division of Labour: Town and Country
'From the first there follows the premise of a highly developed division of labour ...'
C2 The Rise of Manufacturing
The immediate consequences of the division of labour between the various towns ...'
C3 The Relation of State and Law to Property
'The first form of property, in the ancient world as in the Middle Ages ...'

D. Proletarians and Communism
D1 Individuals, Class, and Community
'In the Middle Ages the citizens in each town were compelled to unite ...'
D2 Forms of Intercourse
'Communism differs from all previous movements ...'
D3 Conquest
'The whole interpretation of history appears to be contradicted by the fact of conquest ...'
D4 Contradictions of Big Industry: Revolution
'Our investigation hitherto started from the instruments of production ...'

Glossary

alienation

Marx used the term in a number of ways, to capture the absence of a sense of meaning in life under capitalism. In this chapter, it has been used in the following senses. (i) Under capitalism, people perform tasks that are not fulfilling in themselves, but are done simply to earn money. (ii) The product of human beings' labour is alienated, and dominates human life and relations. Both capitalism and the state are alienated products of human activity. (iii) Human beings lack a 'communal essence'; that is, they relate to each other as egoistic individuals, rather than fellow creatures.

base

The relations of production are the economic base of a society. (See *superstructure*.)

bourgeoisie

The capitalist ruling class; those who own the means of production and employ the proletariat.

burghers

Town-dwelling merchants. They were prominent following the decline of feudalism.

capitalism

The mode of production in which the means of production are the private property of the ruling class. The ruling class of capitalism is the bourgeoisie, and the workers are the proletariat.

citizens

In 'On the Jewish Question', Marx claims that the state gives people the illusion of equality. Everyone is equal in that they are equally citizens of the state, but they are not equal in the sphere of civil society.

civil society

All those relations between people that involve industry and trade, and various informal associations. In 'On the Jewish Question', this is characterized as a sphere of 'war of all against all', in contrast to the state in which everyone is equal.

class

To be a class, a group needs to share a particular role in the prevailing productive relations, and be conscious of themselves as a class.

communism

The stage in the history of society which will succeed capitalism. Marx believed it would be characterized by great abundance, such that all human needs would be met. The means of production would not be privately owned, so there would be no exploitation and no alienation.

contradiction

In Marx's terms, when the relations of production start to fetter the forces of production, they are in a state of contradiction.

development thesis
The thesis that the forces of production have an inexorable tendency to expand.

division of labour
Marx and Engels describe this in two ways in *The German Ideology* (Part 1). (i) The kind of division characteristic of a production line: people perform different tasks in the production of the same item. (ii) The division of work into different vocations, so that each individual has to specialize.

feudalism
A pre-capitalist stage of society. Nobles own the land and allow the serfs to work it, in exchange for some of the products of their labour. There is no sharp distinction between private and public, and serfs are not abstracted into the two roles of free citizen and wage slave, as they will be in capitalism.

forces of production (productive forces)
Anything necessary for making things: the machines, the raw material and the labour power.

functional explanation
An explanation that attempts to explain an event in terms of its effects.

guilds
Institutions set up in the towns to regulate manufacture, following the break-up of feudalism.

historical materialism
Not a term used by Marx, but now standard terminology. The thesis that history develops because of the expansion of the productive forces, which causes changes in the relations of production, which in turn causes changes in the superstructure.

human emancipation
A term from 'On the Jewish Question'. Human emancipation will occur when people are free from the inequalities which dominate civil society under capitalism.

ideology
A set of ideas. The 'dominant ideology' is the set of ideas which dominate civil society at the time.

liberalism
A broad political philosophy, which favours negative over positive liberty. It is characteristic of liberalism to seek regimes characterized by political emancipation.

money
Money is moveable capital. It is the means of exchange that arose with trade and manufacture.

nobility
The ruling class of feudalism. They own the land that they allow the serfs to work in exchange for part of the products of their labour.

political emancipation

A term from 'On the Jewish Question'. Political emancipation occurs when people have rights to equality, liberty, security and property. They are free and equal citizens of the state, but not free and equal in civil society.

proletariat

The working class under capitalism. The proletariat survives by selling their labour to the bourgeoisie. Marx thought the proletariat would overthrow capitalism and usher in communism.

private property

Property that is owned by individuals. In particular, under capitalism, the bourgeoisie own the means of production, and employ the proletariat to make objects to trade.

relations of production

The social arrangements characteristic of an historical stage. In particular, who owns what property. The relations of production always tend to the form that is maximally conducive to the expansion of the forces of production.

revolution

A revolution follows when the relations of production are a fetter on the forces of production. Marx thought this stage would be reached with capitalism, after which the proletariat would overthrow the bourgeoisie and establish communism.

serf

The serfs are the workers in a feudal society.

slave

Slaves were the workers in pre-feudal societies. Unlike serfs and the proletariat, they did not even own themselves.

state

The state is an alienated product of human activity. It is an abstraction, which provides the illusion of freedom and equality. People are free and equal as citizens of the state, but they are exploited and alienated as members of civil society. This split is characteristic of capitalism.

superstructure

What is and what is not in the superstructure is a much-debated issue. At least it contains the legal and political aspects of a society (in capitalism, this would include laws defending private property and constitutions enshrining democracy), and it might also contain the prevailing religious mores of the society (Cohen, Reading 5.3, p.290). Its nature is determined by its function of stabilizing the relations of production (in order to be conducive to the expansion of the forces of production). (See *base*.)

'Young Hegelians'

A radical group of philosophers with whom Marx was associated from 1837 to 1842. In *The German Ideology* (Part 1), Marx attacks them for being concerned with revolutions in the realm of thought rather than in the material world.

Further reading

Cohen, G. A., *Karl Marx's Theory of History A Defence* (Oxford University Press, 1978). Quite a difficult book, but rigorous and interesting. It set a new standard in work on Marx.

Elster, J., *An Introduction to Karl Marx* (Cambridge University Press, 1986). A helpful book in a similar style to that of Cohen, which covers the major aspects of Marx's thought.

Singer, P., *Hegel* (Oxford University Press, 1983). A good, short introduction to this difficult thinker, which points out the influences on Marx.

Wood, A., *Karl Marx* (Routledge, 1981). A general study that is particularly good on the question of Marx's attitude to morality.

Notes

[1] I have attached, in an appendix (p.264), information regarding the position of the headings and sub-headings Arthur introduces. If you have not got Arthur's edition, I suggest you go through your text noting down where the headings and sub-headings occur. Because translations differ (even in their paragraph order), the sentences given in the Appendix are unlikely to be an exact match with those in other editions.

[2] Cf. Hindess (1993) and Callinicos (1989).

[3] Cf. Berlin (1948), chaps III and IV; Cohen (1978), chap. I; Wood (1981) and (1993.)

[4] I will follow convention and use 'Marxian' to describe characteristics of Marx's theory as he stated it, and 'Marxist' to describe elements of the theory as it was developed by others. These terms pick out two ends of a spectrum; most works on Marx will contain elements of both exposition and development, and so will be both Marxian and Marxist.

[5] Darwin's explanation of the hollow bones of birds is roughly as follows. By chance, some birds were born with hollow bones. These then had a greater chance of surviving, as it was easier for them to fly away from predators. Hence, those birds survived and left young, some of which also had hollow bones. They survived, and left young for the same reason, until hollow bones became a general characteristic of birds. Lamarck's explanation, on the other hand, was that modifications produced in an individual by its environment were transmitted to its descendants. For example, a giraffe may acquire a long neck by stretching to reach leaves high in the tree, and this is transmitted to its young who are also born with a long neck.

Readings

'Playthings of Alien Forces: Karl Marx and the Rejection of the Market Economy'

Jonathan Wolff

In this short article, Jonathan Wolff attempts to answer the question of why Marx thought the planned economy was connected with human freedom. Production within the capitalist free market leads to alienation, and Wolff explores various aspects of this problematic term. Alienation can be eliminated if we take control of the social forces that surround production. Hence a planned economy, by removing alienation, will bring an increase in freedom.

An account of Marx's theory of alienation

Recent history throws up an apparent paradox for Marxism. Above all, Marxism is a philosophy of liberation, and in this lies its enormous attraction throughout this century. Yet Marx was also committed to the planned economy, and increasingly people of all political persuasions have come to believe that the planned economy leads not to human flourishing but to demoralization. Hence our paradox: how can such a depressing and inefficient economic system ever have been thought to be justified in the name of emancipation?

Some might say that the charges against the planned economy are exaggerated, that its advantages outweigh its disadvantages. Under communism no one starves, and all have employment and shelter, even if the general standard of living is below that to which we aspire in bourgeois society. But this does not explain why Marx valued the planned economy as *liberating*. His view was not simply that the planned economy ensures that our basic needs are met. He thought that *only in a planned economy can a life fully worthy of human beings be lived*. My purpose is to explain why Marx held this (what now seems quite bizarre) view.

The philosophy of historical materialism

Throughout his writings Marx emphasized the idea of man as an essentially *productive* being: the most characteristic and essential human feature is that human beings produce (rather than forage for or hunt) their means of subsistence. This is the key to our story, and we should start by considering the line of philosophical reflection that confirmed Marx in this view. It will be best to approach Marx's position historically, through a criticism of earlier views from Marx's perspective.

We begin by asking a vague or general philosophical question: what is the relation between the human subject and the world? The question sharpens somewhat when we consider Descartes's answer. The essence of mind is thought, while the essence of the world is extension. Hence there is a radical separation between mind and the world: you can be assured of your own existence even if you doubt all else. But how, then, can one know any more than the contents of one's mind and that one exists? Once such a gulf between the thinking human subject and the external world has been established, how can it be overcome and knowledge gained of that world? Notoriously Descartes was able to advance only by first proving the existence of God, and it is very unclear whether anything of his constructive project remains if the proofs of God are rejected.

At apparently the opposite pole is the materialist view of Hobbes. For Hobbes human beings are simply part of the material world. Thoughts are 'internal motions'. Human behaviour is regulated by the laws of nature like all else, and philosophical problems become, to a great extent, scientific problems.

Whether this cuts off Cartesian doubt is an interesting question, but more important from our point of view are the difficulties with Hobbes's position. Once a scientific materialism, of a world of molecules in motion, is adopted it is very unclear what room can be found for ideas of rationality, morality and, if we want it, human freedom. Consider Hobbes's explanation of morality. Men call 'good' those things they desire, and desire is an internal movement. Hence morality seems reduced to motion.

A consistent materialist might reject morality, rationality and freedom. Yet this puts the materialist *social critic* in a difficult position. Consider Marx's criticism of the materialist utopian socialist Robert Owen. Owen argued that human beings are simply products of their circumstances, and so they can be reformed by the reform of their circumstances. As manager of the New Lanark cotton mill Owen was able to put his ideas into practice. Here is the example of the 'silent monitor':

> This consisted of a four-sided piece of wood, about two inches long, and one broad, each side coloured – one side black, another blue, the third yellow, and the fourth white, tapered at the top, and finished with wire eyes, to hang upon a hook with either side to the front. One of these was suspended in a conspicuous place near to each of the persons employed, and the colour at the front told the conduct of the individual during the preceding day, to four degrees by comparison. Bad, denoted by black, indifferent by blue, good by yellow and excellent by white.

Instead of punishing his workers Owen had his supervisors monitor their daily performance, and Owen made a point of walking through the mill conspicuously looking at the silent monitors, but saying nothing. Sure enough, the workers' performance greatly improved. Owen further comments:

> Never perhaps in the history of the human race has so simple a device created in so short a period so much order, virtue, goodness, and happiness, out of so much ignorance, error and misery.

(Morton 1969, pp.98–9)

Owen's modern editor comments: 'It is often said that in this, and other ways, Owen treated his work-people as if they were children. There is some truth in this, but it must be remembered that a large proportion of them *were* children.'

Nevertheless there is something very apt in this comment: Owen treated his workers in an extraordinarily patronizing fashion, and this leads to Marx's criticism. Owen's view that you can change people by changing their circumstances because people are wholly determined by their circumstances makes problematic the role of the social reformer, who sets out to make the change. For if the social reformer is a human being, then his or her actions should also be determined by the circumstances. But to advocate and engage in reform surely requires one to break free of that chain of determination. Therefore materialist social criticism seems to presuppose a class of people – individual geniuses, as Owen saw himself – superior to society who are exempt from the laws of determination. But there cannot be such people if deterministic materialism is true.

Thus Marx rejected the crude materialism of Owen and others. But in fundamental philosophical terms the main fault with the materialist view, for Marx, is something it shares with the Cartesian picture. These views have in common a theory of perception: that the mind is a passive receiver of information from an independent outside world. We could call this a representative or correspondence theory of mind: the mind is like a camera recording external data.

What could be wrong with this? For Marx it leaves out the fact that human beings are active in the world, changing nature and what they see. Things outside of us are not merely 'given' for us to perceive. The vast majority of things one encounters are human products, created or transformed by human endeavour.

This active side of man's relations with the world – the objectifying power of human thought – was, Marx argues, first systematically developed by idealism, although, according to Marx, in a mystified way. We can see what Marx means by the 'objectifying power' of human thought by considering Kantian epistemology. Kant's central idea is that the human mind structures the world through categories which it imposes on reality. Thus, for example, for Kant space and time have no independent existence but are 'forms' of sense, through which the human subject perceives and organizes the world. We see things in spatial and temporal relations only because of the way the mind is constructed. So the human mind is active in the sense that how the world is presented to us depends on features of the human mind: its organizing capacity. In this sense, the world is a human construction.

The insight – which Kant 'mystified' – is that human beings at least in part create the world which they perceive. Yet Marx rejected Kant's position, endorsing certain Hegelian criticisms and then, in turn, criticizing Hegel. Of Hegel's criticisms of Kant two are most relevant here. First, for Kant, the mind has a universal, ahistoric character. The basic structure of the mind is the same at all times and places. By contrast Hegel argued for a developmental conception, and one which allowed for different levels of development for different cultures.

Even more important is Hegel's explanation for this development: the mind changes through interaction with the world. This is part of the idea of a dialectical development. As mind experiences and tries to understand the world, it develops ever higher-level concepts, thus changing itself. But Hegel's view is also a form of idealism in which the mind makes up the world. So as the mind changes the world changes. Consequently as mind develops so does the world.

Marx agrees that human action in the world changes both the world and human beings. But Hegel, thinks Marx, states this only in an abstract way – idealistically – only in thought, as a history of the development of our concepts. And this is Marx's objection.

To take stock, Marx has contrasted and criticized two dominant philosophical positions. Firstly, the materialist position from Hobbes to Feuerbach is criticized for its unreflective ahistorical nature, failing to give due consideration to the role mankind plays in creating the world it perceives. Secondly idealism, at least in Hegel's hands, understands the importance of historical development, but restricts this to the development of thought.

In sum we might propose a rather stylized opposition between ahistorical materialism and historical idealism. Having put matters like this, it then becomes clear which elements Marx decides to take from each in order to develop his 'philosophy of historical materialism'. Like Hegel he says that man changes himself and the world through interaction with the world. But unlike Hegel this is an interaction that takes placed in concrete reality, as practical activity, not merely thought.

Marx identifies this practical activity with productive activity: labour. Hegel's idealism is a 'mystified expression' of the real relation between human beings and the world. Human beings find self-realization in nature. They change the world not merely by changing their concepts of the world but by physically transforming it. In doing this they change themselves by developing new needs and abilities, which in turn gives rise to further forms of interaction with the world.

The root idea – one Marx finds neglected in all previous philosophies – is that human beings have needs, and need, not contemplation, is their primary relation to the world. Human beings labour on the world in order to satisfy their needs, evolving more and more complex forms of production and social interaction in an attempt to satisfy further needs which are always arising. Thus a philosophical view about man's interaction with the world turns into a theory of society, and a theory of history. For Marx this thought completes the history of philosophy.

Alienation

It is through the development of labour that societies develop. But labour – individual and social – also has a crucial role in individual self-development and fulfilment. 'As individuals express their lives, so they are. What they are, therefore, coincides with their production, both of what they produce, and how they produce' (Marx 1970, p.42).

This sets the scene for Marx's critique of capitalism. Although capitalism has created immense social forces of production, capable of production on a scale previously undreamt of, it nevertheless crushes individual flourishing. For under capitalism the vast majority of people do not live lives worthy of human beings. Their lives, and especially their labour, Marx says, are alienated.

The term 'alienation' commonly indicates dislocation from one's surroundings; the thought of feeling lost in circumstances that ought to be familiar. Marx's concept incorporates this subjective aspect, but goes far beyond it too. It is best introduced – as Marx does himself – through the idea of religious alienation.

Marx took the idea of religious alienation from other 'Young-Hegelian' writers – notably Feuerbach – although the root idea is much older. The central thought is that man makes God in his own image. Protagoras said, 'If triangles had a God, it would have three sides.' Feuerbach agrees. Everything human beings have said about God is a mystified expression of things true of themselves. Human beings project their own powers and attributes on to an abstract, non-existent entity. Instead of enjoying and glorying in these powers, man 'alienates them', raises them to an infinite level, and worships them. Marx says that 'religion is a devious acknowledgement of man, through an intermediary'.

In general, for Marx, that alienation exists presupposes some normative account of how things should be: what an appropriate or flourishing human life would be. Secondly, it also presupposes that something is lost: things that belong together become separated. Finally, and this is distinctive of the theory, that which is lost must reappear in an alien form.

We can apply this in the case of religious alienation. Human beings have what Feuerbach called a species-essence, a human potential. Yet they become 'separated' from this essence. They do not use and enjoy their capacities. Rather, and this is the third point, they project them on to an abstract being, which then comes to dominate them. Human beings come to feel that their lives and destinies are controlled and determined by this external, alien, being: by this object which, unacknowledged by them, is of their own making.

One can suffer from religious alienation without realizing. Marx knows that many are content with their relation to their God. This he calls illusory happiness, happiness based on an illusion. Yet even those who are happy are still alienated.

Marx now deepens Feuerbach's analysis. Feuerbach does not explain why alienation exists, and so is naïve about how it is to be overcome. His view is that when people come to see religion for what it is, it will wither away. Marx's reply is that religious alienation comes into existence because conditions on earth are so bad that people seek solace in heaven. Religion will not disappear until it is no longer necessary: when it becomes possible for human beings to enjoy their species-essence on earth.

Alienated labour

Although religion clearly pre-dates capitalism, under capitalism Marx argues that it is largely sustained by the problem, specific to capitalism, of alienated labour. I want essentially to concentrate on just three of the many claims made by Marx concerning alienated labour: first, that under capitalism people perform a form of labour unworthy of human beings; second, that capitalism itself is an alienated product of human activity; third, that mankind does not recognize its 'communal essence' under capitalism.

Human production is elucidated by Marx by comparing it with the productive activities of other animals. Human beings can produce in accordance with their will and consciousness. They can make elaborate plans, and then knowingly and deliberately carry them out. Also they can 'distinguish their life's activity from themselves'. The spider, say, does not distinguish spinning a web from being a spider: it just goes ahead and spins the web. We, on the other hand, can recognize that our activities are distinct and under our control. Human production is unrestricted. We can produce 'even in accordance with the laws of beauty'.

Under capitalism, according to Marx, we fail to produce this way. We produce blindly, on the level of animals, or worse:

> In the factory we have a lifeless machine which is independent of workers, who are incorporated into it as living appendages.

(Marx 1976, p.548)

> [The Worker] is depressed, therefore, both intellectually and physically to the level of a machine, and from a man becomes abstract activity and a stomach.

(Marx 1975, p.285)

Productive activity should be 'part' of the worker, in that it should be an end in itself: a confirmation of the worker's life, and a source of enjoyment. But under capitalism labour is 'external'. It is shunned when not necessary. It is used to satisfy other needs, but it is not enjoyed in itself. Hence it is degraded to a means. Indeed it has become a commodity – hired out to others for their use. Man is not able to enjoy those features which are most distinctively human. Hence man feels free only when engaged in animal activity.

This, then, is a brief account of the degradation of labour under capitalism. More insidious, however, is our non-human relation to our products: alienation from the product. The basic idea here is that the world of objects is created by human beings, but these objects appear hostile and alien. Human beings are not 'at home' in the world they create. Not only do workers lose control of their products; their products come to control and dominate them. Just as human beings first create a God, and then bow down to it, they create an economic world of objects and then become mystified and dominated by it. They become – and this is the crux – 'playthings of alien forces'.

This idea has two central aspects. First humans become strangers in the world, not appreciating or understanding their own creations. Many human products are treated as miracles or facts of nature: consider the water, sewerage and electricity systems. Secondly, and crucially, human beings come to be dominated and subjugated by these products. As we saw, for example, one of the things that makes productive activity so alienating is production-line technology. But this technology was invented by human beings, and manufactured by human beings.

Most importantly, however, domination also arises on another level, affecting not only the worker. In fact, Marx says, the capitalist suffers a double alienation: shielded from the fact of alienation. Like the worker, the behaviour of the capitalist becomes controlled by 'impersonal social forces'. You can't buck the market. Capitalism has its laws, and you flout them at your peril. If you ignore them, then, just like those who try to ignore the law of gravity, you will come to grief.

But what, as it were, is the metaphysical status of these laws, these market forces? According to Marx they are no more than the accumulated consequences of human behaviour. Human beings act in certain ways, and this has certain large-scale effects. Given these effects certain future action by people seems rationally required and this reinforces the process, which becomes endlessly reinforced by the behaviour it generates. Capitalism is a mad machine, out of control, determining the behaviour of people in ways which intensifies its control. Like Frankenstein's monster, or the Sorcerer's Apprentice's broomstick, our creations come back to take on an independent, oppressive, life. Capitalists must act as capitalists and seek ever-increasing profits, or lose out in competition and sink to the level of the worker. But because the capitalist must seek profit, then he or she must exploit the worker, and impose alienating working methods, which the worker has no choice but to accept.

This is all because we have created something we cannot restrain – capitalism. And, Marx argues in *Capital*, this system has catastrophic effects. Capitalism contains mechanisms which depress wages to a minimum, and ensure that there will always be a large body of unemployed. Capitalism will be afflicted by a continual drop in the rate of profit, and will be hit by recurring and ever-deepening crises, in an ever-shortening boom-bust cycle. All this is a consequence of the normal functioning of this anarchic system of production. To take just one case, who wants stock-exchange crashes? Yet they happen. And as a result of human behaviour, of a type mandated by capitalist structures.

Finally under capitalism we do not recognize our common humanity, and our communal essence. Human beings are hugely dependent on each other. Without realizing it we are all part of an enormous division of labour, producing things for other people, and consuming the products of others. This mutual dependence partly constitutes our communal essence. Yet capitalism also forces us to become alienated from this, and so from each other. Consider the example of need. The human response to a fellow being in need is to do whatever is required to fulfil that need. Under capitalism another response is appropriate: to use that need as a source of power or profit. Those extremely short of money, for example, will work for very little pay. Thus we relate to each other not with mutual need in mind, but individual profit.

The reason for Marx's hostility to the market, and his idea of the planned economy as liberating, have emerged. Capitalism is something we have created, through the unintended consequences of human action. It is a human product, even though it often appears to us as a fixture of nature. Capitalism is, thus, an alienated human product, and it has disastrous effects. Labour – the central human activity – is degraded. Individual lives are tormented and less than fully human. We are screened off from our communal nature. Capitalism contains vast irrationalities, leading to crisis and enormous waste of human potential. We are 'playthings of alien forces'.

Taking control

This is how we have made the world – the unintended consequence of human action. But the world is anarchic, out of control. Thus to create a truly human society it is necessary for us to remake the world: take control of our products, take control of the social forces. This will allow us to treat each other as the communal beings we are, to treat others as ends in themselves.

But what would it be to remake the world in this way? The problem with capitalism is anarchy of production; the solution, therefore, is to have a planned, coordinated economy. To take control of the social forces is to have a centrally planned economy. This, at least, is how it appeared to Marx, and Marx also assumed that this would be possible. If we can plan the economy then we can remake the world in a truly human way.

This way of seeing the social world, I think, partially explains Marx's dismissive attitude to questions of morality, especially of justice. To worry about the injustice of capitalism, and try to remedy this by tinkering with the mechanisms of distribution, is rendered quite irrelevant when one appreciates the contingency of capitalism. If capitalism were irremovable, then all we could do would be to work out how we can improve it. But the existence of capitalism is not a fact of nature, and its defects go far beyond problems of injustice. What we should do is work to remove it and replace it with a better society.

But how is this to be done? Is this project any more realistic than Feuerbach's thought that we will remove religion by explaining to people what religion is? Marx does have a theory of history which purports to show how the new society is to come about. It is beyond the scope of this essay to go into the question, but Marx sees capitalism as ultimately leading to its own destruction, to be replaced by some form of communal society. Of course it might seem too good to be true that history is headed in the direction that a concern for human flourishing would also recommend, but that is another issue.

I hope, then, to have explained why Marx was so attracted to the planned economy, and why he thought that such an economy would be liberating. History seems to have shown us that Marx was wrong. Yet Marx's criticisms of the market seem deep and often cogent (although I have not here tried to indicate which I believe to be sound). If neither the market nor the planned economy can give us what we want then where should we look next? That is a question, I think, to which no convincing answer has yet been given.

References

Marx, K. (1975) *Early Writings*, ed. L. Colletti, Penguin.

Marx, K. (1976) *Capital*, Vol.1, Penguin.

Marx, K. and Engels, F. (1970) *The German Ideology*, ed. C. J. Arthur, Lawrence & Wishart.

Morton, A. L. (1969) *The Life and Ideas of Robert Owen*, International Publishers.

Further reading

Arthur, C. J. (1986) *Dialectics of Labour*, Blackwell.
Cohen, G. A. (1978) *Karl Marx's Theory of History: A Defence*, Oxford University Press.
Hook, S. (1950) *From Hegel to Marx*, University of Michigan Press.
Marx, K. (1977) *Selected Writings*, ed. D. McLellan, Oxford University Press.

Notes

From Wolff, Jonathan (1992) 'Playthings of Alien Forces: Karl Marx and the Rejection of the Market Economy', *Cogito*, pp.35–41.

'Marx's Early Critique of Liberalism'

Jon Pike

Jon Pike is staff tutor in Philosophy at The Open University, and author of *From Aristotle to Marx: Aristotelianism in Marxist Social Ontology* (1999). In this article, he discusses 'On the Jewish Question' principally as an attack on liberalism. Liberals typically believe that freedom consists in being politically free, that is, having such rights as a right to vote and to equality before the law. After setting the essay in context, Pike discusses Marx's contrast between this liberal 'political emancipation' and 'true human emancipation'. He shows how political emancipation relies on a damaging division of the individual into 'citoyen' (citizen) and 'bourgeois'. In the final section, Pike contrasts this liberal view with Marx's alternative: 'a society of universal friendliness'.

Introduction

The emancipation of the Jews had been a long-standing concern of European liberals since at least the French revolution. Revolutionary France was the first nation to grant civil rights to Jews, when the Assembly awarded citizenship to all Jews who swore loyalty to the state. But the debate over this law was still suffused with ambiguity towards the Jews: the Marquis de Clermont-Tonnere argued that 'the Jews must be refused everything as a separate nation and be granted everything as individuals' (cited in Davies (1997), p.843). Prussia lagged behind even this ambiguous type of reform. A Jewish Enlightenment soon emerged with Moses Mendelssohn (1729–86) as its figurehead, and the model for Nathan in Lessing's emblematic Enlightenment play *Nathan the Wise* (1779). Despite this, in 1816 a series of laws were passed in Prussia which put Jews in a considerably weaker position than Christians. Marx's own father, Heinrich Marx had been forced to convert to Christianity in order to continue to practise as a lawyer. In 1843 the Rhenish Parliament voted for Jewish emancipation but the King of Prussia vetoed their proposal. So the cause of Jewish emancipation – of equality before the law regardless of religious affiliation – was an important one, especially for German liberals.

Marx's essay 'On the Jewish Question' was written in 1843 and published in *the Deutsch-Französische Jahrbücher* in February 1844. The *Jahrbücher* was a radical political journal published in Paris by German émigrés. It was not a roaring success: the edition published in February 1844 was the only one that ever emerged, when its editors fell out with one another, partly over its advocacy of atheism. The state authorities in Germany seized many copies, although in October 1844 Engels, Marx's new friend, reported that 'people still continue to snatch up copies of the *Jahrbücher*' (Engels to Marx, October 1844; in Marx and Engels (1955 edn) p.18). But if the journal lacked longevity, it more than made up for that in the importance of its contents. Two pieces by Marx appeared in the *Jahrbücher*. The *Critique of Hegel's Doctrine of the State* contained Marx's powerful intervention into the debates between left and right Hegelians and his radical criticism of Hegel's political philosophy. The essay 'On the Jewish Question' consisted of an extended critique of two works by Marx's friend and collaborator Bruno Bauer, *The Jewish Question* and *The Capacity of Present day Jews and Christians to become free*.

Bruno Bauer, however, aimed to criticize the liberal advocacy of Jewish emancipation. Bauer's atheism meant that he thought of freedom from religious discrimination as an empty freedom – it was a freedom to do something pointless. His view was that Jews should drop their Judaism and instead become atheists:

> If the Jews want to become free, they should profess belief not in Christianity, but in the dissolution of religion in general, that is to say, in enlightenment, criticism and its consequences – free humanity.

(Marx (1977 edn), p.16)

There is certainly something odd about this answer – it has something of the flavour of the reply given to the hopelessly lost driver: 'if you want to get to Glasgow, you certainly don't want to start from here'. The prominence of Bauer's atheism meant that he engaged in a debate that was fundamentally about the content of a variety of religious beliefs, rather than one that was political in character. Marx, too, was an atheist, but, in 'On the Jewish Question', his atheism operates more as a background assumption rather than determining the terrain of disagreement.

'On the Jewish Question' is in two parts and each refers to a specific essay by Bruno Bauer: the first to 'The Jewish Question' and the second to 'The Capacity of present-day Jews and Christians to become free'. Part I of the essay moves from more particular concerns about Jewish emancipation in Prussia, towards general concerns about the 'Rights of Man' and their place in human emancipation. Part I contains the most important parts of the essay.

Marx's response to Bauer is, then, a critique of a critique. He agrees with Bauer that there is something wrong with the simple call for Jewish emancipation, but his diagnosis of the problem does not target the religious beliefs of the Jews. Rather, it focuses on the nature of emancipation and the possibilities of achieving human emancipation under *any* state. It contains, in embryonic form, his critique of liberalism. That critique comes in two parts: first, to the extent that liberalism offers emancipation, that emancipation is partial, and its partiality distorts human existence;

second, to the extent that liberalism holds up individual rights as the foundation of political morality, it makes hidden and false assumptions about the nature of humankind.

Marx's first argument hinges on the distinction between 'political emancipation' and 'fully' or 'truly human emancipation'.[1] He aims to drive a wedge between these two notions by showing that political emancipation masquerades fraudulently as human emancipation. Accordingly, political emancipation needs to be cut down to size.

The political emancipation of the Jews is the process whereby religious discrimination is disallowed within and by the state. Political emancipation is completed by a secular state; a state which takes no position on religious matters – religious belief is a purely private affair, a matter of individual conscience. One recent account of the liberal state – that it is agnostic or neutral between competing accounts of 'the good', or how we ought to live (see, for example, Rawls (1993) and Barry (1995)) – is a vigorous generalization of this older idea of 'political emancipation' (and it is open to the criticisms levelled at that idea in 'On the Jewish Question'.) The early nineteenth-century Prussian state clearly did favour one account of how we ought to live – it was a Christian state and systematically discriminated against Jews, for example, by preventing them from entering the professions. At first sight, political emancipation seems to be the obvious way to get to human freedom. However, Marx questions the notion that political emancipation is somehow a method of achieving genuine or thoroughgoing freedom:

> A proper critique would have a third question – *what sort of emancipation* is under discussion? What preconditions are essential for the required emancipation? It is only the critique of political emancipation itself that would be the final critique of the Jewish question and its true resolution into 'the general problems of the age'.

> (Marx (1977 edn), p.42)

Marx tries to demonstrate one limitation of political emancipation – that it fails to eliminate the mystifications of religion – by an example. North America ought to indicate the limits of political emancipation to atheists such as Bauer. Religious minorities in the US were fully emancipated in 1844, in the sense that the legal system did not discriminate between religions at all and the constitution guaranteed religious freedom. So the state in the US had no religious content. Nevertheless, 'North America is the land of religiosity *par excellence*' (ibid., p.43). So political emancipation fails entirely to accomplish the atheist's intention. This example is enough to deal with the contention that political emancipation is genuine freedom. It doesn't give real freedom, because it leaves subordination to religion intact. However, Marx wants to make more of this point.

> The fact that even in the land of completed political emancipation we find not only the existence of religion but a living existence full of freshness and strength furnishes us with proof that the existence of religion does not contradict or impede the perfection of the state. But since the existence of religion is the existence of a defect, the source of this defect can only be sought in the nature of the state itself.

> (Ibid., pp.43–4)

What, then, is wrong with the nature of the state? At this point in the essay, Marx begins to generalize his critique. He argues that the liberal state rests on a split between two aspects of a person. In the public realm of the state, the individual is a citizen, equal to every other citizen; there he is a communal being. But in the private realm of civil society, the individual acts as an isolated individual and aims to satisfy his or her own particular needs.

Political emancipation of religion means the freedom to pursue one's religious beliefs – as such it means excluding religion from the 'free' state, at the same time as the state steps back from the religious lives of individuals. This bifurcating process does not annul religion – and the annulment of religion is a requirement of truly human emancipation, according to Marx. In the same way, dropping a property qualification for voting does not annul private property, it simply shunts private property out of the public realm. Again, in Marx's view, the annulment of private property is needed for human emancipation, and political emancipation is not fitted for that task. So political emancipation is only a very partial emancipation: religion and private property are still part of the furniture of our lives – but the furniture has been moved from the public room to the private room. What is needed is to throw the furniture out altogether.

Marx's argument works in a number of different ways. First, he assumes that both private property and religion frustrate human freedom. Suppose we accept that private property is essentially about human domination and subordination, and that religion is merely a form of alienation (by transferring – 'alienating' – human powers and potentials to the supernatural world, humans subordinate themselves to an alien being). If this is the case, it is clear that political emancipation does not amount to human freedom, because political emancipation leaves these practices of domination and subordination intact. Rather than abolishing them, it simply shifts them from the public to the private realm.

But suppose we do not concede to Marx the assumptions about private property and religion. 'On the Jewish Question' suggests at least two arguments that have to do with bifurcation *per se*. If human life is to have a rational basis, then there must be rational principles governing it. But the individual who has a say in political life is radically separate from the individual who exists in civil society. The *citoyen* is split from the *bourgeois*, and it is this split self that is the object of Marx's criticism. One set of normative principles and self conceptions covers the state and another, different, and contradictory set covers civil society. Political emancipation reveals 'the general secular contradiction between the political state and civil society' (ibid., p.51). Marx indicates the absence of an overarching principle governing the boundaries of certain normative practices. At the same time, he gestures at the form that any such principle might have, like the old socialist slogan that 'democracy stops at the factory gate'. The critical bite of such slogans arises because they immediately look arbitrary: *why* should democracy stop there? Any such overarching principle embodies the bifurcation which Marx rejects.

Yet here, too, there is a hidden assumption at work. While Marx lays down a clear enough challenge to the liberal to justify the distinction between the state and civil society, there are plausible candidates for meeting that challenge. To put the point another way, suppose we grant Marx his claim that 'merely political emancipation' leaves a bifurcated self. What is *wrong* with a bifurcated self? The answer to this question emerges when we consider the Marxian critique of rights.

In 'On the Jewish Question' Marx asks about the conditions that make rights important and the consequences of making rights the central moral concept in a political morality. He looks at the mystification of liberal rights wherein what was a particular limited construct becomes an immutable and ahistorical truth. Marx is critical of the 'so called rights of man' because none of them

> goes beyond egoistic man, man as he is in civil society; namely, an individual withdrawn beyond his private interests and whims and separated from the community. Far from the rights of man conceiving of man as a species-being; species-life itself, – society – appears as a framework exterior to individuals, a limitation of their original self-sufficiency. The only bond that holds them together is natural necessity, need, and private interest, the conservation of their property and egoistic person.

(Ibid., p.54)

What is the basis for the connection of rights to the 'egoistic' individual? One way in which rights work is as a mechanism for defence. [2] You may not do certain harmful things to me, because to do so violates my rights. Historically, the paradigmatic accounts of natural rights, such as Locke's in the *Second Treatise*, emphasize this defensive form, and for good reasons. They were in part designed as ideological defences of private property against absolute sovereigns. Amongst modern political philosophers the notion of rights as protective barriers is common. According to Hayek, we are 'surrounded' by a 'protected sphere' (Hayek (1962), p.139) of rights, and the spatial metaphor is instructive.

Consider the following thought experiment. Suppose you are able to travel through time, in H.G. Wells fashion, to a future society occupied by beings very like ourselves. As a political philosopher, you are intrigued by their political rules and institutions so you inquires of these beings how they organize themselves.

'Don't worry!' they reply. 'We have established the rights of time travellers quite clearly in our constitution. For example, your right to retain all your fingers and toes is explicitly guaranteed by our constitutional documents. No one may slice off your fingers and toes without being liable to strict penalties, because your rights over your fingers and toes must not be infringed.'

I would not be wholly reassured by this response. Because I don't normally fear having my fingers and toes sliced off, I would be unsettled by the indication that they were under threat. I can take it that they are under threat, because the *point* of a right is to protect something that is under threat. There is no reason to attribute a 'right to X' to an individual if there is no possibility of preventing the individual from 'X-ing' in the first place. So, when offered the *right* to all my fingers and toes, I might reasonably speculate about the *threat* to them. Perhaps the digits of time travellers are particularly rare and tasty. My speculation in this way is reasonable because the attribution of a right only makes sense in the presence of a threat to whatever it is that the right defends.

This claim is true of rights in general and not just of property rights. The right to religious freedom is only worth raising as a right if the exercise of religious freedom is seriously under threat. What is more, practical political examples indicate this connection: the right to work is demanded in conditions of unemployment and it has much less bite in conditions of full employment. So, if rights talk makes sense only in conditions where the activities defended by those rights are under threat, then the thrust of Marx's polemic becomes clear. Those who universalize rights and regard them as foundational for human political morality, thereby universalize threats and regard threats as foundational for human social organization.

This is the nub of Marx's critique of rights in 'On the Jewish Question'. Rights talk only makes sense against a background assumption about threats and the need for defence against them. The conditions that make threats likely, and therefore make rights important, are rather complex.[3] Here I shall just discuss two. It is clear that scarcity of resources makes threats likely, and Marx is often accused of making over-optimistic assumptions about abundance, particularly in times more in tune to ecological limits to growth. But scarcity will not do all the work. What is need is an additional claim about the absence of altruism. J.L Mackie brings these two elements together when outlining 'the problem that morality is needed to solve: limited resources and limited sympathies together generate both competition leading to conflict, and an absence of what would be mutually beneficial cooperation' (Mackie (1977), p.111) and the same pair of assumptions clearly drives Hobbes's political philosophy.

However, there is an alternative to a morality founded on threats, and Marx is not the first philosopher to appeal to that alternative. Suppose the assumption of limited sympathies is challenged. In the *Nicomachean Ethics*, Aristotle argues that:

> if people are friends, they have no need of justice, but if they are just need friends in addition; and the justice that is most just seems to belong to friendship. However, friendship is not only necessary, but fine.

(Aristotle (1984 edn), 1155a26)

Friendship is both 'justice in the fullest sense' and something that eradicates the need for justice. There are clearly two notions of justice at work here, and the first – justice in the narrow sense, which concerns defensive rights – is the target of Marx's attack. Friendship obviates the need for defensive rights. I do not need rights against my friends since they do not pose a threat to me. This is because they will not intentionally act against me. The point is an analytical one: someone who intentionally acts against me simply is not my friend. So rights are only necessary in the absence of friendship and the presence of threats. Although Marx was not a fully fledged communist thinker at the time of the writing of 'On the Jewish Question', it is clear that he draws on an alternative model of society organized according to justice 'in the fullest sense' – justice as friendship. This alternative to a world of threats can then be read in Bertolt Brecht's redolent description of communism as a movement for universal friendship. Egoistic Man – who asserts his rights against threats from others – is not at home there.

Two remarks can be made. Marx's straightforward claim about the import of rights talk is correct. The attribution of a right only makes sense in the presence of a threat to whatever it is that the rights defends. Liberal theorists who regard rights as foundational are clearly committed to regarding such threats as foundational – and ineradicable – and they ought to make that assumption clear.

But whether this point tells against liberalism in a substantive way, rather than convicting it on a technicality, depends on whether the society of universal friendliness is a possible scenario. The plausibility of such a society varies positively with the seriousness of the liberal error in failing to specify the preconditions of the rights-based account of political morality. The more plausible such a society, the more serious the error.

Marx's critique of political emancipation and his attack on rights both rest on an account of human nature.[4] First, truly human emancipation is a matter of being integrated rather than bifurcated. Marx's account of freedom is rather special. Rather than being a matter of the absence of constraint, freedom is a question of *reconciliation*. We are free when we live according to our essence or species being. But this is not the case in the liberal state. The human essence (or species being) which is social, universal, rational and free from domination and subordination is reflected (albeit imperfectly) in the role of citizen. But human social life has bifurcated into the public realm and the private realm, the *citoyen* and the *bourgeois*, the state and civil society. The most important metaphors in 'On the Jewish Question' are those of 'splitting' and 'reunifying'.

The assumption about human essence that Marx makes is the Aristotelian assumption that 'it is evident that the state (*polis*) is a creation of nature, and that man is by nature a political animal (*zoon politikon*) (Aristotle (1996 edn), 1253a2–3, p.13). 'Human species being' is for Marx what 'man is by nature' and for Aristotle a social and political animal who is fully human not in isolation from other humans but only together with them and in common control of their lives.[5] Marx agrees with Aristotle that 'the individual, when isolated, is not self sufficing; and therefore he is like a part in relation to the whole. But he who is unable to live in society or has no need because he is sufficient for himself, must be either a beast or a god: he is no part of a state.' (ibid., 1253a26–9, p.13).

To be what he really *is*, man needs to reunite the political 'abstract citizen' and become fully aware of himself as 'species being'. It is a short but important step from the account of how human beings are to how they ought to behave. Simply put, they ought to behave in accordance with their essence, as part of a whole, and without privileging themselves against others. It is a simplification of the overall account, but not a distortion of it, to suggest that human species being prescribes friendship.

Marx's critique of liberalism in 'On the Jewish Question' is a profound piece of political philosophy. It is by no means a knockdown argument against the forms of thought adopted by contemporary liberals but it clearly raises a significant challenge. In order to resist Marx's challenge, liberals must show the impossibility, or at least instability, of a society of universal friendliness, and they must come up with an adequate overarching principle with which to justify the bifurcation of humankind in the liberal state. Meeting such a challenge involves recognizing the penetration of Marx's critique.

References

Aristotle (1996 edn) *Politics*, S. Everson (ed.), Cambridge University Press.

Aristotle, (1984 edn) *Ethics*, T. Irwin (trans.), Hackett.

Barry, B. (1995) *Justice as Impartiality*, Cambridge University Press.

Davies, Norman (1997) *Europe, A History*, Pimlico.

Hayek, F. (1962) *The Constitution of Liberty*, Routledge & Kegan Paul.

Mackie, J.L. (1977) *Ethics, Inventing Right and Wrong*, Penguin.

Marx, K. (1977 edn) 'On the Jewish Question', D. McLellan (trans.) in *Selected Writings*, D. McLellan (ed.), Oxford University Press.

Marx, K. and Engels, F. (1955 edn) *Marx–Engels Selected Correspondence*, Progress Publishers.

Pike, J. (1999) *From Aristotle to Marx: Aristotelianism in Marxist Social Ontology*, Ashgate.

Rawls, J. (1993) *Political Liberalism*, Columbia University Press.

Notes

This article was specially written for this book.

[1] The fact that Marx and Bauer talk of political emancipation is a drawback for Lukes's otherwise very helpful distinction between a morality of '*recht*' and a morality of emancipation: political emancipation as outlined in 'On the Jewish Question' is clearly a matter of '*recht*'.

[2] The main concern here is with so-called 'negative rights'; rights against interference. However, the argument applies, though less forcefully to so-called 'positive rights': rights to X.

[3] Scarcity, egoism, disagreement about the good and imperfect knowledge are the four conditions outlined by Stephen Lukes (1985) *Marxism and Morality*, Oxford University Press, pp.32–3.

[4] Norman Geras has laid to rest the notion that Marx did not have a theory of human nature: Geras, N. (1983) *Marx and Human Nature, Refutation of Legend*, Verso.

[5] For more on the Aristotle–Marx connection see S. Meikle (1985) *Essentialism in the Thought of Karl Marx*, Duckworth; also McCarthy, G.E. (1990) *Marx and the Ancients, Classical Ethics, Social Justice and Nineteenth Century Political Economy*, Maryland; McCarthy, G.E. (ed.) (1992) *Marx and Aristotle: Nineteenth Century German Social Theory and Classical Antiquity*, Maryland; and Pike, J. (1999) *From Aristotle to Marx*, Ashgate.

'Forces and Relations of Production'

G.A. Cohen

G.A. Cohen is a leading commentator on Marx, and his book, *Karl Marx's Theory of History* (1978), is widely regarded as setting a new standard in the subject. This extract from a later book recapitulates a central theme in that earlier one. Cohen first gives an account of historical materialism, showing that the 'development thesis' – the claim that 'the productive forces tend to grow in power throughout history' – is explanatorily fundamental. In this exposition he also defines the key terms 'forces of production', 'relations of production' and 'superstructure'. He then shows that historical materialism relies on 'functional explanations'. These appear to explain events in terms of their effects, which, as Cohen shows, is impossible. Instead, Cohen construes functional explanations in such a way that this problem is avoided.

I present [here], in summary form, the interpretation of historical materialism which I offered in my book on *Karl Marx's Theory of History*.[1] I define and connect the concepts of forces and relations of production, and I maintain that the basic explanations of historical materialism are *functional* explanations.

KMTH says, and it says that Marx says, that history is, fundamentally, the growth of human productive power, and that forms of society (which are organized around economic structures) rise and fall according as they enable and promote, or prevent and discourage, that growth.

The canonical text for this interpretation of Marx is his famous 1859 Preface to *A Contribution to the Critique of Political Economy*, some sentences of which we shall look at shortly. I argue (in section 3 of chapter 6 of *KMTH*) that the Preface makes explicit the standpoint on society and history which Marx occupied throughout his mature writings, on any reasonable view of the date at which he reached theoretical maturity. In attending to the Preface, we are not looking at just one text among many, but at that text which gives the clearest statement of the theory of historical materialism.

The presentation of the theory in the Preface begins as follows:

> In the social production of their life men enter into definite relations that are indispensable and independent of their will, relations of production which *correspond* to a definite stage of development of their material productive forces. The sum total of these relations constitutes the economic structure of society, the real *basis, on which arises* a legal and political superstructure ...[2]

These sentences mention three ensembles, the productive forces, the relations of production, and the superstructure, among which certain explanatory connections (here indicated by italics) are asserted. I shall first say what I think the ensembles are, and I shall then describe the explanatory connections among them. (All of what follows is argued for in *KMTH*, but not all of the argument is given in what follows, which may therefore wrongly impress the reader as dogmatic.)

The productive forces are those facilities and devices which are used to productive effect in the process of production: means of production on the one hand, and labour power on the other. Means of production are physical productive resources: tools, machinery, raw materials, premises, and so forth. Labour power includes not only the strength of producers, but also their skills, and the technical knowledge (which they need not understand) they apply when labouring. Marx says, and I agree, that this subjective dimension of the productive forces is more important than the objective or means of production dimension; and within the more important dimension the part most capable of development is knowledge. Hence, in its later stages, the development of the productive forces is largely a function of the development of productively useful science. If you want to turn a productively advanced society into a backward one, you will not achieve much by destroying its physical instruments of production. As long as its productive know-how remains intact, the society will before long restore itself, as Germany did when, according to a once prevalent view, its industry had been devastated by the Second World War. Some think that Germany suffered less material destruction than the word 'devastated' suggests, and perhaps they are right. But the old view about the German recovery was not a ridiculous one, and the reason why it was not ridiculous is because there is, as I am here maintaining, no inherent barrier to reconstituting the physical side of productive power, as long as its cognitive side is undamaged. If, by contrast, you somehow remove productive know-how from the heads of producers, but spare their material facilities, then, unless they import knowledge afresh from abroad, their advanced facilities will decay and they will need centuries to recoup.

Note that Marx takes for granted in the Preface, what elsewhere he asserts outright, that 'there is a continual movement of growth in productive forces'.[3] I argue (in section 6 of chapter 2 of *KMTH*) that the right standard for measuring that growth in power is how much (or, rather, how little) labour must be spent with given forces to produce what is required to satisfy the inescapable physical needs of the immediate producers.[4] This criterion of social productivity is less equivocal than others which may come to mind, but the decisive reason for choosing it is not its relative clarity but its theoretical appropriateness: if relations of production correspond, as the theory says they do, to levels of development of productive power, then this way of measuring productive power makes the theory's correspondence thesis more plausible. [5]

I do not say that the only explanatory feature of productive power is how much there is of it: qualitative features of productive forces also help to explain the character of relations of production. My claim is that in so far as quantity of productive power is what matters, the key quantity is how much time it takes to (re)produce the producers, that is to say, to produce what they must consume to be able to continue working (as opposed to what they actually consume, which generally, and in contemporary capitalist society considerably, exceeds what they must consume). It is the amount of time available beyond, or surplus[6] to, that historically dwindling requirement that is so fateful for the form of the second ensemble we need to describe, the relations of production.

Relations of production are relations of economic power, of the economic power[7] people enjoy or lack over labour power and means of production. In a capitalist society relations of production include the economic power capitalists have over means of production, the economic power workers (unlike slaves) have over their own labour power, and the lack of economic power workers have over means of production. Immediate producers may have no economic power, some economic power, or total economic power over their own labour power and over the means of production they use. If we permit ourselves a measure of idealization, we can construct table I, which rather neatly distinguishes the relations of production of historically important immediate producers.

Table I

	Amount of economic power over	
	His labour power	The means of production he uses
Slave	None	None
Serf	Some	Some
Proletarian	All	None
Independent	All	All

The table names three subordinate producers, and one independent. Since one may have no, some, or total economic power over one's labour power and over the means of production one uses, there are nine cases to consider. I think it is diagnostically valuable to inquire which of the remaining five cases are logically or otherwise possible, and which in turn of those are actual, but I shall not enter on that discussion here. [8]

Now the sum total of relations of production in a given society is said to constitute the economic structure of that society, which is also called – in relation to the superstructure – the basis, or base, or foundation. The economic structure or base therefore consists of relations of production only: it does not include the productive forces. It is true that to exclude the productive forces from the economic structure runs against the usual construal of Marx,[9] but he actually said that the economic structure is constituted of relations of production, and he had systematic reasons for saying so. [10] People mistakenly suppose that the productive forces belong to the economic base because they wrongly think that the explanatory importance of the forces ensures their membership in it. But while the forces indeed possess that importance, they are not part of the economic base.[11] To stay with the spatial metaphor, they are below the economic foundation, the ground on which it rests. [12] (Since it consists of relations of economic power, the economic base would be obliterated by a fever of social disobedience in which all economic power melted away, yet means of production and technical knowledge, and, therefore, the productive forces, remain intact in that fantasy. Total social disarray eliminates economic structure while leaving the productive forces entirely unchanged.)

The Preface describes the superstructure as legal and political. So it at any rate includes the legal and state institutions of society, or at least some of them. It is customary to locate other institutions within it too, and it is controversial what its correct demarcation is: my own view is that there are strong textual and systematic reasons for supposing that the superstructure is a lot smaller than many commentators think it is.[13] It is certainly false that every non-economic social phenomenon is superstructural: artistic creation, for example, is demonstrably not, just as such, superstructural for Marx. In this exposition I shall discuss property law only, which is uncontroversially a part of the superstructure.

So much for the identity of the three ensembles mentioned in the Preface. Now relations of production are said to *correspond* to the level of development of the productive forces, and in turn to be a *foundation* on which a superstructure rises. I think these are ways of saying that the level of development of the productive forces explains the nature of the production relations, and that they in turn explain the character of the superstructure co-present with them. But what kind of explanation is ventured here? I argue that in each case what we have is a species of functional explanation.

What is functional explanation? Here are two examples of it: 'Birds have hollow bones because hollow bones facilitate flight', 'Shoe factories operate on a large scale because of the economies large scale brings'. In each case something (birds having hollow bones, shoe factories operating on a large scale) which has a certain effect (flight facilitation, economies of scale) is explained by the fact that it has that effect.

But now let me be somewhat more precise.[14] Suppose that e is a cause and f is its effect, and that we are offered a functional explanation of e in terms of its possession of that effect. Note first that the form of the explanation is not: e occurred because f occurred. If that were its form, functional explanation would be the exact opposite of ordinary causal explanation, and it would have the fatal defect that it represented a later occurrence as explaining an earlier one. Nor may we say that the form of the explanation is 'e occurred because it caused f'. Similar constraints on explanation and time order rule that candidate out: by the time e has caused f, e has occurred, so that the fact that it caused f could not explain its occurrence. The only remaining candidate, which I therefore elect, is: e occurred because it would cause f, or, less tersely but more properly: e occurred because the situation was such that an event like e would cause an event like f.

Now if this account of what functional explanations are is correct, then the main explanatory theses of historical materialism are functional explanations, for the following reasons: Marx never denied, and he sometimes asserted, and it is, moreover, manifestly true, that superstructures hold foundations together, and that relations of production control the development of the productive forces. Yet Marx also held that the character of the superstructure is explained by the nature of the base, and that the latter is explained by the nature of the productive forces. If the intended explanations are functional ones, we have consistency between the effect of A on B, and the explanation of A by B, and I do not know any other way of rendering historical materialism consistent.[15]

I shall now expound in greater detail one of the two functional explanatory theses, that which concerns base and superstructure.

The base, it will be recalled, is the sum total of production relations, these being relations of power over labour capacity and means of production. The capitalist's control of means of production is an illustration. And the superstructure, we saw, has more than one part, exactly what its parts are being somewhat uncertain, but certainly one *bona fide* part of it is the legal system, which will occupy us here.

In a capitalist society capitalists have effective power over means of production. What confers that power on a given capitalist, say an owner of a factory? On what can he rely if others attempt to take control of the factory away from him? An important part of the answer is this: he can rely on the law of the land, which is enforced by the might of the state. It is no great oversimplification to say that it is his legal right which causes him to have his economic power, since what he is effectively able to do depends on what he is legally entitled to do. And this is in general true in law-abiding society with respect to all economic powers and all economic agents. We can therefore say: in law-abiding society people have the economic powers they do because they have the legal rights they do.

That seems to refute the doctrine of base and superstructure, since here superstructural conditions – what legal rights people have – determine basic ones – what their economic powers are. Yet although it seems to refute the doctrine of base and superstructure, it cannot be denied. And it would not only seem to refute it, but actually would refute it, were it not possible, *and therefore mandatory* (for historical materialists), to present the doctrine of base and superstructure as an instance of functional explanation. For we can add, to the undeniable truth emphasized above, the further thesis that the given capitalist enjoys the stated right because it belongs to a structure of rights, a structure which obtains because it sustains an analogous structure of economic power. The content of the legal system is explained by its function, which is to help sustain an economy of a particular kind. People do usually get their powers from their rights, but in a manner which is not only allowed but demanded by the way historical materialism explains superstructural rights by reference to basic powers. Hence the effect of the law of property on the economy is not, as is often supposed, an embarrassment to historical materialism. It is something which historical materialism is committed to emphasizing, because of the particular way in which it explains law in terms of economic conditions.

Legal structures rise and fall when and because they sustain and frustrate forms or economy which, I now add, advance the development of the productive forces. The addition implies an explanation why whatever economic structure obtains at a given time does obtain at that time. Once more the explanation is a functional one: the prevailing production relations prevail *because* they are relations which advance the development of the productive forces. The existing level of productive power determines what relations of production would raise its level, and relations of that type consequently obtain. In other words: if production relations of kind k obtain, then that is because k-type relations are suitable to the development of the forces, in virtue of their existing level of development: that is the canonical form of the explanation in the standard case. But I should also mention the transitional case, in which the relations are not suitable to the development of the forces but, on the contrary, fetter them. In transitional cases the prevailing relations obtain because they recently *were* suitable to the development of the forces, and the class they empower has managed to maintain control despite their no longer being so: it is because ruling classes have an interest in the maintenance of obsolete relations that their *immediate* replacement by freshly suitable relations is not to be expected. People do not rush towards the dustbin of history just as soon as they have played out their historical role.

Now since

1   the level of development of productive power explains why certain relations, and not others, would advance productive power,

and

2   relations which advance productive power obtain because they advance productive power,

it follows that

3   the level of development of productive power explains the nature of the economic structure (of, that is, the sum total of production relations).

Proposition (3) assigns explanatory primacy to the productive forces. Note that neither (1) nor (2), taken separately from the other, establishes that (3), the Primacy Thesis, is true. It should be evident that (1) does not assign explanatory primacy over the production relations to the productive forces, since (1) says nothing about what sort of economic structure will in fact obtain. And, although it is less evident, it is also true that (2) does not confer explanatory primacy on the level of development of the forces. The reason why (2) does not do so – the reason, that is, why (2) is insufficient to establish (3) – is that (2) is consistent with (3) – defeating non-(1) explanations of the character relations must possess to advance productive power. One such non-(1) explanation would be:

4   The dominant ideology, which is not explained by the level of development of the productive forces, determines what relations would advance that development further.

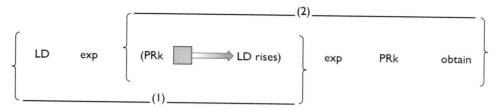

Figure 1

Figure 1[16] shows how (3) is derived from (1) and (2): (1) says that the level of development of the productive forces explains why relations of kind *k* would now raise that level, and (2) says that the fact that relations of that kind are apt to raise the level of development of the forces explains why just such relations obtain. Proposition (3) is derived through deletion of the middle portion of the schema, and it is justified, given (1) and (2), by the transitivity of explanation.

Now to say that *A* explains *B* is not necessarily to indicate *how A* explains *B*. The child who knows that the match burst into flame because it was struck may not know how the latter event explains the former, because he is ignorant of the relationship between friction and heat, the contribution of oxygen to combustion, and so on. In a widely favoured idiom, he may not know the *mechanism* linking cause and effect, or, as I prefer to say, he may be unable to *elaborate* the explanation. In the relevant sense of 'how', we require an answer to the questions: *How does the fact that the economic structure promotes the development of the productive forces explain the character of the economic structure? and How does the fact that the superstructure protects the base explain the character of the superstructure?* Recall the functional explanation of the hollow bones of birds: to say, correctly, that birds have hollow bones because the feature is useful for flight is not to say how its usefulness accounts for its emergence and/or persistence. To that question Lamarck gave an unacceptable answer and Darwin an excellent one, which was later rendered even better, through developments in genetic theory. To corresponding questions about explanations of large scale in terms of economies of scale one may answer by referring to conscious human purposes, or to an economic analogue of chance variation and natural selection, or to some mix of the two.[17] But no one has given good answers to the similar questions (italicized above) about historical materialism. I offer some not very satisfactory answers in chapter 10 of *KMTH*. This seems to me an important area of future research for historical materialists, since the functional construal of their doctrine is hard to avoid. [18]

Let me now summarize my argument for the thesis that the chief explanatory claims of historical materialism are functional in form. Those claims are that

3   the level of development of productive power explains the nature of the economic structure

and

5   the economic structure explains the nature of the superstructure.

I take (3) and (5) to be functional explanations because I cannot otherwise reconcile them with two further Marxian theses, namely that

6   the economic structure promotes the development of the productive forces

and

7   the superstructure stabilizes the economic structure.

(6) and (7) entail that the economic structure is functional for the development of the productive forces, and that the superstructure is functional for the stability of the economic structure. These claims do not by themselves entail that economic structures and superstructures are *explained* by the stated functions: A may be functional for B even though it is false that A exists *because* it is functional for B. (The bridge of my nose is functional for my vision, since it helps to support my spectacles, but, unlike my right eye, it does not exist *because* it is functional for vision.) But (6) and (7), *in conjunction with* (3) *and* (5), do force us to treat historical materialist explanation as functional. No other treatment preserves consistency between the explanatory primacy of the productive forces over the economic structure and the massive control of the latter over the former, or between the explanatory primacy of the economic structure over the superstructure and the latter's regulation of the former.

I hold that the central explanations of historical materialism are functional explanations, and I defend functional explanation as an explanatory device, but I do not defend the sloppy functional explanatory theorizing in which so many Marxists engage.[19]

Many Marxist exercises in functional explanation fail to satisfy even the preliminary requirement of showing that A is functional for B (whether or not it is also *explained* by its function(s)). Take, for example, the claim that the contemporary capitalist state functions to protect and sustain the capitalist system. Legislation and policy in the direct interest of the capitalist class can reasonably be regarded as confirming it. But what about putative counter-examples, such as social welfare provision and legal immunities enjoyed by trade unions? These too might be functional for capitalism, in an indirect way, but that is something which needs to be argued with care, not just asserted. But those who propound the general claim about the state rarely trouble to say what sort of evidence would falsify or weaken it, and therefore every action of the state is treated as confirmatory, since there is always some way, legitimate or spurious, in which the action can be made to look functional.

Methodological indiscipline is then compounded when, having satisfied himself that state policy is functional, the theorist treats it, without further argument, as also functionally explained. He proceeds from 'A is functional for B' to 'B functionally explains A' without experiencing any need to justify the step, if, indeed, he notices that he has taken a step from one position to a distinct and stronger one.

Notes

From Cohen, G.A. (1988) *History, Labour, and Freedom: Themes from Marx*, Clarendon Press, pp.3–14.

[1] This work is referred to hereafter as *KMTH*.

[2] *Critique of Political Economy*, p.20 (my emphases).

[3] *The Poverty of Philosophy*, p.166.

[4] As opposed, for example, to their socially developed needs, reference to which would be inappropriate here (though not, of course, everywhere).

[5] For a set of correspondences of relations to forces of production, see *KMTH* 198, and [Cohen (1988)] pp.155–6 ...

[6] This is not the only important concept of surplus in Marxism, but I invoke it here because it is a concept of something purely material, and I conceive historical materialism as an attempt to explain the social by reference to the material: see *KMTH* 61, 98, and ch.4 *passim* for defence of the distinction between material and social properties of society.

[7] I call such power 'economic' in virtue of what it is power over, and irrespective of the means of gaining, sustaining, or exercising the power, which need not be economic. See *KMTH* 223–4 and [Cohen (1988)] ch.2 ... *passim.*

[8] The discussion is pursued at *KMTH* 66–9.

[9] See *KMTH* 29 n.2 for a list of authors who take for granted that productive forces belong to the economic structure.

[10] See *KMTH* 28–9. I have now, alas, noticed a passage which seems to locate the forces within the economic base, but I shall continue to situate them outside it, since the theoretical reasons for doing so strike me as overwhelming. (The recalcitrant passage is at the foot of *Capital* i, 175.)

[11] And, in my view, they are not economic phenomena of any kind: my reasons for denying that they are will be found in *KMTH*, ch. 4, sect. I.

[12] See *KMTH* 30 for a distinction between the material and the economic bases of society: the productive forces belong to the former and are therefore not part of the latter.

[13] I criticize the common practice of overpopulating the superstructure in my review of Melvin Rader's *Marx's Interpretation of History*. For a systematic way of confining the superstructure, see [Cohen (1988)] ch. 9 sects. 6, 8 ...

[14] But not as precise as in *KMTH*, ch. 9 sects. 4, 7, and ch. 10, where the structure of functional explanation is described in greater detail.

[15] The only author who, to my knowledge, shows a complete understanding of the problem but attempts a different solution to it is Philippe Van Parijs, whose solution to the problem I do not understand. See his 'Marxism's Central Puzzle', and my comments in 'Reply to Four Critics', pp.204–6.

[16] It comes from p.220 of my 'Walt on Historical Materialism', an article which provides further clarification of the *KMTH* claims about the relationship between forces and relations of production.

[17] See *KMTH* 287–9.

[18] For valuable work on the problem of the mechanism in functional explanation, see Van Parijs, *Evolutionary Explanation in the Social Sciences*.

[19] For an impressive catalogue of methodologically lax uses of functional explanation, see Jon Elster's 'Marxism, Functionalism and Game Theory'.

'Alienation'

Will Kymlicka

In this extract, Kymlicka considers the argument that Marx is a 'perfectionist': that is, that he favours a certain ideal form of life that will be brought about by abolishing wage-labour and socializing the means of production. Kymlicka argues that this presupposes that non-alienated labour is the sole good we ought to pursue, and to counter this he argues first that there are other aims we might have (for example, to enjoy more leisure) which we might accept as compensation for some alienated labour. Second, he argues that the focus on non-alienated labour is sexist, as it undervalues 'the predominantly female sphere of reproductive life'. Kymlicka is anxious to point out that his criticism of Marx does not justify the distribution of meaningful work under our current system.

If Marxists are committed to abolishing private property, they must appeal to something other than exploitation. According to Steven Lukes, Marx's critique of capitalism appeals not only to a 'Kantian'[1] concern with exploitation, but also to a 'perfectionist' concern with alienation (Lukes (1985), p.87; cf. Miller (1989), pp.52–4).[2] Whereas the Kantian strand emphasizes the way private property reduces some people (the workers) to a means for the benefit of others (capitalists), the perfectionist strand emphasizes the way private property inhibits the development of our most important capacities. The problem with private property is not simply that it is exploitative, for even those who benefit from exploitation are alienated from their essential human powers. This alienation argument seems a more promising route for defending a prohibition on private property, for while equalizing private property eliminates exploitation, it may just universalize the alienation.

Perfectionist arguments, of which Marx's alienation argument is one example, say that resources should be distributed in such a way as to encourage the 'realization of distinctively human potentialities and excellencies', and to discourage ways of life which lack these excellencies (Lukes (1985), p.87). Such theories are 'perfectionist' because they claim that certain ways of life constitute human 'perfection' (or 'excellence'), and that such ways of life should be promoted, while less worthy ways of life should be penalized. This is unlike liberal or libertarian theories, which do not try to encourage any particular way of life, but rather leave individuals free to use their resources in whatever ways they themselves find most valuable.[...] I will look briefly at how Marxist perfectionism might defend a prohibition on private property.

Any perfectionist argument must explain what the 'distinctive human excellencies' are, and how the distribution of resources should be arranged so as to promote them. In Marx's case, our distinctive excellence is said to be our capacity for freely creative co-operation production. To produce in a way that stunts this capacity is to be 'alienated' from our true 'species-nature'. Hence, Marxist perfectionists argue, resources in a communist society should be distributed so as to encourage people to achieve self-realization through co-operative production. Distribution might still be governed by the needs principle,[3] but for perfectionists the needs principle is not concerned with all needs. Rather, it would involve 'some selection of those forms of human interest and concerns which most fully express the ideal of co-operative, creative, and productive activities and enjoyments' (Campbell (1983), p.138; cf. Elster (1985), p.522).

How should this ideal be promoted? Marxists argue it is best promoted by abolishing wage-labour and socializing the means of production. Wage-labour alienates us from our most important capacity, because it turns the worker's labour-power into a mere commodity the disposition of which is under someone else's control. Moreover, for many workers under capitalism, this exercise of labour-power tends to be mindless and devoid of any intrinsic satisfaction. Socializing the means of production ensures that each person has an effective say in how her work life is organized, and enables her to organize production so as to increase its intrinsic satisfaction, rather than to increase the profits of the capitalist. Capitalism reduces our life's activity to a means which we endure in order to secure a decent living, but socialism will restore work to its rightful place as an end in itself, as 'life's prime want' (or, more accurately, socialism will make it possible for the first time in history for labour to assume this rightful place).

This, then, is the perfectionist argument for abolishing private property in the means of production. What are we to make of it? Phrased as a choice between intrinsically satisfying and intrinsically unsatisfying work, most people will favour creative and co-operative work. The evidence is overwhelming that most workers in capitalism wish that their jobs were more satisfying. The 'degradation of labour' which capitalism has imposed on so many people is abhorrent, an unconscionable restriction on their ability to develop their human potential (Schwartz (1982), pp.636–8; Doppelt (1981)) Liberals try to deal with this by distinguishing legitimate and illegitimate ways that people can come to be employed by others. But on the Marxist view, any wage-relationship is alienating, since the worker gives up control over her labour-power, and over the products of her labour. Wage-labour may not be exploitative, if both parties started with an equal share of resources, but it is alienating, and we can eliminate the alienation by socializing productive resources rather than equalizing private property.

However, while unalienated labour is surely better than alienated labour, these are not the only values involved. I may value unalienated labour, yet value other things more, such as my leisure. I may prefer playing tennis to unalienated production. I must engage in some productive work to secure the resources necessary for my tennis, and all else being equal, I would prefer it to be unalienated work. But all else is not always equal. The most efficient way to produce goods may leave little room for creativity or co-operation (e.g. assembly-line production). If so, then engaging in non-alienated work may require a greater investment in time than I am willing to make. For example, if I can acquire the resources I need by doing either two hours a day of alienated work or four hours a day of unalienated work, the extra two hours of tennis may outweighs the two hours of alienation. The question, then, is not whether I prefer unalienated labour to alienated labour, but whether I prefer leisure so much that I would accept alienated labour in order to acquire it. Opportunities for unalienated work 'are not so much manna from the sky. Resources must be used to make these opportunities available, which means lesser availability of some other goods', like leisure (Arneson (1987), p.544, n. 38).[4]

Consumption is another good that may conflict with non-alienated production. Some people enjoy consuming a wide variety of goods and services, from food to opera to computers. Agreeing to perform alienated labour in return for higher wages may enable them to expand their range of desired consumption. If we prohibit alienated labour, we eliminate their alienation, but we also make it more difficult for them to pursue forms of consumption they truly value. Marxist perfectionists tend not to be concerned with possible decreases in material consumption. The consider people's concern with consumption as a symptom of the pathology of materialism created by capitalism, so that the transition to socialism 'will involve a large shift in cultural emphasis from consumption to production as the primary sphere of human fulfilment' (Arneson (1987), pp.525, 528). But is it pathological to be concerned with expanding one's consumption? The 'keeping up with the Joneses' syndrome may be, for the pursuit of such status goods is often irrational. But that is not true of many desires for increased consumption. There is nothing pathological abut a music-lover wanting expensive stereo equipment, and being willing to perform alienated labour to acquire it. Hence there is no reason for communism to 'exclude or stigmatize those who prefer the passive pleasures of consumption' over the active pleasures of production (Elster (1985), p.522).

The pursuit of unalienated labour can also conflict with relationships with family and friends. I may want a part-time job that allows me as much time as possible with my children, or perhaps seasonal work, so that I can spend part of each year with friends or relatives. As Elster notes, the Marxist emphasis on self-relationships, for there is a 'tendency for self-realization to expand into all available time... [and this] is a threat both to consumption and to friendship' (Elster (1986), p.101).

The issue is not whether unalienated labour is a good, but whether it is an overriding good, a good which is necessary to any decent life, and which outweighs in value all competing goods. There is no reason whatsoever to think unalienated labour is such a good. Marx's own argument for this claim reveals how implausible it is. He argued that freely co-operative production is our distinctive human excellence because this is what differentiates us from other species – it is what defines us as humans. But this 'differentia' argument[5] is a *non sequitur*. Asking what is best in a human life is not a question 'about biological classification. It is a question in moral philosophy. And we do not help ourselves at all in answering it if we decide in advance that the answer ought to be a single, simple characteristic, unshared by other species, such as the differentia is meant to be' (Midgley (1978), p.204). Exaltation of co-operative productive activity 'is a particular moral position and must be defended as such against others; it cannot ride into acceptance on the back of a crude method of taxonomy' (Midgley (1978), p.204). Whether or not other animals have the same capacity for productive labour as humans has no bearing on the question of the value of that capacity in our lives. There is no reason to think that our most important capacities are those that are most different from other animals.

This focus on productive labour is also sexist. Consider Marx's claim that because workers are alienated from their 'species-life' (i.e. 'labour, life activity, productive life itself') therefore 'man (the worker) only feels himself freely active in his animal functions – eating, drinking, procreating, or at most in his swellings and in dressing-up, etc.; and in his human functions he no longer feels himself to be anything but an animal' (Marx (1977), p.66). But why is production a more 'human function' than reproduction (e.g. raising children)? It may be less distinctively human, in the sense that other animals also reproduce. But this just shows how irrelevant the criterion is, for family life is surely as important to our humanity as production. Marx combined a profound sensitivity to historical variations in the predominantly male sphere of productive life with an almost total insensitivity to historical variations in the predominantly female sphere of reproductive life, which he viewed as essentially natural, not distinctively human (Jaggar (1983), ch. 4; O'Brien (1981), pp.168–84). Any theory which hopes to incorporate the experience of women will have to question the elevation of productive labour.

There are many values that may compete with unalienated production, such as 'bodily and mental health, the development of cognitive facilities, of certain character traits and emotional responses, play, sex, friendship, love, art, religion' (Brown (1986), p.126; cf. Cohen (1988), pp.137–46). Some people will view productive labour as 'life's prime want', but others will not. A prohibition on alienated labour, therefore, would unfairly privilege some people over others. As Arneson puts it, the identification of socialism with a particular vision of the good life 'elevates one particular category of good, intrinsic job satisfaction, and arbitrarily privileges that good and those people who favour it over other equally desirable goods and equally wise fans of those other goods' (Arneson (1987), p.525). Given that people differ in the value they attach to labour, 'differential alienation of labour, from an initial position of equal opportunity and fair division of assets, can vastly increase the welfare and life quality of people'. Hence 'a perfectionist defence of nonalienation seems remote' (Roemer (1985), p.52).

Not all Marxists who emphasize the flourishing of unalienated production under communism are perfectionists. Some Marxists who proclaim the end of alienation are simply making a prediction about what people will do with their equal resources, not giving a perfectionist instruction about how to distribute those resources. They predict that people will value unalienated labour so highly that they will never accept improved leisure or family life as compensation for alienation. Should this prediction turn out to be false, however, there would be no reason to interfere with people's choices by prohibiting alienation. It is unclear whether Marx's comments on alienation are predictions or perfectionist instructions (Arneson (1987), p.521). Engels, however, was anti-perfectionist, at least in the case of sexual relations. When discussing the nature of sexual relations in communism, he says that the old patriarchal relations will end, but

> What will there be new? That will be answered when a new generation has grown up: a generation of men who never in their lives have known what it is to buy a woman's surrender with money or any other social instrument of power; a generation of women who have never known what it is to give themselves to a man from any other considerations than real love or to refuse to give themselves to their lover from fear of the economic consequences. When these people are in the world, they will care precious little what anybody today thinks they ought to do; they will make their own practice and their corresponding public opinion about the practice of each individual – and that will be the end of it. (Engels (1972 edn), p.145)

The equal distribution of resources ensures that exploitative relations will not arise, but there is no correct socialist model of personal relations which is to be encouraged or imposed. But why should not economic relations likewise be left to the free choices of people from a position of material equality? We should wait and see what that 'new generation' will choose to do with their lives and talents, and while they may systematically favour unalienated labour, there is no reason for perfectionist intervention to encourage that result.

Again, none of this will justify the existing distribution of meaningful work. I have argued that people should be free to sacrifice the quality of work life for other values, like better leisure. Under capitalism, however, those with the best jobs also have the best consumption and leisure, while those with poor jobs get no compensating increase in leisure or consumption. But the solution is not to give everyone the best possible work, at the expense of improved leisure, since some people would rather have better leisure. As Arneson puts it, 'The core socialist objection to a capitalist market is that people who have fewer resources than others through no fault of their own do not have a fair chance to satisfy their preferences. The solution to this problem is not to privilege anybody's preferences [e.g. those for work over leisure], but to tinker with the distribution of resources that individuals bring to market trading'... (Arneson (1987), pp.537, 533).

This returns us to the 'Kantian' strand of Marxist thought, which leaves individuals free to decide for themselves what is worth doing with their fair share of resources. And, we have see, this leads to a series of questions about fair distribution which Marxists simply have not addressed. Until they do, it is difficult to tell whether Marxism provides a distinctive account of justice from those of other political traditions.

References

Arneson, R. (1987) 'Meaningful Work and Market Socialism', *Ethics*, 97, 3, pp.517–45.

Brown, A. (1986) *Modern Political Philosophy: Theories of the Just Society*, Penguin.

Campbell, T. (1983) *The Left and Rights: A Conceptual Analysis of the Idea of Socialist Rights*, Routledge & Kegan Paul.

Cohen, G.A. (1988) *History, Labour, and Freedom: Themes from Marx*, Oxford University Press.

Doppelt, G. (1981) 'Rawls' System of Justice: A Critique from the Left', *Nous*, 15, 3, pp.259–307.

Elster, J. (1985) *Making Sense of Marx*, Cambridge University Press.

Elster, J. (1986) 'Self-Realization in Work and Politics: The Marxist Conception of the Good Life', *Social Philosophy and Policy*, 3, 2, pp.97–126.

Engels, F. (1972 edn) *The Origin of the Family, Private Property, and the State*, International Publishers.

Jaggar, A. (1983) *Feminist Politics and Human Nature*, Rowman and Allanheld.

Lukes, S. (1985) *Marxism and Morality*, Oxford University Press.

Marx, K. (1977 edn) *Economic and Philosophic Manuscripts of 1844*, Lawrence and Wishart.

Midgeley, M. (1978) *Beast and Man: The Roots of Human Nature*, New American Library.

Miller, D. (1989) 'In What Sense must Socialism be Communitarian?', *Social Philosophy and Policy*, 6, 2, pp.51–73.

O'Brien, M. (1981) *The Politics of Reproduction*, Routledge & Keagan Paul.

Roemer, J. (1985) 'Should Marxists be Interested in Exploitation', *Philosophy and Public Affairs*, 14, 1, pp.30–65.

Schwartz, A. (1982) 'Meaningful Work', *Ethics*, 92, 4, pp.634–46.

Notes

From Kymlicka, Will (1990) *Contemporary Political Philosophy: An Introduction*, Oxford University Press, pp.186–92.

[1] [The great philosopher, Immanuel Kant (1724–1804), claimed that it is morally wrong to treat other people merely as the means to an end, rather than as ends in themselves. To this extent, Marx's view that capitalists merely use workers as a means to making money is a Kantian criticism. (This is not the criticism that Kymlicka develops here.)]

[2] Luke also distinguishes a 'utilitarian' strand in Marx's thought, but I will leave this aside, partly because we have already examined utilitarianism, and partly because this strand of Marx's thought has had less influence on contemporary Marxists than the Kantian and perfectionists strands. Moreover, I doubt there was a utilitarian strand in Marx's thought. He rejected the idea that a person can be harmed just because that would increase the overall good (Murphy (1973), pp.217–20; but cf. Allen (1973), Brenkert (1981)).

[3] [*Needs principle*: in a late work, *Critique of the Gotha Programme* (1891), Marx claimed that people should use their abilities to create benefits and that these should then be allocated on the basis of need: 'From each according to his abilities, to each according to his needs!' (Marx (1891), p.321).]

[4] Marx himself once claimed that 'the realm of freedom really begins only where labour determined by necessity and external expediency ends; it lies by its very nature beyond the sphere of material production' (Marx (1981), pp.958–9). This is not his usual view of the matter, nor is it shared by most contemporary Marxists (e.g. Cohen (1978), pp.323–5), but it is surely true that the 'development of human powers as an end in itself' can occur outside production, and that 'nothing in the nature of things prevents the sphere of leisure from becoming the main arena for the free many-sided self-development of the individual that Marx prized' (Arneson (1987), p.526).

[5] [*Differentia argument*: this is an argument to the effect that, in Kymlicka's terms, 'cooperative production is our distinctive human excellence because this is what differentiates us from other species'. This, as Kymlicka claims, is unconvincing. If it were the case that what differentiates us from all other species is that we have nostril hair, this would not make nostril hair a distinctive human excellence (Marx (1844), pp.58–68).]

CHAPTER 6

John Stuart Mill: *On Liberty* and *The Subjection of Women*

Nigel Warburton

By the end of this part of this chapter you should:

- Have read Mill's *On Liberty* and *The Subjection of Women* at least twice.
- Have a good critical understanding of Mill's position on the Harm Principle and its applications.
- Have a good critical understanding of Mill's position in *The Subjection of Women*.
- Appreciate *On Liberty*'s relation to *The Subjection of Women*.
- Appreciate some relevant features of the original historical context in which these books were written.
- Appreciate the continuing relevance to political philosophy of some of the central issues in these two works and understand their relationship to the ideas of the other thinkers in this book.

Introduction

Liberty and equality are two of the most emotive concepts in political philosophy. The two books studied in this chapter have these concepts at their heart. *On Liberty* presents a powerful defence of liberty in a wide range of contexts; *The Subjection of Women* is a polemic defending greater sexual equality before the law, but includes a discussion of more general issues of equality between the sexes. Mill wrote *On Liberty* in the 1850s – or rather he co-wrote it, since his wife Harriet Taylor had a large part to play in its final form. The book first appeared in 1859, the same year as Darwin's *The Origin of Species*. It presents a vision of humanity transcending our lower appetites to realize our full potential. Social pressures in Victorian Britain were cramping the lives of many of Mill's contemporaries; his aim was to show how greater individual liberty would benefit everyone, not just those who took direct advantage of it. English law in 1869 when *The Subjection of Women* was first published gave women very few rights: they could not own property, nor did they have full legal protection from physical or sexual abuse by their husbands. Mill's first aim in that work was to reform unjust laws; however, much of his argument has continuing significance beyond its original context.

Many present-day discussions of liberty and of sexual equality take Mill's *On Liberty* and *The Subjection of Women* as starting points. Both books repay close study.

On Liberty already has the status of a classic in political philosophy, and *The Subjection of Women* is quickly acquiring this status. Susan Moller Okin, for instance, has described the latter as 'one of John Stuart Mill's finest pieces of argument' (Mill (1988 edn), p.v). Since Mill was one of the greatest thinkers of the nineteenth century, this is high praise. Taken together *On Liberty* and *The Subjection of Women* form a passionate yet reasoned defence of human progress through increased freedom and equality.

This chapter falls into two parts: in the first I shall consider *On Liberty*, and in the second *The Subjection of Women*.

Reading *On Liberty*

In his autobiography Mill described *On Liberty* as 'a kind of philosophic text-book of a single truth' and went on to explain what that truth was:

> the importance, to man and society, of a large variety in types of character, and of giving full freedom to human nature to expand itself in innumerable and conflicting directions.

(Mill (1989 edn), p.189)

Clear enough, you might think. The fact that he describes it as a 'kind of philosophic text-book' suggests a didactic approach; the fact that there is one basic message, the 'single truth', suggests that the book should be relatively easy to understand. And in its broadest outlines *On Liberty* is quite easy to follow. It is a powerful plea for preserving individual liberty from the encroachments of the state and from the homogenizing effects of majority opinion; a prophylactic against the pressures to social conformity of Victorian Britain and a celebration of toleration, eccentricity and diversity. As such it is the key text in the tradition of liberal thought.

However, despite its canonical status at the heart of this tradition, *On Liberty* is not as clear as this makes it seem. The precise interpretation of some of its central themes is contentious: a huge secondary literature has grown up around questions such as 'What did Mill really mean by "harm"?' and 'Are his views on liberty compatible with his professed utilitarianism?' This presents an immediate difficulty. There is a tension between what Mill says he is doing and the content of what he has actually written, a feature of the work that most commentators have noted and many have tried to resolve – this is, for example, the basis of Isaiah Berlin's approach in 'John Stuart Mill and the Ends of Life' (Reading 6.2). If you read *On Liberty* critically you will no doubt discover apparent and perhaps real inconsistencies in his position; you may also be puzzled by his sketchy account of such key issues as 'What is harm?'. When you attempt to apply his 'single truth' to present-day situations, any confidence you had about what Mill really means may dissolve. Even if the principle were simple, the application of it to particular cases is rarely clear cut. Such difficulties arise in part because the book was meant for a wide readership and consequently avoids the more detailed technical analyses which would be appropriate for a philosophical treatise rather than a 'text-book of a single truth'. His aim was not to pre-empt every possible criticism of his position, but rather to sketch it in broad strokes. It is hardly surprising, then, that the book generates at least as many questions as it answers.

The main difficulty you are likely to encounter reading any of Mill's work for the first time is not, however, of a directly philosophical kind. His sentences are often long and complex in syntax, and this can sometimes obscure their meaning. For this reason it is certainly worth skimming ahead to get an overview of each chapter before returning to the detail. This process is made easier by the fact that Mill's organization of his thought is, for the most part, exemplary. For instance, in chapter II of *On Liberty* he not only devotes a passage to each of the four arguments he gives in favour of freedom of thought and expression, but also provides a summary of them (Mill (1974 edn), pp.115–18). He uses paragraphs as units of thought; so when reading his work to get an overview it can help if you identify the main point of each paragraph rather than read for detail at a first sitting.

ACTIVITY

Read 'The Writing of *On Liberty*' below. This is an extract from Mill's autobiography in which he indicates the contribution of his wife, Harriet Taylor.

The Writing of *On Liberty*

The *Liberty* was more directly and literally our joint production than anything else which bears my name, for there was not a sentence of it that was not several times gone through by us together, turned over in many ways, and carefully weeded of any faults, either in thought or expression, that we detected in it. It is in consequence of this that, although it never underwent her final revision, it far surpasses, as a mere specimen of composition, anything which has proceeded from me either before or since. With regard to the thoughts, it is difficult to identify any particular part or element as being more hers than all the rest. The whole mode of thinking of which the book was the expression, was emphatically hers. But I also was so thoroughly imbued with it that the same thoughts naturally occurred to us both. That I was thus penetrated with it, however, I owe in a great degree to her. There was a moment in my mental progress when I might easily have fallen into a tendency towards over-government, both social and political; as there was also a moment when, by reaction from a contrary excess, I might have become a less thorough radical and democrat than I am. In both these points as in many others, she benefitted me as much by keeping me right where I was right, as by leading me to new truths and ridding me of errors. My great readiness and eagerness to learn from everybody, and to make room in my opinions for every new acquisition by adjusting the old and the new to one another, might, but for her steadying influence, have seduced me into modifying my early opinions too much. She was in nothing more valuable to my mental development than by her just measure of the relative importance of different considerations, which often protected me from allowing to truths I had only recently learnt to see, a more important place in my thoughts than was properly their due.

The *Liberty* is likely to survive longer than anything else that I have written (with the possible exception of the *Logic*), because the conjunction of her mind with mine has rendered it a kind of philosophic text-book of a single truth, which the changes progressively taking place in modern society tend to bring out into ever stronger relief: the importance, to man and society, of a large variety in types of character, and of giving full freedom to human nature to expand itself in innumerable and conflicting directions. Nothing can better shew how deep are the foundations of this truth, than the great impression made by the exposition of it at a time which, to superficial observation, did not seem to stand much in need of such a lesson. The fears we expressed, lest the inevitable growth of social equality and of the government of public opinion should impose on mankind an oppressive yoke of uniformity in opinion and practice, might easily have appeared chimerical to those who looked more at present facts than at tendencies; for the gradual revolution that is taking place in society and institutions has, thus far been decidedly favourable to the development of new opinions, and has procured for them a much more unprejudiced hearing than they previously met with. But this is a feature belonging to periods of transition, when old notions and feelings have been unsettled and no new doctrines have yet succeeded to their ascendancy. At such times people of any mental activity, having given up many of their old beliefs, and not feeling quite sure that those they still retain can stand unmodified, listen eagerly to new opinions. But this state of things is necessarily transitory: some particular body of doctrine in time rallies the majority round it, organizes social institutions and modes of action conformably to itself, education impresses this new creed upon the new generations without the mental processes that have led to it, and by degrees it acquires the very same power of compression, so long exercised by the creeds of which it has taken the place. Whether this noxious power will be exercised depends on whether mankind have by that time become aware that it cannot be exercised without stunting and dwarfing human nature. It is then that the teachings of the *Liberty* will have their greatest value. And it is to be feared that they will retain that value a long time.

(Mill (1989 edn), pp.188–90)

DISCUSSION

There are two relevant features of this piece. First, it sheds light on Harriet Taylor's contribution to Mill's writing. Mill married Taylor in 1851, almost two years after the death of her husband, but they had been close friends for nearly twenty years, sharing many intellectual interests. Taylor died suddenly in 1858 while they were working together on the text of *On Liberty*. Although Mill was responsible for the book's final form, this extract reveals the extent of her contribution. The second important feature of this extract is that it gives a succinct summary of the particular fears about modern society that provided the impetus for the writing of *On Liberty*. This provides a useful background against which to read *On Liberty* for the first time.

ACTIVITY

Read all of *On Liberty*, skimming difficult passages and concentrating on getting a clear overview rather than a detailed understanding of every sentence. The main point of the first reading of the book is to map out the central arguments that Mill uses, and to provide a framework within which you can fit the details of his position. You may find it helpful to make brief chapter summaries.

Utilitarianism

The straightforward reading of *On Liberty* which Mill invites us to accept presupposes that the reader is aware of the basic utilitarian position. Utilitarianism is the name given to a range of closely related consequentialist philosophical positions which have at their heart the view that the morally right action in any circumstance is the one likely to maximize happiness, a position sometimes known as the Utility or Greatest Happiness Principle. As Mill himself put it in Chapter 2 of his book *Utilitarianism*:

> The creed which accepts as the foundation of morals, Utility, or the Greatest Happiness Principle, holds that actions are right in proportion as they tend to promote happiness, wrong as they tend to produce the reverse of happiness. By happiness is intended pleasure, and the absence of pain; by unhappiness, pain, and the privation of pleasure.

(Mill (1991 edn), p.137)

One of the clearest and simplest varieties of utilitarianism was formulated by Mill's mentor, Jeremy Bentham (1748–1832). Bentham's hedonistic position was that happiness is simply pleasure and the absence of pain: the experience of blissful mental states. The aim of morality was solely to maximize such states in order to produce the greatest aggregate happiness. Bentham did not discriminate between individuals experiencing happiness: in his calculation each was to count for one. Even animals' pains and pleasures could be included in the calculation. Nor was it relevant how happiness was achieved: for him, famously, the child's game of pushpin was of equal moral worth to poetry provided that they generated equal amounts of pleasure. He produced an elaborate system for analysing and comparing pleasures, a 'felicific calculus' as he called it, based on their duration, intensity, tendency to produce further pleasures, and so on.

Mill reacted against this position, modifying Bentham's utilitarianism to take into account the quality as well as the quantity of pleasure produced. Although still a utilitarian, Mill gave an account of happiness which was focused less on maximizing blissful psychological states and more on the development of human potential, self-realization and flourishing. He was influenced as much by Aristotle's concept of *eudaimonia* and Coleridge's conception of humanity as by Bentham's quasi-scientific calculations of happiness. Mill published his modified version of the theory in his book-length treatment *Utilitarianism*, which first appeared in *Frazer's Magazine* in 1861. However, the book was probably drafted at roughly the time he was working on *On Liberty* (1854 to 1856) and the two can plausibly be read as complementary.

In a famous passage in *Utilitarianism*, Mill set out the case for preferring sophisticated unhappiness to the merely animal satisfactions of a simpler existence. As he put it, it is better to be a dissatisfied human being than a satisfied pig. Mill's main reason for believing this is that those who have had the opportunity to experience both sensual animal pleasures (of the kind that satisfy a pig) and the higher grade of existence, choose the second type, even if this means that their desires aren't always satisfied. Mill's utilitarianism presupposed different qualities of happiness: higher and lower pleasures. In other words for him pushpin was not the equal of poetry, since the latter had the capacity to engage the higher pleasures even if not at the intensity with which the lower pleasures, such as sex and eating, could be indulged.

For Mill, then, 'utility' was not simply aggregate pleasure, but took into account the *quality* as well as the *quantity* of the pleasure involved. When, in the introduction to *On Liberty* he asserts his commitment to utilitarianism (Mill (1974 edn), chap.I, p.70), he states 'I regard utility as the ultimate appeal on all ethical questions', he qualifies this by adding 'but it must be utility in the largest sense, grounded on the permanent interests of man as a progressive being'. This addition stresses the difference from the simpler Benthamite approach: for Mill, the 'largest sense' of utility incorporated the notion that some sorts of pleasure were more meaningful than others, and that the point of increased liberty was not just to maximize animal satisfaction, but rather to permit individuals to flourish as human beings. In *On Liberty* he uses the image of the development of a tree to convey his sense of human development, stressing the requirement of freedom for flourishing and the stunting effects of restriction:

> Human nature is not a machine to be built after a model, and set to do exactly the work prescribed for it, but a tree, which requires to grow and develop itself on all sides, according to the tendency of the inward forces which make it a living thing.

> (Ibid., chap.III, p.123)

Mill's main concern, however, in the passage of *On Liberty* about 'the interests of man as a progressive being' was to distance himself from any appeal to natural rights as the basis for his liberal principles. Bentham had famously dismissed talk of natural rights as 'nonsense on stilts', and Mill was similarly unimpressed by the suggestion that the justification of his plea for preserving individual liberty was tantamount to saying that we have a natural right to liberty. The only sense in which Mill argues for a right to liberty is the indirect utilitarian one: the general principle of defending liberty is one which ultimately maximizes happiness.

Most interpreters of Mill have taken his assertion that his arguments for freedom are grounded on utility at face value. However, at least one commentator, Gertrude Himmelfarb, has simply rejected this account of the link between Mill's utilitarianism and his liberalism:

> Whatever Mill's intentions elsewhere – in his book on *Utilitarianism*, for example – it was not his intention here, in *On Liberty*, to rest his case on utilitarian principles. He occasionally, very occasionally, used the word 'utility', more often 'interests'; but he also used such non-utilitarian words as 'rights' and 'development'. In any event, his primary concern was to establish liberty, not utility, as the sole principle governing the relations of the individual and society.

> (Introduction, Mill (1974 edn), p.30)

Himmelfarb's interpretation here is implausible. Certainly Mill did not ground *On Liberty* on Benthamite utilitarianism; but as we have seen, in *On Liberty* he is explicit that utility in the wider sense was 'the ultimate appeal on all ethical questions'. The fact that he used 'non-utilitarian words' such as 'rights' and 'development' is completely consistent with his utilitarianism: rights for a utilitarian are general principles which are ultimately grounded on utility; development is an ingredient in the flourishing life which maximizes individual happiness of the qualitatively superior kind that Mill was so keen to defend.

Himmelfarb uses a further argument to defend her controversial interpretation of Mill as intentionally abandoning utilitarianism in *On Liberty*. She picks out a sentence in which Mill states that an individual can't be compelled to do or refrain from doing something 'because it will make him happier' (ibid., chap.I, p.68) and takes this as evidence that Mill's larger concerns were not with utility. However, it does not follow from this that Mill had abandoned his utilitarianism: a more plausible interpretation would take into account the fact that individuals typically have more knowledge of what will make them happy than do third parties, and those who might claim to be acting for the individual's greater happiness might just as likely be stifling him or her. Furthermore, a utilitarian could consistently argue that preserving individual liberty in general would maximize overall happiness even if in some particular cases overriding the principle of liberty might have produced short-term benefits. In other words it might be better to have a strictly-adhered-to principle of individual liberty than to make calculations of happiness in particular instances. This is not to gloss over potential difficulties that exist in interpreting Mill's position as utilitarian. It may be that despite his intentions to produce a theory consistent with utilitarianism and underpinned by it, Mill's project ultimately fails. Nevertheless, to deny that his *intentions* were utilitarian in this work is to ignore his explicit indications to the contrary and the plausible interpretation of the grounding of *On Liberty* that these expressed intentions suggest.

ACTIVITY

Re-read *On Liberty*, Chapter I, 'Introductory'. Write brief answers to the questions below. Then compare your answers with my discussion. (My discussions in some cases go beyond what can be directly gleaned from the text and take into account criticisms that have been made of Mill.)

1   What is Mill's 'one very simple principle'?

2   Does Mill allow that an adult individual can be coerced into doing something for his or her own good?

3   Does Mill's principle apply to absolutely every human being? If not, who is excluded from it and why?

4   Is Mill simply concerned with laws which intrude within the area within which he believes the individual should be sovereign?

DISCUSSION

1   Mill's 'one very simple principle', the Harm Principle, or Liberty Principle as it is sometimes known, is that intervention to curtail the freedom of responsible adults in a civilized society can only be justified when there is a serious risk of their harming others. As Mill puts it:

the only purpose for which power can be rightfully exercised over any member of a civilized community, against his will, is to prevent harm to others.

(Ibid., chap.I, p.68)

Mill's assumption here is that actions can more or less be grouped into two classes: those which potentially harm others and those which are purely self-regarding and so should not be the concern of the state or society. Some critics have questioned the existence of truly self-regarding actions, since almost anything an individual does could in principle impinge on the lives of others. As James Fitzjames Stephen, Mill's most brilliant contemporary critic, remarked of the Harm Principle:

It assumes that some acts regard the agent only, and that some regard other people. In fact, by far the most important part of our conduct regards both ourselves and others.

(Stephen (1967 edn), p.66)

Throughout *On Liberty* Mill gives a range of formulations of his Harm Principle, not always using the word 'harm': sometimes he uses phrases such as 'cause evil', 'injure' or refers to acts which may be 'prejudicial to the interests of others'. A number of philosophers have expended a great deal of ink on attempting to reconcile subtleties of interpretation of the various terms Mill uses. When studying the text for the first time, however, it is worth steering clear of these complexities of interpretation and to treat Mill's use of 'harm' and related terms as being put forward in a straightforward non-technical way.

2   Mill is explicit that paternalism, coercion for the good of the individual coerced, is never a sufficient condition for interfering with an adult's free choices, just so long as these choices do not result in harm to others:

He cannot rightfully be compelled to do or forebear because it will be better for him to do so, because it will make him happier, because, in the opinion of others, to do would be wise or even right.

(Mill (1974 edn), chap.I, p.68)

In such circumstances Mill concedes that there will be good reasons for remonstrating with the individual, for trying to persuade him or her not to take a particular course of action; however, this must stop short of compulsion. Coercion for the good of the individual concerned is never justifiable in Mill's view. This is a theme taken up and criticized in Gerald Dworkin's article 'Paternalism' (Reading 6.3).

3   Mill sets limits to the individuals covered by his principle. It is only to apply to human beings 'in the maturity of their faculties' (ibid., p.69): paternalism is justifiable towards those who have not yet reached an age at which they can be considered autonomous individuals. Presumably he would classify some people with learning disabilities or severe psychiatric problems as failing to have 'the maturity of their faculties', though he does not here make this explicit. More controversially for readers today, though, he does exclude adults from cultures which in his view were more primitive than his own: 'we may leave out of consideration those backward states of society in which the race itself may be considered in its nonage' (ibid.)

Expressing the sort of sentiment which established and maintained the British Empire, he added: 'Despotism is a legitimate mode of government in dealing with barbarians, provided the end be their improvement and the means justified by actually effecting that end' (ibid.). This wasn't simply blind prejudice: his point was that in some societies free and equal discussion of a kind that could lead to the improvement of humanity would not be possible. Once such discussion was achievable, then the Harm Principle could appropriately be invoked.

4   Mill is certainly concerned to prevent the intrusion of laws into areas of private morality. But his arguments in *On Liberty* do not stop there. He is not exclusively concerned with philosophical issues about the law. He saw a great threat to individual development as stemming from what, following Alexis de Tocqueville, he labelled 'the tyranny of the majority'. Majority opinion acting through social disapproval, exclusion and pressure to conform could, Mill argues, curb individual development to the detriment of all:

> Society can and does execute its own mandates; and if it issues wrong mandates instead of right, or any mandates at all in things with which it ought not to meddle, it practises a social tyranny more formidable than many kinds of political oppression, since, though not usually upheld by such extreme penalties, it leaves fewer means of escape, penetrating much more deeply into the details of life, and enslaving the soul itself.

(Ibid., chap.I, p.63)

ACTIVITY

Re-read *On Liberty*, Chapter II 'Of the Liberty of Thought and Discussion' and the first paragraph of Chapter III 'Of Individuality, as One of the Elements of Well-Being', and answer the following questions.

I   What are the four main arguments that Mill gives in this chapter for permitting freedom of thought and discussion?

2   In the first paragraph of Chapter III, Mill gives the example of an opinion about corn dealers delivered to an angry mob. This makes an important point about the limits of free expression – the theme of Chapter II. What is that point?

DISCUSSION

I   Mill's four main arguments in favour of freedom of thought and discussion are as follows (I have given them headings for ease of reference).

The Infallibility Argument: those who silence others assume their own infallibility. History reveals numerous instances of people who felt certain that the views they were silencing were false when in fact they were true.

The Dead Dogma Argument: if views are not challenged they will be held as dead dogmas and not living truths.

The Partly True Argument: received opinion rarely amounts to the whole truth on any topic. Even views which taken as a whole are false may contain important true elements which might otherwise be lost.

The Link With Action Argument: views which are unchallenged lose their power to stir people into action.

The underlying assumption of this chapter must be that tolerating freedom of speech will maximize happiness: otherwise the chapter would contradict the utilitarian principle endorsed in the introductory chapter. However, Mill's arguments are all expressed in terms of maximizing truth and keeping it alive and capable of functioning as a stimulus to action. The implicit assumption, then, is that this process will result in greater happiness, or, to put it in terms closer to Mill's than to Bentham's: an increase in humanity's potential for flourishing.

2   The example Mill uses is of the view that corn dealers are starvers of the poor being circulated through the press as contrasted with the same view being delivered in a speech to an angry mob assembled in the front of the house of a corn dealer. Mill, applying the principles of the previous chapter, thinks that freedom of speech should extend to expressing such a view in print. However, someone who expressed this view in a speech to an angry mob could justifiably be punished and presumably forcibly silenced. The point of this example is to illustrate the principle that the limits of free speech are set by the circumstances in which views are expressed: if the context turns the expression of the view into 'a positive instigation to some mischievous act', then Mill believes, it should not be tolerated. He does not consider the view itself a harm to the corn dealer: however, since in the context it is likely to lead directly to harm, the Harm Principle justifies intervention.

ACTIVITY

Read John Gray's 'Freedom of Expression' (Reading 6.1). Gray gives a broadly sympathetic reading of Mill's position, stressing the value of autonomous thought. Then re-read *On Liberty*, Chapter III 'Of Individuality, as One of the Elements of Well-Being' and answer the following questions.

1   On what grounds does Mill advocate the toleration of experiments of living?

2   Why do we need geniuses, according to Mill? Under what conditions will they flourish?

DISCUSSION

1   Mill argues for the toleration of diverse ways of living up to the point where the individual makes himself or herself a 'nuisance to other people' (ibid., chap.III, p.119). He maintains that it is 'useful' that there should be different experiments in how to live and that, where the traditions and customs of other people entirely determine how individuals are to live, one of the principal ingredients in human happiness will be lacking. Accepting established custom as the guide on how to live only requires an ape-like ability to imitate: Mill believes passionately that in conditions in which humans are given freedom to choose how they will live their happiness will be maximized. Indeed, the effect of individual freedom over how to live is beneficial to others in that society as well as to the individual:

> In proportion to the development of his individuality, each person
> becomes more valuable to himself, and is, therefore, capable of being more
> valuable to others. There is a greater fullness of life about his own
> existence, and when there is more life in the units there is more in the
> mass which is composed of them.

(Ibid., chap.III, pp.127–8)

Furthermore, human diversity is such that imposing a narrow range of
choices of lifestyle on all members of a society will inevitably crush and
constrain many of them. In the same vein he argues that conditions of
freedom are the conditions needed for geniuses to flourish.

2   Mill maintains that without geniuses human life would become a stagnant
     pool. Geniuses both bring new things to humanity and inject life into what is
     already there. Although always a minority in any society, they are catalysts
     for the happiness of others. According to Mill geniuses require an
     atmosphere of freedom in which to flourish. This is because they are by
     their nature different from most people, and will not fit easily into the
     patterns of life handed down to them by custom.

James Fitzjames Stephen raised several telling objections to Mill's
assertions about the conditions in which geniuses flourish. One of his
more serious challenges to Mill was his point that far from stimulating
genius, comfortable conditions of freedom could be extremely
detrimental to character and development:

> The great defect of Mr Mill's later writings seems to me to be that he has
> formed too favourable an estimate of human nature. This displays itself in
> the chapter ['Of Individuality, as One of the Elements of Well-Being'] by
> the tacit assumption which pervades every part of it that the removal of
> restraints usually tends to invigorate character. Surely the very opposite of
> this is the truth. Habitual exertion is the greatest of all invigorators of
> characters, and restraint and coercion in one form or another is the great
> stimulus to exertion. If you wish to destroy originality and vigour of
> character, no way to do so is so sure as to put a high level of comfort easily
> within the reach of moderate and commonplace exertion. A life made up
> of danger, vicissitude, and exposure is the sort of life which produces
> originality and resource.

(Stephen (1967 edn), p.81)

ACTIVITY

Re-read *On Liberty*, Chapter IV 'Of the Limits to the Authority of Society over
the Individual' and answer the following questions.

1   Does it follow from Mill's approach that we should have no interest in one
     another's conduct?

2   What point is Mill making with his example of the intemperate family man?

3   What is the point of Mill's discussion of the Mohammedan's attitude to
     pork eating?

DISCUSSION

1   Mill is explicit that it would be 'a great misunderstanding' of his doctrine to suppose that we shouldn't be interested in one another's lives unless our own well being is at stake. His position is not that we shouldn't try to persuade each other to do what is best, only that the evil of forcing someone to do something for his or her own good far outweighs any benefit that might result from such coercion. He maintains that we should be spurring each other on, helping each other develop and flourish:

> Human beings owe to each other help to distinguish the better from the worse, and encouragement to choose the former and avoid the latter. They should be forever stimulating each other to increased exercise of their higher faculties and increased direction of their feelings and aims towards wise instead of foolish, elevating instead of degrading, objects and contemplations.

(Ibid., chap.IV, p.142)

Mill was well aware that his Harm Principle, with its emphasis on protecting self-regarding actions from interference, might be interpreted as an inducement to selfish concern with one's own affairs and took care to show that it was consistent with an interest and active involvement in other people's self development.

2   The hypothetical case of an intemperate man who becomes unable to pay his debts and fulfil his responsibilities to his family serves to make Mill's point that the apparently self-regarding actions of those with 'a distinct and assignable obligation to any other person or persons' (ibid., chap.IV, p.148) can harm the interests of those to whom they have an obligation. As such the intemperate man may justifiably be punished for the breach of his duty to his family, but not for his intemperance *per se*. The implication is that if the man did not have any obligations to his family, the Harm Principle would not provide any reason for curbing his excesses.

3   Mill states that nothing that Christians believe or do makes Mohammedans hate them more than the fact that they eat pork. Mohammedans find the practice deeply offensive. Mill considers whether it would be 'a legitimate exercise of the moral authority of public opinion' to ban the consumption of pork in a predominantly Mohammedan country. His point seems to be that pork eating is a self-regarding action, and thus not the concern of the state or of other groups (in this he clearly ignores the pig's interests).

ACTIVITY

Re-read *On Liberty*, Chapter V 'Applications' and answer the following questions.

1   For Mill, is risk of harm to others a sufficient condition for intervention?

2   What are Mill's views on the acceptability of preventing foreseeable crimes being committed?

3   Should individuals be free to sell themselves into slavery on Mill's view?

DISCUSSION

1   On first reading, Mill might seem to be saying that we ought to intervene *wherever* there is a risk of harm to others, this is not his position at all. He is only offering his Harm Principle as a *necessary* but not a *sufficient* condition for intervention as the following quotation makes explicit:

> it must by no means be supposed, because damage, or probability of damage, to the interests of others, can alone justify such interference of society, that therefore it always does justify such interference. In many cases an individual, in pursuing a legitimate object, necessarily and therefore legitimately causes pain or loss to others, or intercepts a good which they had a reasonable hope of obtaining.
>
> (Ibid., chap.V, p.163)

To back up this claim he uses the example of a competitive examination in which one candidate reaps rewards at the expense of another, who might be said to have his or her interests harmed. He argues that this is an acceptable and legitimate form of harm and not a ground for intervention unless some underhand method had been used to achieve the results (see ibid., chap.V, p.164). The unsuccessful candidate has, in the case of a fair competition, suffered harm to his or her interests, but it in no way follows from Mill's principles that this fact alone would justify intervention.

This clarification of the Harm Principle itself suggests a criticism of Mill's approach: even if we can make sense of his notion of harm, we are left with no clear guidelines for the application of the principle. We can identify cases in which others are harmed or the interests of others are harmed by actions of individuals, but will not be able to determine whether, although the necessary conditions for curtailing freedom have been met, we would be justified in curtailing freedom in particular cases. Identifying necessary conditions does not provide an adequate ground for discriminating between appropriate and inappropriate intervention; the application of the principle in cases where the necessary condition has been met remains unclear.

2   Although Mill believed that governments often infringe liberty while claiming to be preventing crimes, he did allow that a public authority, or for that matter an individual, could intervene to prevent a crime. If poisonous chemicals were only ever used to commit murder, then the state could justly prevent their sale; as it is, there are innocent uses of poisonous chemicals. Consequently Mill suggests precautions such as registering purchasers of poisonous substances.

In the case of a drunkard who has previously been convicted of violence while drunk, Mill allows that it would be appropriate to punish this person if he were found drunk again. Although drunkenness may in some forms be an example of the kind of purely self-regarding action that Mill believes should be immune from state or societal intervention, when there is a serious risk of a crime being committed because of drunkenness, he believes it appropriate to curb the drunkards' behaviour. This is consistent with his Harm Principle – as with the case of the protester making a speech on the steps of a corn dealer's house discussed above, the context of the action determines the justification for forcible intervention: 'The making himself drunk, in a person whom drunkenness excites to do harm in others, is a crime against the others' (ibid., chap.V, p.167).

3   Mill argues that any freedom to sell oneself into slavery would be self-defeating since by choosing to be a slave the person in question would be relinquishing future liberty, something which Mill elsewhere argues is an essential ingredient in a happy life. Consequently Mill believes that individuals should not be allowed to give up their basic liberty: 'The principle of freedom cannot require that he should be free not to be free. It is not freedom to be allowed to alienate his freedom' (ibid., chap.V, p.173).

Mill's discussion of slavery takes on a new aspect after reading *The Subjection of Women* where he refers to the conditions of married women as a type of slavery (Mill (1988 edn), pp.5–17).

Is On Liberty really compatible with utilitarianism?

In many places Mill seems to be arguing for an absolute and inviolable right to individual freedom. His expressed aim, however, as we have seen, is to provide an account which is compatible with utilitarianism and which has maximizing happiness at its foundation. The official story as far as Mill is concerned is that a right to liberty is a right that can be defended entirely in terms of utility. Some commentators, however, have seen non-utilitarian considerations at the core of the work. If restricting someone's liberty in a particular case will almost certainly lead to an increase in that person's happiness in the long run, then surely, a strict utilitarian should be prepared to bite the bullet and restrict that person's liberty. Many readers of *On Liberty* have been left with the suspicion that in his tenacious adherence to the Harm Principle Mill unintentionally comes closer to advocating an absolute right to personal freedom than his professed utilitarianism would consistently allow.

ACTIVITY

Read the extract from Isaiah Berlin's essay 'John Stuart Mill and the Ends of Life' (Reading 6.2). Berlin's approach to Mill is both critical and to some extent sympathetic. Try to identify Berlin's main criticisms of Mill; also pinpoint the virtues he sees in Mill's approach. Then re-read the final paragraph of Reading 6.2. Outline the main arguments Berlin uses in defence of the claim that it is not Mill's utilitarianism which lies at heart of his thought and feeling.

DISCUSSION

Berlin's arguments include:

1   Utilitarians aim to maximize happiness. Mill assumes that preserving personal freedom will in fact maximize happiness. Berlin points out that this assumption is not self-evident: it is possible that restricting freedom greatly could lead to greater happiness overall. In other words, he raises the possibility that Mill's empirical assumption about the relation of happiness to liberty is simply wrong.

2   Mill points out that if happiness is the sole criterion of the moral worth of an action then questions of how we should live – whether we should burn witches, or pursue truth – can only be resolved by 'actuarial calculation'. Yet Mill would have strongly opposed such an approach to life.

Berlin's conclusion is that Mill's belief that 'men are made human by their capacity for choice – choice of evil and good equally' is what is at the heart of this approach. Notice that this is very different from the position adopted by Himmelfarb who maintains that Mill did not *intend On Liberty* to be underpinned by utilitarian considerations, a contention which is easily refuted by close reading of the text (see pp.309–10 above).

Against paternalism

Throughout *On Liberty* Mill argues against paternalism towards adults. We each know best what will make our lives go well; and even if we don't, it is better to be free to make our own mistakes than to be coerced 'for our own good'. For Mill, the limits of individual freedom are governed by the Harm Principle, not by others' views of what is best for us. Mill's rhetoric is so persuasive that it is easy to ignore the counter-arguments which can be mustered in favour of a limited form of paternalism.

ACTIVITY

Read Gerald Dworkin's article 'Paternalism' (Reading 6.3). Dworkin gives a clear statement of Mill's position on paternalism. He goes on to argue that Mill is too stringent in his opposition to paternalism; there are, maintains Dworkin, some circumstances in which paternalism towards adults is justified. This Reading should reinforce your understanding of Mill's views on paternalism and provide a critical angle on his conclusions. It also demonstrates the continuing relevance of the arguments of *On Liberty*.

Mill and political philosophy

On Liberty presents a reasoned defence of the notion that adults should be free from interference in their lives up to the point where they risk harming others. As we've seen, many of Mill's assumptions, such as that this approach to life will maximize happiness, that there exist purely private actions, that paternalism towards adults should never occur, are open to challenge. For Machiavelli it would have been obvious that, at least from the Prince's point of view, setting limits on state interference in individuals' lives could jeopardize state security. The *virtuoso* Prince should certainly not leave individuals free from interference if interfering with their lives could serve the state. In contrast with Hobbes, Mill is concerned with the freedoms that need to be preserved in a civilized society. For Hobbes it is clear that the social contract will involve giving up many of the freedoms that we would have had in the state of nature; it is rational for us to give these up in exchange for the greater good of our personal security. Unlike Locke, Mill does not rest his liberalism on any religious beliefs about God-given rights; for Mill the ultimate justification for his defence of freedom is the, perhaps equally questionable, theory of utilitarianism. Rousseau, who defends a form of positive liberty (in Isaiah Berlin's sense), believed that true freedom (what he calls 'moral freedom') is attained not by following our desires but by relinquishing all our rights to the communal body and following the general will. Mill's account of freedom is principally in terms of negative freedom: freedom from interference.

Mill's position on freedom stands in stark contrast with that of his contemporary, Marx, though both were interested in organizing society so that 'man as a progressive being' might prosper. For Mill it is obvious that we should as adults be left free to pursue our particular desires, provided that we don't risk harming others in the process. For Marx, there was a prior question of how we came to have the desires we do have. These are a product of our circumstances and hence simply reflect the unfairness of our social and economic system. To be truly free, that whole system needs to be replaced with another in which there is no 'private realm' in which people can make decisions that cause others to be alienated from their true selves and means of self-expression. Giving wage-labourers freedom to pursue their own ends will not benefit humanity if they are alienated from their true selves and the means of self-realization. Giving the bourgeoisie freedom to pursue their own ends confirms them in their belief that other people are obstacles to freedom rather than encouraging the kind of cooperation among equals that Marx envisaged. It is only by eliminating the evils of capitalism that humanity will be truly free: the kind of freedom that Mill defends was, for Marx, an ideological illusion, behind which self-seeking individuals prosper at the expense of the workers.

On Liberty and The Subjection of Women

On Liberty, despite its apparently straightforward approach, gives rise to a range of interpretations. Its central themes of the rejection of paternalism and the wider considerations of individual freedom in the face of state and social pressure are at least as important in the early twenty-first century as in 1859 when the book was first published. *On Liberty* remains the starting point for many contemporary discussions of freedom, censorship and the role of the state. In contrast, *The Subjection of Women* seems at least at first reading much more tied to its age, and to the social situation which gave rise to it.

The Subjection of Women presents a powerful plea for greater equality before the law, which in turn would lead to greater freedom for women, particularly for married women. The benefits of greater freedom are utilitarian benefits: increasing liberty in various respects tends to maximize happiness, for the sorts of reasons presented in *On Liberty*. Underpinning both works is Mill's conception of humanity: his view that through our free choices we have the capacity to make ourselves better people and that this will ultimately be for the greater good of all. Curtailing freedom removes the possibility of individual fulfilment through choice. Throughout *The Subjection of Women* Mill refers to the position of married women as one of slavery, a condition that he argued was detrimental not just to the women concerned, but to society as a whole. As we have seen, in *On Liberty* Mill argues that individual freedom should not extend to the point of allowing an individual to choose to become a slave, despite the choice being voluntary, since by selling himself for a slave, he abdicates his liberty; he forgoes any future use of it beyond that single act. He therefore defeats, in his own case, the very purpose which is the justification for allowing him to dispose of himself. He is no longer free, but is thenceforth in a position which has no longer the presumption in its favour that would be afforded by his voluntarily remaining in it. The principle of freedom cannot require that he should be free not to be free.

(Mill (1974 edn), chap.V, p.173)

This passage takes on a new significance in the light of Mill's repeated claim in *The Subjection of Women* that married women are in essence slaves to their husbands. His reference to the laws on divorce becomes explicit when he goes on to assert that a consequence of his Harm Principle was that

those who have become bound to one another, in things which concern no third party, should be able to release one another from the engagement; and even without such voluntary release there are perhaps no contracts or engagements, except those that relate to money or money's worth, of which one can venture to say that there ought to be no liberty whatever of retraction.

(Ibid.)

Mill, however, sees the complexity of the situations that might arise with the issue of divorce, not least when children are involved. His view is that either individual should be legally free to end a marriage, but this does not entail moral freedom to do so, a radical conclusion for his time, if a commonplace today.

ACTIVITY

Read all of *The Subjection of Women*, skimming difficult passages and concentrating on getting a clear overview rather than a detailed understanding of every sentence. The main point is to map out the central arguments that Mill uses, and to provide a framework within which you can fit the details of his position. You may find it helpful to make brief chapter summaries.

Reading *The Subjection of Women*

Mill's stated aim in *The Subjection of Women* is as straightforward as his stated aim in *On Liberty*: to explain the justification for his belief that:

the principle which regulates the existing social relations between the two sexes – the legal subordination of one sex to the other – is wrong in itself, and now one of the chief hindrances to human improvement; and that it ought to be replaced by a principle of perfect equality, admitting no power or privilege on the one side, nor disability on the other.

(Mill (1988 edn), chap.I, p.1)

This aim presents somewhat different difficulties for the present-day reader. Whereas the 'single truth' of *On Liberty*, although in large part a response to the trends of Mill's own time, has, as we have seen – and inasmuch as it is single and true – applications in any age; much of *The Subjection of Women* is directed at the existence of specific inequalities which were part of the English law at the time the book was written. In the 1860s common law in England denied married women property rights and gave them few rights of protection against violence and sexual abuse by their husbands. There was, for example, no concept of marital rape, a situation which allowed men to enforce on their wives what Mill considered to be 'the lowest degradation of a human being, that of being made the instrument of an animal function contrary to her inclinations' (ibid., chap.II, p.33). A superficial reading of the book might suggest that it is irrelevant at a time when women, in the West at least, are not to the same degree victims of such blatant inequality before the law. However, although parts of the work are now principally of historical interest, the central philosophical strands are still relevant today. When reading the work from a philosophical point of view, rather than, say, as social history, it is important to focus on the arguments Mill uses, many of which, with minor adaptations, apply to any situation in which unequal treatment of the sexes or other groups is advocated, not just when such treatment is supported by unjust laws.

Furthermore, the book is not simply a critique of Victorian laws and of the assumptions which underpinned them; it also provides an account of a more positive kind, of a framework of equality and friendship within marriage which permits both individuals to develop and flourish as human beings. This more positive account is consistent with and complements many of the views expressed in *On Liberty*.

A further point worth making at the outset is Mill's unusual status as a man writing a feminist tract. Although Mill's wife, Harriet Taylor, who died in 1858, was a major influence on *On Liberty* – as he acknowledged in its dedication – and on *The Subjection of Women*; he was nevertheless responsible for the final form of both of them. You may feel that it is inappropriate for a man to defend equality between the sexes since it is primarily men who are responsible for existing inequalities. On this view Mill's perspective on women will inevitably be sexist and inappropriate – it will come as no surprise to you that Mill makes what now seem sexist or at least conservative conjectures about what women would choose for themselves once legal obstacles to their liberty had been removed (see p.325 below). In the same vein, you might even want to question my status as a man writing about another man writing about the position of women. In our defence it is worth pointing out that denying that men could ever be qualified to write about equality between the sexes is the kind of silencing of opinion that he attacked so eloquently in Chapter II of *On Liberty*. His arguments in *The Subjection of Women* against deciding *a priori* what men and women can and cannot do would equally apply here.

ACTIVITY

Read *The Subjection of Women*, Chapter I and answer the following questions.

1   What are Mill's main arguments against the notion that unequal treatment of men and women is justly based on limitations imposed on women by their nature?

2   Why, according to Mill, needn't men impose laws to prevent women from doing what is against their nature?

DISCUSSION

1   In the second half of Chapter I Mill gives a series of powerful arguments undermining the position of those who want to argue anything on the basis of women's nature. His principal point is epistemological: it is about the source of the supposed knowledge of women's nature. He maintains an agnostic position: it just isn't possible to know what women's nature is like at the present time, so anyone who bases arguments on views about women's nature is going beyond the available knowledge.

To back up this stance, Mill points out that what is currently called women's nature is at best an artificial thing: the product of unnatural shaping. Here he uses the image of a tree deformed by a combination of hothousing and exposure to wintry air. What some think of as women's nature has been artificially created in a like manner: it is not the freely formed natural expression of women, but rather the product of a male-dominated culture. This is not the true nature of women. In *On Liberty*, as we have seen, he stressed the need for human nature in general to express itself through free development 'according to the tendency of the inward forces which make it a living thing' (Mill (1974 edn), chap.III, p.123). The point here is not that we *should* discover the 'true nature' of women in order to settle the matter, but rather the negative one that his contemporaries' arguments based on assumptions about women's nature were clearly based on inappropriate and incomplete evidence.

A second argument Mill uses against those who claimed to know women's nature was that history has shown the degree to which what has been presumed to be an unchanging natural feature is in fact the product of circumstances, of external influences rather than of some inward force. A serious study of psychology could in principle discover the elements of character which are due to sex and those due to culture, but Mill points out that the psychological evidence available at his time, wouldn't merit a conclusive verdict on this issue, so no one can claim knowledge of woman's nature on its basis.

A further point that Mill makes is that those who claim to know women's nature are arguing from very scanty evidence: most know very few women well. Usually the evidence that men use about human nature is derived from a single detailed case study: that of their wife. Yet to generalize from this to all women is clearly a dubious move.

2   Mill makes the point that it is completely unnecessary to exclude women from certain areas of life which by their nature they are unsuited to since 'What they can do, but not so well as the men who are their competitors, competition suffices to exclude them from' (Mill (1988 edn), chap.I, p.28) He adds that despite the widely held view that women are by nature fitted to be wives and mothers, the constitution of society suggests completely the contrary. If it is women's nature to marry and have children, there shouldn't be any need to prevent them from taking up other occupations. Yet Mill suggests, women of his time are forced into marriage by all other doors being closed to them. His explanation for this is not that men really believe that women would choose not to marry, but rather, given the choice of a reasonable profession as opposed to an unequal marriage, many of them would take the option of the profession. Men who oppose female

equality, Mill suspects, fear that women would demand marriage on equal terms.

ACTIVITY

Read *The Subjection of Women*, Chapter II and answer the following question.

What is the point of Mill's comparison between a marriage and a business partnership?

DISCUSSION

The comparison between a marriage and a business partnership is intended as a counter to the claim that in all freely chosen relationships between two people one must be the absolute master. The common case of a voluntary partnership in business can permit far greater equality than exists by law in a marriage. There can be division of duties and of rights, and sometimes decisions should depend on one person: but there is no reason why that should always be the same person. Mill's clear message here is that marriage should be in some respects closer to a partnership on equal terms rather than a form of enslavement.

ACTIVITY

Read *The Subjection of Women*, Chapter III and answer the following question.

On what grounds does Mill dismiss the notion that, because women appear on average less talented than men, no women should be allowed to enter the top professions?

DISCUSSION

Mill makes the point that being on average inferior in some respect to men would not be a sufficient reason for preventing women from entering the top professions: what would need to be shown would be that no individual woman could reach an appropriate standard. Furthermore, history has shown that women are capable of everything that is done by men, even though they have not always attained the very highest standards that have been achieved in various fields. Banning women from applying for certain professions, he points out, excludes potentially highly competent individuals: this is unfair to the women excluded, and unfair to those who might benefit had they been employed.

ACTIVITY

Read *The Subjection of Women*, Chapter IV and answer the following question.

What, according to Mill, are the main benefits to humanity of giving women greater freedom in how to live their lives?

DISCUSSION

Giving women greater freedom in how to live their lives, attained through greater equality before the law, would benefit humanity by replacing an unjust relationship with a just one. The legal subordination of women to men has a damaging effect on character development: it encourages men to feel that power and authority can rightly be possessed even though acquired by the chance occurrence of being born male. This goes against the progressive principle that:

> conduct, and conduct alone, entitles to respect: that not what men are, but what they do, constitutes their claim to deference; that, above all, merit, and not birth, is the only rightful claim to power and authority.

(Ibid., chap.IV, p.89)

A second benefit to humanity is that opening up a range of occupations to women has the effect of 'doubling the mass of mental faculties available for the higher service of humanity' (ibid.). Mill believes that in the present situation there is not such a surfeit of talent that humanity can afford to rule out half of the available resource. Furthermore women who are not given the educational and employment opportunities open to their husbands and who are forced to gain their own status from their husbands may force their husbands into a kind of mediocrity of respectability.

Mill's most forceful arguments about the benefits of greater equality between the sexes focus on the kind of friendship possible within marriage. He claims that a happier married life is likely when marriage is between people who share interests. If women are given the same sorts of opportunities as men in terms of education and employment, then such liaisons are more likely to occur. When marriage gives women an inferior status to their husbands, the effect can be to the detriment of both. A marriage between equals, on the other hand, Mill believes, can be part of the moral regeneration of humanity.

The most direct benefits of increased equality and liberty are, however, in terms of the personal independence of women no longer forced into a kind of captivity and enslavement: 'the difference to them between a life of subjection to the will of others, and a life of rational freedom' (ibid., chap.IV, p.103). Personal independence is a major ingredient in happiness.

Sexual inequality

Now that we have looked more closely at the detail of Mill's argument in the *Subjection of Women*, I will focus on three important topics raised by the work: sexual inequality, marital friendship, and the limits of Mill's feminism.

Mill is often cited in debates about sexual inequality, though his position is often misunderstood.

ACTIVITY

Write brief answers to the questions below on the topic of Mill's defence of sexual equality. Then read Janet Radcliffe Richards, 'Mill and Sexual Inequality' (Reading 6.4), which eliminates some common misunderstandings of Mill's attack on sexual inequality. In this short piece Radcliffe Richards gives answers to all the questions asked.

1   Does Mill argue that the sexes are equal in any respect?

2   Does Mill argue that by eliminating legal inequalities an equality of outcome will be achieved, with, for instance, equal numbers of men and women becoming civil servants?

3   Is it always obviously wrong for the law to treat different groups of people differently?

4   Does Mill believe that the law's different treatment of men and women is a logical conclusion derived from true premises?

Marital friendship

Although much of the *Subjection of Women* is devoted to attacking preconceptions about the role of women, the book also presents a positive vision of marriage. For Mill, friendship in marriage is both possible and desirable.

ACTIVITY

Read the extract from Mary Lyndon Shanley's article 'The Hope of Friendship' (Reading 6.5). Shanley recognizes both the power and shortcomings of Mill's arguments about the possibility of friendship within marriage and its benefits to society .

Limits of Mill's feminism

The assumptions that Mill makes about what women would choose to do if the legal obstacles to liberty were removed now appear sexist. He is happy to endorse the existing divisions of labour between the sexes, as Shanley points out (Reading 6.5, pages 363–4). However, this aspect of Mill's writing should be seen in the light of the point made in Chapter I of *The Subjection of Women*, that the presumption of sexual inequality was the starting point for most discussion of the status of women in society at the time Mill was writing. It is difficult today to read Mill's book as a radical contribution to the debate – who, for example, would now argue that married women should be denied in law the right to own property? – but that is how it was initially received. Mill was far ahead of most of his contemporaries in his advocacy of equality for women, from his earliest campaigning for the use of birth control through to his later arguments for the removal of unjust laws. We should not be surprised to find him sharing some of the prejudices of his age: what is remarkable is the degree to which he could see beyond commonly held beliefs.

The whole of *The Subjection of Women* is focused on inequalities between the legal treatment of men and women, and as we have noted already, in the West most legal obstacles to equality between the sexes have now been removed, perhaps making it easier for us to see that they are the prejudices of an earlier age. Mill made a very widespread assumption, that marriage can only occur between people of different sexes; however, there is no reason why this must be so. In a sense all those wishing to have a same-sex marriage are treated unequally by the law when compared to their heterosexual counterparts. This is not a topic that Mill addressed, or could have been expected to have addressed. It can, however, serve as a reminder to us not to be too smug about the sorts of equality before the law which exist in our time.

Conclusion

On Liberty and *The Subjection of Women* jointly make the case for preserving individual freedom and cultivating sexual equality for the greater happiness of individuals and for the greater good of society. Mill's vision of humanity was optimistic and progressive: he believed that a rational approach to the question of how we should live could improve our lot. Though present-day philosophers may now find fault with such optimism, the power of his arguments and the vigour of his prose remain as lasting foils against complacency.

Glossary

aggregate happiness

   The sum of all happiness and unhappiness.

autonomy

   The capacity to determine the course of one's own life for oneself.

consequentialism

   A general term for any ethical theory which is based on an assessment of the outcomes of actions. The best known form of consequentialism is utilitarianism.

eudaimonia

   An Ancient Greek word usually translated as 'flourishing' or sometimes, slightly misleadingly, as 'happiness'. This is the term Aristotle used to describe a successful life.

felicific calculus

   Bentham's table for calculating the aggregate happiness brought about by any action based on such aspects as the pleasure's duration, intensity, tendency to produce further pleasure.

Harm Principle

   Mill's general rule that the only justification for preventing an individual acting in a particular way is if it will otherwise cause harm to someone else. This is sometimes known as the Liberty Principle.

hedonistic

Concerned with pleasure.

liberalism

A general term covering a group of political theories which stress individual freedom and limited government control over the lives of adults.

Liberty Principle

Another name for the Harm Principle.

utilitarianism

The consequentialist ethical theory that the morally right action is the one that maximizes happiness.

Further reading

The principles Mill defended in both *On Liberty* and *The Subjection of Women* are ultimately justified by his consequentialist ethics. He gave his clearest account of this in *Utilitarianism* (1861); there are numerous good editions of this work available.

Annas, Julia (1977) 'Mill and the Subjection of Women', *Philosophy*, 52, pp.179–94 also provides a critical assessment of this work.

Crisp, Roger (1997) *Mill On Utilitarianism*, Routledge, gives a lucid account of Mill's utilitarianism and includes chapters on *On Liberty* and *The Subjection of Women*.

Okin, Susan, Moller (1979) *Women in Western Political Thought*, Princeton University Press, includes a chapter on *The Subjection of Women*.

Pyle, A. (ed.) (1994) *Liberty: Contemporary Responses to John Stuart Mill*, Thoemmes Press. Andrew Pyle's collection of responses to Mill by his contemporaries provides interesting insights into how Mill was understood in his time. Most of the criticisms of Mill that have been made in the twentieth century had already been made in the nineteenth century.

Riley, Jonathan (1998) *Mill: On Liberty*, Routledge, is a useful commentary.

Ryan, Alan (ed.) (1997) *Mill: Texts and Commentaries*, Norton Critical Editions, includes complete texts of *On Liberty* and *The Subjection of Women* together with an interesting selection of secondary readings and an annotated bibliography.

St John Packe, Michael (1954) *The Life of John Stuart Mill*, Macmillan, is the standard biography of Mill.

Skorupski, John (1989) *John Stuart Mill*, Routledge, includes a substantial chapter on liberty.

Skorupski, John (ed.) (1998) *The Cambridge Companion to Mill*, Cambridge University Press, includes essays on *The Subjection of Women* and on Mill's liberalism.

Stephen, James, Fitzjames (1967 edn) *Liberty, Equality, Fraternity*, R.J. White (ed.), Cambridge University Press (first published 1873) engages brilliantly with Mill's major contentions in *On Liberty* and was perhaps Mill's most systematic and cogent critic during his lifetime.

Wolff, Jonathan (1996) *An Introduction to Political Philosophy*, Oxford University Press includes a chapter on Mill 'The Place of Liberty'. This provides a useful overview of the main philosophical themes of the work and their continuing relevance.

Readings

'Freedom of Expression'

John Gray

In this extract, John Gray provides an analysis of Chapter II of On *Liberty*. Gray emphasizes Mill's concern with establishing a society of autonomous agents.

It is true of any liberal theory of freedom of expression that it must account for the immunity from legal restriction of acts of expression which occasion manifest damage to interests of a gravity that would warrant such restriction if the acts were not acts of speech (for example) but acts of a non-expressive character. Mill acknowledges that acts of expression are in this respect a privileged class of acts in a number of passages:[1]

> Such being the reason which make it imperative that human beings should be free to form opinions, and to express their opinions without reserve; and such the baneful consequences to the intellectual, and though that to the moral nature of man, unless this liberty is either conceded, or asserted in spite of prohibition; let us next examine whether the same reasons do not require that men should be free to act upon their opinions – to carry them out in their lives, without hindrance, either physical or moral, from their fellow-men, so long as it is at their own risk and peril. This last proviso is of course indispensable. No one pretends that acts should be as free as opinions. On the contrary, even opinions lose their immunity when the circumstances in which they are expressed are such as to constitute their expression a positive instigation to some mischievous act.

In this passage Mill acknowledges that expressive acts enjoy a privileged immunity from liberty limiting legal restrictions on harm preventing grounds. He allows to expressive acts a greater freedom from restriction on such grounds than other kinds of act. How might he justify this apparently unreasonable exemption? At the end of chapter two of *On Liberty*, Mill summarises the major arguments he has adduced in support of 'absolute freedom of opinion and sentiment on all subjects, practical or speculative, scientific, moral and theological'.[2] First, he appeals to the fact of human fallibility; second, he appeals to the value of truth; third, he appeals to the value of rationality, asserting that, even if an opinion contains the whole truth, it will be held as a prejudice, without understanding of its grounds in reason, if it is not belief, claiming that without 'the collision of adverse opinions', men's convictions lack the force of heartfelt views. In listing these four arguments in support of freedom of expression, Mill identifies two features that are partly constitutive of autonomous thought – the rationality and the vitality of the beliefs and judgements with which it operates – in the absence of which no man can attain 'the ideal perfection of human nature'. In making this reference to two constituents of autonomous thought, Mill resolves the paradox of any liberal theory of free expression: if it is legitimate to restrict non-expressive acts when they threaten damage to human interests, why is it illegitimate to restrict the liberty to perform expressive acts when they threaten similar damage (as surely they often do)? Mill's repudiation of restrictions on freedom of speech is a consistent application of his ascription to human beings of an overriding interest in becoming and remaining autonomous agents. Restrictions on free expression by their nature obstruct autonomous thought. For, provided always that the individual can be supposed to have attained 'the maturity of his faculties', it cannot coherently be suggested that he might forfeit his sovereignty in weighing rival reasons for action while continuing to regard himself as an autonomous agent. An autonomous agent who cherishes that status is obliged to discount both the harm to himself accruing from the acquisition of false beliefs and the harm done as a result of acquiring a belief (true or false) via an expressive act as being always overridden by the harm done by any restraint of free expression to the interest he shares with other sin remaining an autonomous agent. While an autonomous agent may accept, accordingly, that the state has authority to subject him to various kinds of restraint, and while he may rely on the judgement of others about the rectitude of the state's imposing limits to his liberty, he cannot (without forfeiting his status as an autonomous agent) abrogate the responsibility he has to evaluate critically the state's actions and the judgements of others. Discharging the responsibility of an autonomous agent, however, presupposes that he possess all the resources of information and conflicting opinion and judgement which are indispensable conditions of rational deliberation and which can only be secured by the protection of liberal freedoms of speech. Such an interpretation of Mill's reasoning in support of freedom of speech is supported by the character of the famous exception which he allows to the principle of freedom of expression: [3]

> An opinion that corndealers are starvers of the poor, or that private property is robbery, ought to be unmolested when simply circulated through the press, but may justly incur punishment when delivered to an excited mob assembled before the house of a corndealer, and then handed about the same mob in the form of a placard.

It is surely possible to regard this passage as making an appeal to the improbability of autonomous thought in 'excited mobs' rather than an appeal to the harm to the interests of corndealers caused by the utterances made in such circumstances: for, after all, corndealers might be as severely harmed by confiscatory legislation (passed as a result of expressive acts uttered in the reasoned arguments of parliamentary debate) as by any sort of mob violence. Once again, the abridgements which Mill is prepared to make to his liberal principles disclose clearly the rationale for their general adoption – his overriding concern for the creation of a society of autonomous agents. Mill does not deny that expressive acts may be harmful; he insists that their harmfulness is not in general sufficient to warrant restricting them.

All this is not to say that there are no difficulties in Mill's theory of freedom of expression. Expressive acts are typically other-regarding and, in respect of some of them at least, a strong causal link can be established with harm to the vital interests of others. What of racist speech which directly engenders a lynching, for example? Within a right-based theory, it might make sense to maintain that, not incitement to violators of rights, but only rights violation, shall ever be punishable; but it is hard to see how such a view could be justifiable within a utilitarian outlook even of Mill's sort. As Marshall says of Mill's discussion of tyrannicide: [4]

> Mill says not only that the lawfulness of it may properly be discussed but that instigation to it in a particular case may be punished only if an overt act has followed and a probable connection can be established between the act and the instigation. This appears to mean some other overt act by someone other than the instigator and other than the act of instigation which may well be overt enough. Mill seems inconsistent here. What he presumably ought to be saying is that if an act is mischievous or damaging to others or to society, society may properly make it criminal and suppress such speech acts as are so closely connected with the commission of the act as to be part of it as to be counted as attempts to do the act; but that something to be called discussion, advocacy, debate, or expression of opinions about its desirability, can never be deemed to be part of a mischievous action in this sense.

What Mill lacks, in short, are criteria to distinguish incitement to act from advocacy and debate about the merit of action.

Mill's arguments in chapter two of *On Liberty* have been subject to other criticisms. McCloskey[5] and Acton[6] point out that, contrary to Mill's assertion, all silencing of discussion is *not* an assumption of infallibility. Wolff[7] has claimed that, if an argument from scepticism or ignorance is indeed crucial in *On Liberty*, then Mill's argument has the illiberal implication that 'error has no rights' – that we may be intolerant, providing that we have a rational assurance of the correctness of our beliefs. Though these criticisms may have some force when they are directed against particular remarks in Mill's argument, they neglect a vital aspect of his case. This is that, in the second chapter of *On Liberty* and elsewhere in his writings, Mill acknowledged that different modes of criticism and justification are appropriate in different areas of thought and practice. Further, even in areas such as the natural sciences, where standards of criticism are acknowledged by Mill to be different in character from those pertinent to practical affairs, the account of inquiry given in *On Liberty* is closer to a Popperian[8] error-elimination process or even, it may be, to Feyerabendian[9] pluralism, than it is to the inductivism Mill espouses in the *Logic*. (The connection between Mill's fallibilist theory of knowledge and his political theory will be explored in chapter 6 of this study.) Finally, these traditional criticisms neglect the point, central to Mill's argument, that liberty of thought and expression is valuable, not just instrumentally as a means to the discovery and propagation of truth, but non-instrumentally, as a condition of that rationality and vitality of belief which he conceives of as a characteristic feature of a free man.

Let us consider these points in greater detail. Mill seems to think that, at least in some areas of thought, questions and arguments cannot be fully understood, still less can maxims or principles be adopted, if liberty of discussion is suppressed. As he puts it: [10]

> The fact, however, is that not only the grounds of the opinion are forgotten in the absence of discussion, but too often the meaning of the opinion itself ... Instead of a vivid conception and a living belief, there remain only a few phrases retained by rote; or, if any part, the shell and husk only of the meaning is retained, the finer essence lost.

It is tempting to suggest at this point that Mill believes that, in some areas of thought, an element of commitment or at least of imaginative sympathy is necessary if uses of language are even to be understood. His claim then becomes that such commitment or sympathy cannot exist, or at any rate will not typically exist in any very strong form, if the concepts and categories implicit in forms of discourse are not subject to recurrent contestation. In the first part of the claim, Mill may be joining hands with those who think that, with religious language (for example), discourse has an expressive and non-reportive function. In the second part of the claim, he may be suggesting that a form of dialectical reasoning is especially appropriate for some subject matters, not just as a means to the adoption of well-ground beliefs, but even as an indispensable condition of understanding. There is here, at least vestigially, a conception of inquiry as being internally related to certain imaginative and emotional as well as intellectual activities. Again, it may well be that Mill is emphasising that the demands of autonomy in thought and practice differ across different areas of thought and forms of life. It would be idle to pretend that any of this is explicit in Mill, however; and it would be dishonest not to admit that some of the things he says in *On Liberty* run counter to these interpretations.

Yet, in a number of places, we find Mill insisting on a distinction between mathematical and other forms of knowledge: [11]

> The peculiarity of the evidence of mathematical truths is that all the argument is on one side. There are no objections. But on every subject in which difference of opinion is possible, the truth depends on a balance to be struck between two sets of conflicting reasons. Even in natural philosophy, there is always some other explanation possible of the same facts ... and it has to be shown why that other theory cannot be the true one; and until this is shown, and until we know how it is shown, we do not understand the grounds of our opinion.

Mill immediately goes on to make a distinction between different areas of thought, which may be seen as turning on the peculiarity of practical reasoning when contrasted with reasoning in theoretical studies: 'when we turn to subjects infinitely more complicated, to morals, religion, politics, social relations, and to the business of life, three-fourths of the arguments for every opinion consist in dispelling the appearances which favour the opinion different from it. [12]

The salience of the distinction between practical and theoretical reasoning I have suggested is supported by a statement in the same chapter: 'Truth, in the great practical concerns of life, is so much a question of the reconciling and combining of opposites, that very few have minds sufficiently capacious and impartial to make the adjustment with an approach to correctness ...'.[13] And Mill emphasises the indispensable utility of the practice of critical discussion in a number of other places: [14]

> He [man] is capable of rectifying his mistakes, by discussion and experience. Not by experience alone. There must be discussion, to show how experience is to be interpreted. Wrong opinions and practices gradually yield to fact and argument; but facts and arguments, to produce any effect on the mind, must be brought before it. Very few facts are able to tell their own story, without comments to bring out their meaning ... the only way in which a human being can make some approach to knowing the whole of a subject, is by hearing what can be said about it by persons of every variety of opinion, and studying all modes in which it can be looked at by every character of mind.

Again: [15]

> If even the Newtonian philosophy were not permitted to be questioned, mankind could not feel as complete assurance of its truth as they do now. The beliefs which we have most warrant for have no safeguard to rest on, but a standing invitation to the whole world to prove them unfounded. If the challenge is not accepted, o is accepted and the attempt fails, we are far enough from certainty still; what we have done is the best that the existing state of human reason admits of; we have neglected nothing that could give the truth a chance of reaching us. If the lists are kept open, we may hope that if there be a better truth, it will be found when the human mind is capable of receiving it, and in the meantime we may rely on having attained such approach to truth as is possible in our own day. This is the amount of certainty attainable by an fallible being, and this is the sole way of attaining it.

Yet again: [16]

> The Socratic dialectics ... were essentially a negative discussion of the great questions of philosophy and life, directed with consummate skill to the purpose of convincing anyone who had merely adopted the commonplaces of received opinion that he did not understand the subject – that he as yet attached no definite meaning to the doctrines he professed ... It is the fashion of the present time to disparage negative logic – that which points out weaknesses in theory or errors in practice, without establishing positive truths. Such negative criticism would indeed be poor enough as an ultimate result, but as a means of attaining any positive knowledge or conviction worthy the name, it cannot be valued too highly; and until people are again systematically trained to it, there will be few great thinkers, and a low general average of intellect, in any but the mathematical and physical departments of speculation. On any other subject no one's opinions deserve the name of knowledge, except so far a she has either had forced upon him by others, or gone through of himself, the same mental process which would have been required of him in carrying on an active controversy with opponents.

The lack in Mill's writing of any fully adequate treatment of these matters should not induce a hasty dismissal of what he has to say about freedom of expression. As I have interpreted him, he regards freedom of expression as partly constitutive of autonomous agency. Further, the pursuit of truth in at least some areas of inquiry cannot be separated from the practice of critical discussion: truth itself is sometimes regarded by Mill as but the upshot of open debate in these areas. For these reasons, freedom of expression is not to be traded off against anything else, save where this is necessary to forestall moral catastrophe. Though Mill's account may appear to accord to expressive acts a privileged status, this impression is seen to be delusive, once it is realised that these acts come within the viral interest in autonomy which the Principle of Liberty protects.

Notes

From Gray, John (1996 2nd edn) *Mill on Liberty: A Defence*, Routledge, pp.103–10.

[1] J.S. Mill (1972 edn) *Utilitarianism, On Liberty and Considerations on Representative Government*, Dent, p.114.

[2] Ibid., p.75.

[3] Ibid, p.144.

[4] Geoffrey Marshall (1971) *Constitutional Theory*, Clarendon Press, pp.156–7.

[5] H.J. McCloskey (1971) *John Stuart Mill: a Critical Study*, Macmillan, pp.119–20.

[6] H.B. Acton, 'Introduction' to Mill (1972 edn), pp.xx–xxi.

[7] R.P. Wolff (1968) *The Poverty of Liberalism*, Beacon Press, pp.8–15.

[8] I refer, of course, to Popper's defence of falsificationism in (1959) *The Logic of Scientific Discovery*, Hutchinson.

[9] On this, see P.K. Feyerabend (1975) *Against Method*, New Left Books, p.48.

[10] Mill, op. cit., p.99.

[11] Ibid., p.46.

[12] Ibid.

[13] Ibid., p.107.

[14] Ibid., p.82.

[15] Ibid., p.85.

[16] Ibid., p.104.

'John Stuart Mill and the Ends of Life'

Isaiah Berlin

In this extract from his classic essay on Mill, Isaiah Berlin (1909–97) draws attention to a number of weaknesses in Mill's arguments, while still showing broad sympathy to his overall project.

I shall not impose upon your patience by giving you an abstract of Mill's argument. I should like to remind you only of those salient ideas to which Mill attached the greatest importance – beliefs which his opponents attacked in his lifetime, and attack even more vehemently today. These propositions are still far from self-evident; time has not turned them to platitudes; they are not even now undisputed assumptions of a civilized outlook. Let me attempt to consider them briefly.

Men want to curtail the liberties of other men, either (a) because they wish to impose their power on others; or (b) because they want conformity – they do not wish to think differently from others, or others to think differently from themselves; or, finally (c) because they believe that to the question of how one should live there can be (as with any genuine question) one true answer and one only; this answer is discoverable by means of reason, or intuition, or direct revelation, or a form of life or 'unity of theory and practice'; its authority is identifiable with one of these avenues to final knowledge; all deviation from it is error which imperils human salvation; this justifies legislation against, or even extirpation of, those who lead away from the truth, whatever their character or intentions. Mill dismisses the first two motives as being irrational, since they stake out no intellectually argued claim, and are therefore incapable of being answered by rational argument. The only motive which he is prepared to take seriously is the last, namely, that if the true ends of life can be discovered, those who oppose these truths are spreading pernicious falsehood and must be repressed. To this he replies that men are not infallible; that the supposedly pernicious view might turn out to be true after all; that those who killed Socrates and Christ sincerely believed them to be purveyors of wicked falsehoods, and were themselves men as worthy of respect as any to be found today; that Marcus Aurelius, 'the gentlest and most amiable of rulers', known as the most enlightened man of his time and one of the noblest, nevertheless authorized the persecution of Christianity as a moral and social danger, and that no argument ever used by any other persecutor had not been equally open to him. We cannot suppose that persecution never kills the truth. 'It is a piece of idle sentimentality', Mill observes, 'that truth, merely as truth, has any inherent power denied to error, of prevailing against the dungeon and the stake' (p.48). [1] Persecution is historically only to effective.

> To speak only of religious opinions: the Reformation broke out at least twenty times before Luther, and was put down. Arnold of Brescia was put down. Fra Dolcino was put down. Savonarola was put down. The Albigeois were put down. The Vaudois were put down. The Lollards were put down. The Hussites were put down. ... In Spain, Italy, Flanders, the Austrian Empire, Protestantism was rooted out; and most likely would have been so in England had Queen Mary lived or Queen Elizabeth died ... No reasonable person can doubt that Christianity might have been extirpated in the Roman Empire. (p.47)

And if it be said against this that, just because we have erred in the past, it is mere cowardice to refrain from striking down evil when we see it in the present in case we may be mistaken again; or, to put it in another way, that, even if we are not infallible, yet, if we are to live at all, we must make decisions and act, and must do so on nothing better that probability, according to our lights, with constant risk of error; for all living involves risk, and what alternative have we? Mill answers that 'There is the greatest difference between presuming an opinion to be true, because with every opportunity for contesting it, it has not been refuted, and assuming its truth for the purpose of not permitting its refutation' (p.39). You can indeed stop 'bad men from perverting society with false or pernicious views' (p.39), but only if you give men liberty to deny that what you yourself call bad, or pernicious, or perverted, or false, is such; otherwise your conviction is founded on mere dogma and is not rational, and cannot be analysed or altered in the light of any new facts and ideas. Without infallibility how can truth emerge save in discussion? There is no *a priori* road towards it; a new experience, a new argument, can in principle always alter our views, no matter how strongly held. To shut doors is to blind yourself to the truth deliberately, to condemn yourself to incorrigible error.

Mill had a strong and subtle brain and his arguments are never negligible. But it is, in this case, plain that his conclusion only follows from premises which he does not make explicit. He was an empiricist; that is, he believed that no truths are – or could be – rationally established, except on the evidence of observation. New observations could in principle always upset a conclusion founded on earlier ones. He believed this rule to be true of the laws of physics, even of the laws of logic and mathematics; how much more, therefore, in 'ideological' fields where no scientific certainty prevailed – in ethics, politics, religion, history, the entire field of human affairs, where only probability reigns; here, unless full liberty of opinion and argument is permitted, nothing can ever be rationally established. But those who disagree with him, and believe in intuited truths, in principle not corrigible by experience, will disregard this argument. Mill can write them off as obscurantists, dogmatists, irrationalists. Yet something more is needed than mere contemptuous dismissal if their views, more powerful today perhaps than even in Mill's own century, are to be rationally contested. Again, it may well be that without full freedom of discussion the truth cannot emerge. But this may be only a necessary, not a sufficient, condition of its discovery; the truth may, for all our efforts, remain at the bottom of a well, and in the meantime the worse cause may win, and do enormous damage to mankind. Is it so clear that we must permit opinions advocating, say, race hatred to be uttered freely, because Milton has said that 'though all the winds of doctrine are let loose upon the earth ... whoever knew truth put to the worse in a free and open encounter?' because 'the truth must always prevail in a fair fight with falsehood'? These are brave and optimistic judgements, but how good is the empirical evidence for them today? Are demagogues and liars, scoundrels and blind fanatics, always, in liberal societies, stopped in time, or refuted in the end? How high a price is it right to pay for the great boon of freedom of discussion? A very high one, no doubt; but is it limitless? And if not, who shall say that sacrifice is, or is not, too great? Mill goes on to say that an opinion believed to be false may yet be partially true; for there is no absolute truth, only different roads towards it; the suppression of an apparent falsehood may also suppress what is true in it, to the loss of mankind. This argument, again, will not tell with those who believe that absolute truth is discoverable once and for all, whether by metaphysical or theological argument, or by some direct insight, or by leading a certain kind of life, or, as Mill's own mentors believe, by scientific or empirical methods.

His argument is plausible only on the assumption which, whether he knew it or not, Mill all to obviously made, that human knowledge was in principle never complete, and always fallible; that there was no single, universally visible, truth; that each man, each nation, each civilization might take its own road towards its own goal, not necessarily harmonious with those of others; that men are altered, and the truths in which they believe are altered, by new experiences and their own actions – what he calls 'experiments in living'; that consequently the conviction, common to Aristotelians and a good many Christian scholastics and atheistical materialists alike, that there exists a basic knowable human nature, one and the same, at all times, in all places, in all men – a static, unchanging substance underneath the altering appearances, with permanent needs, dictated by a single, discoverable goal, or pattern of goals, the same for all mankind – is mistaken; and so, too, is the notion that is bound up with it, of a single true doctrine carrying salvation to all men everywhere, contained in natural law, or the revelation of a sacred book, or the insight of a man of genius, or the natural wisdom of ordinary men, or the calculations made by an elite of utilitarian scientists set up to govern mankind.

Mill – bravely for a professed utilitarian – observes that the human (that is the social) sciences are too confused and uncertain to be properly called sciences at all – there are in them no valid generalizations, no laws, and therefore no predictions of rules of action can properly be deduced from them. He honoured the memory of his father, whose whole philosophy was based on the opposite assumption; he respected Auguste Comte, and subsidized Herbert Spencer, both of whom claimed to have laid the foundations for just such a science of society. Yet his own half-articulate assumption contradicts this. Mill believes that man is spontaneous, that he has freedom of choice, that he moulds his own character, that as a result of the interplay of men with nature and with other men something novel continually arises, and that this novelty is precisely what is most characteristic and most human in men. Because Mill's entire view of human nature turns out to rest not on the notion of the repetition of an identical pattern, but on his perception of human lives as subject to perpetual incompleteness, self-transformation, and novelty, his words are today alive and relevant to our own problems; whereas the works of James Mill, and of Buckle and Comte and Spencer, remain huge half-forgotten hulks in the river of nineteenth-century thought. He does not demand or predict ideal conditions for the final solution of human problems or for obtaining universal agreement on all crucial issues. He assumes that finality is impossible, and implies that it is undesirable too. He does not demonstrate this. Rigour in argument is not among his accomplishments. Yet it is this belief, which undermines the foundations on which Helvétius, Bentham, and James Mill built their doctrines – a system never formally repudiated by him – that gives his case both its plausibility and its humanity.

His remaining arguments are weaker still. He says that unless it is contested, truth is liable to degenerate into dogma or prejudice; men would no longer feel it as a living truth; opposition is needed to keep it alive. 'Both teachers and learners go to sleep at their post, as soon as there is no enemy in the field', overcome as they are by 'the deep slumber of a decided opinion' (p.61). So deeply did Mill believe this, that he declared that if there were no genuine dissenters, we had an obligation to invent arguments against ourselves, in order to keep ourselves in a state of intellectual fitness. This resembles nothing so much as Hegel's argument for war as keeping human society from stagnation. Yet if the truth about human affairs were in principle demonstrable, as it is, say, in arithmetic, the invention of false propositions in order to be knocked down would scarcely be needed to preserve our understanding of it. What Mill seems really to be asking for is diversity of opinion for its own sake. He speaks of the need for 'fair play to all sides of the truth' (p.65) – a phrase that a man would scarcely employ if he believed in simple, complete truths as the earlier utilitarians did; and he makes use of bad arguments to conceal this scepticism, perhaps even from himself. 'In an imperfect state of the human mind', he says 'the interests of the truth require a diversity of opinions' (p.68). Or again, 'Do we really accept the logic of the persecutors [and say] we may persecute others because we are right, and they may not persecute us because they are wrong?' (p.101). Catholics, Protestants, Jews, Muslims have all justified persecution by this argument in their day; and on their premises there may be nothing logically amiss with it. It is these premises that Mill rejects, and rejects not, it seems to me, as a result of a chain of reasoning, but because he believes – even if he never, so far as I know, admits this explicitly – that there are no final truths not corrigible by experience, at any rate in what is now called the ideological sphere – that of value judgements and of general outlook and attitude to life. Yet within this framework of ideas and values, despite all the stress on the value of 'experiments in living' and what they may reveal, Mill is ready to stake a very great deal on the truth of his convictions about what he thinks to be the deepest and most permanent interests of men. Although his reasons are drawn from experience and not *a priori* knowledge, the propositions themselves are very like those defended on metaphysical grounds by the traditional upholders of the doctrine of natural rights. Mill believes in liberty, that is, the rigid limitation of the right to coerce, because he is sure that men cannot develop and flourish and become fully human unless they are left free from interference by other men within a certain minimum area of their lives, which he regards as – or wishes to make – inviolable. This is his view of what men are, and therefore of their basic moral and intellectual needs, and he formulates his conclusions in the celebrated maxims according to which 'The individual is not accountable to society for his actions, in so far as these concern the interests of no person but himself' (p.108), and that

> The only reason for which power can be rightfully exercised over any member of a civilised community against his will is to prevent harm to others. His own good, either physical or moral, is not a sufficient warrant. He cannot rightfully be compelled to do or to forbear ... because in the opinion of others to do so would be wise or even right. (p.30)

This is Mill's profession of faith, and the ultimate basis of political liberalism, and therefore the proper target of attack – both on psychological and moral (and social) grounds – by its opponents during Mill's lifetime and after. Carlyle reacted with characteristic fury in a letter to his brother Alexander: 'As if it were a sin to control or coerce into better methods human swine in any way... Ach Gott in Himmel!' [2]

Milder and more rational critics have not failed to point out that the limits of private and public domain are difficult to demarcate, that anything a man does could, in principle, frustrate others; that no man is an island; that the social and the individual aspects of human beings often cannot, in practice, be disentangled. Mill was told that when men look upon forms of worship in which other men persist as being not merely 'abominable' in themselves, but as an offence to them or to their God, they may be irrational and bigoted, but they are not necessarily lying; and that when he asks rhetorically why Muslims should not forbid the eating of pork to everyone, since they are genuinely disgusted by it, the answer, on utilitarian premisses, is by no means self-evident. It might be argued that there is no *a priori* reason for supposing that most men would not be happier – if that is the goal – in a wholly socialized world where private life and personal freedom are reduced to vanishing point, that in Mill's individualist order; and that whether this is so or not is a matter for experimental verification. Mill constantly protests against the fact that social and legal rules are too often determined merely by 'the likings and dislikings of society', and correctly points out that these are often irrational or are founded on ignorance. But if damage to others is what concerns him most (as he professes), then the fact that their resistance to this or that belief is instinctive, or intuitive, or founded on no rational ground, does not make it the less painful, and, to that extent, damaging to them. Why should rational men be entitled to the satisfaction of their ends more than the irrational? Why not the irrational, if the greatest happiness of the greatest number (and the greatest number are seldom rational) is the sole justified purpose of action? Only a competent social psychologist can tell what will make a given society happiest. If happiness is the sole criterion, then human sacrifice, or the burning of witches, at times when such practices had strong public feeling behind them, did doubtless, in their day, contribute to the happiness of the majority. If there is no other moral criterion, then the question whether the slaughter of innocent old women (together with the ignorance and prejudice which made this acceptable) or the advance in knowledge and rationality (which ended such abominations but robbed men of comforting illusions) – which of these yielded a higher balance of happiness is only a matter of actuarial calculation. Mill paid no attention to such considerations: nothing could go more violently against all that he felt and believed. At the centre of Mill's though and feeling lies, not his utilitarianism, nor the concern about enlightenment, nor about dividing the private from the public domain – for he himself at times concedes that the state may invade the private domain, in order to promote education, hygiene, or social security or justice – but his passionate belief that men are made human by their capacity for choice – choice of evil and good equally. Fallibility, the right to err, as a corollary of the capacity for self-improvement; distrust of symmetry and finality as enemies of freedom – these are the principles which Mill never abandons. He is acutely aware of the many-sidedness of the truth and of the irreducible complexity of life, which rules out the very possibility of any simple solution, or the idea of a final answer to any concrete problem. Greatly daring, and without looking back at the stern intellectual puritanism in which he was brought up, he preaches the necessity of understanding and gaining illumination from doctrines that are incompatible with one another – say those of Coleridge and Bentham; he explained in his autobiography the need to understand and learn from both. [3]

Notes

From Gray, J. and Smith, G.W. (eds) (1991) *J.S. Mill* On Liberty *in Focus*, Routledge, pp.141–8.

[1] Mill, *On Liberty*; all page references in the text refer to Spitz, D. (ed.) (1975) *John Stuart Mill's On Liberty*, Norton Critical Editions.

[2] Carlyle, A. (ed.) (1904) *New Letters of Thomas Carlyle*, 2 vols, John Lane, pp.2–196.

[3] And in the essays on 'Coleridge' and 'Bentham', *CW*, 10.

'Paternalism'

Gerald Dworkin

Gerald Dworkin, author of *Theory and Practice of Autonomy* (1988), argues against Mill that paternalism towards adults can sometimes be justifiable. It can on occasion be right for the state to protect us for our own good.

> Neither one person, nor any number of persons, is warranted in saying to another human creature of ripe years, that he shall not do with his life for his own benefit what he chooses to do with it. (Mill)

> I do not want to go along with a volunteer basis. I think a fellow should be compelled to become better and not let him use his discretion whether he wants to get smarter, more healthy or more honest. (General Hershey)

I take as my starting point the 'one very simple principle' proclaimed by Mill *On Liberty* ...

> That principle is, that the sole end for which mankind are warranted, individually or collectively, in interfering with the liberty of action of any of their number, is self-protection. That the only purpose for which power can be rightfully exercised over any member of a civilized community, against his will, is to prevent harm to others. He cannot rightfully be compelled to do or forbear because it will be better for him to do so, because it will make him happier, because, in the opinion of others, to do so would be wise, or even right.

This principle is neither 'one' nor 'very simple.' It is at least two principles; one asserting that self-protection or the prevention of harm to others is sometimes a sufficient warrant and the other claiming that the individual's own good is *never* a sufficient warrant for the exercise of compulsion either by the society as a whole or by its individual members. I assume that no one, with the possible exception of extreme pacifists or anarchists, questions the correctness of the first half of the principle. This essay is an examination of the negative claim embodied in Mill's principle – the objection to paternalistic interferences with a man's liberty.

I

By paternalism I shall understand roughly the interference with a person's liberty of action justified by reasons referring exclusively to the welfare, good, happiness, needs, interests or values of the person being coerced. One is always well-advised to illustrate one's definitions by examples but it is not easy to find 'pure' examples of paternalistic interferences. For almost any piece of legislation is justified by several different kinds of reasons and even if historically a piece of legislation can be shown to have been introduced for purely paternalistic motives, it may be that advocates of the legislation with an antipaternalistic outlook can find sufficient reasons justifying the legislation without appealing to the reasons which were originally adduced to support it. Thus, for example, it may be that the original legislation requiring motorcyclists to wear safety helmets was introduced for purely paternalistic reasons. But the Rhode Island Supreme Court recently upheld such legislation on the grounds that it was 'not persuaded that the legislature is powerless to prohibit individuals from pursuing a course of conduct which could conceivably result in their becoming public charges,' thus clearly introducing reasons of a quite different kind. Now I regard this decision as being based on reasoning of a very dubious nature but it illustrates the kind of problem one has in finding examples. The following is a list of the kinds of interferences I have in mind as being paternalistic.

II

1   Laws requiring motorcyclists to wear safety helmets when operating their machines.

2   Laws forbidding persons from swimming at a public beach when lifeguards are not on duty.

3   Laws making suicide a criminal offence.

4   Laws making it illegal for women and children to work at certain types of jobs.

5   Laws regulating certain kinds of sexual conduct, for example, homosexuality among consenting adults in private.

6   Laws regulating the use of certain drugs which may have harmful consequences to the user but do not lead to anti-social conduct.

7   Laws requiring a license to engage in certain professions with those not receiving a license subject to fine or jail sentence if they do engage in the practice.

8   Laws compelling people to spend a specified fraction of their income on the purchase of retirement annuities (Social Security).

9   Laws forbidding various forms of gambling (often justified on the grounds that the poor are more likely to throw away their money on such activities than the rich who can afford to).

10   Laws regulating the maximum rates of interest for loans.

11   Laws against duelling.

In addition to laws which attach criminal or civil penalties to certain kinds of action there are laws, rules, regulations, decrees which make it either difficult or impossible for people to carry out their plans and which are also justified on paternalistic grounds. Examples of this are:

1   Laws regulating the types of contracts which will be upheld as valid by the courts, for example, (an example of Mill's to which I shall return) no man may make a valid contract for perpetual involuntary servitude.

2   Not allowing assumption of risk as a defence to an action based on the violation of a safety statute.

3   Not allowing as a defence to a charge of murder or assault the consent of the victim.

4   Requiring members of certain religious sects to have compulsory blood transfusions. This is made possible by not allowing the patient to have recourse to civil suits for assault and battery and by means of injunctions.

5   Civil commitment procedures when these are specifically justified on the basis of preventing the person being committed from harming himself. The D.C. Hospitalization of the Mentally Ill Act provides for involuntary hospitalization of a person who 'is mentally ill, and because of that illness, is likely to injure himself or others if allowed to remain at liberty.' The term injure in this context applies to unintentional as well as intentional injuries.

All of my examples are of existing restrictions on the liberty of individuals. Obviously one can think of interferences which have not yet been imposed. Thus one might ban the sale of cigarettes, or require that people wear safety belts in automobiles (as opposed to merely having them installed), enforcing this by not allowing a motorist to sue for injuries even when caused by other drivers if the motorist was not wearing a seat belt at the time of the accident.

I shall not be concerned with activities which though defended on paternalistic grounds are not interferences with the liberty of persons, for example, the giving of subsidies in kind rather than in cash on the grounds that the recipients would not spend the money on the goods which they really need, or not including a $1000 deductible provision in a basic protection automobile insurance plan on the ground that the people who would elect it could least afford it. Nor shall I be concerned with measures such as 'truth-in-advertising' acts and Pure Food and Drug legislation which are often attacked as paternalistic but which should not be considered so. In these cases all that is provided – it is true by the use of compulsion – is information which it is presumed that rational persons are interested in having in order to make wise decisions. There is no interference with the liberty of the consumer unless one wants to stretch a point beyond good sense and say that his liberty to apply for a loan without knowing the true rate of interest is diminished. It is true that sometimes there is sentiment for going further than providing information, for example when laws against usurious interest are passed preventing those who might wish to contract loans at high rates of interest from doing so, and these measures may correctly be considered paternalistic.

III

Bearing these examples in mind, let me return to a characterization of paternalism. I said earlier that I meant by the term, roughly, interference with a person's liberty for his own good. But, as some of the examples show, the class of persons whose good is involved is not always identical with the class of persons whose freedom is restricted. Thus, in the case of professional licensing it is the practitioner who is directly interfered with but it is the would-be patient whose interests are presumably being served. Not allowing the consent of the victim to be a defense to certain types of crime primarily affects the would-be aggressor but it is the interests of the willing victim that we are trying to protect. Sometimes a person may fall into both classes as would be the case if we banned the manufacture and sale of cigarettes and a given manufacturer happened to be a smoker as well.

Thus we may first divide paternalistic interferences into 'pure' and 'impure' cases. In 'pure' paternalism the class of persons whose freedom is restricted is identical with the class of persons whose benefit is intended to be promoted by such restrictions. Examples: the making of suicide a crime, requiring passengers in automobiles to wear seat belts, requiring a Jehovah's Witness to receive a blood transfusion. In the case of 'impure' paternalism in trying to protect the welfare of a class of persons we find that the only way to do so will involve restricting the freedom of other persons besides those who are benefitted. Now it might be thought that there are no cases of 'impure' paternalism since any such case could always be justified on nonpaternalistic grounds, that is, in terms of preventing harm to others. Thus we might ban cigarette manufacturers from continuing to manufacture their product on the grounds that we are preventing them from causing illness to others in the same way that we prevent other manufacturers from releasing pollutants into the atmosphere, thereby causing danger to the members of the community. The difference is, however, that in the former but not the latter case the harm is of such a nature that it could be avoided by those individuals affected if they so chose. The incurring of the harm requires, so to speak, the active cooperation of the victim. It would be mistaken theoretically and hypocritical in practice to assert that our interference in such cases is just like our interference in standard cases of protecting others from harm. At the very least someone interfered with in this way can reply that no one is complaining about his activities. It may be that impure paternalism requires arguments or reasons of a stronger kind in order to be justified, since there are persons who are losing a portion of their liberty and they do not even have the solace of having it be done 'in their own interest.' Of course in some sense, if paternalistic justifications are ever correct, then we are protecting others, we are preventing some from injuring others, but it is important to see the differences between this and the standard case.

Paternalism then will always involve limitations on the liberty of some individuals in their own interest but it may also extend to interferences with the liberty of parties whose interests are not in question.

IV

Finally, by way of some more preliminary analysis, I want to distinguish paternalistic interference with liberty from a related type with which it is often confused. Consider, for example, legislation which forbids employees to work more than, say, forty hours per week. It is sometimes argued that such legislation is paternalistic for if employees desired such a restriction on their hours of work they could agree among themselves to impose it voluntarily. But because they do not the society imposes its own conception of their best interests upon them by the use of coercion. Hence this is paternalism.

Now it may be that some legislation of this nature is, in fact, paternalistically motivated. I am not denying that. All I want to point out is that there is another possible way of justifying such measures which is not paternalistic in nature. It is not paternalistic because, as Mill puts it in a similar context, such measures are 'required not to overrule the judgment of individuals respecting their own interest, but to give effect to that judgment: they being unable to give effect to it except by concert, which concert again cannot be effectual unless it receives validity and sanction from the law.' (*Principles of Political Economy*).

The line of reasoning here is a familiar one first found in Hobbes and developed with great sophistication by contemporary economists in the last decade or so. There are restrictions which are in the interests of a class of persons taken collectively but are such that the immediate interest of each individual is furthered by his violating the rule when others adhere to it. In such cases the individuals involved may need the use of compulsion to give effect to their collective judgment of their own interest by guaranteeing each individual compliance by the others. In these cases compulsion is not used to achieve some benefit which is not recognized to be a benefit by those concerned, but rather because it is the only feasible means of achieving some benefit which *is* recognized as such by all concerned. This way of viewing matters provides us with another characterization of paternalism in general. Paternalism might be thought of as the use of coercion to achieve a good which is not recognized as such by those persons for whom the good is intended. Again while this formulation captures the heart of the matter – it is surely what Mill is objecting to in *On Liberty* – the matter is not always quite like that. For example, when we force motorcyclists to wear helmets we are trying to promote a good – the protection of the person from injury – which is surely recognized by most of the individuals concerned. It is not that a cyclist doesn't value his bodily integrity; rather, as a supporter of such legislation would put it, he either places, perhaps irrationally, another value or good (freedom from wearing a helmet) above that of physical well-being or, perhaps, while recognizing the danger in the abstract, he either does not fully appreciate it or he underestimates the likelihood of its occurring. But now we are approaching the question of possible justifications of paternalistic measures and the rest of this essay will be devoted to that question.

V

I shall begin for dialectical purposes by discussing Mill's objections to paternalism and then go on to discuss more positive proposals.

An initial feature that strikes one is the absolute nature of Mill's prohibitions against paternalism. It is so unlike the carefully qualified admonitions of Mill and his fellow utilitarians on other moral issues. He speaks of self-protection as the *sole* end warranting coercion, of the individual's own goals as *never* being a sufficient warrant. Contrast this with his discussion of the prohibition against lying in *Utilitarianism:*

> Yet that even this rule, sacred as it is, admits of possible exception, is acknowledged by all moralists, the chief of which is where the with-holding of some fact ... would save an individual ... from great and unmerited evil.

The same tentativeness is present when he deals with justice:

> It is confessedly unjust to break faith with any one: to violate an engagement, either express or implied, or disappoint expectations raised by our own conduct, at least if we have raised these expectations knowingly and voluntarily. Like all the other obligations of justice already spoken of, this one is not regarded as absolute, but as capable of being overruled by a stronger obligation of justice on the other side.

This anomaly calls for some explanation. The structure of Mill's argument is as follows:

1   Since restraint is an evil the burden of proof is on those who propose such restraint.

2   Since the conduct which is being considered is purely self-regarding, the normal appeal to the protection of the interests of others is not available.

3   Therefore we have to consider whether reasons involving reference to the individual's own good, happiness, welfare, or interests are sufficient to overcome the burden of justification.

4   We either cannot advance the interests of the individual by compulsion, or the attempt to do so involves evils which outweigh the good done.

5   Hence the promotion of the individual's own interests does not provide a sufficient warrant for the use of compulsion.

Clearly the operative premise here is (4), and it is bolstered by claims about the status of the individual as judge and appraiser of his welfare, interests, needs, et cetera.:

> With respect to his own feelings and circumstances, the most ordinary man or woman has means of knowledge immeasurably surpassing those that can be possessed by any one else.

> He is the man most interested in his own well-being: the interest which any other person, except in cases of strong personal attachment, can have in it is trifling, compared to that which he himself has.

> These claims are used to support the following generalizations concerning the utility of compulsion for paternalistic purposes.

> The interferences of society to overrule his judgment and purposes in what only regards himself must be grounded on general presumptions; which may be altogether wrong, and even if right, are as likely as not to be missapplied to individual cases.
>
> But the strongest of all the arguments against the interference of the public with purely personal conduct is that when it does interfere, the odds are that it interferes wrongly and in the wrong place.
> All errors which the individual is likely to commit against advice and warning are far outweighed by the evil of allowing others to constrain him to what they deem his good.

Performing the utilitarian calculation by balancing the advantages and disadvantages, we find that: 'Mankind are greater gainers by suffering each other to live as seems good to themselves, than by compelling each other to live as seems good to the rest.' Ergo, (4).

This classical case of a utilitarian argument with all the premises spelled out is not the only line of reasoning present in Mill's discussion. There are asides, and more than asides, which look quite different and I shall deal with them later. But this is clearly the main channel of Mill's thought and it is one which has been subjected to vigorous attack from the moment it appeared – most often by fellow utilitarians. The link that they have usually seized on is, as Fitzjames Stephen put it in *Liberty, Equality, Fraternity*, the absence of proof that the 'mass of adults are so well acquainted with their own interests and so much disposed to pursue them that no compulsion or restraint put upon them by any others for the purpose of promoting their interest can really promote them.' Even so sympathetic a critic as H.L.A. Hart is forced to the conclusion that:

> In Chapter 5 of his essay [*On Liberty*] Mill carried his protests against paternalism to lengths that may now appear to us as fantastic ... No doubt if we no longer sympathise with this criticism this is due, in part, to a general decline in the belief that individuals know their own interest best.
> Mill endows the average individual with 'too much of the psychology of a middle-aged man whose desires are relatively fixed, not liable to be artificially stimulated by external influences; who knows what he wants and what gives him satisfaction or happiness; and who pursues these things when he can.'

Now it is interesting to note that Mill himself was aware of some of the limitations on the doctrine that the individual is the best judge of his own interests. In his discussion of government intervention in general (even where the intervention does not interfere with liberty but provides alternative institutions to those of the market) after making claims which are parallel to those just discussed, for example, 'People understand their own business and their own interests better, and care for them more, than the government does, or can be expected to do,' he goes on to an intelligent discussion of the 'very large and conspicuous exceptions' to the maxim that:

> Most persons take a juster and more intelligent view of their own interest, and of the means of promoting it than can either be prescribed to them by a general enactment of the legislature, or pointed out in the particular case by a public functionary.

Thus there are things

> of which the utility does not consist in ministering to inclinations, nor in serving the daily uses of life, and the want of which is least felt where the need is greatest. This is peculiarly true of those things which are chiefly useful as tending to raise the character of human beings. The uncultivated cannot be competent judges of cultivation. Those who most need to be made wiser and better, usually desire it least, and, if they desire it, would be incapable of finding the way to it by their own lights.

> ... A second exception to the doctrine that individuals are the best judges of their own interest, is when an individual attempts to decide irrevocably now what will be best for his interest at some future and distant time. The presumption in favour of individual judgment is only legitimate, where the judgment is grounded on actual, and especially on present, personal experience; not where it is formed antecedently to experience, and not suffered to be reversed even after experience has condemned it.

The upshot of these exceptions is that Mill does not declare that there should never be government interference with the economy but rather that

> ... in every instance, the burden of making out a strong case should be thrown not on those who resist but those who recommend government interference. Letting alone, in short, should be the general practice: every departure from it, unless required by some great good, is certain evil.

In short, we get a presumption, not an absolute prohibition. The question is why doesn't the argument against paternalism go the same way?

I suggest that the answer lies in seeing that in addition to a purely utilitarian argument Mill uses another as well. As a utilitarian, Mill has to show, in Fitzjames Stephens's words, that: 'Self-protection apart, no good object can be attained by any compulsion which is not in itself a greater evil than the absence of the object which the compulsion obtains.' To show this is impossible, one reason being that it isn't true. Preventing a man form selling himself into slavery (a paternalistic measure which Mill himself accepts as legitimate), or from taking heroin, or from driving a car without wearing seat belts may constitute a lesser evil than allowing him to do any of these things. A consistent utilitarian can only argue against paternalism on the grounds that it (as a matter of fact) does not maximize the good. It is always a contingent question that may be refuted by the evidence. But there is also a non-contingent argument which runs through *On Liberty*. When Mill states that 'there is a part of the life of every person who has come to years of discretion, within which the individuality of that person ought to reign uncontrolled either by any other person or by the public collectively,' he is saying something about what it means to be a person, an autonomous agent. It is because coercing a person for his own good denies this status as an independent entity that Mill objects to it so strongly and in such absolute terms. To be able to choose is a good that is independent of the wisdom of what is chosen. A man's 'mode of laying out his existence is the best, not because it is the best in itself, but because it is his own mode ... . It is the privilege and proper condition of a human being, arrived at the maturity of his faculties, to use and interpret experience in his own way.'

As further evidence of this line of reasoning in Mill, consider the one exception to his prohibition against paternalism.

> In this and most civilised countries, for example, an engagement by which a person should sell himself, or allow himself to be sold, as a slave, would be null and void; neither enforced by law nor by opinion. The ground for thus limiting his power of voluntarily disposing of his own lot in life, is apparent, and is very clearly seen in this extreme case. The reason for not interfering, unless for the sake of others, with a person's voluntary acts, is consideration for his liberty. His voluntary choice is evidence that what he so chooses is desirable, or at least endurable, to him, and his good is on the whole best provided for by allowing him to take his own means of pursuing it. But by selling himself for a slave, he abdicates his liberty; he foregoes any future use of it beyond that single act. He therefore defeats, in his own case, the very purpose which is the justification of allowing him to dispose of himself. He is no longer free; but is thenceforth in a position which has no longer the presumption in its favour, that would be afforded by his voluntarily remaining in it. The principle of freedom cannot require that he should be free not to be free. It is not freedom to be allowed to alienate his freedom.

Now leaving aside the fudging on the meaning of freedom in the last line, it is clear that part of this argument is incorrect. While it is true that *future* choices of the slave are not reasons for thinking that what he chooses then is desirable for him, what is at issue is limiting his immediate choice; and since this choice is made freely, the individual may be correct in thinking that his interests are best provided for by entering such a contract. But the main consideration for not allowing such a contract is the need to preserve the liberty of the person to make future choices. This gives us a principle – a very narrow one – by which to justify some paternalistic interferences. Paternalism is justified only to preserve a wider range of freedom for the individual in question. How far this principle could be extended, whether it can justify all the cases in which we are inclined upon reflection to think paternalistic measures justified, remains to be discussed. What I have tried to show so far is that there are two strains of argument in Mill – one a straight-forward utilitarian mode of reasoning and one which relies not on the goods which free choice leads to but on the absolute value of the choice itself. The first cannot establish any absolute prohibition but at most a presumption and indeed a fairly weak one given some fairly plausible assumptions about human psychology; the second, while a stronger line of argument, seems to me to allow on its own grounds a wider range of paternalism than might be suspected. I turn now to a consideration of these matters.

VI

We might begin looking for principles governing the acceptable use of paternalistic power in cases where it is generally agreed that it is legitimate. Even Mill intends his principles to be applicable only to mature individuals, not those in what he calls 'non-age.' What is it that justifies us in interfering with children? The fact that they lack some of the emotional and cognitive capacities required in order to make fully rational decisions. It is an empirical question to just what extent children have an adequate conception of their own present and future interests but there is not much doubt that there are many deficiencies. For example, it is very difficult for a child to defer gratification for any considerable period of time. Given these deficiencies and given the very real and permanent dangers that may befall the child, it becomes not only permissible but even a duty of the parent to restrict the child's freedom in various ways. There is however an important moral limitation on the exercise of such parental power which is provided by the notion of the child eventually coming to see the correctness of his parent's interventions. Parental paternalism may be thought of as a wager by the parent on the child's subsequent recognition of the wisdom of the restrictions. There is an emphasis on what could be called future-oriented consent – on what the child will come to welcome, rather than on what he does welcome.

The essence of this idea has been incorporated by idealist philosophers into various types of 'real-will' theory as applied to fully adult persons. Extensions of paternalism are argued for by claiming that in various respects, chronologically mature individuals share the same deficiencies in knowledge, capacity to think rationally, and the ability to carry out decisions that children possess. Hence in interfering with such people we are in effect doing what they would do if they were fully rational. Hence we are not really opposing their will, hence we are not really interfering with their freedom. The dangers of this move have been sufficiently exposed by Berlin in his 'Two Concepts of Liberty'. I see no gain in theoretical clarity nor in practical advantage in trying to pass over the real nature of the interferences with liberty that we impose on others. Still the basic notion of consent is important and seems to me the only acceptable way of trying to delimit an area of justified paternalism.

Let me start by considering a case where the consent is not hypothetical in nature. Under certain conditions it is rational for an individual to agree that others should force him to act in ways which, at the time of action, the individual may not see as desirable. If, for example, a man knows that he is subject to breaking his resolves when temptation is present, he may ask a friend to refuse to entertain his requests at some later stage.

A classical example is given in the *Odyssey* when Odysseus commands his men to tie him to the mast and refuse all future orders to be set free, because he knows the power of the Sirens to enchant men with their songs. Here we are on relatively sound ground in later refusing Odysseus' request to be set free. He may even claim to have changed his mind but, since it is *just* such changes that he wished to guard against, we are entitled to ignore them.

A process analogous to this may take place on a social rather than individual basis. An electorate may mandate its representatives to pass legislation which when it comes time to 'pay the price' may be unpalatable. I may believe that a tax increase is necessary to halt inflation though I may resent the lower pay check each month. However in both this case and that of Odysseus, the measure to be enforced is specifically requested by the party involved and at some point in time there is genuine consent and agreement on the part of those persons whose liberty is infringed. Such is not the case for the paternalistic measures we have been speaking about. What must be involved here is not consent to specific measures but rather consent to a system of government, run by elected representatives, with an understanding that they may act to safeguard our interests in certain limited ways.

I suggest that since we are all aware of our irrational propensities, deficiencies in cognitive and emotional capacities, and avoidable and unavoidable ignorance, it is rational and prudent for us to in effect take out 'social insurance policies.' We may argue for and against proposed paternalistic measures in terms of what fully rational individuals would accept as forms of protection. Now clearly, since the initial agreement is not about specific measures we are dealing with a more-or-less blank check and therefore there have to be carefully defined limits. What I am looking for are certain kinds of conditions which make it plausible to suppose that rational people could reach agreement to limit their liberty even when others' interests are not affected.

Of course as in any kind of agreement schema there are great difficulties in deciding what rational individuals would or would not accept. Particularly in sensitive areas of personal liberty, there is always a danger of the dispute over agreement and rationality being a disguised version of evaluative and normative disagreement.

Let me suggest types of situations in which it seems plausible to suppose that fully rational individuals would agree to having paternalistic restrictions imposed upon them. It is reasonable to suppose that there are 'goods' such a health which any person would want to have in order to pursue his own good – no matter how that good is conceived. This is an argument used in connection with compulsory education for children but it seems to me that it can be extended to other goods which have this character. Then one could agree that the attainment of such goods should be promoted even when not recognized to be such, at the moment, by the individuals concerned.

An immediate difficulty arises from the fact that people are always faced with competing goods and that there may be reasons why even a value such as health – or indeed life – may be overridden by competing values. Thus the problem with the Jehovah's Witness and blood transfusions. It may be more important for him to reject 'impure substances' than to go on living. The difficult problem that must be faced is whether one can give sense to the notion of a person irrationally attaching weights to competing values.

Consider a person who knows the statistical data on the probability of being injured when not wearing seat belts in an automobile and knows the types and gravity of the various injuries. He also insists that the inconvenience attached to fastening the belt every time he gets in and out of the car outweighs for him the possible risks to himself. I am inclined in this case to think that such a weighing is irrational. Given his life plans, which we are assuming are those of the average person, his interests and commitments already undertaken, I think it is safe to predict that we can find inconsistencies in his calculations at some point. I am assuming that this is not a man who for some conscious or unconscious reasons is trying to injure himself nor is he a man who just likes to 'live dangerously.' I am assuming that he is like us in all the relevant respects but just puts an enormously high negative value on inconvenience – one which does not seem comprehensible or reasonable.

It is always possible, of course, to assimilate this person to creatures like myself. I, also, neglect to fasten my seat belt and I concede such behavior is not rational but not because I weigh the inconvenience differently from those who fasten the belts. It is just that having made (roughly) the same calculation as everybody else, I ignore it in my actions. [Note: a much better case of weakness of the will than those usually given in ethics tests.] A plausible explanation for this deplorable habit is that although I know in some intellectual sense what the probabilities and risks are I do not fully appreciate them in an emotionally genuine manner.

We have two distinct types of situation in which a man acts in a nonrational fashion. In one case he attaches incorrect weights to some of his values; in the other he neglects to act in accordance with his actual preferences and desires. Clearly there is a stronger and more persuasive argument for paternalism in the latter situation. Here we are really not – by assumption – imposing a good on another person. But why may we not extend our interference to what we might call evaluative delusions? After all, in the case of cognitive delusions we are prepared, often, to act against the expressed will of the person involved. If a man believes that when he jumps out the window he will float upwards – Robert Nozick's example – would not we detain him, forcibly if necessary? The reply will be that this man doesn't wish to be injured and if we could convince him that he is mistaken as to the consequences of his action, he would not wish to perform the action. But part of what is involved in claiming that the man who doesn't fasten his seat-belts is attaching an incorrect weight to the inconvenience of fastening them is that if he were to be involved in an accident and severely injured he would look back and admit that the inconvenience wasn't as bad as all that. So there is a sense in which, if I could convince him of the consequences of his action, he also would not wish to continue his present course of action. Now the notion of consequences being used here is covering a lot of ground. In one case it's being used to indicate what will or can happen as a result of a course of action and in the other it's making a prediction about the future evaluation of the consequences – in the first sense – of a course of action. And whatever the difference between facts and values – whether it be hard and fast or soft and slow – we are genuinely more reluctant to consent to interferences where evaluative differences are the issue. Let me now consider another factor which comes into play in some of these situations which may make an important difference in our willingness to consent to paternalistic restrictions.

Some of the decisions we make are of such a character that they produce changes which are in one or another way irreversible. Situations are created in which it is difficult or impossible to return to anything like the initial stage at which the decision was made. In particular, some of these changes will make it impossible to continue to make reasoned choices in the future. I am thinking specifically of decisions which involve taking drugs that are physically or psychologically addictive and those which are destructive of one's mental and physical capacities.

I suggest we think of the imposition of paternalistic interferences in situations of this kind as being a kind of insurance policy which we take out against making decisions which are far-reaching, potentially dangerous and irreversible. Each of these factors is important. Clearly there are many decisions we make that are relatively irreversible. In deciding to learn to play chess, I could predict in view of my general interest in games that some portion of my free time was going to be preempted and that it would not be easy to give up the game once I acquired a certain competence. But my whole life style was not going to be jeopardized in an extreme manner. Further it might be argued that even with addictive drugs such as heroin one's normal life plans would not be seriously interfered with if an inexpensive and adequate supply were readily available. So this type of argument might have a much narrower scope than appears to be the case at first.

A second class of cases concerns decisions which are made under extreme psychological and sociological pressures. I am not thinking here of the making of the decision as being something one is pressured into – for example, a good reason for making duelling illegal is that unless this is done many people might have to manifest their courage and integrity in ways in which they would rather not do so – but rather of decisions such as that to commit suicide, which are usually made at a point where the individual is not thinking clearly and calmly about the nature of his decision. In addition, of course, this comes under the previous heading of all-too-irrevocable decisions. Now there are practical steps which a society could take if it wanted to decrease the possibility of suicide – for example not paying social security benefits to the survivors or, as religious institutions do, not allowing persons to be buried with the same status as natural deaths. I think we may count these as interferences with the liberty of persons to attempt suicide and the question is whether they are justifiable.

Using my argument schema the question is whether rational individuals would consent to such limitations. I see no reason for them to consent to an absolute prohibition but I do think it is reasonable for them to agree to some kind of enforced waiting period. Since we are all aware of the possibility of temporary states, such as great fear or depression, that are inimical to the making of well-informed and rational decisions, it would be prudent for all of us if there were some kind of institutional arrangement whereby we were restrained from making a decision which is so irreversible. What this would be like in practice is difficult to envisage and it may be that if no practical arrangements were feasible we would have to conclude that there should be no restriction at all on this kind of action. But we might have a 'cooling off' period, in much the same way that we now require couples who file for divorce to go through a waiting period. Or, more far-fetched, we might imagine a Suicide Board composed of a psychologist and another member picked by the applicant. The Board would be required to meet and talk with the person proposing to take his life, though its approval would not be required.

A third class of decisions – these classes are not supposed to be disjoint – involves dangers which are either not sufficiently understood or appreciated correctly by the persons involved. Let me illustrate, using the example of cigarette smoking, a number of possible cases.

1   A person may not know the facts – for example, smoking between one and two packs a day shortens life expectancy 6.2 years, the costs and pain of the illness caused by smoking et cetera.

2   A person may know the facts, wish to stop smoking, but not have the requisite will-power.

3   A person may know the facts but not have them play the correct role in her calculation because, say, she discounts the danger psychologically since it is remote in time and/or inflates the attractiveness of other consequences of the decisions.

In case 1 what is called for is education, the posting of warnings, et cetera. In case 2 there is no theoretical problem. We are not imposing a good on someone who rejects it. We are simply using coercion to enable people to carry out their own goals. (Note: There obviously is a difficulty in that only a subclass of the individuals affected wish to be prevented from doing what they are doing.) In case 3 there is a sense in which we are imposing a good on someone in that given their current appraisal of the facts they do wish to be restricted. But in another sense we are not imposing a good since what is being claimed– and what must be shown or at least argued for – is that an accurate accounting would lead them to reject the current course of action. Now we all know that such cases exist, that we are prone to disregarding dangers that are only possibilities, that immediate pleasures are often magnified and distorted.

If in addition the dangers are severe and far-reaching, we could agree to allow the state a certain degree of power to intervene in such situations. The difficulty is in specifying in advance, even vaguely, the class of cases in which intervention will be legitimate.

A related difficulty is that of drawing a line so that it is not the case that all ultra-hazardous activities are ruled out, for example, mountain-climbing, bull-fighting, sports-car racing, et cetera. There are some risks – even very great ones – which a person is entitled to take with his life.

A good deal depends on the nature of deprivation – for example, does it prevent the person from engaging in the activity completely or merely limit his participation – and how important to the nature of the activity is the absence of restriction when this is weighed against the role that the activity plays in the life of the person. In the case of automobile seat belts, for example, the restriction is trivial in nature, interferes not at all with the use or enjoyment of the activity, and does, I am assuming, considerably reduce a high risk of serious injury. Whereas, for example, making mountain-climbing illegal completely prevents a person from engaging in an activity which may play an important role in his life and his conception of the person he is.

In general, the easiest cases to handle are those which can be argued about in the terms which Mill thought to be so important – a concern not just for the happiness or welfare, in some broad sense, of the individual but rather a concern for the autonomy and freedom of the person. I suggest that we would be most likely to consent to paternalism in those instances in which it preserves and enhances for the individual his ability to rationally consider and carry out his own decisions.

I have suggested in this essay a number of types of situations in which it seems plausible that rational men would agree to granting the legislative powers of a society the right to impose restrictions on what Mill calls 'self-regarding' conduct. However, rational men knowing something about the resources of ignorance, ill-will and stupidity available to the lawmakers of a society – a good case in point is the history of drug legislation in the United States – will be concerned to limit such intervention to a minimum. I suggest in closing two principles designed to achieve this end.

In all cases of paternalistic legislation there must be a heavy and clear burden of proof placed on the authorities to demonstrate the exact nature of the harmful effects (or beneficial consequences) to be avoided (or achieved) and the probability of their occurrence. The burden of proof here is twofold – what lawyers distinguish as the burden of going forward and the burden of persuasion. That the authorities have the burden of going forward means that it is up to them to raise the question and bring forward evidence of the evils to be avoided. Unlike the case of new drugs, where the manufacturer must produce some evidence that the drug has been tested and found not harmful, no citizen has to show with respect to self-regarding conduct that it is not harmful or promotes his best interest. In addition the nature and cogency of the evidence for the harmfulness of the course of action must be set at a high level. To paraphrase a formulation of the burden of proof for criminal proceedings – better ten men ruin themselves than one man be unjustly deprived of liberty.

Finally, I suggest a principle of the least restrictive alternative. If there is an alternative way of accomplishing the desired end without restricting liberty, then although it may involve great expense, inconvenience, et cetera, the society must adopt it.

Note

From Dworkin, Gerald (ed.) (1997) *Mill's* On Liberty *Critical Essays*, Rowman & Littlefield, pp.61–82.

'Mill and Sexual Inequality'

Janet Radcliffe Richards

Janet Radcliffe Richards, Reader in Bioethics at University College London, and author *of The Sceptical Feminist*, clears up some common misunderstandings of Mill's position in *The Subjection of Women*.

Mill is discussing a particular kind of inequality in the *treatment* of women and arguing that it is wrong. That is his main purpose, and I shall say more about it in a moment. But to put this into proper perspective, we need to distinguish it from other kinds of sexual equality that he is *not* defending. People often argue for (or against) sexual equality without realizing, apparently, that there are many things that might be meant by this, and that the justifiability of the claim may depend entirely on which is at issue.

First, Mill is not arguing that the sexes *are* equal in any respect. We may infer from much of what he says that he has no doubt about this matter in many important ways. We know, for instance, what an extremely high opinion he had of the intellect of his wife, and his account of what marriage can be between truly equal partners leaves us in no doubt of what he thinks. He also suggests many ways in which the sexes *may* have different, but equally important, characteristics. But it is important that whatever we may think we can infer from the text about his beliefs, this is not something he is *arguing* for. It is no part of his purpose to make this claim. He does, in considerable detail, discuss his opponents' claims that the sexes are *unequal* in various ways, but his arguments are purely negative. His claim is not that his opponents are definitely wrong, even though we may be certain he thinks they are, but rather that they have not enough grounds to claim that they are right. Women are subjected to a systematically different education and environment, and we are therefore not in a position to say which *observed* inequalities between the sexes stem from nature (as we should now say) and which from nurture. This is quite enough to undermine his opponents' arguments, which is what he wants. But it is important to see that he is not making a positive claim of his own about factual sexual equality.

And secondly, he is not arguing for equality of *outcome* of any kind between the sexes. This is an issue that comes up a great deal in current discussions: people who complain about sexual inequality now have a great deal to say about the small number of women in top jobs or in Parliament, or about women's lower rates of pay, or women as a proportion of the poor or the mentally ill, and the like. Mill says nothing about such matters. Of course you may well point out that most of these issues did not arise, since women were excluded from most public activity and their property was their husbands'; but nevertheless this is a different issue, and one Mill does not address. So if we are going to consider such matters later we shall have to be careful to distinguish them from the kind of equality Mill is discussing.

[...]

What this all implies is, of course [...] the fact that there is no point in complaining about (or insisting on the desirability or inevitability of) sexual inequality as if that were a single thing. Here as in all other contexts we cannot argue about equality without first specifying the kind of equality at issue. And as usual, we need to be aware that equality in some respects may be incompatible with equality in others, and be prepared to choose between different conflicting respects, or at least to produce different arguments for different kinds.

[...]

[Mill] is considering the unequal *treatment* of the sexes by the law. Now [...] treatment is equal or unequal only in particular respects, so we need to be clear about the nature of the inequality. The sexes are unequally treated in that the law specifies one kind of treatment for men, and another – less good – for women. This, as it stands, is a simple description of fact. The issue being argued about is whether this is *wrong* or not.

Now you may be inclined to say that it is *obviously* wrong to treat one group less well than another; and people are often quick to rush in with accusations of discrimination on these grounds. But the problem is that we *certainly don't* think it is always wrong when laws, or other rules, specify that people should be treated differently. We do it all the time and often think it right. There is one sense in which people are treated unequally when the sick are given time off work and the well are not, since being given time off work is a benefit; but we don't think it's wrong. The same thing happens when the guilty are punished and the innocent are not, or when one person is given a desirable job and another is not. So we can't say that all cases of unequal treatment *in this sense* are wrong. And if by 'discrimination' we mean something wrong, this is not an adequate basis for accusations of discrimination. So what is the difference between the ones that are and the ones that are not?

(Note that we do sometimes use 'discriminate against' simply to indicate disadvantageously different treatment. But then the expression is purely *descriptive*, and leaves open the question of whether the treatment is wrong or not. This is why we must not get hooked on the word 'discrimination' – which oscillates between the simply descriptive and the pejorative. It is why we *must* keep to the rule of distinguishing between descriptions and moral judgements.)

You may want to say that the difference between justified and unjustified differentiation is that some distinctions are relevant and others are not; and this is on the right track. But we can express the point differently, and more accurately, by considering what has been going on in Mill's arguments.

Think of some case, like the ones just mentioned, where we do treat people unequally in the sense just mentioned (i.e., we treat them differently, and in such a way that it is better to have one kind of treatment than the other) but think there is nothing wrong. If you look at such cases, you will see that you can appeal to some general principle that tells you *why* some people should have the more favourable treatment. The sick have time off work because they need it, the well qualified get the job because we want the job well done, and so on.

Now what Mill's opponents were trying to do was show that the unequal treatment of the sexes by the law was justified in just the same way. They tried to show that it followed from perfectly general principles about treating people in ways that suited their natures, or the need to get work properly done and the country properly governed. But Mill argued – and I think showed conclusively – that their arguments just did not work. They depended on premises either known to be false or not known to be true, or they depend on mistaken logic, or they were incompatible with principles held by the recommender, or all three at once.

In other words, what Mill showed was that the unequal treatment of women was *not* a consequence of general principles held by the people who were recommending it. It was something superimposed on these other principles, and quite distinct from them. It was in this sense that it was irrelevant.

Mill doesn't put it quite like this, but it is obviously in line with what he thinks. He catches the significance of it in one passing remark in Chapter II when he speaks of *institutions grounded on an arbitrary preference of one human being over another* (Mill (1988 edn), p.45). The point about the 'arbitrary' is that the preference doesn't derive from some general principle applying equally to everyone, but stands alone. The disadvantageous treatment of women seems to have no other purpose than the arbitrary advantage of men, and all these hopeless arguments are just attempts to disguise the fact.

[...]

Contemporary relevance

If we do think it unjust to subject people to *arbitrary* disadvantage – unequal treatment that cannot be justified in terms of a general principle – that suggests an important point of methodology. Whenever some policy or action involves the disadvantageous treatment of some people in comparison with others, the first thing to check is whether it really can be justified in terms of whatever principles are offered in its defence. *Even before we start to ask whether the principle is one we agree with or not*, we can ask whether it supports the policy it is supposed to support, because if it doesn't the policy is, from the point of view of someone who holds that principle, arbitrary, and objectionable on those grounds. And if more justifications are offered, they can be subjected to the same test.

The particular arguments used by Mill can still be used against the societies, in many parts of the world, whose treatment of women is still much as Mill described it. But the method of argument is more generally useful.[...] And in principle it can be tried with any differential treatment whatever.

Furthermore, its usefulness is not confined to the analysis of laws. The question can be raised in the context of *any* unequal treatment. There is still differentiation between the sexes in laws and formal institutions (some in this country, enormous amounts in some other parts of the world); there is differentiation in convention, in treatment of individuals, and so on. Whenever there are such differences, and anyone tries to defend them, we can ask whether the justifications work in their own terms, or whether the unequal treatment must be regarded as arbitrary.

It is, by the way, important to distinguish between the question of what kinds of differential, unequal, treatment still exist, and the quite different question of whether any particular kind is arbitrary if it does. The first is an empirical question, and although it is easily answered in some contexts (it is clear when laws differentiate the sexes, or when clubs have rules excluding women, or when teachers say they want strong boys to come and help with furniture shifting), there are other contexts in which it is very difficult to say what is happening. This is the problem that occurs when an employer says he didn't appoint some female candidate because she wasn't as good as the male who was appointed, and we may suspect that the real differentiating factor was her being female. It is often difficult to establish the truth in contexts like this (how would you tell for certain?). However, large numbers of carefully controlled experiments have been done to show that people do differentiate on grounds of sex even when they are not aware of it themselves. For instance, experiments have been done in which people have been shown student essays or academic articles, and asked to assess them. It turns out that their assessment of the same articles is strongly influenced by whether the name put on them is male or female (and, of course, they are invariably thought less good if their author is thought to be female). Or young women have been watched playing with small children, and it is found that their treatment of the same children is quite different according to whether they are dressed and named as girls or as boys. (Some experiments of this kind are referred to in Ann Oakley's *Subject Women*, Martin Robinson, Oxford, 1981, pp.96 and 126.)

Questions of how much such differentiation there is are interesting and important, but because they are empirical they are beyond the scope of this course. Our main concern is with the question of whether some unequal treatment *would* be justified if it *did* exist, and although we may want to know as much as possible about how much unequal treatment there is, we can discuss the questions of justification independently.

This is a very fruitful line of investigation – not just for attacking opponents, but also for investigating our own ideas. I have already claimed that most of us go around all the time trying to keep the disparate parts of an incoherent conceptual system from falling apart, and we tend in consequence to be amazingly tolerant of invented facts or absurd logic when that seems the only way to cover up the cracks. It seems astonishing to us that Mill's contemporaries could not see the mistakes in their own arguments, since they are so clear to us. And the important thing here is that they are shown to be wrong *not* by someone coming in with a new moral view claimed to be better than theirs, but by the discovery of internal problems in their own system. This is (I think) one reason why we can make progress in ethics. We can discover the problems in our own system without even raising the question of whether someone else's moral views are better than ours. And this is the beginning of progress, because if our views are incoherent there must be *something* wrong with them.

Note

From Radcliffe Richards, Janet (1993) *A423 Philosophical Problems of Equality: Study Guide,* The Open University, pp.87–92.

'The Hope of Friendship'

Mary Lyndon Shanley

Mary Lyndon Shanley, author of *Feminism, Marriage and the Law in Victorian England*, gives a critical overview of Mill's account of friendship within marriage, the positive vision of relations between men and women sketched in the final chapter of *The Subjection of Women*.

Mill's remedy for the evils generated by the fear of equality was his notion of marital friendship. The topic of the rather visionary fourth chapter of *The Subjection of Women* was friendship, 'the ideal of marriage' (Rossi (1970), pp.233, 235).[1] That ideal was, according to Mill, 'a union of thoughts and inclinations' which created a 'foundation of solid friendship' between husband and wife (ibid. pp.231, 233).

Mill's praise of marital friendship was almost lyrical, and struck resonances with Aristotle's, Cicero's and Montaigne's similar exaltations of the pleasures as well as the moral enrichment of this form of human intimacy. Mill wrote:

> When each of two persons, instead of being a nothing, is a something; when they are attached to one another, and are not too much unlike to begin with; the constant partaking of the same things, assisted by their sympathy, draws out the latent capacities of each for being interested in the things ... by a real enriching of the two natures, each acquiring the tastes and capacities of the other in addition to its own.

> (Ibid., p.233)

This expansion of human capacities did not, however, exhaust the benefits of friendship. Most importantly, friendship developed what Montaigne praised as the abolition of selfishness, the capacity to regard another human being as fully as worthy as oneself. Therefore friendship of the highest order could only exist between those equal in excellence.[2] And for precisely this reason, philosophers from Aristotle to Hegel had consistently argued that women could not be men's friends, for women lacked the moral capacity for the highest forms of friendship. Indeed, it was common to distinguish the marital bond from friendship not solely on the basis of sexual and procreative activity, but also because women could not be part of the school of moral virtue which was found in friendship at its best.

Mill therefore made a most significant break with the past in adopting the language of friendship in his discussion of marriage. For Mill, no less than for any of his predecessors, 'the true virtue of human beings is the fitness to live together as equals.' Such equality required that individuals '[claim] nothing for themselves but what they as freely concede to every one else,' that they regard command of any kind as 'an exceptional necessity,' and that they prefer whenever possible 'the society of those with whom leading and following can be alternate and reciprocal' (ibid., pp.174–5). This picture of reciprocity, of the shifting of leadership according to need, was a remarkable characterization of family life. Virtually all of Mill's liberal contemporaries accepted the notion of the natural and inevitable complementariness of male and female personalities and roles. Mill, however, as early as 1833 had expressed his belief that 'the highest masculine and the highest feminine' characters were without any real distinction.[3] That view of the androgynous personality lent support to Mill's brief for equality within the family.

Mill repeatedly insisted that his society had no general experiences of 'the marriage relationship as it would exist between equals,' and that such marriages would be impossible until men rid themselves of the fear of equality and the will to domination.[4] The liberation of women, in other words, required not just legal reform but a re-education of the passions. Women were to be regarded as equals not only to fulfil the demand for individual rights and in order that they could survive in the public world of work, but also in order that women and men could form ethical relations of the highest order. Men and women alike had to 'learn to cultivate their strongest sympathy with an equal in rights and in cultivation' (ibid., p.236). Mill struggled, not always with total success, to talk about the quality of such association. For example, in *On Liberty*, Mill explicitly rejected Von Humbolt's characterization of marriage as a contractual relationship which could be ended by 'the declared will of either party to dissolve it.' That kind of dissolution was appropriate when the benefits of partnership could be reduced to monetary terms. But marriage involved a person's expectations for the fulfilment of a 'plan of life,' and created 'a new series of moral obligations ... toward that person, which may possibly be overruled, but cannot be ignored.'[5] Mill was convinced that difficult though it might be to shape the law to recognize the moral imperatives of such a relationship, there were ethical communities which transcended and were not reducible to their individual components.

At this juncture, however, the critical force of Mill's essay weakened, and a tension developed between his ideal and his prescriptions for his own society. For all his insight into the dynamics of domestic domination and subordination, the only specific means Mill in fact put forward for the fostering of this society of equals was providing equal opportunity to women in areas outside the family. Indeed, in *On Liberty* he wrote that 'nothing more is needed for the complete removal of [the almost despotic power of husbands over wives] than that wives should have the same rights and should receive the same protection of law in the same manner, as all other persons.'[6] In the same vein, Mill seemed to suggest that nothing more was needed for women to achieve equality than that 'the present duties and protective bounties in favour of men should be recalled' (ibid., p.154). Moreover, Mill did not attack the traditional assumption about men's and women's different responsibilities in an ongoing household, although he was usually careful to say that women 'chose' their role or that it was the most 'expedient' arrangement, not that it was theirs by 'nature.'

Mill by and large accepted the notion that once they marry, women should be solely responsible for the care of the household and children, men for providing the family income: 'When the support of the family depends ... on earnings, the common arrangement, by which the man earns the income and the wife superintends the domestic expenditure, seems to me in general the most suitable division of labour between the two persons' (ibid., p.178). He did not regard it as 'a desirable custom, that the wife should contribute by her labour to the income of the family' (ibid., p.179). Mill indicated that women alone would care for any children of the marriage; repeatedly he called it the 'care which ... nobody else takes,' the one vocation in which there is 'nobody to compete with them,' and the occupation which 'cannot be fulfilled by others' (ibid., pp.178, 183, 241). Further, Mill seemed to shut the door on combining household duties and a public life: 'like a man when he chooses a profession, so, when a woman marries, it may be in general understood that she makes a choice of the management of a household, and the bringing up of a family, as the first call upon her exertions ... and that she renounces ... all [other occupations] which are not consistent with the requirements of this' (ibid., p.179).

Mill's acceptance of the traditional gender-based division of labor in the family has led some recent critics to fault Mill for supposing that legal equality of opportunity would solve the problem of women's subjection, even while leaving the sexual division of labor in the household intact. For example, Julia Annas, after praising Mill's theoretical arguments in support of equality, complains that Mill's suggestions for actual needed changes in sex roles are 'timid and reformist at best. He assumes that most women will in fact want only to be wives and mothers.'[7] Leslie Goldstein agrees that 'the restraints which Mill believed should be imposed on married women constitute a major exception to his argument for equality of individual liberty between the sexes – an exception so enormous that it threatens to swallow up the entire argument.'[8] But such arguments, while correctly identifying the limitations of antidiscrimination statutes as instruments for social change, incorrectly identify Mill's argument for equal opportunity as the conclusion of his discussion of male-female equality.[9] On the contrary, Mill's final prescription to end the subjection of women was not equal opportunity but spousal friendship; equal opportunity was a means whereby such friendship could be encouraged.

The theoretical force of Mill's condemnation of domestic hierarchy has not yet been sufficiently appreciated. Mill's commitment to equality in marriage was of a different theoretical order than his acceptance of a continued sexual division of labor. On the one hand, Mill's belief in the necessity of equality as a precondition to marital friendship was a profound theoretical tenet. It rested on the normative assumption that human relationships between equals were of a higher, more enriching order than those between unequals. Mill's belief that equality was more suitable to friendship than inequality was as unalterable as his conviction that democracy was a better system of government than despotism; the human spirit could not develop its fullest potential when living in absolute subordination to another human being or to government.[10] On the other hand, Mill's belief that friendship could be attained and sustained while women bore nearly exclusive responsibility for the home was a statement which might be modified or even abandoned if experience proved it to be wrong. In this sense it was like Mill's view that the question of whether socialism was preferable to capitalism could not be settled by verbal argument alone but must 'work itself out on an experimental scale, by actual trial.'[11] Mill believed that marital equality was a moral imperative; his view that such equality might exist where married men and women moved in different spheres of activity was a proposition subject to demonstration. Had Mill discovered that managing the household to the exclusion of most other activity created an impediment to the friendship of married women and men, *The Subjection of Women* suggests that he would have altered his view of practicable domestic arrangements, but not his commitment to the desirability of male-female friendship in marriage.

The most interesting shortcomings of Mill's analysis are thus not found in his belief in the efficacy of equal opportunity, but rather in his blindness to what other conditions might hinder or promote marital friendship. In his discussion of family life, for example, Mill seemed to forget his own warning that women could be imprisoned not only 'by actual law' but also 'by custom equivalent to law' (ibid., p.241). Similarly, he overlooked his own cautionary observation that in any household 'there will naturally be more potential voice on the side, whichever it is, that brings the means of support' (ibid., p.170). And although he had brilliantly depicted the narrowness and petty concerns of contemporary women who were totally excluded from political participation, he implied that the mistresses of most households might content themselves simply with exercising the suffrage (were it to be granted), a view hardly consistent with his arguments in other works for maximizing the level of political discussion and participation whenever possible. More, significantly, however, Mill ignored the potential barrier between husband and wife which such different adult life experiences might create, and the contribution of shared experience to building a common sensibility and strengthening the bonds of friendship.

Mill also never considered that men might take any role in the family other than providing the economic means of support. Perhaps Mill's greatest oversight in his paean of marital equality was his failure to entertain the possibilities that nurturing and caring for children might provide men with useful knowledge and experience, and that shared parenting would contribute to the friendship between spouses which he so ardently desired. Similarly, Mill had virtually nothing to say about the positive role which sex might play in marriage. The sharp language with which he condemned undesired sexual relations as the execution of 'an animal function' was nowhere supplemented by an appreciation of the possible enhancement which sexuality might add to marital friendship. One of the striking features of Montaigne's lyrical praise of friendship was that it was devoid of sensuality, for Montaigne abhorred 'the Grecian license,' and he was adamant that women were incapable of the highest forms of friendship. Mill's notion of spousal friendship suggested the possibility of a friendship which partook of both a true union of minds and of a physical expression of the delight in one's companion, a friendship which involved all of the human faculties. It was an opportunity which (undoubtedly to the relief of those such as James Fitzjames Stephen) Mill himself was not disposed to use, but which was nonetheless implicit in his praise of spousal friendship.[12]

One cannot ask Mill or any other theorist to 'jump over Rhodes' and address issues not put forward by conditions and concerns of his own society.[13] Nevertheless, even leaving aside an analysis of the oppression inherent in the class structure (an omission which would have to be rectified in a full analysis of liberation), time has made it clear that Mill's prescriptions alone will not destroy the master-slave relationship which he so detested. Women's aspirations for equality will not be met by insuring equal civic rights and equal access to jobs outside the home. To accomplish that end would require a transformation of economic and public structures which would allow wives and husbands to share those domestic tasks which Mill assigned exclusively to women. Some forms of publicly supported day-care, parental as well as maternity leaves, flexible work schedules, extensive and rapid public transportation, health and retirement benefits for part-time employment are among commonly proposed measures which would make the choice of Mill's ideal of marriage between equals possible. In their absence it is as foolish to talk about couples choosing the traditional division of labor in marriage as it was in Mill's day to talk about women choosing marriage: both are Hobson's choices, there are no suitable alternatives save at enormous costs to the individuals involved.

Mill's feminist vision, however, transcends his own immediate prescriptions for reform. *The Subjection of Women* is not only one of liberalism's most incisive arguments for equal opportunity, but it embodies as well a belief in the importance of friendship for human development and progress. The recognition of individual rights is important in Mill's view because it provides part of the groundwork for more important human relationships of trust, mutuality and reciprocity. Mill's plea for an end to the subjection of women is not made, as critics such as Gertrude Himmelfarb assert, in the name of 'the absolute primacy of the individual,' but in the name of the need of both men and women for community. Mill's essay is valuable both for its devastating critique of the corruption of marital inequality, and for its argument, however incomplete, that one of the aims of a liberal polity should be to promote the conditions which will allow friendship, in marriage and elsewhere, to take root and flourish.

Notes

From Shanley, Mary Lyndon (1981) 'Marital Slavery and Friendship: John Stuart Mill's *The Subjection of Women*', *Political Theory*, 9, 2, pp.238–44.

[1] Mill, J.S. (1869) *The Subjection of Women* in Rossi, Alice (ed.) (1970) *Essays on Sex Equality*, University of Chicago Press, ch. 4, pp.233, 235. All references to *The Subjection of Women* will be to this edition.

[2] Montaigne's essay, 'Of Friendship' in Frame, Donald M. (trans) (1948) *The Complete Works of Montaigne*, Stanford: Stanford University Press, pp.135–44.

[3] Letter to Thomas Carlyle, October 5, 1833, C.W. [Complete Works] XII, *Earlier Letters*, p.184.

[4] Letter to John Nichol, August 1869, in Mineka, Frank and Lindley, Dwight N. (eds) (1972) *C.W.* XVII, *The Later Letters*, University of Toronto Press, p.1634.

[5] *C.W.,* XVIII, p.300. Elsewhere Mill wrote, 'My opinion on Divorce is that... nothing ought to be rested in, short of entire freedom on both sides to dissolve this like any other partnership.' Letter to an unidentified correspondent, November 1855, *C.W.* XIV, *Later Letters*, p.500. But against this letter was the passage from *On Liberty*, and his letter to Henry Rusden of July 1870 in which he abjured making any final judgements about what a proper divorce law would be 'until women have an equal voice in making it'. He denied that he advocated that marriage should be dissoluble 'at the will of either party', and stated that no well-grounded opinion could be put forward until women first achieved equality under the laws and in married life. *C.W.*, XVII, *Later Letters*, pp.1750–1.

[6] *C.W.*, XVII, p.301.

[7] Annas, J. (1977) 'Mill and the Subjection of Women', *Philosophy*, 52, p.189.

[8] Goldstein, L. (1978) 'Marx and Mill on the Equality of Women', paper presented at the Midwest Political Association Convention, Chicago, April 1978, p.8. Susan Okin makes a similar point, stating that 'Mill never questioned or objected to the maintenance of traditional sex roles within the family, but expressly considered them to be suitable and desirable' (Okin, S.M. (1979) *Women in Western Political Thought*, Princeton University Press, p.237). Okin's reading of Mill is basically sound and sympathetic, but does not recognize the theoretical priority of Mill's commitment to marital equality and friendship.

[9] Of recent writers on Mill, only Richard Krouse seems sensitive to the inherent tension in Mill's thought about women in the household. Mill's own 'ideal of a reformed family life, based upon a full non-patriarchal marriage bond,' Krouse points out, requires 'on the logic of his own analysis... [the] rejection of the traditional division of labour between the sexes' (Krouse, R. (n.d.) 'Patriarchal Liberalism and Beyond: From John Stuart Mill to Harriet Taylor' unpublished manuscript, Williamstown, MA, p.39).

[10] *Considerations on Representative Government*, *C.W.*, XIX, pp.399–403.

[11] *Chapters on Socialism* (1879), *C.W.*, V, p.736.

[12] Throughout his writings Mill displayed a tendency to dismiss or deprecate the exotic dimensions of life. In his *Autobiography* he wrote approvingly that his father looked forward to an increase in freedom in relations between the sexes, freedom which would be void of any sensuality 'either of a theoretical or of a practical kind.' His own twenty-year friendship with Harriet Taylor before their marriage was 'one of strong affection and confidential intimacy only.' Mill, J.S. (1944 edn) *Autobiography of John Stuart Mill*, Columbia University Press, pp.75, 16. In *The Principles of Political Economy* Mill remarked that in his own day 'the animal instinct' occupied a 'disproportionate preponderance in human life.' *C.W.*, III, p.766.

[13] Hegel, G.W.F. (1952 edn) *The Philosophy of Right*, ed. T. M. Knox, Oxford University Press, p.11 ...

Bibliography

Anglo, S. (1971) *Machiavelli: A Dissection*, Paladin.

Annas, J. (1977) 'Mill and the Subjection of Women', *Philosophy*, 52, pp.179–94.

Aristotle (1984 edn) *Ethics*, T. Irwin (trans.), Hackett Publishing Company.

Aristotle (1996 edn) *Politics and The Constitution of Athens*, S. Everson (ed.), B. Jowett (trans.; revised J. Barnes, 1984), Cambridge University Press.

Arthur, C.J. (ed.) (1974) *Marx and Engels: The German Ideology, Part One*, Lawrence & Wishart.

Arthur, C.J. (1986) 'Marx and Engels, *The German Ideology*', in *Philosophers Ancient and Modern*, G. Vesey (ed.), Cambridge University Press.

Ashcraft, R. (1986) *Revolutionary Politics and John Locke's Two Treatises of Government*, Princeton University Press.

Barry, B. (1964) 'The Public Interest', *The Aristotelian Society, Supp. Vol. XXXVIII*, The Aristotelian Society, pp.1–18.

Baumgold, D. (1988) *Hobbes's Political Theory*, Cambridge University Press.

Berlin, I. (1948) *Karl Marx*, 2nd edn, Oxford University Press.

Berlin, I. (1998) *The Proper Study of Mankind*, Pimlico.

Betts, C. (ed.) (1994) *Jean-Jacques Rousseau: Discourse on Political Economy and The Social Contract*, Oxford University Press, Oxford World's Classics.

Bondanella, P. and Musa, M. (eds) (1979) *The Portable Machiavelli*, Penguin Books.

Bull, G. (ed.) (1999) *Niccolò Machiavelli: The Prince*, Penguin Books.

Burgess, G. (1990) 'Contexts for the Writing and Publication of Hobbes's *Leviathan*', *History of Political Thought*, 11, pp.675–702.

Callinicos, A. (ed.) (1989) *Marxist Theory*, Oxford University Press.

Canovan, M. (1987) 'Rousseau's Two Concepts of Citizenship', in Kennedy and Mendus (1987), pp.78–105.

Cohen, J.M. (ed.) (1953) *The Confessions of Jean-Jacques Rousseau*, Penguin Books.

Cohen, G.A. (1978) *Karl Marx's Theory of History: a Defence*, Oxford University Press.

Cohen, G.A. (1988) *History, Labour, and Freedom: Themes from Marx*, Oxford University Press.

Cole, G.D.H. (ed.) (1973) *Rousseau: The Social Contract and Discourses*, Dent.

Copp, D. (1979) 'Collective Actions and Secondary Actions', *American Philosophical Quarterly*, 16, pp.177–86.

Copp, D. (1980) 'Hobbes on Artificial Persons and Collective Actions', *The Philosophical Review*, 89, pp.579–606.

Coyle, M. (ed.) (1995) *Machiavelli's The Prince: New Interdisciplinary Essays*, Manchester University Press.

Crisp, R. (1997) *Mill on Utilitarianism*, Routledge.

Curley, E. (ed.) (1994) *Thomas Hobbes: Leviathan*, Hackett Publishing Company.

Dent, N.J.H. (1988) *Rousseau*, Blackwell.

Dent, N.J.H. (1992) *A Rousseau Dictionary*, Blackwell.

Dworkin, G. (ed.) (1997) *Mill's On Liberty: Critical Essays*, Rowman & Littlefield.

Elster, J. (1986) *An Introduction to Karl Marx*, Cambridge University Press.

Feinberg, J. (1970) *Doing and Deserving: Essays in the Theory of Responsibility*, Princeton University Press.

Fukuda, A. (1997) *Sovereignty and the Sword: Harrington, Hobbes, and Mixed Government in the English Civil Wars*, Oxford University Press.

Gauthier, D.P. (1969) *The Logic of Leviathan: the Moral and Political Theory of Thomas Hobbes*, Oxford University Press.

Goodin, R.E. and Pettit, P. (eds) (1993) *A Companion to Contemporary Political Philosophy*, Blackwell.

Gourevitch, V. (ed.) (1997) *J.-J. Rousseau: The Social Contract and Other Later Political Writings*, Cambridge: University Press.

Gray, J. (1996) *Mill on Liberty: A Defence*, 2nd edn, Routledge.

Gray, J. and Smith, G.W. (eds) (1991) *J.S. Mill, On Liberty in Focus*, Routledge.

de Grazia, S. (1989) *Machiavelli in Hell*, Harvester.

Hall, J.C. (1973) *Rousseau: An Introduction to his Political Philosophy*, Macmillan.

Hampsher-Monk, I. (1992) *A History of Modern Political Thought: Major Political Thinkers from Hobbes to Marx*, Blackwell.

Hampton, J. (1986) *Hobbes and the Social Contract Tradition*, Cambridge University Press.

Hampton, J. (1997) *Political Philosophy*, WestView Press.

Himmelfarb, G. (ed.) (1985) *John Stuart Mill: On Liberty*, Penguin Books.

Hindess, B. (1993) 'Marxism', in Goodin and Pettit (1993), pp.312–32.

Hobbes, T. (1668) *Leviathan, sive De Materia, Forma, & Potestate Civitatis Ecclesiasticae et Civilis*; in *Thomae Hobbes Malmesburiensis Opera Philosophica Quae Latine scripsit, Omnia*, Amsterdam: Johannes Blaeu.

Hobbes, T. (1839 edn) *De Homine*; in *Thomae Hobbes malmesburiensis opera philosophica quae latine scripsit omnia*, Sir William Molesworth (ed.), London: John Bohn, vol. II, pp.1–132.

Hobbes, T. (1840 edn) 'Considerations upon the Reputation, Loyalty, Manners, and Religion, of Thomas Hobbes, of Malmesbury', in *The English Works of Thomas Hobbes*, Sir William Molesworth (ed.), London: John Bohn, vol. IV, pp.409–40.

Hobbes, T. (1994 edn) *Leviathan*, E. Curley (ed.), Hackett Publishing Company.

Hobbes, T. (1996 edn) *Leviathan, or The Matter, Forme, & Power of a Common-wealth Ecclesiasticall and Civill*, R. Tuck (ed.), Cambridge University Press.

Horton, J. and Mendus, S. (eds) (1991) *John Locke: A Letter Concerning Toleration in Focus*, Routledge.

Hume, D. (1963 edn) *Essays Moral, Political and Literary*, Oxford University Press.

Jaume, L. (1986) *Hobbes et l'Etat représentatif moderne*, Presses Universitaires de France.

Kennedy, E. and Mendus, S. (eds) (1987) *Women in Western political philosophy: Kant to Nietzsche*, Harvester.

Kymlicka, W. (1990) *Contemporary Political Philosophy: An Introduction*, Oxford University Press.

Lessay, F. (1992) 'Le vocabulaire de la personne', in *Hobbes et son vocabulaire*, Y.C. Zarka (ed.), Vrin, pp.155–86.

Levine, A. (1976) *The Politics of Autonomy*, University of Massachusetts Press.

Leyden, W. von (1982) *Hobbes and Locke: The Politics of Freedom and Obligation*, Macmillan.

Locke, J. (1980 edn) *Second Treatise of Government*, C.B. Macpherson (ed.), Hackett Publishing Company.

Lloyd Thomas, D.A. (1995) *Locke on Government*, Routledge.

McLellan, D. (1980) *The Thought of Karl Marx*, Macmillan.

McLellan, D. (ed.) (1977) *Karl Marx: Selected Writings*, Oxford University Press.

Macpherson, C.B. (1962) *The Political Theory of Possessive Individualism: Hobbes to Locke*, Oxford University Press.

Machiavelli, N. (1999 edn) *The Prince*, G. Bull (trans.), Penguin Books.

Machiavelli, N. (1983 edn) *The Discourses*, B. Crick (ed.), Penguin Books.

Martinich, A.P. (1997) *Thomas Hobbes*, Macmillan.

Marx, K. (1843) 'On the Jewish Question', in Simon (1994) and McLellan (1977).

Marx, K. (1843–4) *Critique of Hegel's Philosophy of Right*, in Simon (1994).

Marx, K. (1844) 'Alienated Labour', in Simon (1994).

Marx, K. (1859) 'Preface to A Contribution to the Critique of Political Economy', in Simon (1994).

Marx, K. (1891) 'Critique of the Gotha Programme', in Simon (1994).

Marx, K. and Engels, F. (1848) *The Communist Manifesto*, in Simon (1994).

Marx, K. and Engels, F. (1974 edn) *The German Ideology, Part One*, C.J. Arthur (ed.), Lawrence & Wishart.

Mill, J.S. (1974 edn) *On Liberty*, G. Himmelfarb (ed.), Penguin Books.

Mill, J.S. (1988 edn) *The Subjection of Women*, S.M. Okin (ed.), Hackett Publishing Company.

Mill, J.S. (1989 edn) *Autobiography*, J.M. Robson (ed.), Penguin Books.

Mill, J.S. (1991 edn) *Utilitarianism* in *On Liberty and Other Essays*, J. Gray (ed.), Oxford World's Classics, Oxford University Press.

Milner, S.J. (ed.) (1995) *Niccolò Machiavelli: The Prince and other political writings*, Dent.

Nagel, T. (1979) *Mortal Questions*, Cambridge University Press.

Nozick, R. (1974) *Anarchy, State and Utopia*, Basic Books.

O'Hagan, T. (2000) *Rousseau*, Routledge.

Okin, S.M. (1979) *Women in Western Political Thought*, Princeton University Press.

Okin, S.M. (ed.) (1988) *John Stuart Mill: The Subjection of Women*, Hackett Publishing Company.

Pateman, C. (1980) 'The Fraternal Social Contract', in Goodin and Pettit (1993), pp.45–59.

Pateman, C. (1988) *The Sexual Contract*, Polity Press.

Peters, R.S. (ed.) (1962) *Body, Man, and Citizen: Thomas Hobbes*, Collier Books.

Pike, J. (1999) *From Aristotle to Marx*, Ashgate.

Pitkin, H.F. (1967) *The Concept of Representation*, University of California Press.

Plamenatz, J. (1963) *Man and Society*, 2 vols, Longman.

Plamenatz, J. (ed.) (1972) *Machiavelli: The Prince, selections from the Discourses and other writings*, Fontana/Collins.

Polin, R. (1981) *Hobbes, Dieu et les hommes*, Presses Universitaires de France.

Pyle, A. (ed.) (1994) *Liberty: Contemporary Responses to John Stuart Mill*, Thoemmes Press.

Radcliffe Richards, J. (1993) *A423 Philosophical Problems of Equality: Study Guide*, The Open University.

Rawls, J. (1971) *A Theory of Justice*, Oxford University Press.

Rawls, J. (1993) *Political Liberalism*, Columbia University Press.

Riley, J. (1998) *Mill on Liberty*, Routledge.

Rosen, M. (1996) 'The Problem of Ideology', *The Aristotelian Society Supp. Vol. LXX*, The Aristotelian Society.

Rousseau, J.-J. (1987 edn) *Discourse on the Origin of Inequality*, D.A. Cress (trans.), Hackett Publishing Company.

Rousseau, J.-J. (1994 edn) *Discourse on Political Economy and The Social Contract*, C. Betts (trans.), Oxford University Press, Oxford World's Classics.

Runciman, D. (1997) *Pluralism and the Personality of the State*, Cambridge University Press.

Russell, B. (1945) *A History of Western Philosophy*, Allen Unwin.

Ryan, A. (ed.) (1997) *Mill: Texts and Commentaries*, Norton Critical Editions.

St John Packe, M. (1954) *The Life of John Stuart Mill*, Macmillan.

Shanley, M.L. (1981) 'Marital Slavery and Friendship: John Stuart Mill's *The Subjection of Women*', *Political Theory*, 9, 2, pp.229–47.

Simmons, A.J. (1992) *The Lockean Theory of Rights*, Princeton University Press.

Simon, L.H. (ed.) (1994) *Karl Marx: Selected Writings*, Hackett Publishing Company.

Singer, P. (1983) *Hegel*, Oxford University Press.

Skinner, Q. (1981) *Machiavelli*, Oxford University Press.

Skinner, Q. (1990) 'Thomas Hobbes on the Proper Signification of Liberty', *Transactions of the Royal Historical Society*, 40, pp.121–51.

Skinner, Q. (1996) *Reason and Rhetoric in the Philosophy of Thomas Hobbes*, Cambridge University Press.

Skinner, Q. (1999) 'Hobbes and the Purely Artificial Person of the State', *Journal of Political Philosophy*, 7, 1, pp.1–29.

Skinner, Q. (2000) *Machiavelli: A Very Short Introduction*, Oxford University Press.

Skinner, Q. and Price, R. (eds) (1988) *Machiavelli: The Prince*, Cambridge University Press.

Skorupski, J. (1989) *John Stuart Mill*, Routledge.

Skorupski, J. (ed.) (1998) *The Cambridge Companion to Mill*, Cambridge University Press.

Slomp, G. (2000) *Hobbes*, Macmillan.

Sommerville, J. (1996) 'Lofty Science and Local Politics', in *The Cambridge Companion to Hobbes*, T. Sorell (ed.), Cambridge University Press.

Sorell, T. (1986) *Hobbes*, Routledge.

Stephen, J.F. (1967 edn) *Liberty, Equality, Fraternity*, White, R.J. (ed.), Cambridge University Press.

Taylor, A.E. (1938) 'The Ethical Doctrine of Hobbes', *Philosophy*, 13.

Tukiainem, A. (1994) 'The Commonwealth as a Person in Hobbes's *Leviathan*', *Hobbes Studies*, 7, pp.44–55.

Tully, J. (1980) *A Discourse on Property*, Cambridge University Press.

Tully, J. (1993) *An Approach to Political Philosophy: Locke in Contexts*, Cambridge University Press.

Viroli, M. (1998) *Machiavelli*, Oxford University Press.

Waldron, J. (1983) 'Two Worries about Mixing One's Labour', *The Philosophical Quarterly*, 33, 130, pp.37–44.

Warnock, G.J. (1967) *Contemporary Moral Philosophy*, Macmillan.

Warrender, H. (1957) *The Political Philosophy of Hobbes: his Theory of Obligation*, Oxford University Press.

Wokler, R. (1995) *Rousseau*, Oxford University Press.

Wolff, J. (1992) 'Playthings of Alien Forces: Karl Marx and the Rejection of the Market Economy', *Cogito*, 6, 1, pp.35–41.

Wolff, J. (1996) *An Introduction to Political Philosophy*, Oxford University Press.

Wood, A. (1981) *Karl Marx*, Routledge.

Wood, A. (1993) 'Hegel and Marxism', in *The Cambridge Companion to Hegel*, F.C. Beiser (ed.), Cambridge University Press, pp. 414–44.

Wootton, D. (ed.) (1994) *Machiavelli: Selected Political Writings*, Hackett Publishing Company.

Young, I.M. (1989) 'Polity and Group Difference: a Critique of Universal Citizenship', in Goodin and Pettit (1993), pp.256–72.

Zarka, Y.C. (1995) *Hobbes et la pensée politique moderne*, Presses Universitaires de France.

Index

absolutism
  Hobbes's theory of 93, 95–6
  Locke on 142
accusatory system of justice
  158
*The Adventures of
  Huckleberry Finn* (Twain) 59
'The adviser to princes'
  (Skinner) 4, 6, 10, 24–32
Agathocles 7, 8–9, 18, 29, 36,
  46
agency, and property rights in
  Locke 182
aggregate happiness 326
'Alienated labour' (Marx) 242
alienation
  in Marx and Engels 241,
    242–3, 260, 265, 270, 273–
    4
      alienated labour 274–6
      and ideology 258
      Kymlicka's critique of
        262–3, 297–303
      and private property
        244–5, 261
      religious 274
      and the state 248
amorality 20
  in Machiavelli's *The Prince*
    9–10, 16–17, 19
amour-propre, in Rousseau's
  Discourse 187
anarchy/anarchism 96
  and Hobbes's state of
    nature 78, 80, 81–2, 93
  and Locke's contract
    theory of government
    146–8, 150
appetites/aversions, in
  Hobbes's *Leviathan* 70, 73–4,
  96, 100–2
aristocracy
  Hobbes on 93, 110, 117
  Rousseau on government
    by 204
Aristotle
  essential/accidental
    distinction in 96

eudaimonia concept in 308,
  326
  and Hobbes 82, 91, 94
  and Machiavelli 45, 47, 48,
    51, 55, 284, 285
  Nicomachean Ethics 284
  Politics 60, 94, 111
  and women 362
The Art of War (Machiavelli)
  2, 4
atheism, and political
  emancipation 280, 281
Athens, and contract theories
  of government 165
attributed actions, Hobbes's
  theory of 113–16, 118, 120,
  121–2
Aubrey, John, *Brief Lives* 69
authoritarianism, Hobbes's
  theory of 80, 96, 111, 125–8
authority *see* political
  authority
authorization
  and the corporate will
    217–18
  Hobbes's theory of 89–91,
    96, 120–2
autonomy 326

Barry, Brian, 'The public
  interest' 198, 209, 224–7
Bauer, Bruno 240, 280, 281
Bentham, Jeremy 308, 309,
  313, 326, 329, 341
Berlin, Isaiah
  interpretation of
    Machiavelli 16–20, 39–40
  'John Stuart Mill and the
    ends of life' 305, 317–18,
    336–41
  'The originality of
    Machiavelli' 4, 16, 43–58
  'The pursuit of the ideal'
    17
  'Two concepts of liberty'
    209–10, 231–7, 263, 351
Black, Duncan, *Theory of
  Committees and Elections*
  226

Borgia, Cesare 2, 4, 7–11, 14,
  16, 18, 28–9, 30, 31–2, 34, 46
bourgeoisie, in Marx and
  Engels 252, 258–9, 265, 319
Bramhall, Bishop 92
Brecht, Bertolt 284
  'To those born later' 40
bureaucracy, and 'dirty hands'
  in politics 65
Burke, Edmund 234
  *Reflections on the
    Revolution in France* 208

capital punishment
  Hobbes and Locke on 201
  Rousseau on 201, 209
capitalism
  critique of 262
  and Hobbes 77, 100, 105
  and labour power 298
  and Locke 100
  and Machiavelli 38
  and the 'Macpherson
    thesis' 100
  in Marx and Engels 241,
    259, 260, 265, 274
    and alienated labour
      274–6, 301
    and alienation 242–3,
      248, 260, 265
    and the division of
      labour 243
    and freedom 319
    and historical
      materialism 252, 255–
      6, 294
    and ideology 258
    and political rights 246,
      249
careful anarchist argument, in
  Hobbes's *Leviathan* 80–2
Carlyle, Thomas 340
censor, Rousseau on the office
  of 207, 210
Charles I, King 79
children, paternalism towards
  350–1
Christian morality

and the Harm Principle
310–12, 313, 315–17,
326
and limits to the
authority of society
over the individual
314–17, 339–41
and marriage 363
and political
philosophy 318–19
style of writing 305–6
and toleration of
experiments of living
313–14, 338–9
and utilitarianism 305,
308–10, 317–18, 319
writing of 306–7
and paternalism 311, 318,
319, 342–56
*Principles of Political
Economy* 346
and the private sphere 200
and Rousseau 319
The Subjection of Women
304–5, 319–26
and feminism 324, 325–
6
and marriage 322–3,
324, 325, 326
and sexual inequality
257–61, 304, 324–5
and slavery 317, 366
Utilitarianism 347
on women 258
'Mill and sexual inequality'
(Radcliffe Richards) 325,
357–61
mixing of labour argument, in
Locke's account of property
154, 155–7, 172–9, 180–2
monarchy
Hobbes on 93, 110, 111,
117
see also sovereign
Montaigne, Michel de, on
friendship 36, 365
moral freedom
in Mill 320
in Rousseau 218–19, 319
moral individualism, in Locke
136
moral isolation, and 'dirty
hands' in politics 62–3
moral liberty, Rousseau on
194–5, 197, 211
moral obligations

in Hobbes, and general
rules 86, 87
Locke on the state of
nature and 138
to government 166
moral virtue, and friendship
362
morality
in Hobbes's *Leviathan* 87–
9, 271
and the liberal state 246
and Mill's utilitarianism
308–10
and politics
Berlin's interpretation
of Machiavelli 16–20
'dirty hands' in 1, 21,
59–67
public and private spheres
of, and Machiavelli 41,
50–1
single principle of 19, 53–4
workmanship model of 159
see also Christian morality;
classical tradition in
morality; conventional
morality

Nathan the Wise (Lessing) 279
natural association, Marx and
Engels on 251
natural and instrumental
power, in Hobbes's
Leviathan 75–6
natural law
in Hobbes's *Leviathan* 62,
84, 85–7, 110
in Locke 138–40, 151–2
in Rousseau 219
natural liberty, in Rousseau's
Social Contract 195
natural rights 158
in Hobbes's *Leviathan* 84–
5, 90
in Locke 138–9, 151–2, 283
and property rights 154
nature *see* state of nature
negative liberty 185, 210, 211,
231–4, 263
Marx and Engels's
criticism of 243
and Mill 319
normative accounts 145, 158
Nozick, Robert 153, 173–4, 353

obligation *see* political
obligation

'Of the original contract'
(Hume) 144–5, 148–9, 162–7
Okin, Susan Moller 305
On the Edge of Anarchy
(Simmons) 180
'On the Jewish Question' *see*
Marx, Karl
On Liberty see Mill, John
Stuart
Orco, Remirro de 7–8, 28–9
Origin of Species (Darwin) 304
'The originality of
Machiavelli' (Berlin) 4, 16,
43–58
Owen, Robert 271–2

Paine, Thomas 234
partial associations, in
Rousseau's *Social Contract*
211
particular will, in Rousseau
192, 211, 221–2
partly true argument, and Mill
on freedom of thought and
discussion 312
Pateman, Carole
'Hobbes and the sexual
contract' 94–5, 129–34
*The Problem of Political
Obligation* 129
The Sexual Contract 95,
129
paternalism
and cigarette smoking
354–5
and drug-taking 343, 353–
4
Dworkin on Mill and 318,
342–56
Mill's objections to 311,
318, 319, 342, 347–50
paternalistic laws 343–4,
355–6
pure and impure cases of
345
and suicide 343, 354
patriarchy
classical patriarchalism 94,
129, 137, 151
in Hobbes 95, 97, 129–34
Patrizi, Francesco 24, 26
'people power', and Locke 157
perfectionist arguments for
communism 263, 297–301
persuasion, in Rousseau's
Social Contract 206–8
Petrucci, Pandolfo 27

on the civil state 187, 194–
5, 209, 210, 228, 246
and common interest 222–
3
The Confessions 187
and corporate will 210,
217–19
*Discourse on the Origin of
Inequality* 185, 186–9,
190, 191, 192, 194, 209,
212, 218, 219–20
Emile 208, 218, 219
and the general will 185,
190, 192–3, 195–201, 206,
211, 246
  Barry on 224–7
  discovering 196–9
  and freedom 200, 208–
  9, 223, 260
  and government 203–4
  Hall on 216–23
  limits of 199–202
  and Marx 259, 260
  nature of 195–6
and Hobbes 78, 81, 82, 186,
188, 189–90, 220, 221
and the legislator 190, 201,
202, 211, 228–30
on legitimate social bonds
219–23
and liberalism 185, 209–10,
211, 231–7
and Locke 153, 188, 189–90
on Machiavelli's *The
Prince* 5
and Marx 185, 238, 255,
259, 260, 261
and Mill 319
and particular will 192,
211, 221–2
Social Contract 153, 185,
189–235
  Barry on 198, 209, 224–
  7
  Berlin on 209–10, 231–7
  and coercion 208–10
  Dent on 202, 228–30
  and the English
  Parliament 205–6
  government in 185,
  189–90, 195–6, 202–6,
  211
  Hall on 192–3, 216–23
  and moral liberty 194–
  5, 197, 211
  and persuasion 206–8
  and religion 207–8

and the state 193, 195,
204–6, 212
and the sovereign 185, 193,
196, 212
and the decline of the
state 204–5
and the general will
201, 203–4, 216–17
and the state of nature
186–7, 194–5, 209, 212
ruling class, in Marx and
Engels 257, 266
Rumelin, Gustro 63
Russell, Bertrand 208

Sacchi, Bartolomeo 24
Sartre, Jean-Paul 59
Savonarola, Girolamo 53
Schelling, Thomas, *The
Strategy of Conflict* 225
*Second Treatise of
Government see* Locke, John
self reflection argument, in
Hobbes's *Leviathan* 80–2
self-government, and property
rights in Locke 182
Seneca, on mercy 10, 25
Septimius Severus 28
sexist language, and Hobbes
70
The Sexual Contract
(Pateman) 95, 129
sexual equality, in Hobbes's
Leviathan 82, 93–4, 129–34
sexual inequality
  in Mill's *The Subjection of
  Women* 304, 321–5, 357–
  61, 362–6
    contemporary
    relevance of 359–61
  in Victorian Britain 304,
  321, 358
sexual relations
  Engels on 300–1
  Mill on 365
Shaftesbury, Anthony Ashley
Cooper, Earl of 135, 136
Shanley, Mary Lyndon, 'The
hope of friendship' 325, 362–
7
Simmons, A. John
  On the Edge of Anarchy
  180
  'Reconstructing Locke on
  property' 156–7, 180–4
  *The Lockean Theory of
  Rights* 180

*Six Lessons to the Professors
of Mathematics* (Hobbes) 69
Skinner, Quentin
  *Foundations of Modern
  Political Thought* 113
  'Hobbes and the purely
  artificial person of the
  state' 90–1, 91–2, 113–24
  'The adviser to princes' 4,
  6, 10, 24–32
slavery
  Mill on 317, 319–20, 349–
  50, 366
  Rousseau on 219
Smith, Adam 234
social contract
  Hobbes's theory of 92–3,
  94, 95, 125–8, 189–90
  Locke and consent to
  political authority 168,
  189–90
  in Rousseau 186, 188–9,
  190, 212
  see also contract theory of
  government
Soderini, Giovan 27
sovereign
  in Hobbes 70, 82, 97, 201,
  216
    and absolutism 95–6
    Hampton on 110–11,
    125–8
    Skinner on 113, 117–22
    and subjects 91–3
    and the theory of
    authorization 89–91
  and Locke's contract
  theory of government
  163, 201
  in Rousseau 185, 193, 196,
  212
    and the decline of the
    state 204–5
    and the general will
    201, 203–4, 216–17
Spencer, Herbert 338, 339
Spinoza, Baruch 44, 53
Stalin, Joseph, and Rousseau
185, 208
state, the
  Hobbes's theory of 71, 89–
  91, 93, 94, 113–24
  Marx and Engels on civil
  society and 246–9, 260,
  267
  and Mill's *On Liberty* 305